THE DAUGHTER'S RETURN

The Daughter's Return

African-American and Caribbean Women's Fictions of History

CAROLINE RODY

OXFORD
UNIVERSITY PRESS

2001

OXFORD
UNIVERSITY PRESS

Oxford New York
Athens Auckland Bangkok Bogotá Bombay Buenos Aires
Calcutta Cape Town Chennai Dar es Salaam Delhi Florence Hong Kong
Istanbul Karachi Kuala Lumpur Madras Madrid Melbourne Mexico City Mumbai
Nairobi Paris São Paulo Shanghai Singapore Taipei Tokyo Toronto Warsaw

and associated companies in
Berlin Ibadan

Published by Oxford University Press, Inc.
198 Madison Avenue, New York, New York 10016

Library of Congress Cataloging-in-Publication Data
Rody, Caroline, 1960–
The daughter's return : African-American and Caribbean women's fictions of history / Caroline Rody.
p. cm.
Includes bibliographical references.
ISBN 0-19-513888-0
1. American fiction—Afro-American authors—History and criticism. 2. American fiction—Women authors—History and criticism. 3. Caribbean fiction (English)—Women authors—History and criticism. 4. Women and literature—History—20th century. 5. Literature and history—History—20th century. 6. Return in literature. 7. Daughters in literature. 8. Mothers and daughters in literature. 9. Afro-American women in literature. 10. Women in literature. I. Title.
PS153.N5 .R59 2001
813.009′9287′08996073—dc21 00-024830

An earlier version of chapter 1 originally appeared as "Toni Morrison's *Beloved:* History, 'Rememory,' and a 'Clamor for a Kiss,'" in *American Literary History* 7, no. 1 (1995): 92–119. Reproduced by permission of Oxford University Press.

An earlier version of chapter 5 originally appeared as "Burning Down the House: The Revisionary Paradigm of Jean Rhys's *Wide Sargasso Sea,*" in *Famous Last Words: Changes in Gender and Narrative Closure,* ed. Alison Booth. Charlottesville: University Press of Virginia, 1993, 300–325. Reprinted with permission of the University Press of Virginia.

9 8 7 6 5 4 3 2

Printed in the United States of America
on acid-free paper

For my parents,
Emily Miller Rody and Robert S. Rody,
to whom I always return

Acknowledgments

It is my pleasure to acknowledge the great aid of teachers, colleagues, family, and friends who made it possible for me to write this book, over the busy, transforming years in which I traveled from the University of Virginia to Yale and back again.

Michael Levenson, of generous counsel and expansive vision, has profoundly inspired my work and this unfolding project. Deborah McDowell has been a vital teacher, advisor, and critic, her insights essential to this study's evolution. Susan Fraiman and Alison Booth, long cherished mentors, were invaluable readers of the developing manuscript. Paul Cantor and Gordon Hutner offered key guidance in the early stages, and Arthur Kirsch, Maryse Condé, Clare Kinney, and Kathleen Balutansky were teachers of enduring impact. The University of Virginia and Yale University both provided support for my research and writing. I thank *American Literary History* for granting permission to reprint a revised form of an essay first published there as Chapter 1, and the University Press of Virginia for permission to reprint a revised form of an essay as Chapter 5.

I gladly acknowledge my debt to Oxford's superb readers, Jay Clayton, Johanna X. K. Garvey, and Silvio Torres-Saillant, for their meticulous, fruitful readings of the manuscript. I have been fortunate, too, to find other gifted readers: Herbert Tucker, Jennifer Wicke, Elisabeth Ladenson, Stephen Arata, Andrea Levine, Giavanna Munafo, Jean Kane, Ian Duncan, Suzanne Keen, and Ian Baucom. For their support and counsel I thank Raymond Nelson, Gordon Braden, Patricia Spacks, Mark Edmundson, Eric Lott, Jessica Feldman, Stephen Cushman, Anthony Winner, Tejumola Olaniyan, Richard Brodhead, William Jewett, Margaret Homans, Ayşe Agiş, and Langdon

Hammer. Special thanks go to Julie Dash, to my Oxford editors Elissa Morris and Susan Chang, to production editor Stacey Hamilton, and to Nicole Gharda for her work on the index. And I thank my students at Yale and Virginia for providing crucial energy, dialogue, and provocation.

The life lived amidst the writing was richer for the conversation of Susan Pollock, Stacy Wolf, Betsy Rosenthal. Stephanie Rabinowitz, Judie Smith, Amal Jamal, Ann Porotti, David Wyatt, and Lia and Rusty Rushton, and because of the good cheer of Norma and Bernard Lytton, and of Maria Georgopoulou and Christos Cabolis, who often came to the rescue. My in-laws Nesta and Ruhi Ramazani offered abundant sustenance—moral, professional, culinary—along with devoted and spirited babysitting.

I am proud to pay tribute to the matchless, unfailing support of my parents Emily and Robert Rody, whose love and belief in me is the start of all I do, and to whom this book is dedicated. And I wouldn't know my own words without my sisters Annie and Liz and my brother David, who share with me the precious and comic secret of a common language. In writing of daughterly return, I celebrate the memories of Beatrice Cooper Miller, Nettie Glass Rody, and Dorothy Watkins Townes, whose mothering was a blessing.

Last and best thanks go to my two favorite dance partners: Jahan Ramazani, most generous-spirited and most devoted reader, chef, goad, and friend, who has a rare gift for broadening the view, and who demonstrates, day by day, just how the impossible is done; and to our beloved Gabriel Bijan, who announced his arrival in the very midst of the printing of this manuscript's first draft, and who now, as it becomes a book at last, already knows a library of his own by heart.

Contents

THE DAUGHTER'S RETURN

Introduction

The Daughter's Return

In a climactic moment of Julie Dash's 1991 film *Daughters of the Dust*, the not-yet-born girl who narrates this ancestral story runs in slow motion across the screen, amidst a shiny aura, straight into the big belly of her pregnant mother, who stands with arms outstretched to receive her daughter. In Toni Morrison's *Beloved* (1987) a murdered baby girl returns from death in passionate longing for the ex-slave mother who killed her, and in the ensuing drama nearly strangles her to death; when Morrison's heroine discovers the identity of this "devil-child," she says, "You came right on back like a good girl, like a daughter" (261, 203). These two instances of daughterly return, one of desire blissfully fulfilled and the other of grief turned lethal, both can be seen to allegorize the imaginative return of a late twentieth-century woman writer to her traumatic ancestral past.

In the emerging body of literature identified in this study, history is reimagined in the form of a romance: the romance of a returning daughter and a figure I call the mother-of-history. Coming back like daughters—intensely devoted and yet convinced of the arrival of their own moment—African-American and Caribbean women writers recast the conventions of historical fiction as well as received narratives of their peoples' founding trauma, New World slavery. Staging dramatic, often fantastic encounters with the past, they foreground the mother-daughter relationship as the site of transhistorical contact.

To say that these writers face history as daughters is to emphasize both the ethnic and the feminist character of their historiographic project. Ethnicity is a vexed, imprecise cultural and political term, essential for this study only insofar as it describes a literary condition; that is, a writer's subjective sense of being the inheritor of a certain people's *story*. Reimagining an inherited history, particularly a history of collective suffering and struggle, a writer confronts a literary predicament of a different order from that of the rewriting of more distant and impersonal events: "familial" relationship to the story itself. *The Daughter's Return* treats this affective dimension as inseparable from the political dimension of ethnic literary returns to the past.

I read the plots of the African-American and Caribbean daughter's return, in texts written between the late 1970s and the 1990s, as allegories of historiographic desire, that is, of the desire of writers newly emerging into cultural authority to reimagine their difficult inheritance, the stories of their own genesis. My focus is the recurrent, often fantastic figure of the revisionary "daughter," who, transcending time in a quest to contact lost, enslaved foremothers, embodies the newly born power of feminist reimagination.

Historical Returns

At the turn of the millennium, it has come to seem natural that our most serious, sophisticated, and vital cultural and intellectual work should take the past as its subject. History, Toni Morrison has declared, is more infinite than the future. While the sense of an epoch's ending, certainly, causes us to look back over our shoulders, and while technological and ecological changes also make it urgent that we retell ourselves what has happened, it is above all the global human changes of our era that have reopened the past as a compelling territory of the imagination. The end of the Age of Empire has brought with it a worldwide resurgence of previously suppressed "national" histories, the stories of peoples of the former imperial margins and of minority groups in the West; at the same time, developments in communication technology, large-scale political realignments, and mass migrations create unprecedented currents of literary influence and exchange. This contemporary globalization now profoundly shapes our sense of the past, transforming the "historical mind" necessary—as T. S. Eliot saw it—to the work of the modern writer. Simultaneously, a historicist turn across the disciplines has redefined the nature of the historical, displaying the blindnesses and undercutting the foundational claims of "History with a capital *H*," as Martinican critic Edouard Glissant has put it (76).[1]

No discipline or discourse, however, surpasses the deconstructive work of late twentieth-century world literature itself, engaged in what Glissant terms "the struggle against a single History for the cross-fertilization of histories" (93). Rather than demolishing all meaningful historical narrative, postcolonial and ethnic literatures tear down in order to build differently—even if, self-consciously, upon multiple and monumental layers of debris. As these literatures intermingle traditional forms with other available genres, any dying "end of history" whimpers are drowned out by the sounds of what Native American writer Gerald Vizenor celebrates as "a liberation of tribal stories" (xii), and a hybrid global literature retells the story of the history of the world.

The two groups of writers considered in this study have recently emerged from literary obscurity into respective "renaissances" in the moment of this worldwide eruption of formerly unarticulated histories. In an era obsessed with historicity, African-American and Caribbean women writers share a historiographic enterprise with a distinctive political and psychological burden: revising received narratives of their own peoples' traumatic histories. Their fictions, like many postcolonial texts, are "concerned with neither redeeming nor annihilating history," as Stephen Slemon has said, "but with displacing it as a concept and opening up the past to imaginative revision" ("Post-Colonial Allegory" 165). Writers of historical fiction always work, of course, in the consciousness of previously written histories: one inevitably writes "into" a "given" history, modifying or appending a historical map of the world felt to be inadequate. Yet the authors considered in this study, like many minority and postcolonial writers addressing the experience of their forebears, take the enterprise of reimagination especially seriously, knowing it can be a political act with real consequences: they reinscribe received historical narratives in order to debunk and purge them; to relocate the site of the historical and redefine history's meanings; to challenge prevailing discourses of power and knowledge, infuse oral tradition into the written, and reassert devalued folk memory; and to reinvent ethnic, political, and literary bloodlines.

And yet, within the evident logic of this collective revision lies the mystery of historiographic desire. As groups or peoples gain cultural authority within larger social and political orders, it seems, they develop simultaneously the desire to retell their histories. Historical fiction as genre has always been intimately connected to group identity,[2] to the rise of "imagined communities," in Benedict Anderson's term. Judging by the African-American and Caribbean women's fictions considered in this study, the emergence of historiographic desire indicates not the attainment of some great height of social power, but the arrival at a moment just beyond the initial assertions of group identity (the American civil rights and Black Power movements, the Caribbean nationalist movements) in which it becomes possible—and also necessary—to look back, in which aspiration gathers around the sense of the distance traveled thus far, and the stories yet untold are seen to hold the key to a people's future course.

Anderson observes that new narratives of identity spring from the "amnesias" that attend "profound changes in consciousness"; precisely because the story of a people's development "can not be 'remembered,'" it "must be narrated" (204). An attachment to "history as memory," which Walter Benn Michaels deconstructs as an American myth (7), remains nevertheless a vital, valuable mythographic process for marginalized peoples, who tend to privilege "remembered" (as opposed to "learned") history, not least because of the need to reassert the reality of their historical trauma against the officially sanctioned and taught histories that would erase it (see Felman and Laub 69).[3] Whether the texts in this study are examples of what Barbadian poet [Edward] Kamau Brathwaite has called the "literature of reconnection" to African cultural roots ("African Presence" 99), or what Paul Gilroy calls "imaginative attempts to revisit the slave experience and sift it for resources with which to bolster contemporary political aspirations" (220), they represent a profoundly self-authorizing moment in the construction of a cultural imaginary. Asserting their literary power to reimagine a threatening past, African-American and Caribbean writers of daughterly historical fictions tell the world the prehistory of their arrival at the moment when it became possible to tell.[4]

Daughterhood, my metaphor for these writers' imaginative cathexis of their chosen stories, is a metaphorically rich condition in itself, suggesting at once legacy and youth, inheritance of culture and self-conscious membership in a generation with a new agenda. Its reference to parents is ambiguous in terms of gender; it does not in itself specify "to a mother" or "to a father." At the center of this study is the striking fact that a generation of women writers just emerging into literary power should make a romance of its daughterhood to mothers, should frame a return to the massive calamities of African-American and Caribbean history within a plot of daughterly desire for a mother-of-history. This project is enabled, of course, not only by the rise of black, ethnic, and postcolonial literatures but also by several decades of work by feminist historians and literary historians to recuperate a female past, and by the mother-centered structure of much late twentieth-century literature by women,[5] which together have made a symbolic matrifocality almost inextricable from contemporary feminist consciousness. Though the authors discussed here take widely divergent positions on feminism per se, their fictions all recast received forms of historical narrative in intensely mother-centered "histories" with characteristically female literary emphases, among them primary female characters; central mother-daughter relationships; focus on the private and domestic rather than the public, national, or military spheres; and scenes of childbirth and child-rearing.

Yet what makes these fictions most notable amidst the maternal turn of our moment is their rendering of history in a symbolic structure of *daughterly engagement with the maternal past*. That is, the writers in this study make their peoples' pasts meaningful within an "extended metaphor"—in Hayden White's terms—of mother-daughter relations. For White, all historical narratives depend on metaphors, connecting past events to "the story types we conventionally use to endow the events of our lives with culturally sanctioned meanings" ("The Historical Text" 91, 88). This book argues that African-American and Caribbean women writers figure their creative relationships to the past by means of the unconventional, feminist story of a daughter's return to repair a severed matrilineage. Asserting daughterhood to history in the form of a feminist family romance, these writers claim a most intimate, authoritative relationship to a maternal past, declaring themselves history's legitimate heirs.[6] Even as their texts confront the "psychic fracturing" born of a traumatic inheritance (Holloway 116), still they dramatize the attempt to recover the African-American and Caribbean past as a vital and courageous daughterly labor.

Mother-Daughter "Histories"

Among the most remarkable aspects of contemporary African-American and Caribbean women's fictions identified in this study is their development of the relations of mothers and daughters into a radically new system of tropes for the representation of history, invested with new power to articulate female historiographic authority. The scene of childbirth, for example, appearing again and again in these narratives, becomes the signature trope for contact with historical origins; at the same time, it affirms the processes of genealogical and literary inheritance that generated the possibility of "daughterly" rewritings. The richness of the mother-child motif as a code for women's historical experience becomes evident in its vivid inscriptions of historical trauma. If normative history is a woman giving birth, then instances of childbirth gone awry, of the deaths of mother or child, of mother-child separation, or of a woman's refusal of childbearing become tropes for the entrance of "bad history" into women's lives, for female resistance to history, and for authorial inheritance of a traumatic past.

The symbolic import of this tropology is readily apparent. Clearly, to tell history in a vocabulary derived solely from female experiences is to claim the past as a female realm, owned and made meaningful by the women who lived it. Historical fictions of this kind foreground that which has been most excluded from male-centered histories, considered least "historical" (because most "natural"): the female body. Going "directly to the source of powerlessness," to borrow Susan Stanford Friedman's terms, writers of female-bodied histories effect "a linguistic reunion of what culture has sundered": "creativity and procreativity" (390, 372). Their texts claim not only that women have, know, and tell histories, but also that in their bodies, indeed, women generate history.[7]

Further, given the histories of enslavement and colonization retold here, the mother-daughter figural mode must be seen to reclaim connections to maternal origins in the face of the historical destruction of families and lineages, in particular slavery's systematic separation of mothers from their children. This is to say that texts that retell African-American and Caribbean women's history in this mother-daughter vocabulary suggest a will to reverse the rupture of these intimate bonds and claim a historical family—like Morrison's novel, to call the lost past beloved—even while the recurrent plot of severance evokes innumerable, irredeemable mutual losses between mothers and their children.

In psychological terms, the allegory of daughterly return to the body of the mother suggests a feminist privileging of the maternal-infant bond, as theorized by Freud, Lacan, Kristeva, and others, and an affirmation of female relationality, as theorized by Chodorow. But what can it mean, psychologically, to circumscribe the *historical imaginary* within a quest for union with the mother? Kristeva writes that to refuse separation from the maternal body would be to refuse "*the founding separation of the sociosymbolic contract*" (52). A narrative of *historical* return to the mother, then, might be a feminist rejection of the separations enforced by the socio-*temporal* contract—that is, a rejection of the socially normative linear time that Kristeva calls the "time of history." Are historical fictions that in some sense refuse time's linear movement neurotic or dysfunctional texts? Perhaps so if, as Kristeva says, the linear "time of history" makes the rupture from the mother explicit, while "other temporalities work to conceal" that founding rupture (35). And perhaps so, indeed, if we read these texts as bearing belated witness to trauma, evincing trauma's characteristic "refusal of historical boundaries" (Caruth 8), both in their plots of return and in their very emergence in our moment.

Yet, tellingly, Kristeva also calls the kind of linear time that these texts resist "'obsessional time,'" finding "in the mastery of time the true structure of the slave" (35). If the maternal returns of recent African-American and Caribbean feminist historical fictions suggest an impossible desire to deny time's overwhelming losses, they also suggest a desire to rupture the time in which slaves are bound, to open up and liberate time in order to reach and release enslaved foremothers. The time-transcendence that enables such projects suggests the temporal consciousness Kristeva usefully articulates (but perhaps overessentializes) as "Women's Time,"[8] a kind of time akin to "archaic (mythical) memory" and to "the cyclical or monumental temporality of marginal movements" (38).

African-American historical fiction has always contained this mythic dimension, as Jane Campbell argues; it has traditionally recast a bitter history within a millennial vision (xvii). Critics of Caribbean literature, too, note a profoundly mythifying impulse in that tradition of historical fiction (see Zimra, "Calabash" 145). The authors in this study write within these visionary traditions as well as within the revisionary aesthetic of second-wave feminism, which, Kristeva observes, alternately appropriates and refuses "history's time" (38). While these fictions pay realist attention to the historical timeline, in moments they also reject linear time for time-stopped immersion in maternal reunion, a temporal strategy that may well merit the name "women's time." They thus accord with Kristeva's prophesy of a future feminist attitude toward the problem of difference: an "*interiorization of the founding separation*" from the mother (52), that is, an acknowledgment that the primal separation, and the beginning of all differences, lies within. In these fictions of daughterly return to a mother-of-history, a historicized female identity bears its own *temporal* difference, its own historical "relationality" within; these texts reinscribe the history of slavery and colonization within a metamyth of mother-daughter separation and of imaginatively willed, transhistorical mother-daughter reunion. Thus they render contemporary fiction a space for the lamentation, mythification, and imaginative reclamation of an ancestral past.

Fictions of this sort offer a marked contrast to the conventional historical novel, which was above all a realist novel, one that situated a moral or psychological problematic within a convincing simulation of the life of a bygone age, if not of the precise material reality of that age.[9] The twentieth century played diverse changes on this form, most notably in "postmodern" visions that flatten time as a field for a time-scanning consciousness and in "magic realist" visions of the past's miraculous eruption in everyday life. The two groups of women writers in this study are indebted to both of these historiographic modes: they demonstrate the self-conscious postmodern belatedness that engages the past as an intertext to the present, as well as the magic of the history-rich texts of recent Latin American, American ethnic, and other postcolonial literatures, in which a struggling present carries on a lively, intimate, "familial" dialogue with the past, as it mythologizes the decolonizing subject.

The daughterly returns of which I speak are accomplished most often by the introduction into realist "historical" narration of fantastic, magical, or other anti-realist narrative modes. The fantastic/realistic friction of magic realism is generally read as registering the horrific and absurd cultural collisions set in motion by European colonialism; but if magic describes such dissonance, I would argue, it can also serve to allegorize newly arising ethnic historiographic power. This is all the more true for women's usages of the magically real, recently called "magical feminism" (Hart 11), which tend to draw upon magic as a traditionally female province to mythify women's assertion of imaginative power. Many of the texts in this study unfold plots of desire and quest through a magic realism of the female body. Refiguring the past in fantastic treatments of female generative power, their "histories" recast "History" within a metamyth of female generation. In transhistorical spaces like Morrison's 124 or the jail cell in Maryse Condé's *I, Tituba*, these fictions rupture history with timelessness; and in these time-stopped moments, these restored maternal spaces, repressed herstory erupts, revealing a perpetual chain of births, one from within the other, in an unwritten chronology spiraling from the depths of female time.

Such moments, however, are only brief respites from ongoing historical trauma, which is encoded chiefly by the dominant plot of the separation of mother and daughter. To note that such separations are sometimes deliberate, caused by a mother's murder, rejection, or abortion of a child, or her refusal to engender one, and further that returning daughters sometimes aggressively cast their mothers as failed, unnurturing, unwelcoming, compromised, sick, dying, or even murderous, is to suggest the complexity of the female relationships to history newly articulable with this vocabulary of tropes.

History and Horizontality

This two-part study takes up the new revisions of history in fictions by two groups of women writers with distinct but related projects. Though the late-century "renaissances" in African-American and Caribbean women's writing have drawn considerable critical attention, what remains unappreciated is these movements' convergence in revisionary New World historiography, their development of a distinctive feminist idiom for retelling history. Both

African-American and Caribbean women writers began to publish in unprecedented numbers in the 1970s. The African-Americans, developing the rich "minority" tradition of black American letters, have in two decades created a literature that has won spectacular, unprecedented, and international recognition. The Caribbeans, emerging as a force from within the relatively young literary tradition of their heterogeneous island region, remain a smaller, less known literary school, but one equally meteoric in its development.

The Daughter's Return conceives these two groups of writers as culturally and historically distinct, yet also related by commonalities of gendered, cultural, historical, political, and literary experience. My argument depends on broad and deep similarities, as well as important differences. I claim that contemporary works of both groups of writers vigorously revise received narratives of their peoples' originary trauma, New World slavery, in texts structured on the feminist allegory of a daughter's recuperation of a severed mother-daughter relationship. Within their separate literary and cultural contexts, however, they engage varying problematics of historical revision.

Part I of this book considers the meanings of the African-American women's "renaissance" return to history, reading Toni Morrison's *Beloved* as the central, paradigmatic text but also as the demonic shatterer of the collective romance of maternal return. Chapter 1 proposes the theory of "daughterly" historiographic desire, focusing on *Beloved*'s ghost-girl as the embodiment of conflicted desire for a lost matrilineage. The several sections of Chapters 2 and 3 discover the origins and adventures of a Beloved-like archetype I call the "magic black daughter," who can be seen traveling through time to recover the mother-of-history in an extraordinarily diverse range of contemporary fictional "histories" by African-American women, including Octavia Butler, Lucille Clifton, Julie Dash, Jewelle Gomez, Paule Marshall, Gloria Naylor, Phyllis Alesia Perry, and Alice Walker.

Part II situates recent Caribbean women's maternal "histories" within the twentieth-century literary enterprise of rewriting a heritage of colonization and enslavement. In Chapter 4, I argue that the complex history of the figure of the Mother—identified in successive moments of Caribbean literature first with Europe, then Africa, then with the islands themselves—bequeaths to contemporary Caribbean women writers of many racial, national, and cultural identities the problem of imagining a desirable mother-of-history to whom to return.

The heterogeneity of the literature of Caribbean daughterly return leads me to treat each of three Caribbean writers in the book's second half in a separate chapter, rather than in the linked readings that suit the variations on the African-American "magic black daughter" archetype treated in the first half. Chapter 5 takes up Jean Rhys's influential *Wide Sargasso Sea*, a novel that makes an allegorical return to maternal origins in both history and literary history, resituating Charlotte Brontë's white Creole madwoman within a complex interracial maternal matrix. Michelle Cliff's radical recasting of the bildungsroman is the subject of Chapter 6, which examines the reclamation of maternal history within the saga of a mulatto daughter of Jamaica. And Chapter 7 traces the maternal romance of history in Guadeloupean novelist Maryse Condé's rewriting of a Barbadian slave/witch's adventures in colonial Salem, Massachusetts.

Pursuing the implications of Condé's heroine's encounter with the United States and its early literary heroine Hester Prynne, I address in the Epilogue the cross-cultural impulse that links these African-American and Caribbean women's "histories" to many other contemporary women's texts, drawing on a novel by the Indian-American Bharati Mukherjee, as well as on Morrison's *Beloved*, once more. What, I ask, is the allure of our Hester—standing unbowed with her scarlet "A" at the inception of American literature—for "history"-writing women of diverse backgrounds? Reading the postcolonial Hester Prynne, my study's ending becomes a meditation on the position of "America" in women writers' new maps of the world's history.

In crossing national and regional boundaries to compare African-American and Caribbean women's literatures, I follow numerous critics of "black women's literature" and "African diasporic literature," and especially Paul Gilroy's "outer-national, transcultural reconceptualisation" of a "black Atlantic," which treats works like those studied here as part of a "web of diaspora identities and concerns" (218). Insofar as the Caribbean half of this book also includes authors of mixed and non-black racial identity, I follow critics of "New World literature" and "postcolonial literature," who study cultural production in the light of a heritage of interracial contact and hybridization.[10]

While I find merit in all of these rubrics, I couple the two bodies of writing here not to advocate any one conception of the field, but for several heuristic purposes. First, simply, I want to respond to deep consonances between the historiographic projects and idioms of two groups of literary texts characterized by intense "daughterly" engagement with the heritage of New World slavery, and thus to raise to view a distinctive late-century feminist subgenre. Second, I follow what Stelamaris Coser calls the "inter-American bridges" built when these women's narratives themselves span the Americas through memory or migration (4), blurring literary borders, "try[ing] to connect and make sense of a common fragmented history" (25), and underscoring "the restless, recombinant qualities" of the two cultures (Gilroy 31).[11] Further, I believe that criticism written amidst the rapid changes of contemporary world literature should seek to trace the development of heterogeneous alliances and influences, whether they bespeak long-standing shared historical or cultural experience, or a recent repercussion of electronic-age communications. Just as, reading recent American literature, one must increasingly attend to the in-migration of stories from the wider world, reading contemporary women's writing—which has taken on the aspect of an international phenomenon—one finds the critical gesture of attending to both specificity and cross-cultural connections more and more necessary.

Finally, I agree with postcolonial critics like Glissant, Gilroy, Slemon, Homi Bhabha, Edward Said, and Vera Kutzinski that it is worth risking the potentially "recolonizing" move of grouping texts despite complex cultural, historical, and political differentials, because of the benefits of boundary-crossing analysis, of "a theory . . . less intimidated by and respectful of the boundaries and integrity of modern nation states," as Gilroy puts it (4), or of what Kutzinski calls a "paracanonical" critical practice (556), and Said calls, simply, "worldliness":

> By linking works to each other we bring them out of the neglect and secondariness to which for all kinds of political and ideological reasons they had previously been condemned. . . . Otherwise they will be regarded only as informative ethnographic specimens, suitable for the limited attention of experts and area specialists. *Worldliness* is therefore the restoration to such works and interpretations of their place in the global setting, a restoration that can only be accomplished by an appreciation not of some tiny, defensively constituted corner of the world, but of the large, many-windowed house of culture as a whole. (43)

Taking a similar position, Kutzinski points not to the world's great house but to its busy streets, encouraging critics to note "the transgressive dynamics of literary history" (552) and rescind the "policed" borders of literature:

> The way to rescind borders is of course to cross them and, in so doing, blur them, confuse them, make them permeable, open for traffic from all directions, and, as a result, realize that they have in fact been open all along. . . . (555)

Desiring, then, both to build something encompassing and new and to keep all lanes open in an era of dynamic literary change, I attempt to see what it is possible to learn by juxtaposing these two bodies of literature. At the same time, I draw upon other texts and literatures of the contemporary moment in order to illuminate significant patterns or influences.

And a pattern of utmost importance is, precisely, the interest of these texts themselves in the cross-cultural. A thread that becomes increasingly visible over the course of the study, and which I discuss at length in the Epilogue, is the plot of encounter with women of other groups. One of the greatest surprises, for me, in reading African-American and Caribbean women's histories for this study, was to find that the plot of female return to a specific ethnic history repeatedly generates cross-cultural encounters with women—especially heroines and martyrs—of other racial or ethnic groups. In Morrison's *Beloved*, for example, when the escaping slave Sethe goes into labor in a Kentucky wood, she finds help in delivering her baby from Amy Denver, a "whitegirl" with "good hands" who also happens to be running away from a violent home; hidden from general view, these "two throw-away people," "a slave and a barefoot whitewoman," do "something together appropriately and well" (*Beloved* 76, 84–85). The profound implications of the Amy Denver plot become apparent when one reflects that she did not have to be in the novel at all; Morrison could have told the story of this African-American family's struggle for freedom very well without the help of a stray "whitegirl." But Sethe's encounter with Amy transforms the scene of childbirth that is mythologically central to an ethnic narrative, and so doing, embeds the seeds of interracial possibility within American women's maternal heritage. The black daughter born in this liminal moment between slavery and freedom is given the "whitegirl"'s name, "Denver"—a fact all the more astonishing in that she is the first baby to whom Sethe does not have to give a white person's name. Her gesture of tribute underscores the privileged place of the interethnic plot in contemporary women's historical imaginary.

In another such instance, Michelle Cliff's Jamaican mulatto heroine Clare Savage, an adolescent "reaching, without knowing it, for an explanation of her own life," is moved to question her racial identity when she comes upon the diary of Anne Frank; impelled by Anne's story and by the "dark" face on the cover that reminds her of her own, young Clare buys a diary and commences to put her own life in writing (*Abeng* 72, 68). As I collected such significant crossings, I began to observe that these "ethnic" historical fictions contain a paradoxical urge toward interethnic history—a dramatically different story.

Ethnicity is, of course, an inherently relational property; as Werner Sollors puts it (citing Georges Devereux), ethnicity rests on contrast, on "dissociative belonging," for which the formula is "A is an X because he is not a Y" (288, 303). Even defined more positively, as by Michael M. J. Fischer, ethnicity as "something reinvented and reinterpreted in each generation by each individual," "something that emerges in full—often liberating—flower only through struggle" (195), is still "a process of inter-reference between two or more cultural traditions" (201). Such inter-reference is of course basic to the literature of New World slavery, which is characterized by relentlessly binary differentiation of blacks and whites. But the interethnic encounter plots I note in these women's "histories" do not merely help to define differences between racial or ethnic groups; rather, this imagined convergence of ancestors works to inscribe an aesthetic of hybridity, significantly revising cultural narratives of ethnic, racial, or national identity. Heroines who find friends, role models, or surrogate mothers among the women of other groups embody their authors' bids to reclaim a hybrid history.

The female body in these cross-cultural encounters does not merely contain one particular people's history, but mediates "the cross-fertilization of histories." In female bodily dramas of travel, encounter, and exchange, African-American and Caribbean women's texts point to numerous other, yet-to-be-written revisionary daughters' stories. Earlier I argued that these fictions locate difference from the mother within in the form of history within, that is, in the plot of the daughter's separation from or reunion with the mother-of-history. It becomes apparent that in the plot of bodily encounter with other women's histories, these texts bring another sort of difference inside identity: they bring ethnic others inside ethnic history.

Ultimately, I believe, these plots register an important contemporary, rather than "historical," reality. In our era of complex and rapid changes, when the seemingly opposed trends of globalization and ethnic affirmation merge, any "ethnic" return to the past is conceived, written, published, and received within surprising new currents of multiethnic influence and exchange. Contemporary African-American or Caribbean novelists do not merely write against one master tradition (or within one "minor" tradition), but inevitably and self-consciously respond to a heterogeneous intertextual universe, and they address a readership that they know may be as varied as their personal libraries. I would argue that women's literary revisions of history now benefit almost as much from this cross-cultural and international reading and influence—what I call the "horizontal" axis—as from culture-specific, "vertical" traditions of reading and writing. Such cross-fertilizations now help redescribe the history of the world, as the postcolonial return to history discovers not some "absolute pre-colonial purity" (Ashcroft 195), but the history of interrelation. When African-American and Caribbean women's fictions place an interethnic impulse in the realm of imagined ancestry—the very womb, after all, of ethnic difference—they suggest a desire for a past that reflects the most promising developments of contemporary literary culture.

It is central to my understanding of African-American and Caribbean women's texts, then, that they participate in trends of global scope, that their writers read (and review and endorse) one another as well as other "others" across ethnic, national, and linguistic boundaries. Indeed, these writers' consciousness of being—or being received as—a composite group of "multiethnic women writers" may help create the horizontal attention of their plots. The field of contemporary multiethnic literature is, of course, partly the product of publishers' market strategies, which may exoticize and flatten differences as often as they actually promote "diversity" or cultural openness.[12] But publishers respond to the changing demands of reading audiences as well as shape them. Discussing contemporary black women's literary success, Hortense Spillers has argued that a tradition "arises not only because there are writers there to make it, but also because there is a strategic audience of heightened consciousness prepared to read and interpret the work as such"; moreover, traditions "survive as *created social events* only to the extent that an audience cares to intersect them" ("Afterword" 250). The development of such an audience for a multiethnic women's literature is signaled and encouraged by ethnic and postcolonial women writers themselves, who contribute to the construction of this field in their capacity as reviewers and blurb-writers. I did not have to look beyond my bookshelves to construct a chain of celebratory blurbs by which women writers of many minority groups seem to link themselves into a literary movement.

Indian-American writer Bharati Mukherjee, for example, hails the "new and utterly engrossing territory" charted within the covers of Guadeloupan novelist Maryse Condé's *Tree of Life*, and Maya Angelou says "Welcome" to Trinidadian Elizabeth Nunez-Harrell on the cover of *When Rocks Dance*. Gwendolyn Brooks calls Chicana author Sandra Cisneros "brilliant" on the cover of *The House on Mango Street*, and Toni Morrison acclaims the "beauty" of the prose inside the covers of both Native American writer Louise

Erdrich's *Love Medecine* and Jamaican writer Michelle Cliff's *No Telephone to Heaven*. Indian author Indrani Aikath-Gyaltsen's *Crane's Morning* displays praise for her previous novel from no fewer than three ethnic American women writers, among others: the Chinese-American Amy Tan, the African-American Gloria Naylor, and the Dominican-American Julia Alvarez. No surprise that Alice Walker graces the cover of Sherley Anne Williams's African-American slavery novel *Dessa Rose*, speaking in her inimitable way of "the Obvious Collaboration of the Ancestors," but what of Chinese-American writer Maxine Hong Kingston, apparently imitating her, on the cover of Leslie Marmon Silko's Native American epic *Almanac of the Dead*?:

> To read this book is to hear the voices of the ancestors and spirits telling us where we came from, who we are, and where we must go.

Whose ancestors, one may well wonder, and who *are* "we"? The collision and conflation of female ethnic identities on my bookshelf reaches a climax when Gloria Naylor announces on the cover of Julia Alvarez's *How the Garcia Girls Lost Their Accents* that the novel contains "a family presented with such eloquence and such profound honesty you'll want to claim them as yours."

That the desire to claim a family as one's own—a desire essential to Naylor's novel *Mama Day* and to all the daughterly returns to ethnic history considered in this study—should be construed as a trans-ethnic readerly desire as well suggests the degree to which the "horizontality" of the contemporary literary gestalt now shapes "vertical" ethnic authorial projects. This trail of criss-crossing encomia indicates not only that contemporary ethnic women writers are identified by publishers, oddly, as sharing the common property of "diversity," but also that their "families," their "ancestors and spirits," too, are regarded as in some sense alike in their diversity. Patiently awaiting daughterly return, imagined ethnic ancestral families are the sublime objects of the celebrated contemporary project of ethnic feminist historical recuperation, of the universal desire to claim a family. What these book-cover blurbs suggest with such pith and pizzazz, the relationships among ethnically different female characters in African-American and Caribbean women's historical fictions confirm: the impulse to mythify (in an imagined ancestral past) the multiethnic female exchange that, even as it is commodified in the literary marketplace, enriches and animates contemporary women writers' work.

In this study, I hope to achieve a constructive interethnic attention like that of these novelists and their heroines. I am indebted both to the methodology of a critic like Stuart Hall, who advocates a practice that "works with and through difference . . . without suppressing the real heterogeneity of interests and identities" ("New Ethnicities" 28), and to historian David Hollinger's "postethnic perspective," in which notions of fixed or inherited ethnic identity give way to a "rooted cosmopolitanism" that can cross many boundaries, allowing multiple affiliations (4–7). Over the course of this study, as I consider first African-American and then Caribbean women writers within their own ethnic traditions and in relation to one another, I pay increasing attention to their engagement with others outside of either group—

a progression that responds to the intensely interethnic texture of Caribbean literature. Conscious of my own cultural, ethnic, or national difference from these texts and writers, and the difference of my academic analysis from these historiographic ventures, still I want to affirm with a fundamentally affiliative critical discourse the power of these texts to move me and to seem "familiar" to me, a reader who is both an inheritor of another people's story—that of the Jews—and a participant on the "horizontal" axis of contemporary literary exchange. This is not only because I believe these texts actually can help me understand "where we came from, who we are, and where we must go," but also because they present their families "with such eloquence and such profound honesty" that they make me want to claim my own, with similarly daughterly daring.

BOLSTERED BY A "horizontal" spectrum of literary returns to history, African-American and Caribbean women writers re-enter the menacing realm of their inheritance in fictions fueled by daughterly desire, conviction, lament, and rage. Devising new forms in which to meet the past, they mythify both the history-generating power of the female body and the birth of female imaginative power from a traumatic historical matrix. In the heroines of this literature, female desire stages a rendezvous with the hazard of history itself, daring to be overcome with history, to experience the self as the juncture of historical forces, to realize daughterhood in a kind of historical sublime. Conjuring ancestry, these daughters of traumatized, marginalized lineages assert above all that they can indeed "tell time," and that they know that their time to tell has come.

PART I

African-American Women Writers

1 Toni Morrison's *Beloved*

History, "Rememory," and a "Clamor for a Kiss"

i am accused of tending to the past
as if i made it,
as if i sculpted it
with my own hands. i did not.
this past was waiting for me
when i came,
a monstrous unnamed baby,
and i with my mother's itch
took it to breast
and named it
History.
she is more human now,
learning language everyday,
remembering faces, names and dates.
when she is strong enough to travel
on her own, beware, she will.

Lucille Clifton, "i am accused of
tending to the past . . ."

momma
help me
turn the face of history
to your face.

June Jordan,
"Gettin Down to Get Over"

On the back of the Plume edition of Toni Morrison's *Beloved*, reviewer John Leonard proclaims, "I can't imagine American literature without it!" Evidently intended as consummate praise, this remark would seem to congratulate Morrison for having written into the incomplete canon of American literature the very chapter of American history it had long lacked: the story of the African Americans who survived slavery. And in an important sense, *Beloved* is manifestly "about" the filling of historical gaps. "Sixty million and more" reads Morrison's dedication, simply, suggesting at once the numerous ancestors the novel attempts to memorialize, and a vast absence its words could never fill.[1]

But how odd that we should now be unable to "imagine American literature" without the strange, idiosyncratic, imaginative world of *Beloved*. A reading of the novel as a recuperation of unrepresented history does not begin to account for its cultivation of the bizarre and uncanny; its revival of gothic conventions—the haunted house, the bloody secret, the sexually alluring ghost; its obsessive, claustrophobic plot-focus; and an emotional climate that changes from pained repression, to volcanic fury, to a suspended lovers' swoon. All of this seems somehow excessive to the requirements of a historical novel that would recover the story of African-American slavery and survival.

Beloved is, however, a historical novel; Morrison rewrites the life of the historical figure Margaret Garner, who killed her child to prevent her recapture into slavery, and sets this story as the focus of an epic-scale recreation of African-American life under slavery and in its aftermath.[2] What are we to make of the shape of this "history"? Why focus on an astonishing act of violence committed not *upon* but *by* a slave woman? Why should *this* slave story be central for Morrison, and why should we be brought to reimagine this chapter of American history through the prism of a haunting, passionate, violent, and ultimately unresolved relationship between a mother and daughter?

The peculiarities of Morrison's "history" suggest a design different from those described by most theories of the historical novel. This book begins with *Beloved* because, as the most complex, even paradoxical—and probably the greatest—of recent African-American and Caribbean women's historical fictions, it can help us to grasp what is most at stake, what imaginative risks are embraced and claims enabled by these new "daughterly" historiographic ventures. With insights drawn from *Beloved*'s searing portrayal of mother-daughter struggle, I will go on to theorize the allegorical structure of daughterly historical return in "renaissance" narratives by African-American and Caribbean women writers.

A NUMBER OF theories can offer partial explanation of *Beloved* as historical novel. Morrison doubtless achieves the realist portrayal of great "social trends and historical forces" that Georg Lukacs endorses, in the classic historical novels, as offering a "*prehistory of the present*" (34, 337). The plot of the ghost girl can also be seen to draw upon the modes of historical romance and supernatural tale, which have traditionally served in the African-American novel to "[transform] black history into mythic fiction" (Campbell xvii). *Beloved* further suggests the influence on African-American historical fiction of magic realism, read in recent Latin American and third-world fictional "histories" as a revisionary postcolonial narrative mode, mediating and transfiguring the cultural and epistemological clashes of colonial history (Slemon 20–21). Yet while we can read revisionary mythification in Morrison's "history," we still have not accounted for its interest in a murderous mother and ghostly daughter.

Poststructuralist critics of African-American historical fiction would have us read *Beloved* as less a mimetic or mythic recreation of the real than an entrant into ongoing historiographic discourse, inescapably "about" the problem of writing history in the complicated moment in which we tell the past.[3] Though touched by the prevailing postmodern irony toward questions of truth and representation, fiction and history, *Beloved* and most contemporary novels of slavery are not "historiographic metafictions" denying the possibility of historical "Truth" (Hutcheon 109, 113). For these novels, much as for abolitionist slave narratives, the burden of communicating an authentic truth remains, and the inherited conviction of slavery's evil renders the word of fictional slaves true in a sense not solely epistemological or even political, but moral. Postmodern fictions with battles still to fight, today's African-American slave "histories," though they may center upon questions of memory, knowledge, and identity, share with many ethnic, feminist, and postcolonial texts the impulse "to create an authoritative voice, not to undermine an already existing one" (Zimmerman 176). Thus Morrison calls on writers to de-emphasize the *institution* of slavery and put the "authority back into the hands of the slave" (qtd. in McDowell, "Negotiating" 160).[4]

But Morrison's remark gathers irony when we reflect that the difficulty of interpreting *Beloved* as "historical" text is, precisely, the terrible authority its author places in the hands of a slave-heroine. Surely we can read *Beloved* as an historiographic intervention, a strategic re-centering of American history in the lives of the historically dispossessed. But by what logic does the plot of child-murder serve any late twentieth-century ideological interest? In what sense does this plot assert the historiographic authority of an African-American woman's hands? If the above-mentioned theoretical approaches do not greatly illuminate the historicity of the ghost story without which our literature was incomplete, it may be because they view historical writing solely in terms of ideologies of representation, without considering the affective aspect of history writing, insofar as the historiographic project enacts a relationship of desire, an emotional implication of present and past. While *Beloved* is evidently a politically engaged novel, it is also a novel of extraordinary psychological reach. I suggest that to account for *Beloved*, and for all of the fictional daughters' returns studied in this book, we integrate an ideological reading of historical fiction with a reading of the inscribed psychological project of reimagining an inherited past.

Ancestral Return

In contemporary black "histories," we may, indeed, have difficulty separating the political, the psychological, and the ethnic. Discussing the recent "flood" of African-American novels about slavery, Deborah McDowell muses, "Why the compulsion to repeat the massive story of slavery in the contemporary

Afro-American novel . . . ?" ("Negotiating" 144). This hint at a collective psychological source of the trend, if dropped somewhat playfully, probably confirms our sense that larger processes in African-American history and culture are at work here, that the slavery novels of our moment mark the arrival of African-American literature at a juncture of particularly profound cultural reckoning.

For the group of black writers who have attained unprecedented literary authority and audience in an era of intensifying social crisis for the African-American community, the return to the subject of slavery would seem to articulate an ironic coming-of-age. Time and success have brought black literature to a place where the vista seems to be all of memory and return. When Hazel Carby asked in the late 1980s why relatively few African-American novels had focused on slavery, it seems she merely spoke too soon (125). By the early 1990s the roster of such texts had grown long, and we are now looking at a genre in full swing, exhibiting an astonishing diversity and range.[5] Following Margaret Walker's epic *Jubilee* (1966) and gaining greatest popular notice with the phenomenon of Alex Haley's *Roots* (1976), African-American writers have undertaken a collective return to the story of slavery unimaginable in preceding decades. The long deferral of this project in itself speaks volumes, suggesting the overwhelming impact of a trauma still too close and life conditions and looming threats too unchanged, as well as the greater, perceived need for "uplifting" representations of the race.[6]

Thus the current generation's return carries an unmistakable symbolic resonance. In the surge of African-American cultural production that followed the civil rights era, amidst an overriding concern with new articulations of racial identity, a moment arrived when it became possible—and, apparently, crucial—for writers to take on the fictional persona of a slave. As nations when they rise, for good or ill, look back and re-explain to the world the past that produced their emergence in strength, so Afro-America in the 1970s, 1980s and 1990s has been "called . . . to remember" (Charisse Jones A43) and has created libraries of scholarship on African-American slavery, as well as artistic and cultural productions ranging from films, plays, documentaries, paintings, children's books, and an oratorio, to public and family rituals, pilgrimages, and re-enactments to mourn and honor slaves.[7]

Amidst this general "unsealing of memory" (A43), today's most celebrated black writers have engaged in the profound mythopoetic enterprise of identification with slave ancestors, returning African-American literary culture to its "roots" by reviving with new dignity the foundational genre of this literature: the slave narrative (Gates xxxiii). Having attained a certain measure of authority, perhaps a certain measure of safety, of distance from the slave past sufficient to risk intimacy, along with increased access to publication and a growing mainstream audience, black writers have claimed their place in American culture and letters upon the same ground—in history's spiral—as that upon which the slave's voice first emerged. They thus invoke a heritage not only of suffering and resistance but also of self-definition in the face of racist ideologies of literary authority.[8]

A devotee of slave narratives, Toni Morrison long anticipated their literary resurgence. As a Random House editor in 1976, Morrison told an interviewer:

> You know . . . just for sustenance, I read those slave narratives—there are sometimes three or four sentences or half a page, each one of which could be developed in an art form, marvelous. Just to figure out how to—you mean to tell me she beat the dogs and the man and pulled a stump out of the ground? Who is she, you know? Who is she? It's just incredible. And all of that will surface, it *will surface*, and my *huge* joy is thinking that I am in some way part of that when I sit here in this office. . . . ("Intimate" 229)

In this remark the gender of slave narrators who most fascinate Morrison ("Who is she . . . ? Who is she?") is explicit and somewhat remarkable, given that fewer than 12 percent of published slave narratives were written by women (Blassingame 83) and that the popular image of "the slave" has been male from Abolition days to the present (see McDowell, "In the First Place"). Recent feminist scholarship on female slaves has been revising the gendering of this genre,[9] and the large proportion of today's fictional "neoslave narrative[s]" (Bell 289) to reimagine slavery from a black female point of view constitutes a symbolic reauthorization of the female slave's voice and a recovery of her centrality to the slavery story, by writers of the post-1960s black women's literary "renaissance."

As the genre of the slavery novel has evolved over the past four decades, it has borne a changing burden. While Walker's pioneering *Jubilee* faced the necessity of educating its audience in basic ways about the lives of African Americans under slavery, Haley saw a need to dignify the slaves' roots in Africa and thus to name his people the heirs to a legitimate—and a great—history. Both found their historical research subject to challenges not unlike those faced by the original slave narrators.[10] But in the hands of successive returnees to the plantation scenario, the story of slavery has come to reflect writers' growing sense of freedom from these rudimentary concerns, and indeed their sense that the freedom to rework the primal form of the slave narrative is theirs by birthright. Several contemporary novels explicitly dramatize the modern predicament of inheriting this story: Gayl Jones's *Corregidora* (1975), which explores slavery's legacy of rape in a blues mode; Ishmael Reed's uproarious parody of the stock figures and conceits by which we recall slavery in *Flight to Canada* (1976); Octavia Butler's stark science-fiction return to the slave South in *Kindred* (1979); Phyllis Alesia Perry's similar return via reincarnation in the recent *Stigmata* (1998) (these two novels are discussed in Chapters 2 and 3); and Charles Johnson's giddily brilliant picaresque about inner enslavement and freedom, *Oxherding Tale* (1982). Despite the comic mode that sets Reed's and Johnson's work apart from recent slavery fiction by African-American women, all of these novels suggest that received versions of the story left depths still to be plumbed, that if lately released from certain exigencies in retelling slavery, black writers now find themselves bound to address one subject above all: slavery's lingering mark on the heart. It is in this context that I want to consider the mother-daughter romance plot of Morrison's *Beloved* and the other "daughterly" returns to slavery studied here.

Though the rise in historical novels by black writers testifies to a sociopolitical rise to the authority—and the desire—to represent their people's genesis, this aura of ascent should not obscure the psychological descent, the paradoxical willingness to hit psychic bottom that distinguishes this body of work. The stories these novels recuperate are, after all, about deprivation and suffering often literally unspeakable. Morrison notes that slave narrators, "shaping the experience to make it palatable" for white readers, often dropped a "veil" over "their interior life" ("Site" 110). Whether we view her attempt to unveil that interior in a novel as homage or audacity, the "anxiety of influence" operative in her retelling is shaped by a distinctive sense of interiority, an ethnic, "familial" relationship to an inherited, traumatic story. For an African-American writer, slavery is a story known in the bones, and yet not at all. "How could she bear witness to what she never lived?" asks Jones's *Corregidora* (103), crystallizing the paradox of contemporary black rewritings of slavery. A descendant compelled to bear witness to ancestral trauma attests to its relentless intrusion into his or her present, even while acknowledging the impossibility of truly knowing or adequately telling this story. But this only makes descendant-writers more like actual survivors of trauma who, caught in the thrall of traumatic repetitions, "carry an impossible history within them, or . . . become themselves the symptom of a history that they cannot entirely possess" (Caruth 5).

This likeness suggests that we should read texts that bear witness to the inherited trauma of slavery as approaching the past with an interest much more urgent than historical curiosity or even political revisionism. Inserting authorial consciousness into the very processes of history that accomplished the racial "othering" of the self, novels of slavery make their claims to knowledge and power face-to-face with destruction.[11] We might think of such fictions as structures of historiographic desire, attempts to span a vast gap of time, loss, and ignorance to achieve an intimate bond, a bridge of restitution or healing, between the authorial present and the ancestral past.[12]

Years before *Beloved*, Morrison spoke of her fiction in terms of the transmission of cultural inheritance: because black people no longer live in places where parents "sit around and tell their children . . . archetypal stories," the novel must take up the traditional "healing" function of African-American folk music and tales ("Rootedness" 340). The culture-bearing impulse generates in Morrison's novels characters of mythic stature, with tale-telling names and marked bodies,[13] along with the voice of a communal chorus and a narrative voice of an "oral quality" ("An Interview" 409); her model is the "black preacher [who] requires his congregation to . . . join him in the sermon," "not the separate, isolated ivory tower voice of a very different kind of person but an implied 'we' in narration" ("Rootedness" 341, 43).[14] Aspiring to a voice that sounds like "we," Morrison attempts a communal textuality: "If anything I do, in the way of writing novels . . . isn't about the village or the community or about you, then it is not about anything" (344). Upon finishing a book, she has said, "I feel a little lonely, as though I've lost touch . . . with some collective memory" ("Toni Morrison" 131). Writing that contacts collective memory conflates the personal and the communal, works to open the "interior life" of the individual into the "anterior life" of the people (Clemons 75), or, in Morrison's words, "the life of that organism to which I belong which is black people in this country" ("Interview" 413).

In the writing of *Beloved*, however, Morrison's Whitmanesque will to communal subjectivity confronts its antithesis and perhaps its deepest source—the catastrophic destruction of community under slavery. With a capacity for pain and a sustained focus on the dead unprecedented in the African-American novel, *Beloved* includes in the storytelling "we" numberless lost forebears. More than a "history," *Beloved* serves for its author as a substitute:

> There is no place here where I can go, or where you can go, and think about, or not think about, or summon the presences of, or recollect the absences of—slaves. . . . Something that reminds us of the ones who made the journey, and those who did not make it. There is no suitable memorial—or plaque, or wreath, or wall, or park, or skyscraper lobby. There's no three hundred foot tower. . . . And because such a place doesn't exist that *I* know of, the book had to. (Lecture)

Reconceiving the historical novel as memorial, Morrison illuminates the psychological structure of ethnic historical fiction. Like all memorials, *Beloved* is not a "place" of the dead, but a place where survivors can go to "summon" and "recollect," to look upon the sculpted shape of their own sorrow. *Beloved* cannot recover the "interior life" of slaves, but by dramatizing the psychological legacy of slavery, it portrays that "interior" place in the African-American psyche where a slave's face still haunts.

Of slavery as a literary subject, Morrison has said, "It was an era I didn't want to get into—going back into and through grief" ("It's OK" 45). In the personal psychological return required to write *Beloved*, it was not "history" Morrison had to go "back into and through," but an almost palpable atmosphere of "grief," an intensity of hovering emotion attributed neither to the ancestors nor to herself, but filling the space between them. Merging the psychological, the communal, and the historical, Morrison's novel goes "back into and through" time and pain together. Returning to the surface, it brings to the present an archetypal figure for the emotional labor of its own recuperative writing: the return of a dead ancestor. I read the haunting, resurrection, and exorcism of the beloved ghost as the inscription of the writer's "haunted" negotiations with her people's past. Setting a metahistorical struggle between mother and ghostly daughter at the center of an epic reimagining of an entire ancestry, Morrison's history centrally dramatizes the problem of imagining, writing, and publishing—"witnessing"—a story about her own daughterly heritage. And, as I shall argue, the ghost Beloved, who gives a body and face to that which is in excess of African-American "history"—its haunting absences—also functions, in a dramatic reversal, as a marvelous figure for the struggle of daughterly historiographic desire itself.

Storytelling, Absence, and "Rememory"

In the "village" of *Beloved*, the multigenerational, culture-bearing black community of Morrison's ideal appears in devastated form, in the persons of a few traumatized survivors, eking out an existence in the aftermath of slavery. Thematized in the novel, the telling of stories becomes memory's struggle with catastrophe and loss. For Morrison's characters, as for the novel in its contemporary moment, cultural transmission requires the retrieval of traumatic memories. This "history" thus acquires the function of communal "talking cure": its characters, author, and readers delve into the past, repeating painful stories to work toward the health of fuller awareness. As the stories accumulate, *Beloved* foregrounds its own arduous project of historical recovery.

The novel opens on the haunted house where, shunned by the neighborhood, Morrison's heroine Sethe is raising her daughter Denver in an atmosphere of stagnant grief. Together they have come to accept what drove two sons away from home: the "spiteful" baby ghost (3) who makes herself known by the clashing of pots and furniture, pools of red light by the doorway, and tiny handprints in the cake. Into this scene walks Paul D, that rare "kind of man who could walk into a house and make the women cry" (17). His arrival changes the climate of repression: he chases the invisible haunter from the house and sparks in Sethe "the temptation to trust and remember," "to go ahead and feel" (38), for the first time in years. His past, too, has required profound repression: he has a "tobacco tin buried in his chest where a red heart used to be. Its lid rusted shut" (72–73). Together, Sethe and Paul D begin a mutual talking and listening cure, the kind that can release survivors of catastrophe from traumatic repetition and into a livable future (Felman and Laub 69).[15] At the same time, Morrison gives their private losses "a collective force," as Gurleen Grewal puts it; when her characters confide in one another, they create "a historical and political testimony that we as readers participate in as belated witnesses" (Grewal 14).

As Sethe and Paul D's halting storytelling is taken up by others, the novel's present gradually unfolds entwined in multiple strands of time, voice, and perspective. Storytelling becomes the text's self-conscious task; many scenes present a character narrating his or her life to a listener. The novel's distinctive tone arises from the very difficulty of telling, for those recovering from the traumas of slavery—witnessing the murder, torture, or sale of kin; being whipped, chained, and led with an iron bit; housed in an underground "box"; measured and catalogued in terms of "human" and "animal" characteristics; forcibly "nursed" of one's breastmilk by white adolescent boys. These experiences block and fragment the memories of Morrison's ex-slaves, whose stories emerge in bits, out of sequence, in a painful eking out and holding back often rendered in spare synecdoche:

> Paul D had only begun . . . when her fingers on his knee, soft and reassuring, stopped him. . . . Saying more might push them both to a place they couldn't get back from.
>
> Sethe rubbed and rubbed. . . . She hoped it calmed him as it did her. Like kneading bread . . . working dough. Nothing better than that to start the day's serious work of beating back the past. (72–73)

As the narrative loops around events, dramatizing the work of pain upon memory, one senses a hesitance to force the past out of characters whose memories stand in for the suffering of innumerable unknown people. Any recuperations arise against a background of storylessness, of the African-American absences that still mar our recorded history. Morrison chooses just one family's haunted house to explicate, but as Grandma Baby Suggs says, "Not a house in the country ain't packed to its rafters with some dead Negro's grief" (5). Every American house is a haunted house. While *Beloved* revives the past in the modes of haunting, memory, and storytelling, it develops a stark poetics of absence.

Narrating absence, Morrison's prose inventively represents the multiple shades of loss known to slaves: "Anybody Baby Suggs knew, let alone loved, who hadn't run off or been hanged, got rented out, loaned out, bought up, brought back, stored up, mortgaged, won, stolen, or seized" (23). Characters tend to gather around them clusters of the lost. "Did Patty lose her lisp?" Baby Suggs wonders about the children sold from her; "what color did Famous' skin finally take?" (139). On his postwar trek north, Paul D saw "twelve dead blacks in the first eighteen miles," and "by the time he got to Mobile, he had seen more dead people than living ones" (269). A traveling man, Paul D brings to the text a voice of tribal griot-cum-historical eyewitness:

> During, before, and after the War he had seen Negroes so stunned, or hungry, or tired or bereft it was a wonder they recalled or said anything. Who, like him, had hidden in caves and fought owls for food . . . stole from pigs . . . slept in trees in the day and walked by night. . . . Once he met a Negro about fourteen years old who lived by himself in the woods and said he couldn't remember living anywhere else. He saw a witless coloredwoman jailed and hanged for stealing ducks she believed were her own babies. (66)

Passages like this offer cinematic visions of an entire struggling people, among whom Morrison names just a precious few characters for detailed narration. The reader learns, like Ella as she aids escaping slaves, to listen "for the holes—the things the fugitives did not say; the questions they did not ask. . . . the unnamed, unmentioned people left behind" (92). To demarcate the "holes" Morrison has characters repeat isolated remembered details, metonymies for unrecountable emotional experiences, the more poignant for their banality. Baby Suggs recalls, "My first-born. All I can remember of her is how she loved the burned bottom of bread. Can you beat that? Eight children and that's all I remember."

"That's all you let yourself remember," Sethe replies (5). In this landscape of loss it is Morrison's pensive heroine, the "queenly woman" (12) with blood on her hands and a "tree"-scarred back, who articulates the novel's theory of loss and memory in a distinctive vocabulary. To the girl who arrives at the door from nowhere and claims to have no past, Sethe says, "You disremember everything? I never knew my mother neither, but I saw her a couple of times. Did you never see yours?" (118–19). The suggestive verb "disremember" is complemented in Sethe's usage by the term "rememory," which works as both noun and verb: "I don't 'spect you rememory this, but . . ." (160). These idiosyncratic verbal elaborations on "memory" underscore the novel's preoccupation with the problematics of recovering the past.[16] Sethe explains her experience of "rememory":

> If a house burns down, it's gone, but the place—the picture of it—stays, and not just in my rememory, but out there, in the world. . . . Someday you be walking down the road and you hear something or see something going on. So clear. And you think it's you thinking it up. . . . But no. It's when you bump into a rememory that belongs to somebody else. . . . (36)

For Sethe a "rememory" (an individual's past experience) hangs around as a "picture" that can enter another's "rememory" (the part of the brain that "rememories"). Complicating personal identity and consciousness, "rememory" as trope postulates the interconnection of minds, past and present. Thus it neatly conjoins the novel's supernatural vision with its aspiration to communal epic, realizing the "collective memory" of which Morrison speaks. For even while the added prefix "re" suggests that "rememory" is a belated mental *act*, Sethe's account of "rememory" describes a natural (or supernatural) *phenomenon*. Paradoxically then, for Sethe as for her author, "rememory" is the imaginative act that makes it possible to realize one's latent, abiding connection to the past.

"Rememory" thus functions in Morrison's "history" as a trope for the reimagination of one's heritage. The novel's entire poetics of memory—all of Sethe and Paul D's troubles with remembering—can be seen to figure the problem not of Morrison's own memory, of course, but of her imagination as it encounters her people's past. The characters who do not want to or cannot remember their stories reverse the desire of the writer who wants to know and tell a communal history. She must work to "rememory" these ancestors who wish they could forget. In the absence of their particular faces, she must create the characters she wants to mourn. The elevation of memory to a supernatural power that connects all minds—making it possible to "bump into a rememory that belongs to somebody else"—is generated by authorial desire to write like a "we" about unknown ancestors. "Rememory" transforms "memory" into a property of consciousness with the heightened imaginative power sufficient to the ethnic historical novel's claim to retell the story of the past.

Along with this heightened notion of memory, *Beloved*'s inscription of the project of narrating ethnic historical loss relies on heightened tropes of naming and love. Morrison's epigraph, a passage from Romans 9:25, combines the two: "I will call them my people, / which were not my people; / and her beloved, / which was not beloved." Suggesting that the naming function of the text be read as an offering of narrative love, the epigraph proposes a kind of history-telling that can turn estrangement into intimacy. "Beloved," Morrison names the lost past, and "Beloved" is the novel's final word. This implied function of narrative love seeks to repair the violation of love wreaked upon Morrison's characters by slavery, separation, and death. Considering newborn Denver's chances of survival, Ella tells Sethe, "If anybody was to ask me I'd say, 'Don't love nothing'" (92). Like memory, love must defend itself against history. For Paul D in the prison camp, survival meant "you protected yourself and loved small":

> Picked the tiniest stars out of the sky to own. . . . Grass blades, salamanders. . . . Anything bigger wouldn't do. A woman, a child, a brother—a big love like that would split you wide open. . . . To get to a place where you could love anything you chose—not to need permission for desire—well now, *that* was freedom. (162)

Equating "freedom"—a consummate signifier in African-American literature and culture—with the right to love as one chooses, Morrison's text exercises its freedom to cast "long-distance love" backward in time (95) and bestow names on—thus "free"—some of the African Americans history forgot. In the dialectic between the lost past and the rememorying function of narrative love, *Beloved* reconceives the historical text as a transformative space: a space in which the present takes the past in a transforming embrace, constructed for mutual healing.

Faith in narrative's power to transform is underscored in the many scenes of storytelling "exchange," to use Ross Chambers's terms (8), scenes that dramatize the power of cultural transmission to create family relationships.[17] For example, at the novel's mythological core is the story often told to Denver of her birth under horrid conditions while her mother Sethe was on the run from slavery. This story—a significant feminization of the archetypal slave escape narrative[18]—is "exchanged" in the understanding that the hardships endured by the mother should contribute to the child's sense of self.

Denver is the daughter who emerges from the storytelling a woman, embraces her community, learns to read and write, and even plans to go to college. Though she inhabits less the folkloric and more the realist narrative world—unlike Sethe, Beloved, and other Morrison women, she has no emblematic scar—Sethe calls her a "charmed child" (41). Her character figures African-American survival, the unlegendary descendants who have put the memory of such as Beloved behind them. Sethe's storytelling exchange with this daughter is a model for the intergenerational transmission of African-American oral culture[19]; it is Denver who actually retells the escape-childbirth story in the novel. Born in a canoe on the Ohio River, between slavery and freedom, Denver the survivor and story-inheritor becomes a proto-Morrison, bearer of the family exodus saga into literate American culture.

Notably, Denver's character also marks the family's dialogue with whites. Named for Amy Denver, the white girl with "good hands" who assists at her birth (76), Denver has a white "mother" along with her black one and in a sense is born out of their sharing of stories. The dramatic encounter of Sethe and Amy in the American wilderness, bonding over the archetypal female experiences of giving birth and fleeing male violence, provides a female reimagination of the Huck-and-Jim interracial duos of American fiction and popular culture.[20] In the light of Williams's *Dessa Rose* (1986), which also represents a relationship between a pregnant, escaping slave woman and a sympathetic white woman, we might trace the formation of a significant myth of American female interracial bonding, a subject I discuss in later chapters, especially in the Epilogue, as the "horizontal plot." When Denver reports that a white female teacher is preparing her for Oberlin, her connection to white culture is confirmed. The role of white female characters in the birth and nurturance of this fictional daughter seems to cast white women in a supporting relationship to the fictional project itself. Moreover, like the "spores of bluefern growing in the hollows along the riverbank" where Denver is born, "seeds in which the whole generation sleeps confident of a future," these "historical" exchanges with white women seem seeds of promise, pointing toward a future of relationships across the lines of race.

In the storytelling transaction between Sethe and Paul D, the lovers engage in a mutual unburdening of the past in the hopes of a mutual healing and of a future of their own together. "He wants to put his story next to hers," Morrison concludes their protracted and arduous romance (273). The reconciliation of the sexes resulting from this story exchange is a particularly notable transformation, given recent controversy about the representation of black men in black women's texts.[21] Morrison, who has consistently written complex and nuanced black male characters,[22] here creates a man whose entry into the house of fiction starts a rush not just of female tears but of female autobiography. A muse to the telling Sethe—or to Morrison—Paul D also offers hope of futurity at the telling's end: "Sethe," he says, "me and you, we got more yesterday than anybody. We need some kind of tomorrow" (273). The exchange between these two, developing from shared confessions to an actual romantic ending, gestures at a further transformation: the reconstitution of the black family after a time of devastation. When Paul D announces that the traumatic story has run its course and suggests its resolution in a vague futurity, his words manage the interface of this "history" and its crises with those of the present.

But to say that the novel's narrative exchanges affirm the promise of storytelling is to tell only part of the story *Beloved* tells. For Morrison undercuts every claim that stories heal, or bind community, or create futures, in the story exchanges involving the ghost, which come to threaten the heroine's relationships and even her life. To understand the story transactions with

Beloved—and the text's transactions with the lost past—we must examine the elusive character at the novel's heart.

The Daughter's Return

The mysterious, beautiful woman who emerges fully dressed from the stream behind Morrison's haunted house, remembering little besides crouching in the dark, longing for a certain woman's face, and crossing a bridge, turns out to be the resurrected baby Sethe murdered eighteen years earlier. She wants her mother with all the intensity of an abandoned two-year-old. In this rememory of Margaret Garner and her daughter, however, the ghost comes to embody much "more," as Denver puts it (266). Morrison gives her the distinctive name everyone privately gives to their most beloved; it expresses at once the greatest anonymity and the dearest specificity. It is her name because she died still unnamed, and when Sethe heard the preacher speak the word "beloved" at her burial, she had it cut on her baby daughter's tombstone. But when the preacher said "Dearly Beloved," he must have been addressing the living assembled there and not, as the grieving Sethe thought, the dead child. "Beloved" names everyone, in the official, impersonal rhetoric of the church, and names everyone who is intimately loved, but does not name the forgotten. Morrison has the name perform precisely this last function; the novel's defining conceit is to call the unnamed "beloved." Part of Beloved's strangeness derives, then, from the emotional burden she carries as a symbolic compression of innumerable forgotten people into one miraculously resurrected personality, the re-membering of the "sixty million" in one youthful body.[23] And part is just the weirdness of a ghost: like all the ghosts in literature, she embodies a fearful claim of the past upon the present, the past's desire to be recognized by, and even possess, the living.

Yet to write history as a ghost story, to cast the past as longing for *us*, instead of the other way around, is to inscribe a reversal of desire that informs this text's structure on a deep level. Indeed, in dramatizing the longing of the murdered child for her mother, Morrison reverses the usual direction of grief, in which the living mourn the dead; the child or descendant mourns the dead mother or ancestor.

I would argue, then, that the uncanny figure of the mourning baby girl, embodying the novel's reversal of desire, can function to figure not only the lost past but *also the mourning author, the "daughter"* of this lost ancestry, who desires the face of the mother from whom time has separated her. This is to say that the historical project of *Beloved* is in a profound sense a mother-quest, that Morrison sends a surrogate, time-traveling daughter back to the figure of a "mother of history" to enact a demonic errand of love and revenge: seeking to regain her, to heal historical separation, to know the story of the mother history forgot. The novel spares no expense in articulating Beloved's primal, pre-Oedipal craving for her mother's face: "I am not separate from her . . . her face is my own and I want to be there in the place where her face is. . . . I want to be the two of us I want the join" (210–13). Embodying an insatiable, childlike desire for the absent mother's face, to see and be seen, to commune and kiss and know and be known, Beloved is a marvelous allegorical figuration of the woman writer's struggle with and desire for the face of the absent past, for her matrilineage, for the lost mothers she would rewrite.

In the return of the daughter Beloved, Morrison's "rememory" of the murderer-mother thus demonstrates the psychological structure of a daughter's historiographic desire.[24] "How could she do that?" Morrison says she wondered about Margaret Garner, and "because I could not answer that question, I introduced into the book one who had the right to the answer, her dead daughter" ("African-Americans"). That the dead daughter of *Beloved* functions as a surrogate self becomes startlingly clear in Morrison's 1985 "Conversation" with Gloria Naylor on the evolution of her oeuvre. Discussing the imaginative project that impelled her first novel, *The Bluest Eye*, Morrison speaks of the recovery of a "dead girl" who was a lost aspect of herself: "I remembered being a person who did belong on this earth," "but there was no me in this world. And I was looking for that dead girl and I thought I might talk about that dead girl" ("Conversation" 198–99). Years later, developing the psychological world of *Beloved*, Morrison imaginatively conceived the "self" as a separate entity, like "a *twin* or a thirst or a friend or something that sits right next to you and watches you"; "I . . . just projected her out into the earth," she explains, in the form of "the girl that Margaret Garner killed" (208). After years of sustained creative work, Morrison concludes, "[the girl] comes running when called—walks freely around the house. . . . She is here now, alive" (217). Personifying her unfolding imaginary as a gradually resurrected girl, Morrison seems to narrate the historical development of the allegorical figure of the revisionary black daughter, a figure who becomes, as I shall argue in Chapter 2, emblematic of the contemporary African-American women's "renaissance."[25]

Shaping that girl into the ghost Beloved, Morrison dramatizes the black literary daughter's imaginative return to maternal history. Though *Beloved* began as an inquiry into the motives of the mother ("How could she do that?"), it attributes the fiercest energy of desire to the phantom daughter, who returns through time to question the mother. And though the plot turns upon the loss of a child, this history-as-daughter's-rememory is pervaded with grief for lost mothers: Beloved's aching desire for Sethe; Sethe's mourning for Baby Suggs, the mother-in-law almost as present in memory after her death as is her ghostly granddaughter; and Sethe's loss of her own mother, remembered in excruciating fragments: a hat in the rice fields, a scar under her breast (61). This multiple mourning for mothers inscribes in our literature the tragic experience of African-American children and women under slavery, systematically denied mothers and denied the mother-right by the pitiless traffic in human labor and by enforced wet-nursing. Her mother sent to the fields, Sethe was suckled by the plantation nurse: "The little whitebabies got it first and I got what was left. Or none. There was no nursing milk to call my own. I know what it is to be without the milk that belongs to you . . ." (200). Echoing through this "history" is a cry for mother's milk, fusing a mass-scale historical deprivation with that of the "thirsting" self, the daughter deprived of her "disremembered" matrilineage.

The welling-up of mother-daughter longing reaches a climax at the moment when Sethe realizes Beloved is her daughter returned from death; in this moment of perfect restitution, though she holds a cup in her hand, "no milk spilled." A rush of mothers' voices is unleashed, recalling lost daughters or urging remembrance on them:

> From where she sat Sethe could not examine it, not the hairline, nor the eyebrows, the lips, nor . . .
> "All I remember," Baby Suggs had said, "is how she loved the burned bottom of bread. Her little hands I wouldn't know em if they slapped me."
> . . . the birthmark, nor the color of the gums, the shape of her ears, nor . . .
> "Here. Look here. This is your ma'am. If you can't tell me by my face, look here." (176)

Set amid the echoes of so many separations, the miraculous reunion of Beloved and Sethe gathers emotional force: one child restored, one grieving mother's wish come true.

The mother-daughter dialectic that shapes this "history" generates intensely relational forms of identity among female characters. Morrison's women are linked by a three-generation chain of scars, marking both bond and breach: Sethe's mother urges her daughter to recognize her body in death by the scar under her breast, and Sethe's resurrected daughter bears on her neck the mark of her mother's handsaw. Between them, Sethe has "a chokecherry tree" on her back, the scar of a brutal whipping. Schoolteacher's nephews whip Sethe for reporting their first act of violence against her—the one that looms much larger in her memory: forcibly "nursing" her breast milk. The tree is thus associated with Sethe's violated motherhood, the visible sign of the crime she repeatedly laments: "they took my milk!" (17). In this novel of mother-quest, Morrison replaces the prototypical white master's crime against black slave women—rape—with a virtual rape of Sethe's motherhood (in effect rewriting black wet-nursing as institutionalized rape).[26] The tree is a cruciform emblem of her suffering, but it is also an emblem of her place in generation; as the second of three links, a "trunk" with roots, and with "branches," "leaves," and "blossoms" (79), Sethe carries the family tree on her back.[27] As a child, she misunderstood the pain such scars record, and when her mother said, "you can know me by this mark," Sethe replied, "but how will you know me? . . . Mark the mark on me, too" (61). Though Sethe's mother slapped her, Morrison's portrayal of the lost mothers of African-American history inscribes, indelibly, the daughter's reckless willingness to bear the mark of the mother's pain.

The mother-daughter structure also surfaces in a surprising interchangeability of generational positions among female characters. This occurs not only in the ominous passage in which Beloved grows into the mother and Sethe shrinks into the child (250), but also in a curious play on the word "baby," most striking in the name of the matriarch Baby Suggs. "Grandma Baby," as she is oxymoronically called in her old age, got her name from an affectionate husband; the "baby ghost" returns as an infantile young woman; and Denver too is called "baby," at the moment in her eighteenth year when she leaves her mother's house and enters the community to seek work and food for her family: "'Oh baby,' said Mrs. Jones. 'Oh, baby,'" and Denver "did not know it then, but it was the word 'baby,' said softly and with such kindness, that inaugurated her life in the world as a woman" (248). The circulation of female identity through the positions "baby," "daughter," "woman," "mother," and "grandmother" links Morrison's female characters in an imaginative fusion that reflects the daughter-motherly psychic dialectic of this "history," a time-transcending structure in which the novel of history meets the poetics of motherlove: "Grown don't mean nothing to a mother," Sethe says, "they get bigger, older, but grown? . . . In my heart it don't mean a thing" (45). Thinking back like a mother, to misquote Virginia Woolf, Morrison's history adds motherlove to its repertoire of tropes for the conquest of time.[28]

If the ghostly daughter can figure both the return of the past and the desire of the past-questing writer, the obsessive mother-daughter dialectics of *Beloved* also make sense as a structure of *literary* inheritance. The search for the lost "mother" of history might be read as an agonistic struggle—or better, an ambivalent "female affiliation complex" (Gilbert and Gubar, *War of the Words* 168–71)—with the literary foremothers whose influence and whose loss to history Morrison feels so intensely ("Who is she . . . ? Who is she?"): the writers of the slave narratives. Vital and impressive in their escape tales, these earliest African-American women writers represent for Morrison a culturally originary moment and a rich, barely tapped literary inheritance. Yet though their existence is foundational to Morrison's sense of authorship, as chosen antecedents they elude authorial desire, "veiling" in their near-anonymity much more than they reveal. These foremothers can be glimpsed today, usually, only in brief texts published under names recorded nowhere else, collected in volumes holding myriad variations on the same protean plot. In their day the slave narrators had much less literary authority than does the best-selling Morrison, and even today the truth-status of their tales is debated. Still, the "historical" value of the narratives far surpasses that of a belated "neoslave narrative" that reimagines historical "truth." Though it is Morrison's "*huge* joy" to help slave authors to "surface" in contemporary writing ("Intimate" 229), it is also her lot to view them from across a great divide and see in them the dim faces of origin she will never fully capture. In the jealous longing of the abandoned daughter, the novel figures its relationship to the unknown ancestress-muse of the African-American women's literary renaissance.[29]

Just as the ghost daughter's return to the mother can be read as a mirroring of authorial historiographic desire, the daughter also reverses the structure of narrative seduction identified by Chambers: rather than seduce a listener, Beloved seduces Sethe into telling her story. Coming from the place of the dead, this ghost begs to have history told to her. The novel's normative story-exchange between mother and child, carried out by Sethe and Denver in the daylight realm of the present, transacts the inheritance of a real daughter and promises real-world continuity; the exchange between Sethe and Beloved, however, is symbolic of the deep workings of the psyche in struggle with the past, involving guilt, longing, and fury, threatening disintegration and death. From the moment she arrives, her strange appeal works on Sethe, who accepts her into the household, accepts her increasing physical intimacy, and finally recognizes her as her lost daughter. All the while, Beloved coaxes information from Sethe, stories she had never wanted to tell before, but that now flow out of her. Toward the novel's emotional climax, Denver is excluded from the central drama, and Beloved has Sethe all to herself. The relationship intensifies to a frenzy; standing outside the house, the old man Stamp Paid hears "a conflagration of hasty voices," among which "all he could make out was the word *mine*" (172):

> He kept on through the voices and tried once more to knock at the door of 124. This time, although he couldn't cipher but one word, he believed he knew who spoke them. The people of the broken necks, of fire-cooked blood and black girls who had lost their ribbons. What a roaring. (181)

In this mother-daughter struggle Stamp hears the concentrated agony of the entire people.[30] The reunion of Sethe and Beloved crystallizes the vast problem of facing and reclaiming African-American history in a terrible mother-daughter seduction-struggle for the story. Morrison's desire to represent Margaret Garner and her generation, to write a story that could lie "next to hers," so to speak, generates the bodily form of a ghostly child, who floats through time, finds the mother for whom she longs, wins her embrace, and nearly strangles her to death. The mother's murder of her daughter, the daughter's resurrection, and all the novel's gothic horror seem excessive to "history" in the sense of an objective "prehistory of the present" because they illustrate quite a different sense of history: the subjective, ethnic possession of history understood as the prehistory of the self. Encountering the story of Margaret Garner, Morrison could not get it out of her mind, and her return to embrace this impossible mother-figure in fiction suggests the impossibility and the urgency of embracing one's inheritance of such a history, one's living relationship to so much death. In a moment when a black woman writer at last possesses the authority to take her history into her own hands, Morrison risks—and confirms—that authority with the figure of a fearsome foremother, thereby revealing a daughter's vulnerability to her history, its haunting, violent grip on the mind, the dangerous pull of love that draws her back. If our literature was incomplete without *Beloved*, it was because we had not been told the story of slavery by a writer willing to undertake the life-and-death story of the surviving self.

We can read in the obsessive relationship at the center of this text the figuration of authorial desire / grief for a lost mother-of-history, the active principle in Morrison's reimagining of her ancestral community. But our account is incomplete without attention to the implications of the gendering and sexuality of the ghost: Beloved's haunting brings back the past in the form of an excess of female desire. Figuring the disremembered past as "the girl who waited to be loved" (274), Morrison suggestively renders the problematics of historical loss and representation in a drama of inconsumable female desire. Calling the past "Beloved" and remembering it in a female body, the text gives one name to historical loss and to buried female desire, suggesting a symbolic equivalence, and it stages the simultaneous resurrection of both.

Moreover, when the lost past returns in *Beloved*, it demonstrates a startling sexuality. Susan Willis has argued that Morrison tends to figure history, particularly "the loss of history and culture" resulting from the African-American northern and urban migrations, in sexual terms; sexuality erupts in her novels to evoke earlier, more vital modes of black life (35). When the bourgeois black women in *The Bluest Eye* maintain vigilance against "eruptions of funk" (68), Willis claims, "funk" signifies "the intrusion of the past in the present" (41). The "funk" in Morrison's earlier novels denotes, then, a distinctively black female sexuality inseparable from a sense of historical continuity. Yet the ghost Beloved is an eruption of powerful, physical female desire that radically threatens the distinction between past and present, as well as the household and the throats of the living. The disruptive sexuality of a murdered girl returned from the dead is a funky nightmare, an agony of limitless sexual desire expressive of the lot of the disremembered in time.

Strikingly, this ghostly longing does not restrict its objects by gender. Beloved seduces Paul D but "[cannot] take her eyes off Sethe":

> Stooping to shake the damper, or snapping sticks for kindlin, Sethe was licked, tasted, eaten by Beloved's eyes. . . . [S]he felt Beloved touch her. A touch no heavier than a feather but loaded, nevertheless, with desire. Sethe stirred and looked. . . . into her eyes. The longing she saw there was bottomless. . . . (57–58)

When one day Beloved's massaging strokes turn to "lips that kept on kissing," Sethe startles, saying, "You too old for that" (97–98). We might explain this moment in terms of the cognitive clash produced by the returned baby-ghost plot—an eighteen-year-old woman has the desires of a two-year-old girl—but we cannot help but note the approach of Morrison's prose to a homoerotics of mother-daughter, present-past relations, an aesthetic that becomes even more evident in the novel's central section.

When Sethe discovers Beloved's identity and interprets her reappearance as a sign of forgiveness, in immense relief she turns her back on the world, locks her door, and devotes herself to loving Beloved. The novel then embarks upon eighteen pages of "unspeakable thoughts, unspoken" (199) by

Sethe and her daughters, now an isolated and passionate trio, who enter a communion of love, outside time. Echoing the *Song of Songs*, each speaks a monologue in turn: "Beloved, she my daughter. She mine"; "Beloved is my sister"; "I am Beloved and she is mine" (200–210). Their voices then join in a fugue of woman-woman love: "You are my sister / You are my daughter / You are my face; you are me"; "I have your milk / I have your smile / I will take care of you"; "You are mine / You are mine / You are mine" (216–17).

In this fantasy of fulfilled female desire, the text seems to find its heart. When Beloved's desire for Sethe first disrupts Sethe's household, the homoerotic suggestion is one with the volcanic return of the repressed past she brings into the house of the present. But when Sethe locks the door of 124 against the world—in particular the male world of Stamp Paid and Paul D—a woman's desire for another is no longer disturbing; rather, the *jouissant* communion that ensues seems a momentary utopian resolution of the war between present and past. If the fluctuations of sexuality in Morrison encode historical process, this "lesbian" section of *Beloved* might constitute a momentary "separatist" resolution of historical tensions, in a realm "free at last," as Morrison suggestively puts it (199), of male interpretation or authority—free, in fact, of "history." But if, as I have argued, Beloved figures both the lost past and the desiring present, her desire for Sethe suggests a narrative desire that is essentially "matrisexual" (a term that describes the original sexuality of children) (Chodorow 95). The seduction of the ancestress for her story, which Beloved undertakes for Morrison, generates an aesthetic of woman-woman desire, a desire that comes to rest here in an ahistorical, pre-Oedipal fantasy of perfect mother-child reunion. As the form joins their separate voices in ritualized call and response, female historiographic agon is, for a moment, perfectly resolved.

There is, of course, no adequate language in which to represent pre-Oedipal daughter-motherly desire; any attempt is likely to evoke the erotic.[31] A "lesbian" reading of *Beloved* would probably be rejected by Morrison, who has denied that she wrote a lesbian novel in *Sula*, insisting it depicts the close female friendship historically characteristic of black women ("It's OK" 45). Certainly the many strong female bonds in Morrison's novels—particularly the recurring three-woman households—strike us as affirmations of women's love and culture without necessarily implying lesbianism, except perhaps as construed in Adrienne Rich's "lesbian continuum" ("Compulsory"). But it is interesting that after rejecting such readings of *Sula* Morrison would write a novel in language that even more strongly evokes lesbian erotics. I have attributed this to the poetics of daughterly historiographic desire, but lesbian theories can suggest other dynamics at work. Without claiming that Morrison represents a lesbian subjectivity or essence, we might read the part of the novel set behind the closed door of 124 as a narrative form of lesbian psychological "merger" (see Burch 94–100), or as what Tamsin Wilton has called a "lesbian space," a textual space that actively invites our "disruptive" and "destabilizing" readings along lesbian lines (Wilton 135–36, 133).[32]

Most suggestive, to me, is the way this section fuses erotic disruption with an overthrow of the boundaries of time and mortality, each form of transgression figuring the other, as *Beloved*'s women bring time to a halt and hold onto one another. It bears noting, too, that Morrison's figuration of human relationships often tends to blur the "kinds" of love, as when Sethe, upon realizing her daughter has returned to her, "ascended the lily-white stairs like a bride" (176), or when, speaking "unspoken" thoughts to Beloved, she says that Paul D "found out about me and you in the shed" (203), and unwittingly connects her motherly murder to their clandestine lovemaking. "Love is or it ain't," Sethe tells Paul D (164). Clearly female homoerotics remains a vital element in the vocabulary of interchangeable tropes for love demanded by Morrison's passionate, expansive, and redemptive historical vision.

THE PERFECT, timeless lull inside the historical mother's house must pass. When the food runs out, Denver must go into the world to find some and so begins to bring her haunted family back into its community and into time. At home the love-feast has passed the satiation point; Beloved demands more and more from Sethe, while accusing her of desertion. Slowly she begins to grow bigger, while Sethe diminishes, so that it seems to Denver that "the thing was done": "Beloved bending over Sethe looked the mother, Sethe the teething child. . . . Beloved ate up her life, took it, swelled up with it. . . . And the older woman yielded it up without a murmur" (250). The murdered baby turned passionate ghost has become a vampire. A difficult emotional crossing is made when the text acknowledges that the murdered innocent, the forgotten past, can become, if allowed to return and take over our present-day households, a killer. When the women of the town hear that Sethe's murdered baby has returned, they overcome their longtime disgust and decide that "nobody got that coming" (256). Thirty-strong, they march to the house and perform a collective exorcism; Beloved vanishes. Paul D then returns to bring Sethe out of a traumatic withdrawal, and into "some kind of tomorrow" (273).

Having shaken the fictional present of Sethe's life free of the burden of its past, Morrison ends her story. She then closes the text with a two-page coda that leaves Sethe's living family behind and meditates only on Beloved and her meaning for our present moment. There is a recognition here that, like the ghost-vampire of Sethe's past, writing, too, can feed on the historical mother, grow larger than her, potentially kill her; and "when you kill the ancestor," Morrison has said, "you kill yourself" ("Rootedness" 344). Taking leave of history, the novel leaves the slave mother to her own moment, to herself—whoever she was. When she reads a slave woman's narrative Morrison wonders, "Who is she? . . . Who is she?" But at her slave novel's end, she lets the foremother question herself: "Me? Me?" Sethe asks, her story's final words, and her reply when Paul D tells her, "You your best thing, Sethe" (273). *Beloved* ultimately leaves the mother of history to possess herself, stops haunting her with the losses of the past, or with our present longing.

YET IF THE text finally gives up the historical mother, its ending manages to perpetuate the figure of history's desirous daughter, mirror-image of the present-day daughterly imagination that searches backward in time. In the final two pages Morrison diminishes Beloved's body to "a loneliness" that hovers amongst us, but that we banish from thought as we banish denied desire: "Disremembered and unaccounted for, she cannot be lost because no one is looking for her. . . . They forgot her like a bad dream" (274). "Transfiguring and disseminating the haunting," as Morrison has described her work in this coda (Lecture), she brings "history" to an unclosed closure and moves the haunt into our own houses:

> Sometimes the photograph of a close friend or relative—looked at too long—shifts, and something more familiar than the dear face itself moves there. They can touch it if they like, but don't. . . . (275)

Her ending unravels the novel's illusion of historical mimesis, casting its history-telling as the inverse of cultural transmission, the shadowy underside of family inheritance, "not a story to pass on" (274–75) because it has merely delineated an abiding loss—a thing best described by negation. Yet the negatives of the closing paragraph make this nothingness exquisitely tangible:

> By and by all trace is gone. . . . The rest is weather. Not the breath of the disremembered and unaccounted for, but wind in the eaves, or spring ice thawing too quickly. Just weather. Certainly no clamor for a kiss.
>
> Beloved. (275)

The lovely un-substance "not the breath of the disremembered and unaccounted for," passes into the nothing of "just weather," which rolls away before the stunning silence, "certainly no clamor for a kiss." For us of course, closing the book, there is nothing but weather. The past does not exist unless we choose to hear its clamor. But Morrison stages an encounter with the past in a text of such clamorous desire that she does make us seem to see loss's quickening body and hear it clamor back. And in ending, once she has hushed the obscure absences and denied desires that her fiction aroused, her final word seals our relationship to the past with the offering of a name: "Beloved." Thus her history achieves its embrace.

2 Adventures of the Magic Black Daughter

History and "Renaissance" in Contemporary African-American Women's Fictions

That history in Toni Morrison's hands becomes a "mother and child reunion" should be, in a sense, no surprise at all. Narratives of history always depend on the symbolic structure of the parental relation, the most immediate imaginable unit of history. If traditional, androcentric histories—literary and non-literary—tend to discover founding fathers, Morrison's recovery of mothers would seem simply to follow the logic of feminist "re-vision," in Adrienne Rich's inflection of the term.[1] "We think back through our mothers, if we are women," said Virginia Woolf (*Room* 76), and in the last several decades the work of feminist historians and literary scholars to uncover women's neglected history and writing—particularly the multifaceted exploration of motherhood and mother-daughter relationships—has established the recovery of the maternal as a central project of feminism, one with diverse cultural, political, and psychological dimensions. Simply put, a revised female self requires a revised mother.

So it is not matrifocality *per se* that most distinguishes Morrison's "history" among contemporary women's texts—in this *Beloved* has abundant company, especially in recent literature by ethnic American women.[2] Rather, what is distinctive is Morrison's elaboration of a daughter-mother romance, the child's active reunion with the mother, by which historical return is literalized and embodied in the meeting of the two female characters. Centering her history in the *bodies* of daughter and mother, Morrison locates the historical where it has least been recognized. In the central scene of childbirth in *Beloved*, and in the novel's obsessive mother-daughter dialectic, Morrison recovers what was always true: that the female body is the primary generator of history, that childbirth is history in the making.

In contemporary women's literature maternal motifs now predominate in the representation of history, scenes of childbirth serving to affirm the processes of genealogical and literary inheritance that generated the possibility of the texts' present emergence. Among today's writers, African-American women tend more emphatically than any other group to frame their historical rewritings as daughters' retellings and to figure their generation's authorial agency in a daughter's reclamation of her inheritance. Yet the curious twist in *Beloved*, as I noted, is that the childbirth metaphor functions in reverse: the daughter is reborn, the present-day daughter returns to the mother of the past. Remarkably, in recent "historical" narratives by African-American women, the imaginative reversal of childbirth in the form of a black daughter's return to her mother has become a recurrent trope. Though no text matches the desire and fury of Beloved's rendezvous with history, a marvelous time-traveling black daughter reappears in many contemporary African-American women's writings, incarnated in a range of characters with diverse powers. This newborn girl-child seems to have sprung, fully formed, from the collective minds of a group of black women writers at approximately the same moment; these include Octavia Butler, Lucille Clifton, Julie Dash, Jewelle Gomez, Paule Marshall, Toni Morrison, Gloria Naylor, and Alice Walker.

Who is this girl, and what is her errand? First appearing in the late 1970s, the phantom black daughter's amazing career has gone undocumented until now. The following two chapters, beginning with an inquiry into the circumstances of her birth, pursue the magic black daughter's traces through the history of an extraordinary literary moment. Rather than a totalizing theory, she is meant as a hypothesis, a guide who can illuminate anew the realm through which she travels. Following the magic girl, I hope to show how this literary movement has positioned itself to claim an authoritative, intimate relationship to history, how it has reopened the menacing past of slavery as a field for black daughterly desire. Above all, I offer this figure of youthful return as an incarnation of the very spirit of the African-American women's "renaissance."

MOTHERING THE RENAISSANCE

Rebirth of the Dead Black Girl

somebody / anybody
sing a black girl's song
bring her out
to know herself

. . .

she's been dead so long
closed in silence so long
she doesn't know the sound

of her own voice
her infinite beauty
. . .
let her be born
let her be born
& handled warmly. (4–5)

This passage from the opening of Ntozake Shange's 1975 choreopoem *for colored girls who have considered suicide / when the rainbow is enuf*, predating by ten years Morrison's figure for her own entry into writing, reads today like a birth announcement for the black women's "renaissance."[3] Reviving a "dead girl," *for colored girls* transforms the stigma of her color into a radiant emblem of identity; the "rainbow" of "ladies" in brown, yellow, purple, red, green, blue, and orange celebrates an emerging consciousness of collective identity among African-American women.

To ask why an emblematic black girl was "dead" before her "renaissance" and why her death was publicly recorded and redressed around 1970 is to engage a cultural and political history at once complicated and all too simple. The symbolic resonances of Morrison's and Shange's figure extend to the wide-ranging effects of American racism in the lives of black women; to their socioeconomic, cultural, and artistic disenfranchisement and their exclusion from publication; to sexism within African-American communities; and to the especially limiting parameters of the lives of black girls. Searching American literature before this period one finds a paltry few mentally and imaginatively alive black girls, girls who lived lives of their own invention.

Morrison's first novel *The Bluest Eye* (1970), set in 1940s Ohio, depicts the energy and invention of black girls withering in hostile soil. The "dead girl" whom Morrison would later describe, recalling the writing of *The Bluest Eye*, might be a composite of a number of dispirited young characters here. When the narrator Claudia and her sister Frieda decide to save the life of Pecola Breedlove's baby girl—product of her father's rape—they attempt to work a black girls' magic, reciting spells over marigold seeds. "We could think of nothing but our own magic" (9), Claudia says, little suspecting that "the land of the entire country" might be "bad for certain kinds of flowers." But "no green was going to spring from our seeds" (160); Pecola's baby dies and she loses her sanity. Magic does not work for these girls at this moment. "Among the garbage and the sunflowers," "among all the waste and beauty of the world" in which black girls of the 1940s live in the novel's last lines, Morrison writes, "it's much, much, much too late" (159–60).

As it turned out, it was in fact too early for a magical recuperation of what it was too late to retrieve in a realist mode. In the years following Morrison's germinal first novel, a turn among black women writers to an increasingly figurative, even visionary aesthetic made language work magic. Perhaps beginning in Morrison's next novel, with the world-creating, world-burying games of Sula and Nel, later developed in high magical form in the spiritual healing plots of Toni Cade Bambara, Alice Walker, Gloria Naylor, Paule Marshall, and Shange's *for colored girls* itself, climaxing in the resurrection of Beloved, African-American women's fiction became capable of working varying degrees of imaginative transformation on historical tragedy.

The magic black daughter epitomizes such a transformation. The persona of a dead girl who can be rebirthed embodies a redemptive myth of literary language; to project her into life from death is to project a new literature out of the massive trauma of African-American history. The salient paradox of such a figure's emergence, in Morrison, in Shange, and in the widely disparate texts of the black women's renaissance to be discussed in this chapter and the next, is that she arises miraculously *by virtue of* her traumatic origin; her magical powers are inextricable from her inheritance of loss, her confidence from her knowledge that she stands astride a historical abyss.

It is important to note that this girl is not a *traditional* figure of African-American culture or letters, not a conventional female type of popular culture or of literature like a mammy, matriarch, conjure woman, or tragic or noble mulatta, nor a self-mythologizing speaker like an ex-slave, self-created, or "invisible" autobiographer, nor a folkloric or mythic trickster like the "signifying monkey." Certainly she carries on a traditional recourse to the past for the purpose of "mov[ing] clearly *up* . . . from slavery," as Houston Baker puts it, and thus bears the African-American literary "family signature" of "a renewing renaissancism" (101, 106). But the magic black daughter is most significantly a new figure and a figure for newness, for invention, for her very own renaissance: a serious, dedicated, powerful black girl where there was not one before—a girl who comes to redress her own absence. Born like Morrison's Denver in a "charmed" hour (*Beloved* 41), destined to transform American letters with her story, she announces a generation's emergence into unprecedented daughterly authority.

A Renaissance

Shange's *for colored girls* and many other texts of the renaissance era were animated by the "new Black women's consciousness" that began to evolve in the 1960s as a "revolution within the Revolution" for civil rights and Black Power (Henderson xxiii–xxiv) and that grew, in the confluence of the African-American struggle and the women's liberation movement, amidst frustration with tensions between the two and the blindnesses of both. This origin in the actualities of political struggle decisively shaped the "black women's movement,"[4] which would eventually extend a revisionary influence across a broad spectrum of American culture and public life, with particular impact in literature.

Before 1970 few black American female literary figures were widely known, apart from Gwendolyn Brooks, Margaret Walker, and Lorraine Hansberry.[5] That momentous year, which saw the publication of first books by Toni Morrison (*The Bluest Eye*), Alice Walker (*The Third Life of Grange*

Copeland), and Maya Angelou (*I Know Why the Caged Bird Sings*), initiated a boom time for black women's writing. Public notice grew and publications soared in the 1970s and 1980s, among both new writers and those who had begun to open up the publishing houses in previous decades. What a recent anthology of Caribbean women's writing says about their "sudden literary blossoming" is also true of the African-American women's "renaissance": that it is in an important sense a publishing phenomenon, a market response to the perceived change in black women's cultural and economic status (see Mordecai and Wilson xi).[6]

By the 1980s black women's entrance on the American literary scene was being hailed by a new company of black feminist scholars, whose rise was equally meteoric and whose comments register a sense of the momentous. In 1985 Hortense Spillers declares that "the community of black women writing in the United States now can be regarded as a vivid new fact of national life" ("Afterword" 249), and in 1990 Joanne Braxton announces simply, "Black women writers have arrived" ("Afra-American Culture" xxii). For Braxton, the decades leading up to 1990 constituted both a "coming of age" and a "rebirth" ("Afra-American Culture" xxi), while Morrison, interviewed in 1985, celebrates "a marvelous beginning," "a real renaissance" ("Conversation" 213). Barbara Christian claims that same year that black women have "revitalized the American novel" ("Trajectories" 247), and Spillers argues that "the sheer proliferation of the work" demands a reevaluation of the American literary canon ("Afterword" 251). As early as 1983 Stephen E. Henderson asserts that with the advent of African-American women's writing, "our literature made a quantum leap toward maturity and honesty" (xxiv).

Of the many innovations attributable to the new black women's writing, the simplest and most far-reaching has been the fact of its "*finally* placing black women center stage in the text," as Morrison has put it, describing her main goal as a beginning writer ("Interview" 419). Introducing into American literature the vivid language of black women's experience, writers exercised an unprecedented public authority to define black female identity.[7] Related developments included a new focus on the black community as subject and audience; a critique of sexism, sexual violence, and internalized racism in the community; and an expanded range of representation of black heroines, to include ambiguity of character, rebellion against convention, new geographical mobility, open expression of sexuality, including lesbianism, and a focus on relationships among women (Henderson xxiv; Christian, "Trajectories" 240–46).[8]

In retrospect, these developments seem all the more remarkable for having occurred during decades when hopes for large-scale transformation of African-American life began to recede, giving way to a sense of deepening communal crisis. The renaissance of black women's writing thus tends to seem the "charmed child" in whom the promise of the 1960s and 1970s, elsewhere disappointed, became concentrated; these authors have consequently tended to take on—or to be granted—a prophetic role, albeit not one without detractors.[9] If social progress has stalled, the literary canon has indeed been reevaluated, to the extent that Toni Morrison is today one of the handful of authors an American undergraduate is most likely to encounter in a liberal arts education, and to the extent that one newspaper, applauding her Nobel Prize, called African-American women's writing about "black female experience" "the dominant school in American letters today" ("Nobel"). Black women are "more widely read by a broader cross section of the American reading public than any other Black writers have ever been," notes Henry Louis Gates, Jr., crediting contemporary black women writers with "effectively creating a new reading public" (Preface x–xi).[10] Perhaps the enduring contribution of late twentieth-century black women writers will be to have transformed forever the concept of an American literary mainstream—among both writers and readers. This sea-change became unmistakable in 1993, the year that Maya Angelou read her presidential inaugural poem to the nation, Rita Dove became U.S. Poet Laureate, and Morrison won the Nobel Prize. What John Leonard says of *Beloved* is true of twentieth-century African-American women's writing as a whole: we can no longer imagine American literature without it.

Nor, in truth, can we easily conceive late-century world literature without this body of work, which stands in the forefront of world literary experimentation. Emerging simultaneously with postcolonial literatures, African-American women's writing not only participates in a global phenomenon, but also has accelerated the globalization, the boundary-crossing tendencies of late-century literary influence. For the new centrality of this group of "minority" authors to American writing gives our literature a new face on the international scene. As writers and readers around the world increasingly look to African-American women's work, American literature becomes more vitally linked to the literatures of the decolonizing world.[11] So too, within American literary culture, black women writers serve as models for women of other ethnic groups, now in the midst of simultaneous, mutually inspiriting literary "renaissances."[12] It is from this unprecedented, paradoxical cultural position that the "charmed child" has turned to confront her awesome and clamorous inheritance.

Toward the Black Mother-of-History

In 1975, when Mary Helen Washington chronicled the new black women's fiction in the early anthology *Black-Eyed Susans*, she identified as a major theme the battle of idealist daughters with the pragmatist mothers and grandmothers who sacrificed to raise them but thwarted their personal growth (xxiv).[13] Such conflicts between fictional black mothers and daughters, Washington observed, are "not only personal but historical. And the resolution of the conflict can be discovered only as one comes to terms with history" (xxv). The course of the renaissance has proven Washington prescient, as a preoccupation with black mother-daughter relations led gradually to a stunning encounter with black maternal history. But the historical ventures, I would argue—reversing the order of Washington's terms—have depended on a process of rapprochement with the figure of the black mother that dates from the very start of the era. I would locate the inception of the contemporary black feminist reimagination of history in the first fictions to place black heroines "center stage"—in dramatic confrontation with their mothers.

Serious literary engagement with black mothers seems to have been hampered, before this period, by the sway of the popular stereotype of the mammy (Christian 238–39), an ambiguous cultural icon whose strength and nurturance were compromised by implication in white households, suggesting complicity with white domination. But other, seemingly less derogatory stereotypes have been as stifling, in their different ways. The "all-knowing, infallible black matriarch" was a figure Morrison explicitly sought to avoid when beginning to write about black people ("Interview" 419), and the "invincible . . . larger-than-life" black mother had already "tended to become a cliché" for Washington in 1975 (*Black-Eyed* xxi–xxii). Perhaps most disheartening have been the notoriously emasculating "matriarch" of the 1965 Moynihan report and the slack, corrupt "welfare mother" whose currency continues today.[14] The popularity of such distorted images may help explain the vehemence of the daughterly antagonism that Washington identifies in fiction. Moreover, it helps explain the urge toward realist depth and complexity in mother-daughter relationships portrayed in the novels that begin the new era in black women's fiction, in Barbara Christian's account: Gwendolyn Brooks's *Maud Martha* (1953) and Paule Marshall's *Brown Girl, Brownstones* (1959). These are followed by 1970s novels like Morrison's *Sula* (1973) and Alice Walker's *Meridian* (1976), which at once dramatize heroines' rebellion against motherhood and suggest the centrality of maternal heritage (see Christian, "Trajectories" 241–42). Silla Boyce, the difficult mother of *Brown Girl, Brownstones*, has successors in several unmotherly or otherwise troubling mothers in Toni Morrison's novels: Pauline Breedlove of *The Bluest Eye*, Hannah and Eva Peace of *Sula*, and *Beloved*'s Sethe. Indeed, the 1980s fiction of Morrison and other black women has been described as a world of mother-daughter romance "mixed with ambivalence, fear, and anger" (Hirsch 178), in which mothers and daughters often challenge, rage against, and reject one another (De Weever 157–58, 173).[15]

Beyond their distinctive problem with racist maternal stereotypes, African-American women writers of this period have had abundant company in their struggles with the variously imagined figure of the mother. Marianne Hirsch discusses 1970s white American feminist rejections of mothers because of their perceived conformity to patriarchal norms (164–65). Adrienne Rich's 1976 theory of "matrophobia" is apposite to such mother troubles in women's writing. Rich contends that as "the one through whom the restrictions and degradations of a female existence were perforce transmitted," the mother often "stands for the victim in ourselves, the unfree woman, the martyr"; daughters' anger at mothers may signify "the desire to become purged once and for all of our mothers' bondage" (*Of Woman Born* 235–36).

Fiction by black women in the 1950s, 1960s, and 1970s may translate a felt lack of social and literary authority into the figuration of oppressive and complicit black mothers.[16]

It is notable, then, that the course of the renaissance has transformed the fictional black mother from the antagonist of the early battles for individuation to a figure who is at once more complex and also more mythified—even celebrated—in 1980s matrifocal romances, such as *Beloved*, Sherley Anne Williams's *Dessa Rose* (1986), and Gloria Naylor's *Mama Day* (1988). To say so is to suggest that the increasing viability of black literary mothers parallels the growing sense of public authority possessed by daughterly writers. Though a competition of discourses about the black mother continues—clichés alternately waning and reviving, new images appearing to refute them—the overall trend in black women's fiction has been a rise of powerful maternal figures whose strength and whose faults alike are associated with a reclaimed, honored history. It becomes apparent that the progress of this renaissance can be traced not only in the rise of a magic black daughter, but also in the gradual creation of a black mother-of-history to whom she might wish to return. The import of such a figure for the renaissance cannot be overestimated; to borrow Stuart Hall's words, she serves to "restore an imaginary fullness or plenitude, to set against the broken rubric of [the] past," creating "resources of resistance and identity" ("Cultural Identity" 394).

This figure contrasts in interesting ways with Laura Doyle's suggestive theory of the "race mother" figure implicit in modern literary narratives, "the point of access to a group history . . . [but] also the cultural vehicle for fixing, ranking, and subduing groups and bodies." Many twentieth-century writers, Doyle argues, attempt to "unsettle the racial matrix of Western culture," "to unhinge the mother from her pivotal role as a reproducer of borders (both metaphysical and racial)" (4–6). Adapting Doyle's terms, we might say that the black maternal stereotypes mentioned above are race mother figures whom contemporary African-American women writers had to reject on their way to imagining a different mother, one who could enable a historically grounded identity without reproducing the limiting structures of racialized culture. Moving toward the possibility of mothers "as alternate objects of desire," in Hirsch's terms (11), or—as Doyle says of Morrison in *Beloved*—"from submersion of the race mother's story to full exposure and foregrounding of that story" (208), black women writers worked to develop a racial matrix that could, above all, nurture black daughters.[17]

Steps toward creative recovery of this black mother-of-history can be identified in early texts of the period. "Gettin Down to Get Over" (1972), a poem June Jordan dedicated to her mother, synthesizes a wide range of tropes for black motherhood, beginning with the following catalog:

> MOMMA MOMMA MOMMA
> momma momma
> *mammy*
> nanny

granny
woman
mistress
sista

luv

blackgirl
slavegirl

gal (67)

Positioning the mother at the center of a transhistorical collection of names for black female identity, Jordan seems to construct a historicized version of Shange's company of "colored girls." She makes "momma" part of the sisterhood, in contrast to *for colored girls*, early black women's renaissance novels, and 1970s white feminist texts, which privileged sisterhood over the mother-daughter bond. Another innovation is Jordan's vivid tribute to the black maternal body as desired by her child:

> Consider the Queen
>
> her babies pullin at the nipples
> pullin at the momma milk
>
> the infant fingers gingerly
> approach caress the
> soft / Black / swollen / momma breast (71)

Here the poet anticipates the corporeal maternal presences and the nursing scenes of African-American women's historical fictions of the 1980s, which pointedly recover the black mother's body for her own biological child, and not for a white nursling.

In another recuperative step, a 1986 essay by Joanne Braxton discovers "the archetype of the outraged mother," a woman "I had known . . . all my life," but who could not be found in the "wilderness" of American literary criticism:

> With her hands on her hips and her head covered with a bandanna, she is the sassiest woman on the face of the earth, and with good reason. She is the mother of Frederick Douglass travelling twelve miles through the darkness to share a morsel of food with her mulatto son and to reassure him that he is somebody's child. . . . She sacrifices and improvises for the survival of flesh and spirit, and as mother of the race, she is muse to black poets, male and female alike. She is known by many names, the most exalted being "Momma." ("Harriet" 382, 379–80)

Jordan's and Braxton's "mommas" both draw upon and revise stereotypes of maternal strength, clearly rejecting the compromised "mammy" and the culpable "matriarch," but most significantly, imagining the black mother as her daughter's ally and muse, who supports and inspires the writing that conjures her. These examples confirm that in the moment when African-American identities could at last be represented by black women writers from a position of strength, the traditionally "strong" black mother turned strong *for her daughter.*[18] As the heroines of African-American women's literature have become more various, unconventional, and independent, fictional black mothers have become more inspiring muses and more stalwart ancestresses for them—a symbiotic development that speaks volumes about the psychopolitics of literary change.

More recent black fictional mothers have been called "larger than life, goddesses in their own right, arbiters of life and death" (De Weever 154). Interest in the relations of black mothers and daughters has grown to the point of becoming the focus of novels like Morrison's *Beloved* (1987), Terry Macmillan's *Mama* (1987), Naylor's *Mama Day*, and Charlotte Watson Sherman's *One Dark Body* (1993), and a key subplot in dozens of others; the 1991 publication of the anthology *Double Stitch: Black Women Write about Mothers and Daughters* underscores the trend. In this regard, African-American women's texts share with texts by American women writers of many backgrounds the late 1970s to 1990s–era shift from struggle with mothers toward affirmation of mother-daughter relationships, exemplified by psychological studies like Nancy Chodorow's *The Reproduction of Mothering* (1978) and novels like Amy Tan's *The Joy-Luck Club* (1989). Yet even in this context, the matrifocality of recent black women's fiction seems exceptional. Hirsch points to recent black women's writing as the "one tradition among the various feminisms that have developed in the last twenty years . . . [to] feature the mother prominently and in complex and multiple ways" (176), and singles out *Beloved* as the text that "opened the space for maternal narrative in feminist fiction" (198).

The intensity of contemporary black feminist matrifocality must be seen, I believe, to reflect the intensity of engagement with history. Long a troublesome subject for African-American writers,[19] the past has become a "constant and consistent" presence in the renaissance, even in texts that are not centrally "historical" (Christian, "Somebody" 328).[20] If we understand figures of the black mother in African-American women's fiction to carry the valence of a charged, ambivalent relationship to the past, it becomes clear why the two fictional strands of mother-daughter relationships and maternal history have developed in tandem, why the number of matrifocal novels and of historical fictions rose simultaneously. Whereas historicity in novels by black women before the 1980s was limited mostly to "the period of their mothers' lives, from the 1920s to the 1960s" (Christian, "Somebody" 327), more recent African-American women's fictions have rediscovered a deeper maternal past. The emergence of the mother-daughter plot in 1980s historical novels like *Beloved* and Williams's *Dessa Rose* suggests that what Marjorie Pryse says of Alice Walker is true of many contemporary black women writers: "Writing out of the urgency to record her mother's life, [she] discovers her ability to write her 'mothers' ' lives" (3).

The recovery of a history populated by formidable black foremothers has now become fundamental to constructions of African-American female identity. As Karla F. C. Holloway notes, the archetype of the "goddess/ancestor" has become the predominant "metaphor of cultural continuity" (2, 134) in black women's writing; in Braxton's formulation, black women "perform their creative acts in the presence of courageous and outraged female ancestor figures who want their stories told" ("Ancestral Presence" 305). In its most essentialist manifestations, this phenomenon takes the form of what Pryse has called the "emerging perception that women have the ability to reclaim their 'ancient power'" (20), by reincorporating female ancestral spirit. Numerous fictional heroines have invoked such idealized ancestral power, including Sechita of Shange's *for colored girls*, embodying Isis in her carnival dance; Lissie of Walker's *Temple of My Familiar* (1989), recalling maternal comfort during the Middle Passage; Minnie Ransom of Toni Cade Bambara's *The Salt Eaters* (1980) and Naylor's Mama Day, calling upon ancestresses and female spirit guides to help save young women's lives. A failed heroine, by contrast, is Jadine of Morrison's *Tar Baby* (1981), who dreads the maternal figures that come in a nightmare to show their breasts and offer eggs and who "forgets her 'ancient properties'" (Christian, "Trajectories" [citing Morrison], 245).

A more nuanced tribute to maternal legacy occurs in essays by black women who trace the origins of their own creativity to their foremothers.[21] Morrison speaks of her sources in a 1984 interview-essay titled "Rootedness: The Ancestor as Foundation," and Alice Walker's influential essay "In Search of Our Mothers' Gardens" (1974) declares the author's debt to her non-writing, differently creative mother. In the essay "I Sign My Mother's Name," Washington explains such texts as part of a collective effort to

> piece together the story of a viable female culture . . . in which one's mother serves as the female precursor who passes on the authority of authorship to her daughter and provides a model for the black woman's literary presence in this society. (147)

Only a writer who is confident of her own literary authority, of course, could risk the "story" of inheriting it from a black maternal culture.[22]

The full complexity of a writing daughter's relationship to the literary figure of a black mother is suggested by Jordan, author of the "momma" ode, in a more recent, autobiographical poem. In "War and Memory" (from *North Star [New Poems, 1985–1989]*), Jordan recalls her father's violent bullying of her actual, timid mother, who endured his wrath "backing up or hunching smaller / than frail bones should easily allow," while six-year-old June defended her mother with her body (205). Moving on to her adult struggles as a political activist, Jordan closes, "and I / invent the mother of the courage I require not to quit" (211). If necessity, indeed, is the mother of invention, it should be unsurprising that late twentieth-century black feminist texts have come to be characterized by the invention of a "mother courage" for the female self. The re-creation of the black mother as the preeminent muse and supplicant to her writing daughter restores a sullied figural relationship as it enables new narratives of daughterly empowerment. When the offbeat, 1993 illustrated history *Black Women for Beginners* asks comically, "So . . . WHAT'S WRONG WITH BEING A MATRIARCH?" (109), we hear a re-evaluation and reclamation of maternal power during the renaissance years; we note pleasure in the strength of black mothers on the part of daughters newly confident of the strength of their own positions.

Sorting through vestigial images, this literary movement has made complex ideological and psychological negotiations to create the mothers required by new visions of its relationship to the past. The paradoxical peak of the trend may be the historical black mother imagined as heroic daughter-murderer,[23] whose final words once the demon child is gone—"Me? Me?"—have been said to bring subjectivity at last to the maternal voice in women's fiction (Hirsch 6–8). Despite its transgressions, Morrison's *Beloved* exemplifies the mode of historiography preferred by this renaissance: a proliferation of foremother and mother-figures, returns to mothers, recitations of maternal genealogy, and so on, all forming and framing a relational daughterly identity. Never a self-birth, or a head-birth, but a rebirth, this movement continually declares its origin in mothers—actual, literary, cultural, mythic—and figures its own creative agency as a daughters' return.

Black Matrifocal Histories: *Jubilee*

These, then, are the circumstances of the birth of the magic black daughter: a moment when writers who newly position themselves as "daughters" rewrite their history by remythifying the figure of the mother. This configuration finds its paradigm in a novel said by some critics to mark the beginning of the renaissance (several years later than the texts cited by Christian): Margaret Walker's 1966 *Jubilee*.[24] A pathbreaking work of African-American historical fiction, *Jubilee* initiates the tropology of mother-daughter relations for representing a black female past and provides a crucial, enabling model of daughterly recuperation of the black mother-of-history.

The first novel by a black author to reimagine the slavery era in epic form, *Jubilee* was also the first to foreground matrilineal descent and is in fact based on the oral transmission of what the author found "the most valuable slave narrative of all, the living account of my great-grandmother, which had been transmitted to me by her own daughter" (*How I Wrote* 56). Walker's account in *How I Wrote "Jubilee"* of her decades-long struggle against obstacles economic, social, and conceptual to complete her grand design stresses a powerful sense of mission as daughterly literary inheritor: "Most of my life I have been involved with writing this story about my great-grandmother," she says. "I promised my grandmother that when I grew up I would write her mother's story" (50–51). Conducting exhaustive research "to authenticate the story I had heard from my grandmother's lips," "to undergird the oral tradition" (56), Walker adapts the Lukacsian popular historical novel to privilege in unprecedented ways black, maternal, oral culture. The extended defenses in *How I Wrote "Jubilee"* of both the historicity of the novel's facts and the fictionality of its fiction suggest how provocative Walker's historiographic project was for readers of the 1960s, even as it recalls the burden of authentication that has dogged African-American writing since the slave narratives.

If indeed *Jubilee* is the first renaissance text, then the focus on the mother-daughter romance begins in the very first pages of the renaissance, when Walker opens a portal into the lost world of black women's history in a scene of ominous portent: the scene of a woman dying in childbirth. This woman is Sis Hetta, the mother of the novel's heroine, Vyry. Opening with the death of the mother, Walker inaugurates the vocabulary of mother-daughter tropes for women's history in its tragic mode.

"A woman who had never talked much," Hetta on her deathbed is a portrait of silenced, subjugated motherhood. Dying at twenty-nine after giving birth to a stillborn sixteenth child, she is heard "muttering" and making "raspy noises. . . . in her throat" (5, 11); the first word we hear her utter is "Yassah," to her master and rapist. In her one full sentence she asks to see her daughter before she dies, and the two-year-old is brought in to hear her mother rasp her name, "Vyry?" and to speak the one word "Mama," as the slaves keeping vigil around her gradually give up hope and pray God to speedily "take her home" (7, 10–11). The young white "marster," father of Hetta's children, makes a brief appearance to assure her, through the deathroom stench that nearly makes him gag, that she will "get well in a jiffy." "Marster"'s tangential relationship to the death scene and the condescension of the white doctor who arrives two days late and blames the midwife for "carelessness" contribute to the portrait of slave women as helpless victims (6–7). Tending Hetta and reflecting on the cause of her death, her friend Caline silently wonders why she herself has never had children: "Maybe it was something Old Marster made them do to her when she was a young girl and first started working in the Big House. Maybe it was the saltpeter" (4). Every aspect of sexuality here is appropriated by the Master, who sterilizes black women, rapes and impregnates them, sends and sells away their children, then abandons them as they die, bearing his babies.

When Hetta dies, the midwife Granny Ticey suddenly gives "a bloodcurdling yell," runs out of the cabin into the dawn, and throws her clothing over her head. "Showing her aged nakedness while covering her face," writes Walker, "she ran blindly and screaming down the road," upon which "the death wail went up out of every cabin in the Quarters" (14). This stark scene of grief and horror is not easily forgettable, and, as the opening of Walker's epic, it represents the origin of African-American women's history in images of childbirth turned catastrophic, of the agonized death of the mother, of the appalling exposure of the body of the ancient foremother—seemingly in enraged protest against the inversion of nature in the young woman and child's deaths—and of black women's helplessness in reproduction and before their fate. The strangled maternal voice, taken up by the "granny" and then by the slave community as a horrific, angry, and anguished cry, registers at the beginning of *Jubilee* and of the African-American slavery novel tradition the protesting voice of black slave mothers. As the orphaned daughter of this brutalized matrilineage, Vyry will walk a long, arduous road to her "jubilee." She eventually becomes a substantial heroine and ancestress, but she descends from this gruesome scene of women's violation, suffering, and death; the novel's first third names her "Sis Hetta's Child." Daughter, too, to this lineage, Walker makes it half a life's labor to reclaim and dignify her foremothers' stories, and so to affirm the survival of their defiant spirit.

The maternal motif finds dramatic usage again in *Jubilee* when Vyry's marriage to a free black man brings her the conflicting circumstances of motherhood and a chance at freedom. Walker echoes women's slave narratives, particularly Harriet Jacobs's *Incidents in the Life of a Slave Girl*, and anticipates more recent African-American women's novels in locating slave women's most profound conflicts in motherhood.[25] Unwilling to leave her two small children behind, Vyry ruins her chance to escape and join her husband by attempting to carry them on a desperate, muddy hike on a rainy night. Caught, she is whipped savagely, receiving scars that later bear witness to her maternal martyrdom. Rather than becoming the heroic archetype of the escaped slave, Vyry develops from this moment the heroic stature of the self-sacrificing black mother.

After Emancipation, Vyry struggles with mythic fortitude to make a free life for her family, through years of persecution by racist forces including the Ku Klux Klan. She feeds her family abundantly—and in multiple courses—whatever the conditions, farms alongside her second husband, cures her children's malaria, and gives birth silently except to instruct her husband as aide, thus redeeming her mother's story. When Vyry becomes a midwife or "granny" for a poor white community, her vocation as "mother" is in a sense a postslavery acquiescence to the role of "mammy" in white households, but in another sense it marks her ascent to a position of transracial ancestress. As "granny," Vyry succeeds in bridging the races and winning her family security from white violence; thus she also redeems the defeat of the slave granny in the opening scene. At the novel's climax, then, when Vyry bares her back to reveal her whip-scars to her former and present husbands (the latter of whom must have been singularly unobservant), her "ridges like a washboard" are the domestic stigmata of a heroic mother (406). This eruption of maternal bodily discourse is as articulate as the first granny's self-exposure but as indicative of maternal love's triumph as is Vyry's profession of forgiveness for her torturers:

> I honestly believes that if airy one of them peoples what treated me like dirt when I was a slave would come to my door in the morning hungry, I would feed em. God knows I ain't got no hate in my heart for nobody. . . . and I'm gwine preach it to my childrens. . . . (406)

In the Lukacsian celebration of Vyry's heroism that follows this speech, Walker canonizes the figure of the black mother-of-history:

> She was touched with a spiritual fire and permeated with a spiritual wholeness that had been forged in a crucible of suffering. She was . . . a living sign and mark of all the best that any human being could hope to become. In her obvious capacity for . . . redemptive and forgiving love, she was alive and standing on the highest peaks of her time and human personality. Peasant and slave, unlettered and untutored, she was nevertheless the best true example of the motherhood of her race, an ever present assurance that nothing could destroy a people whose sons had come from her loins. (407)

Descended from a dying mother in a hellish anti-maternal scene, Vyry lives to become the immortal mother of her race. Despite the conventional reference to "sons" that clashes with the protofeminist thrust of Walker's whole plot, this first black women's renaissance text is above all the story of the rebirth of the violated great mother, phoenix-like, from her own ashes.

The last lines of *Jubilee* shift the focus from Vyry to her daughter Minna (identified by Walker as figuring the grandmother who told her the family stories), who lies on her mother's bed and listens to her mother's voice outside the window:

> This time she was feeding her own chickens and calling them home to roost. It was this call Minna heard her mother crooning:
>
> Come biddy, biddy, biddy, biddy,
> Come chick, chick, chick, chick! (416)

Having begun with the death of the heroine's silenced mother, the novel concludes by restoring the sound of the maternal voice, as heard by her daughter, in a scene that presages the oral transmission of this story to the great-granddaughter-author. The inset daughter, lying in the place of generation, listens to the maternal call raised, quaintly enough, to the "laying-hens," future bearers of progeny. So the novel, having accomplished the beatification of the black mother-of-history, in closing fuses the listening functions of daughter, narrator, grandmother—and reader—who hear together the voice of the ancestress, calling all home.

THE ARDUOUS PROGRESS in *Jubilee* from the figure of the dying to the immortal black mother established a paradigm for the black matrifocal historical fictions that followed. In this chain of "inspiriting influences," to borrow Michael Awkward's term, writers have repeatedly figured the tragedy of the African-American past in the black daughter's loss of her mother, and the figuration of historical overcoming—and of daughterly historiographic power—in the restoration of the mother-daughter dyad. Morrison's *Beloved*, which, as we have seen, develops this model in extended and elaborate form, is only one of many recent texts to do so. Williams's *Dessa Rose*, published a year earlier, draws on it for a surprising but critical subplot.

In Williams's novel the figure I call the "black mother-of-history" becomes a strikingly abstract archetype, whose position might be held by two different "mothers": the actual mother from whom Dessa Rose was separated when sold to a slave coffel and the recently deceased "Mammy" who raised the white slave mistress Rufel. Though the novel's interest centers on the possibilities for relationship between the black slave woman and the down-on-her-luck white woman when one escapes to shelter in the other's house, Williams makes this plot turn on their competing daughterly desires for the "Mammy" whom both have lost. When Dessa awakens, after giving birth on the run, to the shocking sight of the white woman nursing her infant, a furious conflict arises not—as we might expect—over the body of the black child, but over the body of the black mother-of-history, who becomes the site of a symbolic contest and of a screaming fight between two grown women who are mothers themselves.

Dessa suddenly interrupts Rufel's monologue about her happy life with "Mammy," voicing the rage of all slave children who lost mothers to the white children they had to nurse and raise: "You ain't got no 'mammy,'" she shouts, and when the amazed Rufel insists, "I do—I did so," Dessa retorts: "Mammy have a name, have children"; "What was mammy's name?" (125). But Rufel cannot answer, and so Dessa supplies her own mother's name: "Her name was Rose" (125), the link to "Dessa Rose" confirming the black heroine's authentic status as Mammy's daughter. She then begins to quote the absent mother's discourse, repeating her habitual listing of her many dead and lost children, "remembering the names now the way mammy used to tell them" (126). Recovering the lost black mother's identity in a ventriloquized recitation of her lost children's names, the novel poignantly gestures toward reclaiming the love between slave mothers and children, erased from white histories. *Dessa Rose* makes this daughterly act of recovery essential to its narrative of liberation; it begins the power struggle with the white woman that eventually leads to comradeship and to freedom. Moreover, when Dessa later acknowledges that Rufel's mammy loved her too (167), Williams puts a different spin on daughterhood to the black historical mother, opening the possibility of a kind of cross-race daughterly inheritance, not unlike that of Denver and Amy Denver in *Beloved*.

Like Walker, Williams ends by transforming her black daughter into an ancestress and restores the mother-daughter dyad by figuring her own role as that of writing granddaughter. While she tells her life story to a grandchild-scribe, the aged Dessa braids a child's hair and recalls sitting "between mammy's thighs" to have her own hair braided (257). Spoken from within a transgenerational maternal space, Dessa's closing words stress the sacrifices her generation made for "our children's place in the world" (260). Like Vyry, Dessa as historical mother attempts to confer on her audience the sense of daughterly legacy embodied in her author's project.

AS THE MOTHER-DAUGHTER historical nexus established in *Jubilee* has come to dominate black women's representations of the past, historical trauma has tended increasingly to be figured in violence to, and historical recovery figured in the healthy functioning of, female reproduction: pregnancy, childbirth, and nursing. Thus we find Morrison and Williams's strikingly similar *pregnant* escaping slaves, birthings under threat of capture, violations of nursing by whites, enumerations of lost children, and moments of safety from history in scenes of maternal-child restoration. Similarly, injuries to the black female body in women's historical fictions have taken on a more distinctly gendered character, often focused on the female sex organs. Dessa Rose has whip-scars that form a "history writ about [her] privates" (14); Sethe is forcibly "nursed"; the scar beneath Sethe's mother's breast and the other scars in *Beloved* function as visible links from mother to daughter.

This vocabulary dominates Gayl Jones's novel *Corregidora* (1975), in which family stories cast slavery as the root of a traumatic history of sexual violation in which the present-day heroine is still mired. Involved in abusive relationships with men, Ursa is haunted by stories of a slaveowner's rape of her great-grandmother and then of the daughter she bears him, Ursa's grandmother. Ursa must struggle to come to terms with her grandmother's injunction, despite this legacy of forced reproduction and incest, to "make generations" (41). But her tormented and ambivalent relationship to her heritage is expressed in her physical inability to keep this commandment, having been injured by her husband and subsequently undergone a hysterectomy. For Ursa, the question of motherhood is the question of reconciling herself to her maternal legacy; her inability to bear children becomes a physical emblem of her refusal to perpetuate her tragic history.

The matrifocal nature of recent black women's historical fiction leads it to maternalize even the most conventional scenes of the African-American story of slavery. In *Beloved* and *Dessa Rose* the slave's escape becomes the escape of a woman who wants freedom to be a mother, and the encounter of black and white women becomes an interracial bonding over motherhood. In Alice Walker's *The Temple of My Familiar*, even the story of the Middle Passage centers upon motherhood. Walker's Lissie describes the captive nursing mothers who, their own babies killed by the slavers, "moved among" the captives on the slave ship, "as best they could," offering their breast milk to salve branding-wounds and to nourish the children on board. Lissie recalls:

> It was a sight one does not often see, but I will always remember the way it made me feel; the small, and not so small, boys and girls plastered against the sides and stomachs of our grieving young women. . . . (68)

Though already thirteen years old, Lissie, too, nurses. Afterward, she thinks to herself that "in the hold of the ship, somewhere in the awful darkness . . . the mothers who had suckled me also lay"; "sometimes," she says, "I imagined their moans of despair were songs of comfort for me and for their own lost children" (68). Like Lissie as she lies listening to the moans, Walker reimagines in the scene of utmost pain and despair the possibility of maternal comfort. Walker, Morrison, and Williams all rewrite archetypal scenes of the suffering of African-American slaves as scenes of a black mother's nurturance despite her own agony. The past having become the black mother's realm, even its most terrible passages can be reimagined under the sign of her influence.

Notably, these uses of childbirth and mothering as the endlessly malleable tropes of historical representation participate in a trend across the spectrum of contemporary American ethnic women's writing, in which history divides and reunites mothers and their children. In texts like Cynthia Ozick's *The Shawl* and Amy Tan's *The Joy-Luck Club* (both 1989),[26] the pattern of the rupture and reunion of the mother-daughter dyad signals daughterly re-engagement with ethnic maternal inheritance and an ongoing imaginative struggle with traumatic history.

Birth of the Magic Black Daughter

From the construction of the great black mother-of-history and the tropology of mother-daughter separation and reunion, one key step gives rise to the figure of the magic black daughter: African-American women writers' adoption of a magical aesthetic. To grasp the way this shift in modes released a generation's imaginative power, we might look to a transitional moment, the succinctly stunning ending of Jordan's early paean to "momma":

> momma
> help me
> turn the face of history
> *to your face*. (37)

In the work of an expanding group of black women writers, this early 1970s desire to reimagine "history"—turning its fearsome face into one that would smile upon the black daughter and mirror back her self—would soon cease to depend on metaphor or to call for a mother's help. Working in a more fantastic figurative mode and in the genre of historical romance, writers would soon generate magical daughters *who could themselves journey back to the mother-of-history*, embodying their authors' will to recreate the face of the African-American past.

I read the proliferation of magic black daughters allegorically, as embodying the newly awakened historiographic desire—and power—of a generation of African-American women writers. Empowered to return bodily to a lost mother-of-history, this girl takes the new "mobility" of black female characters to the temporal plane, time-traveling to contact the prehistory of herself. Re-encountering the terrible past within a romance world, she enacts impossible desires for reunion and healing.

If the magic girl incarnates the imaginative force of today's African-American women writers, her youth is emblematic both of the newness of their opportunities and of her self-definition as the child of an ancestry that made these opportunities possible. That her defining act is a return to reclaim her mother is a measure of the matrifocality of contemporary constructions of black female identity. When Braxton writes, "I imagined our ancestor mothers lost forever in that fearsome place in search of a tradition to claim them" ("Harriet" 380), it is clear that the new "tradition" whose self-portrait is a time-traveling black daughter constitutes itself in reclaiming its mothers.

For Morrison, for example, it was not until 1985, during the writing of *Beloved*, that she "said something [she] didn't know [she] knew. About the 'dead girl'" whom she had begun to reanimate by writing her first novel in the late 1960s ("A Conversation" 217). It was thus the development in the 1980s of the *historical mother-questing* self for her novel of slavery that brought this phantom to the surface and caused Morrison to see her entire oeuvre as a coherent, step-by-step "rescu[e] . . . from the grave of time and inattention" and "into living life" of a once-dead girl. Though the magic black girl is a figure for an empowered self, for an activated daughterly imagination, it seems that self could not be realized, in both senses of the word, until a moment when the plot of return to the mother-of-history gave that girl's reappearance a telos, a psychological direction and purpose, igniting her magical power. The project of recovering history thus seems, in retrospect, the telos of the renaissance itself, the overarching, mythic labor of contemporary African-American women's literature.

Staging an "overwhelming emotional and physical confrontation" with the past, Holloway has argued, black women writers tend to emphasize "the consequences of psychic fracturing without any necessary trajectory toward conciliatory wholeness" (116). Indeed, "conciliatory wholeness" is something only rarely glimpsed in the works considered here. And yet I would assert that the emergence of a magical girl on this fractured ground must be seen to signal one trajectory of hope, even as her impossible, embodied form reminds us of the lack that she comes to fill. For this figure's great paradox is to represent a rise to a new sense of empowerment that permits her to acknowledge—perhaps more fully than any African-American literary figure before her—the traumatic grip of the past that calls her back in longing.

WHAT SORT OF figure does the magic black girl cut in the arena of American cultural politics? One as unlikely and as impressive as the renaissance she heralds. Born in the liberating cross-currents of the 1960s and 1970s—her authors now aged from approximately forty through seventy—this bold girl manages to sustain her education in hope through more chastened and cautious decades. Her departure from the realist narrative mode associated with the black political struggle might be read by some as registering disappointing actualities, but by no means are her adventures an escape into fantasy. Rather, as I will argue in the next part of this chapter, her adoption of romance and magic enables powerful, culturally crucial revisionary work: the remythologizing of African-American history. The uncanny powers of the magic black daughter are only marginally more impressive than the cultural influence achieved by these writers, who have attained mass audiences and opened up the exclusive realm of publication as they have changed popular consciousness about American history. It is this extraordinary imaginative leap into literary and cultural authority, even across a terrain littered with the debris of other strong dreams, that the magic black daughter embodies.

Her allegorical role—as emblem of an ascendant literary generation—is underscored by a curious connection found in Morrison's remarks on the "dead girl" whom her novels have brought "little by little . . . back into living life":

> Now she comes running when called—walks freely around the house, sits down in a chair; looks at me, listens to Gloria Naylor and anybody else she wants to. She cannot lie. Doesn't know greed or vengeance. Will not fawn or pontificate. There is no room for pupils in her eyes. She is here now, alive. I have seen, named and claimed her—and oh what company she keeps. ("A Conversation" 217)

This girl is uncannily like Morrison's portrayal, in the same essay, of contemporary black women writers, whose "gaze . . . is unblinking and wide and very steady. . . . not narrow . . . very probing and . . . does not flinch" ("Interview" 418), and of whom she writes:

> I look at [Naylor] and think for the thousandth time how fine it is now. So many like her and more coming. Eyes scrubbed clean with a Fuller brush, young black women walking around the world who can (and do) say "I write is what I do." ("A Conversation" 217)

The spirit-girl who is Morrison's imaginary, her self, her work, seems manifest too in Naylor and her sister-writers; the "company she keeps" suggests the richly populated world of their combined imaginations.

"We Are the Young Magicians," poet Ruth Forman titles a 1993 collection. A writing community highly "conscious of itself" and of its remarkable rise to authority (Spillers, "Afterword" 250), the writers of the black women's renaissance dispatch the figure of a marvelous, time-traveling girl into the forbidding world of African-American history to declare, against all odds, the arrival of a black "women's time."

RETURN OF THE MAGIC BLACK DAUGHTER

The figure of a time-traveling daughter within a fiction of history obviously bears the influence of the magical realist fiction of Latin America and the larger decolonizing world over the past half-century. But the enthusiastic adoption of the narrative mode of magic realism by black women writers as a group has been insufficiently considered. What does it mean for black women writers to take up "magic"? How has magic transformed the challenge of confronting the African-American past, and how has it become the presiding metaphor, in this literature, for the recuperative imagination, even for black female authorship itself? The second part of this chapter will investigate the meanings and uses of "magic" in renaissance historical returns, focusing primarily on two texts: one a film that exemplifies the magic daughter's romance of return to black maternal history, and the other a novel written just before the magical explosion, in which the daughterly heroine's stark voyage to the past reveals the threatening terrain that gave rise to magical desires.

Daughters of the Dust

Two decades behind American literature, American film finally entered black women's time with Julie Dash's 1991 film, *Daughters of the Dust*. Ten years in the making, rejected by Hollywood, completed after protracted struggles for funding, *Daughters* was the first commercially released feature-length film by an African-American woman.[27] Dash's film stands out as a recovery of the African-American past within a remarkably unambivalent romance form. Using "magic" filmic effects, it creates an archetypal image of the marvelous black daughter's return to the mother-of-history.

Set in the stunning land and seascape of the South Carolina Sea Islands in 1902, *Daughters of the Dust* depicts a day in the life of writer/director Dash's ancestors the Gullahs, an African-American people whose separation from the mainland United States preserved many elements of West African culture. The last day spent by the Peazant family on its island before a momentous exodus to the mainland is a space of time out of time. In this pause between tradition and an unknown future, Dash's characters seem suspended between Africa and America, making the choices that will constitute them as a people.

The film unfolds in a slow sequence of vignettes, in which black characters (women in flowing white dresses, men in black suits) stroll, play, picnic, and pose choreographically on the contours of the beach, framed by an enormous sky. Visually lavish, short on plot, and dreamy in mood, the film engages time under the aspect of cyclicity. Dash explains that *Daughters* tells its story "the way an old relative would retell it, not linear but always coming back around" (Rule C17). Circular, too, is the logic of the film's narration; this "old relative"'s tale is narrated in voice-over by "the Unborn Child," a luminous phantom black girl in a white dress and blue ribbon, who flits through scenes of the living family and through flashbacks of slave ancestors, intrudes magically into a family photograph pose—quite startling the photographer—and except for that moment is as invisible to her family as Morrison's reanimated "dead girl" to any visitor at her home. This spirit-child is the one to whom Eula Peazant is about to give birth at this pivotal moment in the family's life. While she represents the Peazants' future, the Unborn Child is profoundly drawn to the past: "My story begins before I was born," she recites; "I remember, and I recall" (Dash 80, 138).

Compared to *Beloved*, *Daughters of the Dust* offers a simpler structure of historical recovery; this phantom child's role in her family's saga clearly figures that of the descendant-filmmaker. The girl's relationship to the mother she re-encounters is also simpler, free of the tragedy of *Jubilee* or the tortuous struggles of *Beloved*. Eula is a life-affirming mother whose amply pregnant body "speaks" maternal discourse throughout the film, who communicates with her own dead mother's spirit, and who proclaims before the assembled family that all its women are "good" women, despite the sexual violation that many, including herself, have suffered (155–57). Though her rape by an unnamed (presumably white) assailant causes her anguished husband to suspect the Child is not his, Eula remains remarkably serene. The emblematic historical trauma of her rape seems overcome by her maternal mission; what seems to matter most is that the Child is hers.

If in the Unborn Child Dash creates a brilliant visual portrait of the figure of the magic black daughter, she also offers to the renaissance a definitive iconographic image of daughterly return. In a moment that is climactic and yet muted by the film's dreamy pace and hypnotic musical score, the magic girl runs through the family's woodland graveyard in slow motion, ringed by her shiny aura, straight into the belly of her mother, who stand with arms extended, waiting to receive her child. According to the screenplay, the Unborn Child "fades back into her mother" (139); in this moment Dash's "rememory" achieves the perfect, seamless, bodily reunion with the mother that Beloved could only desire. Voice-over narration by a young black girl is unusual in American film, to say the least, but this image of a spirit child who plays invisibly among her ancestors and then crosses time and death to reunite with her mother's body offers a vision of joyful, reverent female embrace of inheritance utterly unlike anything our film or literary culture has produced.

In a suggestive reading by Renee Curry, the Child is an Afra-American narrative innovation, a "unifying" and "not . . . contradictory" site of convergence for several forces at work in the film (348). The first of these is traditional African belief in the spiritual connection between ancestors and unborn souls. Second, the Child is a compensatory figuration of Dash's own aborted fetus, a child given up for the sake of the film. In a book on the making of *Daughters of the Dust*, Dash recalls discovering this pregnancy:

> I had two choices—to put off the production for at least another year or to have an abortion. I made my decision to go forward with the filming. . . . *Daughters* would become the child that I would bear that year. (9–10)

The third aspect of the Unborn Child's character that Curry identifies is defiance of the white feminist orthodoxy that resists any notion of the "unborn." Giving a voice to this child, Curry argues, Dash articulates a position in which "aborting the child does not mean silencing the belief that the child had a voice" (348).

This is to suggest that Dash invents for the renaissance poetics of loss and legacy a third term between "spirit" and "fetus": a phantom child, outside life and death, who is free and powerful, who both narrates heredity and speaks with her own voice. A figure more purposeful and confident than Morrison's "dead girl" and more connected to an embracing heritage, the Unborn Child embodies—and intrudes into the past—the not-yet-born black female imagination of her author's moment. Enacting the descendent-writer's narrative of return, she celebrates above all her own free and vital daughterly self.

Of all the texts of the magic black girl's return, *Daughters* is least traumatized by history. Dash sets the film after Emancipation, in a community of ex-slaves with a uniquely independent heritage, who date events "1867, second year of freedom" (145), and so on, and name their daughters "Iona" (I-own-her) and "Myown"—names that mark a distance from the haunted world of *Beloved*, in which "mine" remains "unspeakable" among mothers and daughters. Though the child-narrator figures most evidently the agency of the filmmaker, she may also represent the forty-year-old Dash's grandmother, who might have been born to such a family in 1902 and might have been the "old relative" who told these stories in circular fashion. Grandmother as child, daughter time-traveling to her ancestors: these tropes shared by Dash, Morrison, and (minus the magic) Margaret Walker construct a potent alternative to the dominant narratives of American history: a mythic continuity of identity through black female generations.

In this mythic structure, the Unborn Child's symbolic double is the film's "great-gran," Nana Peazant. The Child tells us that this matriarch—who practices African religion, retells the past like a griot, and vehemently refuses to leave the island—summoned her from the spirit world to aid her parents in their moment of crisis. As the film elaborates the plot of the child's uncertain paternity and of black women's stigmatized sexuality, nothing is more certain than that the old woman's symbolic position is being handed to the Child, that the goings-on of this strangely beautiful island day comprise a middle, a crossing, between the world of the "old souls" (133) and that of the Unborn. As Nana puts it, "the ancestors and the womb . . . they're one, they're the same" (94).

Reciting such unities, the film demonstrates little anxiety about losing or recovering mothers. Contact with ancestors here, in contrast with *Beloved*, seems utterly assured, and daughterly desire for reunion completely fulfilled. The film focuses anxiety instead on the "womb," the future of a group whose journey north opens an uncertain margin into our own time. Indeed, *Daughters* articulates a persistent fear of losing daughters: the unborn girl whose father fears she is not his own; Yellow Mary, the "ruint" woman whose flamboyant return to the island complements the Unborn Child's; and mild-mannered Iona, who receives a written marriage proposal from a Native American suitor at the film's opening. Her elopement with him on horseback at the last possible moment, riding off into the primeval American wilderness while her possessive mother inconsolably cries "Iona! Iona! I . . . Own . . . Her!" (163) from the departing boat, is the film's most memorable tribute to a black daughter's imaginative freedom to reinvent her relationship to America.[28]

Herein is encoded the structure of desire in Dash's psychohistorical film: with the connection to ancestry a strongly felt fact but the children's commitment to their heritage uncertain, Dash depicts a descendantship that is both reverential and creative, daughterly and free. Raised in a New York City housing project, Dash was as a child "embarrassed" by her family's Gullah culture (Mills C3); years later her tribute to ancestry foregrounds the question of the children's link to it, elaborating daughters' varying choices to return to, remain with, or leave the old people.

In some magical way, the Unborn Child–narrator carries out her great-grandmother's charge, reuniting her parents and causing them to stay, while most of the family moves on, so that she can be born on Nana's island. Thus she firmly fuses traditional West African reverence for ancestry to the imaginative "spirit" of the late twentieth-century African-American women's renaissance. Dash's remarks about the film resonate with the sense of the magic that a daughter's retelling can work:

> I like telling stories and controlling worlds. In my world, black women can do anything. They ride horses and fly from trapezes; they are in the future as well as in the past. (Rule C17)

The magic black daughter is the descendent whose imaginative power is so great, she can remake the harsh world of the past as if it always had been under the control of a black woman. Reentering her own prehistory, she can rememory the ancestors and transform the family picture by the addition of her own laughing face.

Magic Realism, Magic Authorship

The scene in *Daughters of the Dust* of the daughter's return to the mother's body is a filmic image from the language of our dreams, an image somehow familiar though perhaps never filmed before. A magical realization of the Kristevan semiotic desire for return to the maternal body, it stands as an emblem of African-American women's daughterly returns to history.

But why, we might ask, should these fictions of return be attracted to or in need of magic? Why should they turn away from realism even as they work to restore what previous histories have distorted or obscured? This paradox goes to the heart of the paradoxical mode of magic realism itself. Critics often ascribe the tension between the realistic and the anti-realistic in magic realism to postcolonial literary hybridization, in the sense that it encodes the meeting of ethnic or "native" oral folktale and Western literary narrative. But fictional magic is not simply an efflorescence of the anti-rational elements of an indigenous culture or region[29]; neither does a narrative mix of magic and realism merely imitate a strange cultural encounter. Rather, magic realist narrative is an emphatically revisionary postmodern mode. In Lois Parkinson Zamora's words, it evokes an "excessive reality" and challenges "the nature and limits of the knowable" in direct critique of the limitations of European realism, that is, realism's inscription of "the binarisms, rationalisms, and reductive materialisms of Western modernity" (498; see also Chanady; D'Haen 195), as well as the "authoritarian aura" it derives from association with imperialism (Faris 179–80).

Nowhere is this revisionary work as dramatic as in magic realism's engagements with history. Presenting "idiosyncratic" or "alternate versions of officially sanctioned accounts" of history, Wendy B. Faris claims, magic realism sets out to do no less than "battle death," in the sense of opposing totalitarian discourses (169–70, 163). For Glissant, magic realism represents the complexity of Caribbean reality by rendering "a historical dimension (of not obvious history) that realism alone cannot account for" (105). That is, magic works to figure the shaping persistence of colonial history in the postcolonial present; in Frederic Jameson's terms, it depends on a historical "disjunction," the lingering traces of an earlier mode of production (such as slavery) bringing about the "superposition of whole layers of the past within the present" ("Magic Realism" 311). Magic realism breaks down the realist barriers that would keep such potent history at a distance and so offers a model of "mythic, cumulative, participatory" subjectivity (Zamora 498).

Clearly the colliding modes of reality in African-American women's historical narratives operate similarly to those in postcolonial literature. In both sets of texts, the "magical supplement to realism" (Faris 165) enables writers to tell near-untellable and previously untold stories, in a richer evocation of history as it lives for its inheritors. The figure of the returning magic black daughter exemplifies such a project; she serves to embody a descendant's imaginative engagement with the African-American past, "elaborating for the self a transhistorical context" (Zamora 504), even as she dramatizes the lingering trauma of historical severance. She requires of us another kind of reading of our positioning in history, a reading that appreciates the figural dissonance of the occasional resurrected child, the expressive possibilities of the occasional override of time, fact, and nature.

To some, "magic" suggests escapism, denial of the real. Jameson's earlier reading of romance as a turning away from realism in moments of transitional socioeconomic formation is relevant here (*Political Unconscious* 104, 148). But Faris, citing Jameson, shows that magic realism differs on this point precisely insofar as "history is the weight that tethers the balloon of magic" in this dialogical mode. Using the resources of realism to perform its labor of memory, magic realism does the work realist historiography does, and then some (Faris 170, 180–81). Most importantly, I think, as this mode delivers its "unsanctioned" version of history and historical process, its magic conveys above all a sense of a marvelously empowered revisionary imagination at work. As I argued at the end of the first part of this chapter, the embrace by African-American women writers in the 1970s, 1980s, and 1990s of an antirealist fictional aesthetic and of the subject of history indicates less a disappointed turning away from the actual than an assertion of power in the realm of the literary. In my view, narrative magic should be understood, whether it appears in Buenos Aires or New York, to represent not only an affirmation of folk epistemes within a reality of complex cultural and historical dimensions, but also an expression of the imaginative and interpretative potency of the formerly dispossessed. The magic black daughter herself, figuring an authorial will to imaginative transcendence of loss, also has a wider figurative import: she embodies a people's rising, resistant consciousness of power.

Understandably, however, Morrison herself has been ambivalent about the term "magic realism"; initially she mistrusted it as "another one of those words that covered up what was going on. . . . a way of *not* talking about the politics" in Latin American fiction—and presumably, in her own ("Interview" 414). But she has also said that "Black people believe in magic"; "it's part of our heritage" ("Talk" 48). In traditional black folk culture, she explains, supernatural and practical ways of knowing blend, "neither taking precedence over the other" ("Rootedness" 342; see also "An Interview" 409; "Interview" 414). Magic realism would thus seem to imitate the hybrid, diasporic structure of black American epistemology, of the hyphenated condition "African-American" itself. Though Morrison later became "indifferent" to the term ("Interview" 414), critics who seem to share her mistrust have recently attempted to create substitute terms. Gates describes her aesthetic as "magical naturalism," a coinage that stresses, precisely, Morrison's engagement with social and political reality (Preface ix).[30] In a somewhat different vein, K. Anthony Appiah describes a recent African novel with the term "spiritual realism," which would seem to dignify the supernatural elements concerned, calling them not just magic but authentic aspects of the African tradition of a spirit world "more real than the world of the everyday" (147).[31]

For Appiah, this mode "gives the writer access to a world of almost unlimited powers" (147–48). Indeed, any of these terms would seem to describe a technique that allows a writer to appropriate special powers in remaking the world. Jane Campbell claims that by infusing historical fictions with aspects of African supernatural belief, black writers create "a genuinely radical literary form" that suggests "Afro-Americans' potential power"; it "transforms history and culture as whites have presented them into history and culture as blacks envision them" (155–56, xi). This would suggest that renaissance magic realism has nothing to do with escape and everything to do with politics, as Morrison implies; granting "magic" might to her people, a writer figures the potential of their "real" might.[32]

But perhaps the figure of the magic black daughter, focused on her ancestral mission, may seem to reject postmodern deconstructions of authorship, subjectivity, and historical narrative. On the contrary, I would call her an avatar of marginal, ethnic, or "multicultural" postmodernism, which tends to persist in valuing subjectivity, voice, and personhood-in-history, even while deconstructing master narratives in the interest of difference and opposition. This is the dual impulse Stephen Slemon finds central to much minority and postcolonial literature: to dismantle the descriptive authority of received histories, even while asserting the magical power of revisionary language to reconstitute lost worlds, forgotten stories ("Modernism's Last Post" 5–7). Indeed, we might say that the magic girl works the kind of productive syntheses between postmodern critique and black identity politics advocated by bell hooks, among others. As I argued about "neo-slave narrative novels" in Chapter 1, the magic black daughter's historical ventures depend with moral and political urgency on certain historical truth-claims and, with the same urgency, continue to champion the historical subject. But making these claims in the magic realist mode—which has been called an "ex-centric" but "cutting edge" postmodern narrative mode (D'Haen 194, 201)—she makes gestures typical of the ethnic postmodern: granting voice to the occluded, dismantling historical objectivity by personalizing history and affirming non-rational (ineffable, magical, ancestral) connections to the past, and recovering "premodern conceptions of subjectivity" (Zamora 544). The suspension of a desiring phantom within a text that tells history suggests that what moves the tale is not knowledge but desire, that history-writing is the trace of someone's desire for relationship with someone else. The magic daughter's emplotment in a maternal romance is, rather than a retreat from the political, a black postmodern rendering of an inheritor's implication in history, and in historiographic desire.

The magic in African-American women's writing may be best understood, then, as a way of fusing in one revisionary myth of identity an affirmation of traditional African-American magical practice—magic conceived as a black woman's possession; a "transhistorical" consciousness of an awesome inheritance; and a growing sense of literary power. Invoking a legacy, magic as trope mythifies black women's contemporary literary emergence.

ARTICULATING THIS link in the 1985 collection *Conjuring: Black Women, Fiction, and Literary Tradition*, edited with Spillers, Marjorie Pryse connects the "magic" in contemporary black women's writing both to traditional African-American women's folk magic—called "conjure" in literature since Chesnutt's *The Conjure Woman* (1899)—and to the "magic" of transmitting tradition in writing:

> In the 1970s and 1980s black women novelists have become metaphorical conjure women . . . who make it possible for their readers and for each other to recognize their common literary ancestors . . . and to name each other as a community of inheritors. (5)

As Pryse observes, Alice Walker "associates authorship with magic" (1) when she ends *The Color Purple* with the provocative afterword: "I thank everybody in this book for coming. A. W., author and medium." Walker's claim to authorial magic seems to me ultimately a mythification of literary ethnicity, a way of recasting her literary and cultural inheritance in terms that at once rise above and mythify the merely "racial."[33] That is, the conceit of magic black female authorship tropes imaginative writing as the "magical" deployment of inherited powers. Thus I would qualify Pryse's argument that in the persona of "medium" Walker "implicitly disclaims genius" (Pryse 1). Rather, I think, the "magical" ability to mediate or ventriloquize ethnic ancestral voices *is* the distinctive, collectivist "genius" claimed by Walker and her peers. In this self-consciously daughterly renaissance, a writer portrays herself as operating within a "cumulative, participatory" subjectivity, receiving from ancestors the magic that allows them to speak through her pen, the magic that enables her to reimagine history as easily as Morrison's Sethe can "bump into a rememory that belongs to somebody else."

Alice Walker exceeds most other contemporary black women writers in her predilection for the trope of daughterhood magically activated as authorship; for example, the dedication to her 1984 poetry volume *Horses Make the Landscape Look More Beautiful* reads:

> Rest in Peace
> In me
> the meaning of your lives
> is still
> unfolding.
>
> Rest in peace, in me.
> The meaning of your lives
> is still
> unfolding. (9)

The magical roles of daughter and author fuse, too, in Walker's early story, "The Revenge of Hannah Kemhuff," in which the author recasts an episode from her own mother's life. In the story, however, Walker makes her first-person narrator not the daughter of the mother-figure, Hannah, but the assistant to the rootworker Tante Rosie, whom Hannah hires to lay a curse on her enemy. Daughter-writer masked as magician's "apprentice" (60), the narrator gathers materials to work revenge-magic on behalf of the mother.

Assertions of magic authorship also appear in recent writing by American women of other ethnicities and by other New World women writers, who draw on their cultural traditions to create magical shadings of ethnic authorship. Native American writer Leslie Marmon Silko begins her novel *Ceremony* (1977) by positing authorship as a spiritual connection to a female creation source. The opening invokes the Laguna creatrix "Ts'its'tsi'nako, Thought-Woman": "whatever she thinks about / appears," and continues:

> She is sitting in her room
> thinking of a story now
>
> I'm telling you the story
> she is thinking. (1)

Similarly, Guadeloupean novelist Maryse Condé introduces *I, Tituba: Black Witch of Salem* (1991; the subject of Chapter 7), a novel about an eighteenth-century African-Caribbean woman who learns magic from her mother-spirits, with an epigraph: "Tituba and I lived for a year on the closest of terms. During our endless conversations she told me things she had confided to nobody else" (v). Exceeding the conventional authorial claim merely to have found or edited the text, this note locates Condé's authorship in the supernatural realm in which Tituba lives, and in a relationship of female spiritual tutelage like that the novel describes.

As the above examples will suggest, the texts of the time-traveling black daughter's romance with the mother-of-history participate in a newly emerging *feminized* mode of magical realism in world literature. Patricia Hart has coined the phrase "magical feminism" for Chilean novelist Isabel Allende's use of magical realist techniques within a female-centered literary aesthetic (11). But I would identify a more substantially feminist revision of "Garcia-marquian" technique, in historical fictions by African-American women writers as well as in fiction by a variety of New World women writers. Beyond merely redistributing magic equally in the hands of women as well as men, these narratives locate "magic" *in the female body*; as we have seen in *Beloved* and *Daughters of the Dust*, they produce fantastic myths in which female generative power becomes a force for re-encountering the past and deriving a daughterly heritage. The plot of Allende's *The House of the Spirits* (1985) turns upon the magic of female literary heritage. The spirit of a "magic" grandmother whose story dominates the book's first part returns at the end to save the life of her granddaughter, who is tortured over many excruciating pages, giving her the will to live and the idea of writing; the granddaughter lives to write her grandmother's story, the novel itself. Such also is the ending of Mexican novelist Laura Esquivel's *Like Water for Chocolate* (1989), in which the narrator is the magical heroine's grand-niece, who inherits her magic recipes with her story. Magic feminism sets itself apart from male uses of the magically real by casting the ineffable connection to the past we call "inheritance" or "ethnicity" within a myth of female generative power, and casting authorship as a daughter's magical cathexis of her foremothers, an affirmation of generational continuity.[34]

Kindred

In the literary history of the African-American women's renaissance, Dash's image of the Unborn Child returning to her mother's body marks a high romantic moment, a period beginning some time after 1980 when the awful past became renderable as the realm of an enabling black mother, and that mother began to act as a magnet, a polestar, an anchor in time for desiring daughters.

We are reminded of the hazards of imaginative engagement with the African-American past prior to the creation of this metaphor in Octavia Butler's *Kindred* (1979). The earliest black daughterly text to literalize the return to traumatic origins through time-travel,[35] *Kindred* discovers a dawning 1970s power to reclaim the past, but its allegorical return, compared to those of Morrison or Dash, is dangerous, joyless, and nearly motherless. Written, as it were, before black history took on the mother's face, *Kindred* is notably pre-magical. From the heroine's opening announcement that her arm has just been amputated, *Kindred* re-encounters the past in neither the dreamy glow of *Daughters of the Dust* nor the communal storytelling voice of *Beloved*. Butler's narrative mode is not magic realism, but science fiction, and this generic difference, I would argue, suggests the stakes of historical engagement in *Kindred*'s moment. Before the claim to an enabling maternal connection and before magic, a returning daughter faced a menacing history indeed.

One of very few black female science fiction writers,[36] Butler exploits the genre's powerful effects in this early novel to render an African-American nightmare: a black woman of our day is suddenly transported by unknown means to her ancestral plantation in the antebellum South and finds herself among enslaved kindred whose lives she has scarcely imagined. The conventions of science fiction decree the narration of Dana Franklin's terrifying adventures within a violent logic, and in a matter-of-fact tone: Dana's arm gets stuck as she returns from time-travel through her living room wall, California, 1976. The impossibilities of Butler's narrative follow strict laws that allow none of the surprises of magic realism. When Dana insists, upon returning to the present, that her husband Kevin take her bizarre story seriously, he replies:

> I wouldn't dare act as though I didn't believe. After all, when you vanish from here, you must go someplace. If that place is where you think it is—back to the ante bellum South—then we've got to find a way to protect you while you're there. (47)

Kindred consistently demonstrates this strangely pragmatic dream-logic: if a woman like Dana vanishes from a room, then she must have turned back into the slave-self of her worst, unconscious fears. And because things work in archetypal oppositions here, the husband Dana keeps time-traveling away from and back to is a white man, a fact that creates potent ironies throughout the novel. This interracial marriage seems, indeed, the central problem of—even the sufficient cause for—Dana's saga: having married a white man, she must *need* this journey to work out an identity crisis and to test her marriage, to discover what black and white have meant in her history and what they ought to mean in her life.

The preoccupation with white men is the second element distinguishing the novel from later texts in this group. *Kindred*'s daughterly return finds the face of history to be not black and female, but white and male, and it consistently privileges its heroine's relationships to white men. In contrast to Beloved or the Unborn Child, Dana's power to travel in time is generated neither by herself nor by her connection to mothers; she is "called" to the past not by a great-grandmother, but by her "several times great grandfather" (28), who is, of all things, a red-headed white boy. The plot of Dana's relations with her foremothers is always subordinated to the central love-hate struggle between the heroine and the white father, as he grows into a man. This difference, too, suggests the shaping force of genre: the influence of a European male-founded and -identified genre, as opposed to a postcolonial, New World, "native"-founded and -identified genre, on an African-American woman writer's imagination of the past.

Not only is *Kindred*'s visit to history preoccupied with white fathers, sons, and lovers, but it is also framed by a black woman's "anxiety of authorship" in relation to white men: the heroine and her white husband are both writers—not surprisingly in a novel set in 1976, he is published and she still aspiring. Their adventures are entirely mediated by the reading of books. Dana is first called to the past from the living room of the newly married couple's first home, where she is unpacking their library; to the boy who sees her across a century she appears surrounded by books (22). When in the midst of "history," Dana often recalls facts from her history books to make sense of her experiences.[37] Conflicts over writing are central to her relationship with her slaveholding great-great-grandfather: her attempt to teach him to read and write, his growing jealousy of her (illegal) literacy, his secret confiscation of her letters. During one return to the present Dana begins to write about her experiences, in what the reader expects will become this novel, and her first successful work. As an allegory of historiographic desire, then, *Kindred* positions itself explicitly in a rivalry with white male historiographic authority.

This struggle of course underlies all African-American historical fictions, which engage in a broadly "counter-discursive" revisionary project (Tiffin 96),[38] in relation to traditions of white historiography. Recent women's fictions literalize this relationship; witness *Beloved*, in which Sethe claims authorship of the ink that Schoolteacher uses to record her "human" and "animal" "characteristics"; Naylor's *Mama Day*, which begins by displaying the bill of sale for a revered ancestress whom the heroine comes to know more deeply; Barbara Chase-Riboud's *Sally Hemings*, which juxtaposes its reimagined life of Jefferson's slave mistress with a series of quoted letters and other texts by famous white historical figures; and most explicitly *Dessa Rose*, in which the Author's Note implies Williams's intent to refute William Styron's portrait of slaves in *The Confessions of Nat Turner* (1967) (ix). In the first section of *Dessa Rose*, narration alternates between the slave heroine Dessa, chained and condemned to death for rebellion, and the white interviewer Nemi, who wants to use her story in his planned manual on the prevention of slave escapes. Williams foregrounds this struggle over interpretation and ownership of the slave's story, humorously exposing the white writer's numerous failures of understanding and giving Dessa a climactic courtroom triumph over him. When the judge dismisses Nemi's written claim to know her identity, its pages scatter and Dessa walks out toward her freedom, later to tell her own story, as we assume Dana does in *Kindred*.

But while Dessa becomes a storytelling mother, motherhood does not seem to be in the picture for Butler's writing heroine; her plot, emphasizing the father-daughter struggle, scants motherhood, which becomes a telling absence in the novel. In her twentieth-century life Dana has no mother and little sense of "roots"; an orphan, she is raised by an aunt and uncle obsessed with fleeing history. Indeed, from the vantage point of the late 1990s, Dana's motherlessness seems, even more fundamentally than her mixed marriage, the "reason" that science fiction selects her as a woman with a need to search the past. But the reunion of daughter with historical mother is not the focus of desire here, nor do mothers become sources of historical transformation.

Butler shows no inclination to locate a "mother of courage" among Dana's foremothers. Instead, the earliest mother Dana discovers is first seen—though she is a "freewoman"—standing helpless and naked by her cabin at night while her slave husband is whipped, and then she, too, is knocked unconscious. Going to her aid, Dana observes that, like herself, this woman "was fine-boned, probably not as strong as she needed to be to survive in this era"; "but," Dana notes, "she was surviving, however painfully. Maybe she would help me learn how" (38). A far cry from Jordan's "momma," Baby Suggs, or Nana Peazant, this foremother seems the projection of a nominally "free" but still vulnerable black female self back into her ancestry.

We can place this novel in renaissance chronology, then, as the canary in the coal mine, the first venture into the dangerous past by a black daughter whose fragile sense of freedom and authority over her history is not matched by confidence in a welcome from enabling maternal ancestors. Though the call to the past comes to this daughter as she confidently shelves books in her first real home, Dana's journey home in history brings her not to a powerful, redeeming mother, but to foremothers weaker than herself, to whom she finds she cannot lend her power or her freedom, whom she cannot save from victimage to the white father. The "fine-boned" foremother is one of two doubles of the self that Butler's returning black heroine finds in her ancestry, both of whom are devastated by the violent sexual predation of white men. The foremother's daughter Alice is an even more ominous double, who might have been a kindred spirit to Dana—their resemblance is such that the slavemaster Rufus remarks, "You really are only one woman" (228)—but instead becomes an abused and tragic figure whom the master eventually provokes to suicide. The dangers of personal identification with one's maternal African-American heritage are palpable in every moment of *Kindred,* which undertakes a brave quest for kin by a self-consciously orphaned daughter.

On the brink of the era of matrifocal slavery fictions, *Kindred* has interesting company in Chase-Riboud's *Sally Hemings*, also published in 1979. An exquisite rendering of the paradoxes of interracial relationships under slavery, *Sally Hemings* predates by nearly two decades the DNA evidence that Thomas Jefferson fathered a child or children by his slave. The novel is based, instead, on oral and written accounts of a relationship of substance between Hemings and Jefferson. Chase-Riboud renders their story in the realist mode best suited to persuasive historiography—albeit in a lush, tempestuous realism. But this realist treatment of African-American women's history places *Sally Hemings* in a pre-"renaissance" moment, just before the advent of the possibility of magical plots and marvelously empowered daughter-figures. Moreover, Chase-Riboud, like Butler, focuses on her heroine's relationships with white men, Jefferson foremost, but also, in a framing subplot, a young white census taker who visits some years after Jefferson's death and is captivated by the aging Sally Hemings and her story. One might conjecture that such a novel written a decade later would more likely have dispatched a black female returnee to the scene of history to learn the story of Jefferson's "slave wife" (297), than an infatuated white man with the power to define her public status (he outrages the light-skinned Hemings by listing her and her sons in the census as "white," so as to erase evidence of Jefferson's miscegenation).

But in another sense Chase-Riboud moves a step closer than Butler to the matrifocal historical fictions that were to follow, by dividing the heroine's attention and affection between powerful figures of her master and her mother. *Sally Hemings* offers a striking black mother-of-history in the character of Elizabeth Hemings, who ran the Monticello household for many years, and who was also the slave concubine of a white man (John Wayles, father of Jefferson's short-lived wife Martha Wayles Jefferson as well as of Sally Hemings and her siblings). Like *Jubilee*, this novel presents in an early scene the heroine's witness at her mother's deathbed. But in contrast to Vyry's silent mother, Sally Hemings's dying mother delivers a lengthy monologue of her life story, and this prominent scene of maternal narration then leads Sally in flashback into the story of her own life, for much of which Elizabeth Hemings continues on as a compelling character, at the center of the lives of Jefferson's "white family" and "black family" both. Such are the psychological complexities and hypocrisies of the world Chase-Riboud draws, that this mother's compromised status as slave concubine does not detract from her authority on the plantation or in the novel. Indeed, it is one of the achievements of *Sally Hemings* to place its heroine convincingly within a tradition of women who, while powerless to end their enslavement to their lovers, are dignified, sophisticated, self-aware survivors of the sexual politics of a despotic regime.

Butler's *Kindred*, by contrast, discovers in the slave past no such mothers, and no profound mother-daughter bonds; instead it casts its returning heroine's hopes in the riskier realm of interracial cross-gender relationships. When Dana's husband Kevin, noticing the sci-fi change coming upon her, grabs on and is transported with her to 1815 Maryland, he is asked, "Does Dana belong to you now?" "In a way," Kevin replies, "she's my wife." "Niggers can't marry white people!" comes the reply (60). As events progress, the heroine's fears for her own fate dwindle in proportion to her fears of the effect this time and place might have on Kevin and his idea of their relationship. Though he does not turn "bad," his experience is a bitter, changing one, for perhaps he also unconsciously "asked" for this return, unaware that it is his nightmare, too. The difference between their journeys is apparent from the first moment that the two manage to sneak off together, away from nineteenth-century eyes:

> I settled close to Kevin, relaxing, letting go of tension I had hardly been aware of. We said nothing for a while, as he leaned back and seemed to let go of tensions of his own.
>
> Finally, he said, "There are so many really fascinating times we could have gone back to visit."
>
> I laughed without humor. "I can't think of any time I'd like to go back

> to. But of all of them, this must be one of the most dangerous—for me anyway." (77)

Kevin yearns for his former relationship to history, parodied here as a mainstream white, male history-surfing postmodern aesthetic—all the past his own Smithsonian, to explore with no risk of his own implication. But Dana's relationship to time is characteristic of contemporary ethnic and feminist history-quests: doubting that any moment in history would be congenial to her, she yet unconsciously chooses the moment to which she *must* return, the one that is "most dangerous—for me."[39]

The logic of the intermarried black woman's historical quest "for me" requires that she experience the full range of possibilities for encounter with a white man to whom she does legally belong. The boy who summons Dana to her past bears the name of the first father recorded in her family Bible, a primordial name she had never imagined belonging to a white man. The purpose of her visits, Dana realizes, is to save his life. Each time she is jolted into the nineteenth century, she finds Rufus about to drown, burn down the house, be beaten to death, and so on. She has become unstuck in time, Dana understands, "not only to insure the survival of one accident-prone small boy, but to insure my family's survival, my own birth" (29). It *is* a bit hard to fathom:

> Would he have drowned without me? Or would his mother have saved him somehow? Would his father have arrived in time to save him? It must be that one of them would have saved him somehow. His life could not depend on the actions of his unconceived descendant. No matter what I did, he would have to survive to father Hagar, or I could not exist. That made sense. (29)

This near-comic logical perplexity, typical of science fictions, evinces a deeper question in the novel: does it make a difference that Dana returns to meet this patriarch? That is, can the daughter-writer *change* history?

From the distance of two decades, this question shapes itself clearly as an "early" renaissance kind. In texts by late 1980s rewriters like Morrison and Dash, magic allows escape from determinacy and pre-scripted stories—what must be painstakingly justified here, Dash can "explain" with cinematic tricks. But Butler's science fiction aesthetic grants inevitability to history. If Dana returns to the past only to assure that she will someday be born—and thus be able to report her return to the past—she has not changed history but only learned that she was always already implicated in it. In later fictions, by contrast, a daughter's desire becomes powerful enough to suspend and to transform history, as when Beloved returns from death, or the Unborn Child arrives to restore harmony to her family.

While she worries the implications of her confinement within the uncanny, irresistible laws of time-travel, Dana seems unaware of her emplotment in rivalry with the figure of the white boy/master, archetypal subject of History and of the Euro-American novel. What "calls" Dana to Rufus is a constant but unlocatable threat to his life, and this, in the ironic logic of the unconscious, is what drives Dana's character, what is "narratable" in her plot (in D. A. Miller's term). But Dana's conscious role is that of his rescuer, and indeed, she even develops a mission to educate him, to help him grow up a kinder slave-master and better husband to her foremother Alice. Though Rufus is at first susceptible to her influence, in young manhood he ceases to respect her freedom, regards her as one of his slaves, and sells others against her wishes. Inevitably, he does not marry but rapes and makes a concubine of Alice, Dana's double and the first mother named in her family Bible. When the modern intermarried woman investigates her own American history, she encounters the rape of her great-great-grandmother as its primal scene.

Without magic, this daughter can no more save the mother than she can prevent her own descent from her. But once the inevitable is done, Butler does draw one important line of freedom. Though her heroine suffers many abuses along with her kin—overwork, humiliation, whipping—she is not made sexual subject to history's repetition. When Rufus attempts to rape her too, Dana brandishes the knife she has concealed all along and kills the forefather whose life had always seemed in danger when she was around. She thus avenges her victimized mothers and wins escape from the past.

Even in death, however, the master's arm still lies upon the heroine's as, immediately after the stabbing, she is transported for the last time back to the present. On the way back into the living room Dana's arm gets stuck in the plaster wall at "the exact spot Rufus's fingers had grasped" (261). She will never recover from his grip upon her (though significantly it is her left, and not her writing arm).[40] Ironically, in the opening scene from which the entire novel is a flashback, the police have "detained" and questioned Kevin for what looks like criminal assault. Is he guilty? Butler's novel insistently compares these doubles, the white male partners Kevin and Rufus.[41] Could a returning black daughter change a bad white father into an ally in history? Could her modern white husband turn out to be a bad white father, if allowed absolute power? Neither change occurs: the bad old master of history remains so, though newly dead by the black daughter's hand, and Kevin emerges from his trials purged, having proven himself a worthy mate, and suffers only mild police interrogation. But it is no accident that his experiences in the past so disturb him that he feels unable to write. The struggle for the story is won, at least for the moment, and a space for new writing cleared, by the black daughter.

To live in peace in her marriage, Butler's heroine must plumb the depths of her own and America's interracial history and experience the kin-dread of her violent origins. Bravely revisiting her own "most dangerous time," she finds it as bad, and herself as full of rage and vengeance, as she might have expected. While Dana's unmagical visit to the past positions her as witness and avenger but not transformer, her narrative asserts a certain measure of authority and freedom on the part of a black woman of the late 1970s: the freedom to choose whom she loves,[42] and the authority to begin writing history as if it were her own story.

3 Further Adventures of the Magic Black Daughter

ONE DARK BODY

Charlotte Watson Sherman's novel *One Dark Body* (1993), a black mother-daughter romance that endorses spiritual and psychological return to ancestry, makes fresh use of W. E. B. Du Bois's well-known lines on "double consciousness," which it quotes as epigraph:

> One ever feels his twoness,—an American, a negro; two souls, two thoughts, two unreconciled strivings; two warring ideals in one dark body . . . (qtd. in Sherman xiii)

While Du Bois speaks of one individual male body whose "twoness" is a matter of his unreconciled Negro and American identities, "one dark body" in Sherman's usage becomes a metaphor for racial unity in the specific form of black mother-daughter reunion. The novel ends:

> "I'm glad you come back, mama," I say, and start to hum like her mama hummed, and then she start, and we hum till we turn into one dark body inside the holy sounds. (209)

Sherman's adaptation of the Du Boisian trope recapitulates a significant shift made by renaissance women's writing: away from black male writers' focus on interracial conflict and toward a focus on the black family, especially mother-daughter relationships and maternal history. In so doing, Sherman gives us a metaphor for the intensely intimate reunion of black mothers and daughters envisioned in renaissance historical fictions.

Having discussed in Chapter 2 the recovery of the black mother-of-history and the magical powers of her time-traveling black daughter, I turn in Chapter 3 to significant variations on the romance of these two archetypes. The first section of the chapter will consider a variety of figures who magically contain mother-daughter union within their own bodies, who manage to be "one dark body" all by themselves, containing their own matrilineage. Whether inhabitants of realist fictions who undergo a magical turn to ancestry, or extravagantly imagined daughters who preserve their mothers within transhistorical bodies, these figures illustrate the remarkably fruitful imaginative translation of African-American women's renaissance historicism. In them, the engagement with traumatic maternal history gives birth to a rich, heterogeneous collection of female creatures who claim to be history's daughters.

Embodying History: *The Gilda Stories*

When we first meet the heroine of Jewelle Gomez's novel *The Gilda Stories* (1991), she is "the Girl," a nameless, runaway slave, anybody's ancestress, fleeing a Mississippi plantation in 1850. But this girl's story departs completely from African-American historiographic convention when, rescued by a kindly white woman, she joins the woman's extended family—of vampires. Certainly the weirdest historical fiction by a contemporary black woman, Gomez's New Age/lesbian/gothic romance developed from her observation that "black women characters of heroic dimensions in fantasy fiction were almost impossible to find" ("Black Women" 8). Gomez's outlandish response to this lack is the figure of an ex-slave female vampire, and if her novel sometimes cloaks its earnest politics in mawkish prose, it offers an ingenious variation on the paradigm of time-travel to the past, imagining the black ancestress herself as the traveler, a superwoman who brings the past to the present in one dark body.

The strange generic intersection that puts an ordinary black slave girl in the path of the ancient company of vampires allows Gomez to create an immortal witness to the unfolding of African-American history. She explains her unlikely fusion:

> I chose to make my black woman hero a vampire because no one would understand the cycles of blood and life more than a woman and because I wanted a character who had known the intimate horrors of our past and still had the capacity to dream grandly of our triumph. (13)

In Gomez's conceit black history is feminized, so that the traditionally "millennial" vision of African-American historical romance is encapsulated within one woman's body. At the same time, *The Gilda Stories* revises the normative female "cycles of blood and life" so as to imagine African-American history triumphant not through generational succession, but through a superhuman heroine whose immortality partakes of—even subsumes—the lives of her whole people.

Reimagining black women's history in the terms of a venerable if somewhat seamy European genre, rather than the more recent, populist, postcolonial genre of magic realism, Gomez draws new lines of allegiance, while substantially reworking the older genre's conventions. Whereas the traditional vampire's immortality depends on nightly murders—he must suck the blood of mortal victims, who become undead night-stalkers like himself—Gomez creates a singularly benevolent company of vampires, who go out each night not to kill but to "share" "the blood" in a "fair exchange." "As you take from them," Gilda's vampire-mentors teach her, "leave them with something new and fresh"; "energy, dreams, ideas" (44–45, 50). To make another into a vampire is "to choose someone for your family" (69); those who join the family pledge "to pursue only life, never bitterness or cruelty" (43). As they follow their blood hunger, Gomez's ethical vampires practice restraint, never drinking enough to kill. Far from turning people into monsters, then, these undead work to humanize the human race.

Needless to say, Gomez's vampires feel seriously misunderstood by the public. Gilda's "creator" tells her: "There are only inadequate words to speak for who we are. The language is crude, the history false" (43). Yet her words suggest that Gomez's reinvention of the historical black heroine as a vampire—sworn into the fellowship of a maligned history—recuperates one history through another: as it rehabilitates the evil figure of the vampire, it also creates a supernatural avenger of the history of black women. Moreover, Gomez inserts into the mainstream of African-American historical narrative the occluded story of black lesbians.[1] Gomez's vampires are nightly cruisers who must hide their "sharing" from mortal rather than heterosexual view, and just as Gilda's "creator" "never said the word 'vampire'" (32), no character in the novel ever speaks the words "homosexual" or "lesbian," which would seem to describe most of them. Yet *The Gilda Stories* clearly sets out to rehabilitate the homoerotic menace that hovers over many vampire narratives.[2] Both the sexuality and the vampiric acts of Gomez's characters are recast as ethical practices of love and sharing. Judith E. Johnson observes that in this and other rewritings of the vampire myth by contemporary women, "Orality itself, if it is a metaphor for homoerotic passion, loses its aura of the taboo and becomes a form of mutual nurturance" (78). Gomez's remarkably egalitarian version of the vampire's bite implicitly indicts the oppressions of patriarchal heterosexuality, represented by the nightmare rape attempt that the heroine fends off in the opening pages. As it reimagines African-American historical "triumph" through a fantasy genre redolent of forbidden sexuality, then, Gomez replaces the European male vampire's rape-like predation (see Johnson 74) with an idealized vision of mutually nurturing lesbian communalism.

While Gomez's hybrid text reinvents the vampire novel, it also radically transforms the novel of slavery, which becomes the vehicle for a transhistorical African-American heroine, "a living history" (177), who embodies her people's past more fully than any other figure in this literature. Gomez's magic black daughter remembers the faces and events of the last century as we remember childhood, and in her 200-year diary she bears witness to critical moments of her people's history: slavery and escape to freedom; the postbellum era of reform, of nightriders, and of the Klan; urban life in the North;

the advent of Black Power; and the recent black women's cultural resurgence. In her earnest and adventurous participation in each age through which she passes, Gilda resembles the traditional vampire less than she resembles the time-transcending hero/ine of Virginia Woolf's *Orlando* (1928). Like Orlando, whose metamorphosis from man to woman in the modern age of English (literary) history embodies the unfolding of a new literary moment for women, Gilda as she develops continually embodies the arrival of new historic possibilities for black women, not the least of these being their power to reclaim their history in writing.

Bringing a continuous vision with her from slavery to the present, Gilda also recalls the long-lived heroine of Ernest Gaines's *The Autobiography of Miss Jane Pittman* (1971). When she chastises Julius, a black male civil rights activist, for undervaluing the work of women in the movement, Gilda tells him, "A row of cotton is a row of cotton," and remembers under the cover of metaphor her sisters ahead of her in the cotton row, picking in the plantation fields (170–71). News photos from 1971 of inmates at Attica "killing and being killed, lined up in the prison yard," bring Gilda "memories of the slave quarters: dark men with eyes full of submission and rage" (169). Yet unlike *Miss Jane Pittman* and most other African-American slavery fictions, *The Gilda Stories* begins not in slavery but once the heroine has already taken the road to freedom. It thus casts slavery not as a determining history, but as the prehistory of a momentous escape. When Gilda's "creator" presents her with the option of a vampire's immortality, she tells her, "You must choose your path again just as you did when you ran from the plantation in Mississippi" (45), and Gilda senses that "It was larger than simply a long life. It was a grand adventure for which her flight into freedom had only begun to prepare her" (46). A century later, she in turn tells Julius, inviting him to join the vampiric adventure, "It is commitment as you've always fantasized it—in college dormitories when you talked of revolution, in the theater when they speak of changing the world" (191). Gomez's reworking of the African-American escape narrative thus extends the ancestral choice to be free into a fantastic myth of perpetual commitment to liberation, of undying labor for the humane values affirmed by the ex-slaves who wrote of escape to freedom.

As she pursues this quest, Gomez's long-memoried heroine carries all those forebears within her. Before the mirror, Gilda admires her unchanging body, not merely because "her dark skin remained unlined" and "her dark eyes looked back at her as alive and sparkling as they had been . . . 150 years before" (112, 197), but also because in those eyes she sees "her mother's eyes staring back out at her" (179). Gilda's transhistorical body becomes a figure for ancestral continuity: her "rounded stomach and full legs were unchanged from those of her ancestors" (197), and:

> when she looked into the mirror her familiar image formed easily, reminding her of what the Fulani people had always known: the spirit was just that—an intangible thing that did not die with the body. Her essence as an African still shone through her soft, wide features. (222–23)

Gilda's incorporation of her foremothers becomes an essentialist myth of the endurance of black female spirit over generations of black bodies, the inverse of the inheritance of black female victimization in *Corregidora* or in *Beloved*. In the face of a friend in 1981 Gilda sees the faces of her mother and sisters, as well as those of a cook in an 1850 whorehouse and a 1921 church woman; "It was a link she searched for in each new place she lived . . ." (196). Indeed, the novel's structure as a sequence of stories suggests that the "Gildas" of various chapters might even be read as multiple incarnations of one eternal black woman in various specific bodies—the 1921 Missouri farm widow, the 1955 Boston beautician, the 1981 New York jazz singer, and so on. In her travels, Gilda "loved learning each new town, seeing how black people were manifest around the world" (225)—"manifest" as if from one ideal, of which she is most nearly the embodiment.

Yet while she carries many faces in memory, Gilda remains from beginning to end, like all the magic black girls in contemporary literature, her mother's daughter. Gomez's first lines introduce the sleeping "Girl" enmeshed in sensory memories of her mother, but when she awakens into the novel her mother is already dead. As in *Jubilee*, *Dessa Rose*, and *Beloved*, the daughter's loss of her mother remains the emotional touchstone of this text and its inscription of historiographic desire. More fortunate than Vyry or Sethe, however, Gilda remembers her mother well, "the dark comfort of her mother's Fulani face" (128), her hands braiding Gilda's hair, her stories of Africa and the Middle Passage. This mother is a creation of the "high" moment of the renaissance: a strong, adored woman, a firm anchor in the world, the center of memory. For Gilda, history and memory always wear the mother's face: in Boston in 1955 she thinks of her friendship with a mortal woman from Mississippi as "[resting] on the earth from which they'd come, the place where their many mothers had first been bent beneath the yoke" (130–31). Similarly, the bits of native soil that vampires must conceal in their clothing to stay alive take on the additional meaning, in Gilda's pockets, of her link to maternal origins. And most notably, *The Gilda Stories* even maternalizes the convention of the vampire's bite, recasting the scene of vampire-making as one of childbirth (discussed in the second section of this chapter among magical variations on childbirth).

While this text's matrifocality strongly links it to the tradition of African-American women's slavery novels, this feature notably differentiates *The Gilda Stories* from the "prototypical lesbian novels" theorized by Judith Roof (167). Roof's lesbian narrative prototype (based primarily on her reading of white lesbian authors) tells a story of development that begins, like Gilda's story, with "a lack in the place of the mother," but then goes on to deny "the importance of this originary lack" (170), to reject the past "as a useful explanation for the present," and to "focus instead on an already differentiated and very independent protagonist daughter" (171).[3] By contrast, the maternal romance of black history lives as powerfully in Gomez's lesbian novel as it does in the other fictions in this study. And yet Roof's lesbian narrative model may shed some light on a departure Gilda does make from the other magic black daughters: her willingness to move beyond the identity derived from the original mother to another "differentiated" and "independent" identity. For this heroine's escape from the scene of slavery and maternal death to freedom with the vampires gives her a second mother, the "creator" whose identity and whose name, "Gilda," she later inherits. Going on to create new vampires, she makes herself into a very different sort of immortal "mother" from the heroine of *Jubilee*.

As this swerve from one maternal line to another suggests, *The Gilda Stories* holds the plot of transhistorical black female identity in interesting tension with a "horizontal"—and homosexual—plot of multiracial relations, embodied in the eclectic "family" of vampires. The effusively gracious European male vampire Sorel and his companion Anthony hold late-night champagne gatherings—vampires only—that Gilda attends over the centuries. When she first brings Julius in 1971, she feels compelled to warn him, "It's a rather old crowd, a kind of a white crowd, so there won't be much discoing" (187). This old, white crowd is a literary historical residue: the trace of the European roots of the vampire tale—and its homosexual, dandyish aura—as inevitable here, it seems, as are the white father-figures in Butler's 1976 science fiction. At the same time, the multiracial sisterhood of American vampires who are Gilda's lovers and companions suggests another generic affiliation: the feminist romance that tends to be published by Gomez's press, Firebrand. Rather than create a solely black vampire world, Gomez invents a generic hybrid that can afford the conventional slave girl of African-American history an exogamous, transcendent new life in multiracial camaraderie, like a black female figure introduced into the pantheon of cartoon superheroes.

As she traverses the continent, Gilda exchanges mental messages with her Native American vampire lover Bird, who is working among her own "tribe." Gilda's "creator" is a light-skinned, brown-eyed woman of indeterminate origins who, like Morrison's Amy Denver and Williams's Miss Rufel, serves as second mother to a black child. Indeed, Gilda's inheritance of this woman's name and place hints at an allegory of succession from European-American to African-American centrality in the narrative of American history, or even—as in the literary evolution of *Orlando*—in the development of American literature. The first Gilda is weary of her long life and ready to give it over to a replacement when she comes upon the runaway Girl; she later tells her, "The night I found you. . . . I sensed in you a spirit and understanding of the world; that you were the voice lacking among us" (43). Yet if Gilda's story in a sense succeeds the European vampire tale and/or the American historical romance, what it offers instead is not simply an African-American vision, but a vision of an inclusive new culture, a multiracial tribe, as represented by the "family" of vampires. While *The Gilda Stories* honors the integrity of racial and ethnic histories, it projects their convergence in a multiethnic future. In this respect, Gomez inverts the conventional racial politics of many vampire tales, in which an aristocratic foreigner's deadly bite is a form of racial pollution (see Johnson 75–76). Perhaps when Gilda's "creator" complains of the inadequacy of the language "for who we are," the maligned history she seeks to recuperate, above all, is that of those like herself and Bird who love across racial and ethnic "barriers" and those—perhaps like her author as well as herself—born of the mingling of peoples.

All who join this new tribe must sacrifice an easier adherence to their original peoples, giving up racial exclusivity along with their mortality. But in the tension between the two plots of African-American matrilineal inheritance and cross-race love and solidarity, the novel worries the meaning of Gilda's choice: does it privilege an African-American vision of racial uplift or the opening out of African-American history into a multiracial American future? Gilda's emplotment in both a slave's and a utopian feminist narrative gives her dual loyalties to black mortals and to a multiracial vampire band, making her a uniquely torn magic black daughter. As the novel develops the multiracial vampire plot, it is always concerned about Gilda's relations with the African-American populace she has had to leave behind, as in this passage set in 1921:

> Among the free blacks on farms and in small towns, she came closer to knowing, through them, who she was. Her preternatural life made her an outsider, but still she enjoyed their evocation of the secrets of the past and their unequivocal faith in the future. Gilda was chagrined by her concept of *they* and how her life separated her from them. Still she took comfort in the familiar smells and sounds and the rare sense of unity that sometimes crept into her. (112)

By 1955 Gilda laments that her vampire life has amounted to a "one-hundred-year journey—away from my people into the world" and is glad that her day job as a beautician in Boston's South End allows her to "retrieve them, touch and be touched by them as I was before . . . to understand the rhythm of their lives, their desires" (157). To Bird, who comes to visit, it seems that Gilda has found a sense of "tribal unity," as she herself has among Native Americans (155). It becomes apparent that the price Gilda pays for her superhuman powers, and that Gomez pays for rewriting black history in this remarkable generic hybrid, is history filtered through an always-alienated consciousness—perhaps not unlike that of a belated, lesbian, daughterly history-writer. Even as she re-creates her foremothers, Gomez reinscribes her historical separation from them in the mirrored pain of an immortal, longing for her original family, and of a lesbian, separated from "the folk"—all of whom seem here to be heterosexuals.

When in 1921 Gilda reveals her true identity to a mortal black woman friend in a farewell note, she writes that "she was different from them all, a part of them yet apart from them"; by this she means "to leave Aurelia with hope, an honest hope, born of who they really were" (128). By this point in the novel it seems that this hope, and the underlying myth of the text, is of the transhistorical continuity of African-American women in a progressive, ever-widening millennial social vision. *The Gilda Stories* thus adds a twist to the paradigmatic African-American historical romance of Jane Campbell's definition, for while it represents black history as holding the secret of a gradually unfolding "triumph," its triumph is more multiculturally and polysexually imagined.

Appropriately, at the height of her development, Gilda, like Orlando, becomes a successful writer. The novel shows a remarkable degree of self-consciousness about its own capitalization on market trends when it embodies the culmination of African-American history in a black woman's use of romance to "rememory" forgotten history—in bestselling fiction:

> Writing romances was, for Gilda, a way of sharing some of the many stories she had gathered through her long life. . . . To many, the stories she wrote seemed curious, archaic. . . . Having conspired to forget their past, the generations plowed ahead at top speed to some mythical future as if the wild west existed in the stars. Gilda had written the stories of their history, cloaking it in adventure and mysticism, and they sold. (220)

Always astride the moment's current, Gilda cashes in on the late twentieth-century public craving for a mythified African-American past. And like her sisters in the renaissance generation, she conceives the literary mission of linking ancestry to the future as a fitting consummation of this history. On the novel's last page, as Gilda and friends escape a dystopian United States in 2020 and cross a border into a promising South American territory, the black vampire Ermis hums gospel hymns, recalling that her mother "loved the music": "She said it was so pure, it made her think of the history" (252). *The Gilda Stories* elevates "the history" of African Americans to a sacred inheritance, one that a daughter who hopes to nurture the future must carry within her, on all her adventures.

Magic Photography

For the reader of *The Gilda Stories* the narrative's magic is mediated by an intriguing cover photograph of a tall, young woman in a dotted white blouse and a long, flared, and belted skirt: the dress of the turn-of-the-century. Her dark face is intelligent, kind, and perhaps shy, her eyes large and expressive; her hands are hidden, her long arms clasped behind her back. Reading the book, one comes to rely on the photograph as a portrait of Gilda, to feel that this young woman looks exactly like the mild-mannered vampire of Gomez's stories. But the copyright page announces that the cover photo pictures "the author's great-aunt, Effie Johnson, Boston circa 1900." This postmodern trick, assimilating a historical photograph to a fiction, recalls Virginia Woolf's illustrations of her hero/ine Orlando at various stages of life (most of which are reproduced paintings from the ancestral estate of Vita Sackville-West). Following Woolf, Gomez coaxes the reader to see in the face of an ordinary woman extraordinary qualities—even hints that Aunt Effie might actually have been an incarnation of Gilda! But Gomez's book displays another photograph, too: the standard back cover "author's photograph," transformed by its pairing with the front cover image into a photo of the great-niece of Gilda. Jewelle Gomez is pictured as a contemporary-looking woman with an identifiably bohemian/New Age/lesbian style: over a black tunic, she is adorned with exotic signifiers—a multi-patterned scarf tossed dramatically over one shoulder, a mysterious amulet around her neck, a bracelet, and several rings. Her skin color is notably lighter than "Gilda's," and her features less distinctly African, but her eyes, the intensity of her gaze, strongly resemble "Gilda's." As double portrait, these photographs seem to instance the continuity of transhistorical black female essence described in the novel. Transcending physical differences, this inheritance opens, finally, into the multiracial family of the future, which in *The Gilda Stories* is born from within the mainstream of African-American history.

Gomez's transformation of her great-aunt's photograph into that of an immortal, magic black woman is a trope repeated in magic daughter fictions, which often play with the "magic" of photography to figure the "magic" of a descendant's reimagining of history. These texts draw upon the photograph's paradoxical nature as a record of presence under the sign of mortality,[4] its mediation between the ephemeral and the permanent, to represent imaginative transcendence of time. In the coda to *Beloved*, as she dissolves the ghost into a lingering communal memory, Morrison writes, "sometimes the photograph of a close friend or relative—looked at too long—shifts, and something more familiar than the dear face itself moves there" (275). Reread after Gomez's fantasy novel, this moment in Morrison seems to summon the timeless, essential black female identity embodied by Gilda. But in Morrison's much more nuanced evocation of the past, the photograph offers only a glimpse of the eternal and only when "looked at too long," when searched for a mythic presence it cannot sustain. In a more comic vein, Julie Dash, playing with photography as *mise en abyme*, films a black male photographer at the family gathering, who brushes up against magic in the form of her own more powerful technology of moving images. When the Unborn Child suddenly steps beside her father in a group of men on whom poor Mr. Snead, behind his curtained camera, is focusing, the photographer is baffled by his encounter with a new, black female imaginative power to revisit the past.

The renaissance portrays itself baffling another black male photographer in Alice Walker's *The Temple of My Familiar*. This time the unfixable subject is not a spirit girl but an old woman, like Gilda a "living history" in a transhistorical body. Miss Lissie Lyles, introduced in the novel as an ordinary old woman, soon reveals a remarkable secret: she remembers multiple reincarnations, stretching back several thousand years. The trope of reincarnation allows Walker to create a history-spanning character with a scope far greater than that of Gilda or of Orlando. Throughout her many lifetimes, Miss Lissie reports, "I have always been a black woman. I say that without, I hope, any arrogance or undue pride, for I know this was just luck" (53). Reincarnated along the path of the African diaspora, Lissie experiences all the ages of her people's past, remembering not only her sale into slavery and suffering on the Middle Passage, but also numerous earlier lifetimes in Africa.

Over the course of Walker's sprawling plot, Lissie tells her lives' stories to Suwelo, the young man who has just inherited the house of his uncle, Lissie's recently deceased lover. When Suwelo asks the identity of the people pictured in the house's many framed photographs, his uncle's friend Hal tells him, "Most of the women are Lissie." "But there're a lot of women," he protests. "Lissie is a lot of women," Hal replies (38). Lissie never told her secret to the photographer who, shooting her picture repeatedly, noticed that she "could never present the same self more than once" (91). Even she came only slowly to the interpretation that her "memory and the photographs corroborated each other exactly":

> I had been those people, and they were still somewhere inside of me. When Henry Laytrum aimed his camera, different ones were drawn out. . . .
>
> The selves I had thought gone forever, existing only in my memory, were still there! Photographable. (91–92)

These photos confirm that Lissie was once an ancient pygmy, a slave woman who lost her leg to a bear trap, a "high yellow flapper," a uniformed maid, and many other selves. When the photos were taken, Lissie's pleasure in realizing her magic, multiple selfhood helped her to transcend the circumstances of her present incarnation: the Great War, the Depression, and campaigns of violent terror against black people. Amidst the chaos, "this," Lissie recalls, "is what was happening to me. And because I was a colored woman, nobody would ever know about it. I was sort of glad, for I'm the kind of woman that likes to enjoy herselves in peace" (92).

Like Gilda at the mirror, Lissie reads the photographic portrait of self as the image of an ancestral composite in one body. In Walker's romance of history, what might have been diagnosed and disciplined as a multiple personality disorder, refused as an illusion born of looking "too long" at history and identity, or, for that matter, advanced as a post-structuralist reading of the instability of the self is rendered as mystical consciousness of ancient spirit. The novel indeed celebrates such a consciousness as a healthy response by a black woman to disabling realities, present and historic. "When Henry Laytrum aim[s] his camera" Lissie does not become his victim; rather, she mobilizes different selves to counter the male artist's mastery of her image. And though the history she recalls is unrelievedly terrible, by containing and remembering it all Lissie achieves a sense of triumph, over both history and the limitations of her present existence. Notably, it takes this particular lifetime, which brings photography in her photogenic youth and the black women's literary renaissance in her talkative old age, to make the eternal woman realize and articulate her multitudinous identity.

Casting authorial "magic" backward, Walker makes this elderly "mother" a daughter, over and over again. Lissie's youth (in this lifetime) was spent in "the islands 'cross the bay from Charleston" (41). Here as elsewhere in contemporary African-American women's texts, the South Carolina and Georgia Sea Islands have become a "real special" place (41), where African-American life retains its link to "magic," a place of mythic origins for magic daughters.

Yet Lissie was born in this life to parents she despises. In her comic account, being born is always a misfortune, each baby realizing, "this is the next classroom, these people are the next lesson you will be required to learn. Oh, the horror of it!" (54). Firmly on the side of daughters and their choices in all generational conflicts, Lissie champions the ancestral depth of the self as an alternative to a woman's entrapment in the family or other confining circumstances of her present.

One Body, Horizontal Relations

If Lissie resembles Gilda the vampire in embodying a transgenerational black female essence, the two superwomen are also alike in that their authors work to disrupt the static quality of their stories with multiracial counterplots. In Lissie's case these involve an Indian rock star, a Latin American Indian woman, and a wealthy white woman. Moreover, when Lissie dies, she leaves a taped confession to an earlier lie: she also lived lifetimes as a white woman, a white man, and even a lion! *Temple* finally disavows nationalist visions and opens outward to the wider world; the novel ends in a cross-race romantic swap between the black couple Fanny and Suwelo and the Indian couple Arveyda and Carlotta. Like *The Gilda Stories*, *Daughters of the Dust*, and *Kindred*, *The Temple of My Familiar* celebrates the "magical" power of a black daughter to redefine herself, privileging her power to choose multiracial families and futures.[5]

The cross-cultural strand of these late 1980s–early 1990s novels has been present in African-American women's historical texts since Butler's *Kindred* and Chase-Riboud's *Sally Hemings,* which begin a remarkable revalorization of the rape/miscegenation plot (the plot of the white father of Vyry, of Sally Hemings's children, of Dana, possibly of the Unborn Child). While the works of Morrison, Williams, Gomez, Dash, and Walker reclaim a black matrilineage, they also honor new familial and sexual relationships to whites and others, and with these important interethnic connections retell black women's history as one that includes the histories of others.

Most strikingly, *Beloved* implants the possibility of interracial solidarity within American women's maternal inheritance when the "whitegirl" Amy Denver's "good hands" help the escaping slave Sethe give birth in a canoe on the Ohio River. Midwife to the novel's emblematic scene of childbirth, Amy asks to be remembered to the child and in the naming of Denver is honored as surrogate mother to the plot of African-American generational continuity.[6] Similarly, Williams's ex-slave Dessa Rose and ex-slave mistress Rufel care for one another's babies; in her old age Dessa wonders about Rufel, "Do she call my name to Clara?" (259). In such instances—and they will proliferate in the second half of this study—the "horizontal" plot, the plot of the other woman's remembered name and extended hand, becomes a significant, de-essentializing counterforce to the dominant "vertical" plot of quest for the historical mother, embodied by

Walker, Gomez, and Dash in the photograph of a black woman—and all her forebears.

Mothers-Turned-Daughters: *Praisesong for the Widow* and *Mama Day*

In black women's fiction of the 1980s and early 1990s, the twin currents of magic and maternal return become strong enough to make returning daughters even of middle-aged and older heroines. Paule Marshall's *Praisesong for the Widow* (1983) and Gloria Naylor's *Mama Day* (1988) present no fantastic embodiments of mother-daughter reunion, but rather, maternal figures in basically realist narrative worlds who become subject to the magical transformations of romance, in plots that allude to *The Tempest*.[7] These novels remake into daughters women who long ago ceased to think of themselves as anyone but "mama," and the greater age of the heroines seems to create a differently textured relationship to history; living among scant remainders and relics of the past, both are inspired by the joined forces of an ancestress and a daughter to overcome the failure of memory and make magic among the ruins. These mothers-turned-daughters are key figures in whom the renaissance generation honors its own mothers, reconciling the generational tensions of its feminist emergence by returning to them the gift of a newly discovered magical inheritance.[8]

Like Butler's time-traveling heroine Dana, the heroine of Marshall's *Praisesong* is unaware of her need for a transforming journey and is moved where she must be moved by narrative forces beyond her control. Like the travelers shipwrecked by Prospero's storm, the bourgeois black American widow Avey Johnson is compelled to cut short a sea voyage and sojourn on an isle of magic. But whereas the guilty Duke of Shakespeare's *Tempest* needs an island idyll to atone for his wickedness, Avey Johnson needs a spiritual return to ancestry.

Unlike Dana or Dash's Unborn Child, Marshall's heroine does not embody the awakened energy of a new generation. She is, instead, located between two active generations: urged by the spirit of her Aunt Cuney and by her daughter Marion to return to roots. The magic that overtakes this mother, then, is simultaneously an inheritance from the ancestors and a gift from the daughterly renaissance.

Avey is awakened aboard a Caribbean cruiseship by a dream of a life-and-death struggle with Aunt Cuney, the griot of her childhood. Aunt Cuney used to take her walking across her South Carolina Sea Island home to Ibo Landing, where she told her own grandmother's story of the legendary Ibo. Cuney's "Gran" saw a shipload of captured Ibo take a long look at the New World at this spot, turn around, and walk back across the water to Africa (a story that Dash repeats in its entirety in *Daughters of the Dust*). Before Avey's birth, this same grandmother appeared in Cuney's dream to say that the child was "her little girl" and should be named after her (42). Sent into the world by an ancestress, then, like the Unborn Child, Marshall's heroine is named Avatara, after the foremother who claimed "her mind was long gone with the Ibos" (39). Though destined to be a (paradoxical) avatar of return,[9] Avey drifts for decades into a soul-less middle-class existence, until the ancestral call in her dream prompts her to abandon ship and undertake a journey in the spirit of African "reconnection" for which Kamau Brathwaite has celebrated Marshall's work.[10]

Though Avey's daughter Marion—social activist and African traveler—decries the banality of her mother's Caribbean vacation plans, urging a destination more "imaginative, for God's sake" like Brazil or Ghana, where Avey could "learn something," she in fact drives her mother to the pier (14–15). As it turns out, Marion, like many Americans, underestimates the culture of the Caribbean. *Praisesong* shares with Barbadian-American author Marshall's first novel *Brown Girl, Brownstones*, as well as texts like Audre Lorde's *Zami* (1982) and Morrison's *Tar Baby*, the plot of physical or mental return to the Caribbean—rather than Africa itself—as the site of cultural and spiritual renewal.[11] In such texts, Stelamaris Coser notes (citing Stuart Hall), "the Caribbean islands . . . perform their historical and carnivalesque roles as the original and central space where 'creolisations and assimilations and syncretisms were negotiated' in the *New World*" (3). To this trend *Tar Baby*'s Jadine again offers a counterexample, showing her shallowness by rejecting the Caribbean for Paris.

Marshall's Caribbean is a mythic space that can transform a black American widow's complacent sense of time and self, making her mind "swing like a pendulum gone amok" until "she felt to be dwelling in any number of places at once and in a score of different time frames" (232). Caught up in the annual "Excursion" by boat from Grenada to the tiny island of Carriacou, Avey envisions around her a suffering "multitude," "crowded in with her in the hot, airless dark," "packed around her in the filth and stench of themselves" (209). And once on shore, the old man who leads her to the Carriacou ritual of the "Big Drum" seems to grow a thousand years older before Avey's eyes, becoming an "ageless, misshapen creature" and then turning lively again, to lead the song, prayer, and dance (233). Avey had been baffled, earlier, when asked, "And what you is?"; "What's your nation?" (166–67). But the questions begin to make sense when she witnesses the old people, singly and in small groups, entering the circle to dance their "nation dances" (238). Though it is a poor "bare bones of a fete," Avey realizes:

> It was the essence of something rather than the thing itself she was witnessing. Those present—the old ones—understood this. All that was left were a few names of what they called nations which they could no longer even pronounce properly, the fragments of a dozen or so songs, the shadowy forms of long-ago dances and rum kegs for drums. The bare bones. The burnt-out ends. And they clung to them with a tenacity she suddenly loved in them and longed for in herself. (240)

Though Avey longs to realize in herself the "essence of something," the beauty of *Praisesong* is its acknowledgement that this "something" is recoverable only in potent fragments. For as strong as the inkling of essence and the work of magic in this ceremony is the sense of loss. Marshall's rendering of a collective, diasporic African memory of loss echoes the dominant strain in Caribbean literature from Aimé Césaire to Maryse Condé and Michelle Cliff and predates such evocations in Morrison's *Beloved*. *Praisesong* describes the definitive sound made, in the midst of "extravagant . . . complex [and] . . . joyous" music, by an old man's thumb drawn across a drum:

> And the single, dark, plangent note this produced, like that from the deep bowing of a cello, sounded like the distillation of a thousand sorrow songs. . . . The theme of separation and loss the note embodied, the unacknowledged longing it conveyed summed up feelings that were beyond words, feelings and a host of subliminal memories that over the years had proven more durable and trustworthy than the history with its trauma and pain out of which they had come. After centuries of forgetfulness and even denial, they refused to go away. The note was a lamentation that could hardly have come from the rum keg of a drum. Its source had to be the heart, the bruised still-bleeding innermost chamber of the collective heart. (244–45)

Here Marshall spells things out more plainly than most fictions of African-American daughterly return: one who yearns toward her heritage must acknowledge that the loss at its heart also sounds within herself.

Avey signals her embrace of this knowledge when she joins "the dancing, which was not even really dancing" (240), but a "flatfooted glide and stamp," a "rhythmic trudge, the Carriacou Tramp, the shuffle designed to stay the course of history" (248–50). This time when asked "And who you is?" she responds with her full daughterly name: "Avey, short for Avatara" (251). In her ending, this newly rooted heroine decides to "take it upon herself to speak of the excursion to others elsewhere"—to proselytize to the Granadian cab-driver, who will surely think "the American black woman gone crazy," and, upon her return to New York, to "those young, bright, fiercely articulate token few for whom her generation had worked the two and three jobs," catching them "as they rushed blindly in and out of the glacier buildings, unaware, unprotected, lacking memory" (255). She will be like the Ancient Mariner, Avey thinks—but she will also be like Vyry and Dessa and other maternal transmitters of memory—as she passes on the legend of the Ibo and calls other black children to Aunt Cuney's ancestral home, which she will restore as a summer camp. Not surprisingly, Avey feels sure she can "enlist . . . in her cause" her daughter Marion (255), a representative of the generation whose literary emergence created the character of Avey Johnson and the possibility of her return to origins. Magically rejuvenated by the renaissance, this mother joins in its restorative labors.

THE EPONYMOUS HEROINE of Naylor's *Mama Day*, a "far more wise than wicked" old conjure woman of the Sea Islands (111), does not need an "excursion" to appreciate her heritage. Naylor outdoes all other contemporary renderings of this region by making her fictional island, Willow Springs, legally independent of the mainland United States, owned by no state. The magic and the independence of the island also distinguish Mama Day, who, descended from a mythic slave-conjure woman, knows the rootwork and rituals that can move the forces of nature.

Yet, like Marshall, Naylor sets her older black daughter's romance in a world of dwindling memory. An early page of the novel shows readers the complete Day family tree—but the characters in the novel can recall only the names on its lowest branches. Next comes a 1819 bill of sale for Sapphira, a "negress" of "Pure African stock," suspected of witchcraft (2). When this "historical" text reappears later as a time-worn piece of paper Mama Day finds in an attic, she cannot make out her ancestress's name. These two inset texts give Naylor's readers historical data to which her characters have only partial access through memory. But Naylor's point is not to assert the primacy of written over oral memory-keeping; rather, Naylor portrays this community's engagement with the loss of historical knowledge as creative, even heroic.

Though the narrator tells us that Sapphira "don't live in the part of our memory we can use to form words" (4), the remembrance of a mighty ancestress is sacred to the people of Willow Springs. Sapphira's famous but "disremembered" walk (away from the white husband/master she had just murdered? into the sea and back to Africa like Marshall's Ibo?) is commemorated each year in the ceremony of Candle Walk, Naylor's description of which poignantly and humorously traces the evolution of a communal ritual that shifts farther from the original event in each generation. Though the ritual imitation of Sapphira's walk loses by degrees its emotional force and authenticity—young people are driving Candle Walk with flashing headlights, by the end—like Marshall's "Big Drum" dance it curiously retains the power to bind community, and finally seems to become a ceremony in honor of time itself, a commemoration of its passage. Mama Day's opinion is that this gradual loss of memory is "nothing to worry about":

> It'll take generations, she says, for Willow Springs to stop doing it at all. And more generations again to stop talking about the time [when it was done]. . . . By then, she figures, it won't be the world as we know it no way—and so no need for the memory. (111)

This remarkably light grip on memory—in a fiction that depends on it to retain African-American history—sets Mama Day apart from other matriarchs in recent black women's fiction, like Marshall's Aunt Cuney and Dash's Nana Peazant, who hold fervently to their "scraps of memories" (Dash 128) and make certain that their descendants treasure them as well. But Mama Day's comfort with her own transience is her distinctive wisdom and the quality that allows her to become, in her nineties, the oldest of the magic, time-transcending daughters.

Nobody's biological mother, Mama Day is the island's midwife and healer, which makes her "everybody's mama now" (89). She lost her own mother early, but her actual name, Miranda, suggests that she has always been a magical daughter. She inherited her healing powers from a woman who can be described as a "great, great, grand Mother—as if you were listing the attributes of a goddess" (218). And when her grand-niece Cocoa becomes gravely ill, she knows that she must seek the cure in the secrets of her matrilineage. Thus, a threat to a woman of the author's generation prompts this older daughter's return; a mother becomes a daughter to save a daughter. Though belief in magic does not triumph always and for everyone in this novel, within Naylor's key mother-daughter circle it must and it does.

In pursuit of Cocoa's cure, Mama Day conjures a dream-vision of the great Mother, Sapphira. Dreaming, Mama Day "opens door upon door upon door," asking "each door the same thing: Tell me your name" (283). Yet when she "finds herself in a vast space of glowing light," the name that comes to her is not Sapphira, but "Daughter"—a surprising inversion of female identities reminiscent of the naming of Morrison's Grandma Baby Suggs. Naylor offers a lush, intensely physical evocation of Mama Day's moment of restored daughterhood:

> Daughter. The word comes to cradle what has gone past weariness. . . . There's only the sense of being. Daughter. Flooding through like fine streams of hot, liquid sugar to fill the spaces where there was never no arms to hold her up, no shoulders for her to lay her head down and cry on, no body to ever turn to for answers. Miranda. Sister. Little Mama. Mama Day. Melting, melting away under the sweet flood waters pouring down to lay bare a place she ain't known existed: Daughter. And she opens the mouth that ain't there to suckle at the full breasts, deep greedy swallows of a thickness like cream, seeping from the corners of her lips, spilling onto her chin. Full. Full and warm to rest between the mounds of softness, to feel the beating of a calm and steady heart. (283)

In this central revelation of the novel, Naylor creates a verbal equivalent of Dash's visual image of the black daughter's bodily return to the mother-of-history. Recalling the nursing scenes of *Beloved*, *Dessa Rose*, and *Temple of My Familiar*, this passage reclaims the maternal body of history as the heroine's source of self. When Mama Day accepts the startling discovery of her identity as daughter, she also gains the magic insight needed to discover a way to Cocoa's cure. Equating matrilineal connection and magical cure, then, Naylor's novel honors the mothers who enable the "magic" of her own generation—as represented by self-centered Cocoa, whose troubles open the novel, and who at the end begins to mature into Mama Day's heir.

These two 1980s novels envision diaspora Africans of the Sea Islands amidst poverty and richness of memory at once, in possession of a dwindling oral culture that yet persists like a living creature, its "magic" potential accessible even to the "unaware, unprotected" unremembering generations. The older women who return to ancestry in this daughterly way, the "American black wom[e]n gone crazy," their minds "gone with the Ibos," are figures in whom maternal and daughterly identities are reconciled; binding the fragments of memory, they help memory mother the future.

A Daughter Turns Mother

Just when it had begun to seem that the moment of magic in African-American women's historical fictions was passing, that the magic black daughter was primarily a phenomenon of the 1980s, give or take an early appearance in *Kindred* (1979) and a late appearance in *The Gilda Stories* and *Daughters of the Dust* (1991), Phyllis Alesia Perry published *Stigmata* (1998), a novel that conspicuously derives from this recent body of literature, but extends its central tropes in intriguing ways. For Perry's contemporary heroine Lizzie inhabits one dark body together with her great-great-grandmother Ayo, stolen from Africa to slavery in Alabama, and her grandmother Grace; she is their reincarnation, continually re-experiencing their lives, and thus possessing a memory that stretches back over a century and a half. Like Butler's Dana, Lizzie is repeatedly jolted against her will into the ordeal of slavery and suffers permanent physical damage. But unlike Dana, who acquires whipping scars and loses an arm on voyages to and from the past, Perry's Lizzie never actually disappears from the present. Yet she mysteriously acquires what a priest tells her to think of as stigmata, wounds that arise miraculously on her body through her complete identification with a person tortured in the past. The creature of an inclusive present, then, Perry's heroine does not need time-travel to experience her slave-ancestress's pain. The ancestress, Lizzie insists, is simply within her, "a shadow on my heart" (141).

Somewhat surprisingly, this recent novel is the goriest magic black daughter text yet. Blood drips from Lizzie's arms, ankles, and back throughout the course of the novel, horrifying those around her in her middle-class home and in the mental institutions to which her parents commit her for a period of fourteen years. Perry moves the violent return plot of *Kindred* out of the context of a 1970s exploration of black identity within an interracial marriage, and into black suburbia of the 1980s and 1990s, to the home of two uptight, bourgeois parents for whom a magic black daughter's involuntary return to her tormented maternal past is a dangerous and embarrassing craziness, one that must be disciplined and cured. The daughter knows what is true about her identity; it is Lizzie's mother Sarah, "a sixty-year-old woman completely unaware of her own immortality" (30) who needs to be initiated into this novel's truth: that African Americans can and must realize within their own minds and bodies the spirits of their martyred ancestors. *Stigmata* thus takes the mythification of black matrilineal identity to a new level, making it something on the order of a religious faith. Indeed, we might call Lizzie a born-again black daughter.

This daughter understands herself to have two missions: first, to tell the African mother whose daughter was kidnapped into slavery so long ago, "I made it, Mama. . . . I'm alive" (47), and second, most pressingly, to tell the mother of her 1990s present, that she, as the reincarnation of her grandmother Grace, is *her* mother; that is, Lizzie is her own mother's mother. Grandmother Grace abandoned daughter Sarah as a young child, fleeing when she herself could no longer control the bizarre and violent experience of reincarnating Ayo. Lizzie is thus a daughter in the position of proving herself to be the mother of her motherless mother.

This bizarre predicament presents a notable reversal of the mother-turned-daughter fictions discussed above. And, in a sense, this daughter-turned-mother brings the saga of the magic black daughter full circle. For this novel's drama does not lie in an orphaned daughter's search for a mother-of-history; indeed, the text begins with Lizzie already convinced through the strange experiences of a decade that she is her reincarnated ancestresses. Her focus, instead, is her "main occupation—reclaiming my sixty-one-year-old daughter" (93). As in the allegory of Marshall's *Praisesong*, a middle-aged woman who does not know that she is somebody's daughter needs to have the good news brought to her by the "renaissance" generation. But whereas Marshall does not make Avey's daughter Marion claim to be the reincarnation of Aunt Cuney, Perry's heroine announces, "I want to stand up and declare myself to her, cry, 'I am the circle! The circle stands before you!'" (94). Embodying the embrace of present and past, this motherly daughter yearns to bear witness to the cyclical vision common to all the magic black daughter fictions.

Yet the vision of cyclical identity is undermined, in my view, by *Stigmata*'s aspect of adolescent fantasy, by the way it actively fuels the generational tensions that novels by Marshall, Naylor, and others work to reconcile. For when Lizzie seeks to convince her family that her role as daughter conceals her truer and more powerful identity as mother, she deploys her special connection with ancestry so as to appropriate her own mother's place. Several scenes present Lizzie inwardly fuming about her mother's refusal to believe their roles should truly be reversed, and when, at the penultimate chapter's end, Sarah's head rests at last in her daughter/mother Lizzie's lap, we see precisely the ending that Beloved threatened, and that Sethe just barely escaped. Before *Stigmata*, no novel had envisioned the black daughter's imaginative triumph in the mother's submission.

An ongoing question in the novel is whether Lizzie has manufactured this revolution in identities herself. Her parents are convinced that her "ancestral" wounds—even the whip scars on her back—are self-inflicted. But Lizzie understands herself to be the helpless bearer of history's continuance: "we can't stop the sea from rolling beneath us and we can't stop the fear. The chains go on over our skin. . . ." (57). Indeed, when asked why she must continue to be hurt by unseen chains and lashes, Lizzie responds, "So I won't forget again" (193); her ordeal is a necessary discipline for one faithful to her transhistorical identity.

But another possible source of the trouble presents itself in the fact that the eruption of her stigmata is precipitated by her reading of a text: her great-grandmother's diary, containing the transcribed oral history of her great-great-grandmother, Ayo. *Stigmata* thus points to the way that reading

African-American women's "histories" can change consciousness, can provoke "rememory." While Lizzie's Aunt Eva, who believes in her reincarnation, calls the diary and the heirloom quilt that accompanies it "Just the keys that unlock the door to what you call the past" (118), a psychiatrist tells Lizzie, "Reading about your African ancestor obviously put you in a certain frame of mind. We're all much more highly suggestible than we like to think" (105). Wishing to side with neither analyst, I would hazard that the body of African-American women's slavery fictions has by now become so influential that anyone writing fiction of black female identity is liable to be in that "certain frame of mind" that "unlock[s] the door" to the maternal past. That is, *Stigmata* is heir to a powerful, collective, literary myth, as Perry suggests in quite overt allusions to precursor texts including *Kindred*, *Beloved*, and *Daughters of the Dust*.[12] This novel works, in part, as the drama of a daughterly reader, "reborn" as her own mothers through engagement with the myth of black matrilineal inheritance.

The other possibility, of course, is that Lizzie is mentally ill. She herself thinks, as she sits with a sympathetic cousin on a summer evening, monitoring the pain in her wrists, "*We're sick. . . . Very sick*" (84). On one level, the novel is a critique of psychiatry's narrow definitions of mental normalcy; Lizzie reflects that psychiatric treatment is as entrapping as slavery (106). But the novel enters compelling territory when it raises, for the first time in this literature, the threat of scientific analysis and treatment of the "illness" that is the returning daughter's defining condition. Not even Alice Walker's many-faced, multiply reincarnated Lissie Lyles (her name the precursor of Lizzie's?) falls subject to doctors.

The conflict of magic (and religion) versus science arises logically in *Stigmata*, given the bourgeois context inhospitable to magic realism and ancestral "rememory." But it seems to me that the highly embattled nature of the present in which Lizzie's ancestral adventures arise suggests more than a conflict over the changing values that can accompany changes in African Americans' class status. Rather, I think that the heightened tension with realism in the form of medical science, the harshness of Lizzie's relations with parents and the gory displays of her contact with ancestresses, and even the return of the science fiction narrative mode suggest difficulties born of the belated moment of this novel's creation. For if by 1998 the paradigm of a black, female imaginative power to reclaim a matrilineage has become an article of faith—canonical, even—for a broad sector of the reading public, perhaps a younger writer takes up the magical conceit with a certain agonistic edge, with a perceived need to battle her way in, against entrenched powers, to claim a place in the magic circle.

VARIATIONS ON CHILDBIRTH

How many strange births have we encountered thus far on the magic black daughter's trail? Again and again, as African-American women's fictions make inventive use of mother-child tropes to figure their own relationships to history, childbirth has been the remarkably malleable emblem of contact with historical origins, whether inscribing an inheritance of "magic" or of historical trauma. The ghostly reversal of childbirth in *Beloved* and the Unborn Child's dramatic dash into her mother's belly in *Daughters of the Dust* are but two of many "magic feminist" applications of the mother-child motif, which together work to recast the formidable losses of African-American history within a metamyth of transhistorical mother-daughter separation and reunion.[13] This part of Chapter 3 will examine some remarkable variations on childbirth presented in contemporary black women's texts, each of which articulates a differently nuanced relationship to the African-American past.

Refusal of Generation

The childbirth metaphor, it must be said, is potentially as problematic in women's literature as it is fertile and flexible. Susan Stanford Friedman has discussed women's ambivalence about using childbirth as a metaphor for writing, as they have struggled to close the cultural divide that would make creativity and procreativity mutually exclusive (383). For Friedman, "This biologic poetic . . . run[s] the risk of biological determinism, as de Beauvoir and others have feared":

> It theoreticlly [*sic*] privileges motherhood as the basis of all creativity, a position that symbolically excludes women without children and all men. It also tends toward a prescriptive poetic that potentially narrows the range of language and experience open to women writers. (390)

For the writers of historical fictions I consider here, ambivalence arises additionally from the metaphor's disturbing way of figuring inherited historical trauma. But as witnessed by the numerous births we have seen thus far, most recent black women writers have "risked the metaphor's dangerous biologism" (372), in Friedman's terms, and "subverted" its "regressive" potential, transforming it "into a sign representing their own delivery into speech through (pro)creativity" (390).

Some writers, however, vigorously refuse the biological imperative, with radical implications for their historiographic projects. Female characters who forego literal, physical childbearing in these fictions of history—like Dana, Gilda, and Mama Day—participate in a notable collective refusal to bear children among recent black fictional heroines. Younger women in novels written before the mid-1980s, in particular, resist marriage and maternity as ideology and entrapping fate. These include Selina of Marshall's *Brown Girl, Brownstones*, Jones's Ursa, Alice Walker's Meridian and Shug Avery, and Morrison's Jadine and Sula, the last of whom explains it quite clearly: "I don't want to make somebody else. I want to make myself" (92). Jacqueline De Weever notes that Meridian "gives away her first child, aborts the second, and then has her tubes tied," that Jones's Ursa is forced to have a hysterectomy, and that Jadine resolutely refuses to act as either mother or daughter (156–57); these heroines reject motherhood "for soul-making on their own terms" (De Weever 161).

Certainly this collective refusal of childbearing registers resistance to patriarchal definitions of female lives. But in the context of historical representation, it takes on another meaning: the refusal to bear descendants or, conversely, to become ancestresses. Failing to "make generations," Ursa privileges her art, singing, over the perpetuation of a heritage of victimization. A character like Gilda, or like Dana or Meridian, who refuses to make the traditional female entrance into history as someone's mother, seems instead to claim the right to make her own entrance into history, that is, *to make history*, herself. Though the magic daughter–figures strongly desire mothers-of-history, it is hard to imagine any of them growing up to become mothers. That would seem to be beside the point, which is to act imaginatively upon history, to reclaim, heal, or transform it, to celebrate history's arrival at the moment at which one can choose consciously to enter it. The daughters who refuse to become mothers play an important role in recent black women's matrifocal historical fictions, resisting an overdetermined myth of female generation, declaring the freedom even of those who know they emerge from a magic matrix to hold and nurture their own powers. Moreover, some of these characters—like "everybody's" Mama Day, Avey Johnson's Aunt Cuney, Gilda, and perhaps even Gomez's Aunt Effie, too—can become ancestral guides of a more spiritual kind.[14] I shall return to the motif of the refusal of generation in this study's second half, considering Caribbean heroines ranging from mythic ancestresses to present-day daughters, who privilege over conventional motherhood the spiritual role of mother of a nation.

Beyond Biology: Gilda and Lissie

When contemporary African-American women's texts deploy the metaphor of reproduction to represent history, it sometimes takes strange and inventive forms. Gomez's *The Gilda Stories* depends, as we have seen, on an essentialist construction of black female identity, an idea of inherited spirit manifest in all black women. At the same time, however, its version of vampire creation portrays a de-naturalized (and interethnic) form of reproduction that counters the biological essentialism of some other black women's matrifocal historical fictions.

Gomez's variation on female generation produces new vampires in an uncanny female bodily process evocative both of childbirth and of lesbian sex. When her "creator" gives the heroine new birth, "the Girl" first "[curls] her long body in [the creator's] lap like a child safe in her mother's arms" while this mother drinks her blood, and then, held to the woman's breast, "the suckling girl" drinks blood from a scratch on her chest (46).[15] Eventually, the girl becomes the "daughter" of two female vampires; the Native American vampire Bird must "complete the circle," Gilda's "creator" tells her, to "make you our daughter" (47). When Bird and Gilda go to bed to exchange blood and make love, Gomez writes: "To an outsider the sight may have been one of horror: their faces red and shining. . . . Yet it was a birth. The mother finally able to bring her child into the world, to look at her" (140).[16] The roles of mother, sister, daughter, and lover fuse more literally in these eerily tranquil scenes than they do in *Beloved*, but the female-relational structures of desire in the two "histories" are similar. In both cases, daughterly historiographic desire generates a maternal history in which all the varieties of love become interchangeable, and none is stigmatized.

While she eschews heterosexual procreation for a magical form of reproduction that mythifies lesbian relations, Gilda yet manages to create "the family she had hungered for as a child" by giving eternal life to two new black vampires (223). Thus she manages to sustain both interethnic relationships and a commitment to black historical continuity. At the same time, her revised form of reproduction connects Gilda to the trend of refusing biological motherhood among historical heroines in African-American and Caribbean literature.

The reincarnation of Walker's Lissie Lyles is another means of reproduction that transcends biology. Yet, like Gomez's vampire creation, Walker's version of reincarnation stresses, precisely, the mother-child bond, rooting immortality in generation. Lissie remembers being a mother to numerous children in different lifetimes, and she lives forever by continually being reborn. Indeed, *Temple* promotes the cyclical view of female identity also found in texts like *Beloved* and *Daughters of the Dust*; one Walker character begins a story: "Our mothers taught us that in the old, old days, when they were their grandmothers. . . . for we are our grandmothers, you understand, only with lots of new and different things added. . . ." (48). Reincarnation here is less a transmigration of souls than a supernatural form of female generation, a magical feminist version of genealogical descent.

But amidst all this generation, Walker's retelling of history is dominated by the trope of mother-child separation. History in Lissie's capacious memory is mostly a matter of the births and deaths of herself and her children, often at the hands of violent men. Her eyewitness account of the Middle Passage (discussed in Chapter 2), which oddly places Walker's novel of contemporary life among matrifocal slavery fictions, recasts the foundational story of African-American history as an ordeal of mothers and children. And in even older memories, Lissie maternalizes traumatic history back to its dawning, recalling among other episodes the fall of African mother-worshipers to conquering androcentric tribes, the replacement of black Isis with Athena and the Virgin Mary, and the history of the abuse of black women in Africa and Europe. Indeed, the novel's 400-some pages present such continual repetition of the mother-child separation trope for "bad history" that Lissie's emergence into consciousness of her reincarnations—reconnecting mother to child to mother to child—takes on the aspect of redeeming the relentless, age-old story of women's disempowerment.

Intertextual Generation

When Lissie Lyles mentions the disappearance of her daughter Lulu in World War II–era Europe (a strong sign of "bad" history), readers of Walker and of contemporary black women's novels may well expect a sequel about Lulu's life under the Nazis. For a conspicuous trend in renaissance fiction has writers linking their texts by matrilineal chains of characters, whose appearance in sequential novels suggests intertextual childbirth. Of course, novelists have often written fictional series based on the generations of a family and have long troped writing as childbirth. But contemporary black women writers do both of these in a way that seems to locate even their own production of novels in a romance world, a world in which, just as lost children are found and magic is inherited from mothers, books too are linked through the mystery of genealogy.

Thus Gloria Naylor's George Andrews, the man who looks "just like love" and who sacrifices his life for his wife Cocoa in *Mama Day* (310), is an orphan who never knew his mother, but Naylor's readers discover at the end of *Bailey's Cafe* (1992) his miraculous birth to an Ethiopian Jewish virgin who later drowns herself in Harlem. Intertextually and unbeknownst to him, Christlike George redeems his mother's as well as his wife's story. Similarly, Olivia of Walker's *Temple* redeems the story of her mother Celie, heroine of *The Color Purple*, when she redescribes her own violent, incestuous origin—in Celie's rape by her stepfather, the traumatic event that occasions the diary-text of *The Color Purple*—as an "immaculate conception" (171). Olivia has a magic daughter, too, and Celie a magic granddaughter in *Temple*: Fanny, a character of Walker's own generation, whose "second sight" shows her the spirits of vanished Native Americans, who travels outside her body, whose wishes come true (282, 277). Constructing a literary genealogy on the magic matrilineal descent model predominant in contemporary black women's "histories," these writers construct a compensatory (and "immaculate") history, a substitute for the lost connections (and the rapes) concealed in African-American descent lines. At the same time, the characters' unawareness of these marvelous linkages, the loss of the mothers to the children, reinscribes historical loss. The novels do not announce upfront their genealogical connections, and so the reader, uncovering these mysteries late in the reading, comes to sense amidst the losses a mysterious and enduring connection between books, like the inheritance of ethnic magic so often portrayed in the fictions. Thus, a magic feminist treatment of reproduction becomes the guiding logic in the shaping of a literary oeuvre; books beget one another as mothers their children, and sequences of novels seem to arise from a magic intertextual matrix.

Notably, Walker's black daughters are fully conscious of their relationship to the earlier heroine, but black boys in this mythic web are orphans, without knowledge of the maternal magic that made them. As poignant as the story of George Andrews is that of Morrison's Joe Trace, motherless hero of *Jazz* (1992), so named because his parents abandoned him, disappearing "without a trace" (124). If in *Beloved* the return of the ghost embodies the return of the traumatic slave past, at the novel's end the interestingly pregnant Beloved seems to threaten to give birth to an apocalyptic monster-of-history that readers might well not want to see. Morrison spares us when her chorus of women exorcises the ghost and sends Beloved running behind the house, naked and pregnant, never to be seen again. At the novel's end we assume that that birth has been swallowed back into the past. But in the 1985 "Conversation" with Naylor, discussing a continuity between her unfinished novels *Beloved* and *Jazz*, Morrison says that she intends to "extend [Beloved's] life," "her search, her quest," from 1851 "all the way through as long as I care to go, into the twenties where it switches to this other girl." "Therefore," she says, describing what would become *Jazz*, "I have a New York uptown-Harlem milieu in which to put this love story, but Beloved will be there also," as "the mirror, so to speak" (208–9).

Who is this mirror? Most likely it is the dead girl Dorcas, whose body lies in state on the first page and whose photograph haunts the entire novel. Or it might be the mysterious narrative voice, close to and yet distant from the characters, impossibly combining the traits of a limited first-person and an omniscient third-person speaker, a voice that seems to inherit the ghostlike, here-but-not-here, human-but-not-human presence of Beloved.[17] Alternatively, various suggestions open the possibility that the naked, pregnant "wild woman" of the woods rumored to have given birth to Joe Trace is the woman of the same description last seen running toward the stream behind 124 in *Beloved* (see Aguiar 12; McDowell, "Harlem" 3).[18]

If indeed Joe Trace is the child born to Beloved, then Morrison employs the tropes of childbirth and the ruptured mother-child bond in a particularly striking figuration of historical process: the woman who returns from the dead in one novel, in the next novel living alone and biting people who come too close, "too brain-blasted to do what the meanest sow managed: nurse what she birthed," embodies the lingering, devastating presence of "bad history." The child of "this indecent speechless lurking insanity" (179), traumatic history's "trace," taken in and raised by good people, becomes a man who loves deeply but also kills a woman he loves. A complex, sympathetic character—possibly the son of the very human Paul D as well as of the "devil child"—Joe bears the trace of bad history into a realistic aftermath, a blues scenario, where history is remembered only in musical fragments and problems seem simply to arise out of the heat of a Harlem moment. Readers can grasp the authorial magic worked by Morrison in his creation, or by Naylor in the creation of George, but black men living among the remnants of memory in these fictions do not have access to the big picture, to the historical matrix that abandoned them to the world, after giving them miraculous birth.

Mothering the Daughter-of-History: Lucille Clifton

Poet Lucille Clifton knows she is the daughter of just such a maternal heritage. "Oh, she was magic," Clifton writes of her mother. Addressing the "brilliant" African great-great-grandmother who told her descendants, "Get what you want, you from Dahomey women," she writes, "i like to think you gave us / extraordinary power" (*Generations* 75, 14; "daughters" 13). Clifton often uses that power to recover African-American history in poems of human encounter, of visits with family. Sightseeing on a former plantation, she calls out to unmarked slaves' graves "tell me your names / foremothers, brothers," "and i will testify" ("at the cemetery"). In another poem, she personalizes the label "aunt nanny's bench," posted above an artifact in a slave cabin:

> aunt
> is my parent's sister
> nanny
> my grandmother
> bench
> . . .
> the soft curved polished
> wood
> that held her bottom
> after the long days.

At the poem's end, Clifton conjures Aunt Nanny sitting on that bench,

> humming for herself   humming
> her own sweet human name. ("slave cabin")

Reimagining named relatives behind the inadequate labels of African-American history, Clifton participates in the contemporary project of daughterly recuperative art.

But in a most compressed and dramatic instance of the mother-daughter configuration for history, an untitled poem from *Quilting: Poems 1987–1990*, Clifton performs a stunning reversal of the terms:

> i am accused of tending to the past
> as if i made it,
> as if i sculpted it
> with my own hands. i did not.
> this past was waiting for me
> when i came,
> a monstrous unnamed baby,
> and i with my mother's itch
> took it to breast
> and named it
> History.

she is more human now,
learning language everyday,
remembering faces, names and dates.
when she is strong enough to travel
on her own, beware, she will. (7)

Clifton's searing words sketch a figure so startlingly like Morrison's Beloved, and so evidently drawn in warning to all concerned, that she seems to have drafted the revelation-text of this new, collective black women's testament.

When Clifton "came" to writing, she found waiting for her the African-American past, in a female-bodied metaphor so strange it must be unique to recent black women's texts: the "monstrous unnamed baby" whom the poet, with a creative urge that is a "mother's itch," "took . . . to breast." The trajectory from Jordan's "momma / help me / turn the face of history / *to your face*" is dramatic: a decade and a half later, Clifton turns the face of history to that of a baby girl and declares herself its mother, names and nurtures it, and claims to raise it into something "more human." Clifton's poetry enacts a new form of mother-daughter union without striking the agonistic note that appears later in Perry's *Stigmata*: the meeting of the empowered black female poetic imagination and the young, undeveloped subject of African-American women's history, which needs the nurturance of her "language."

But the complicated mother-daughter interplay of all of these "histories" enters Clifton's poem, too. It is possible to read in lines six and seven that Clifton "came" into the world "a monstrous unnamed baby," and to read in the next lines a confusion of self, mother, and baby, which does not seem out of place in the symbolic structure of this poem. As in Morrison, Jordan, Dash, Butler, Gomez, Walker, Naylor, Marshall, and others, the figures of self and of history in Clifton's poem are, if not entirely interchangeable, very close relatives. Relating to the past in the form of a "beloved" "baby," "daughter," "momma," "aunt," or "great, great, grand Mother," these texts elaborate family dramas of monstrosity and nurturance, vengeance and love, as alternating modes of the history-retelling self. In some texts the narrative function is more closely linked to the mother, and in others, to the daughter, but most oscillate between these positions, as seen in the competing longings for a mother, and for a daughter, in *Beloved*. The circularity, repetition, rotation of female identity in all of these "historical" accounts gestures, finally, toward the circumscription of African-American history within a mythic vision of female generation.

Clifton here attributes the new and threatening energy to the baby and renders "natural" the humanizing influence of a black feminist "historian" like herself, who gives "language" to unspoken history, restoring to it the forgotten "faces, names, and dates" so painstakingly gathered in the historical fictions of her contemporaries. But make no mistake, this baby is studying with a plan that is the poet's own. If anyone should doubt whether the imaginative project of African-American women writers to reconstruct their history has much of a future, whether the time-traveling daughter will bring us any further revelations, see Clifton's closing promise: "beware, she will."

CODA

The coda to *Beloved* diminishes the embodied past to a "loneliness" that leaves vanishing footprints and winks at us from the faces in family photographs. It seems appropriate, then, in closing, to diminish the figure of the time-traveling magic black daughter, constructed piece-by-piece over the length of the preceding two chapters, into the inklings from which she arose. In beginning, I proposed to follow this girl's traces through a literary history; like the footprints of Beloved, the traces of the magic black daughter mark in contemporary American literature a profound mother-quest. But also like the ghost's footprints, they lead, finally, into the dim territory of all that is lost. If the magic black daughter paradigm illuminates a range of contemporary African-American women's writings, like any paradigm, it may also distort, not only insofar as it oversimplifies a complex body of literature or obscures other important elements, but also if it projects too solid an aspect and tends to conceal the struggles of will at work, within its various manifestations, to assert a sturdy figure against all odds.

Morrison's haunting ending is designed to sustain our perplexity about her character long after we have put down the book; saying "This is not a story to pass on," she leaves us with a paradox where we expect resolution. For me, *Beloved* was the beginning of speculations about African-American women's historical fiction as a genre, about historical fiction by contemporary women of diverse groups, and about daughterly historiographic desire. Perhaps because of this, *Beloved* now seems to me the coming-to-consciousness of the paradigm of daughterly return to a mother-of-history. This idea perhaps did not know itself until *Beloved*, just as Morrison did not know, until writing the novel, that she had long been about the revival of a "dead girl." A collective return to the subject of African-American slavery over several decades helped prepare the way, in texts both well known and little known. And both before and after *Beloved*, black women writers have developed magical figures of returning black girls in an array of generically innovative fictions. But *Beloved*, in its mythic force and its mass success, raises this important chapter in cultural history to view.

Only Morrison, however, would imagine the time-traveling girl returning to the mother-of-history to accuse her of murder. The relationship between Sethe and Beloved is of an order so much more complex than that of the other mother-daughter relationships in renaissance texts that *Beloved* seems both the climax of the era and its aberration, at once the paradigm-creating and paradigm-dissolving fiction. Morrison's novel stands out in this group as the demonic narrative that disrupts the romance world with an eruption of furious, unresolved grief, that calls up the ancestress in order to attack her for having been so long lost. No fiction musters more powerful desire for the historical black mother, yet only in its monologue/fugue sequence, its "unspeakable words, unspoken," does *Beloved* give way to perfect reunion. If the plot of the magic daughter in *Beloved* is obscure, her journey inverted and finally abortive, if it is harder to read her as a figure of empowered imagination, it is because she was conceived in utmost commitment to the emotional complexity of inheriting traumatic history. Yet, like the others, Morrison's phantom girl yearns for her mother absolutely and above all else; one cannot imagine her without a polestar mother to draw her back—even if, as "dead girl," she cannot win the bliss that comes to the Unborn Child.

A figure like Dash's Unborn Child is, finally, a simpler and more reassuring one. Indeed, Dash and most other creators of magic daughters discussed here must be said to write more recuperative, even more celebratory fictions than Morrison's. Discussing them in these chapters, I have built, it seems, a critical myth that parallels their own mythopoeic project, assembling fragments into a figure of daughterly strength and solidity, perhaps not pointing often enough to the trail of footprints that vanishes behind her. To the extent that my reading refrains from deconstructing these texts' romance resolutions of traumatic history, their discourse of racial heroism, or the essentialism of their black matrifocal visions, it is because I came to see the magic and mysticism of their return plots and constructions of ethnic authorship as enabling a vitally important claim to authority: the authority to rename and reimagine a bitter inheritance. Thus my reading shares the paradox of this literature; constructing and raising to view the history of a literary "boom" while focusing on its engagement with loss, I have followed the renaissance authors in foregrounding the extraction of imaginative triumph from a historical void. Building a chain of signifying tropes, a "tradition" of influence in black women's historical fictions designed to parallel the black male canon, these two chapters have been a kind of "misreading" of the renaissance, an imitation of its recuperative mission.

But if the renaissance gives birth to a girl with a mighty will and a dazzling belief in her own powers, it knows it cannot free her to travel a realm unmarked by inherited loss and trauma. The magic black daughter must make her way through an imaginative space in which desire is most often met by the sound of the wind and some noise that is "certainly no clamor for a kiss." To say that the sheer verbal negation of Morrison's ending, indeed, of her novel as a whole, stuns and disarms readerly desire is to point to the reason for its centrality in this body of literature and in our literary era. Although in its last word *Beloved* reaffirms once more the shadowy figure of the past, it also reminds us that the daughter whose return gives the past a new name draws her marvelous power from her familiarity with the grave.

PART II

Caribbean Women Writers

4 Caribbean Women's Literature and the Mother of History

RECOVERING THE MOTHER-ISLAND

Something inside is laid wide like a wound,

some open passage that has cleft the
  brain,
some deep, amnesiac blow. We left
somewhere a life we never found,

customs and gods that are not born again,
some crib, some grille of light
clanged shut on us in bondage, and withheld

us from that world below us and beyond,
and in its swaddling cerements we're still bound.

Derek Walcott, "Laventille"

Children of the Mother Country

In a recurrent scene of education in Caribbean fiction, children of the islands solemnly offer obeisance to a European nation they have never seen, reciting the absurd formulae of genealogy by which colonial authority teaches them to know themselves. African-Caribbean children of the French-speaking islands learn "to respect the flag of France our mother, to revere her greatness and majesty and the glory that went back to the beginning of time, when we were still monkeys with their tails cut off" (Schwarz-Bart 52), while in British Jamaica, a "class of multicolored boys" chants: "mulatto, offspring of African and white; sambo, offspring of African and mulatto; quadroon, offspring of mulatto and white; mestee, offspring of quadroon and white; mestefeena, offspring of mestee and white." These boys are among the "fortunate," as their teacher informs them, for "in the Spanish colonies there were 128 categories to be memorized" (Cliff, *No Telephone* 56).

The perverse family narratives imparted in a European colonial education were crystallized in the deceptively benign conceit of the "mother country." As presiding eminence in the colonial schools, this "Great Mother" was a stern nurturer indeed.[1] "Not an eyelid must bat not a finger must twitch when we honour the Mother Country," intones a Trinidadian schoolmaster in Merle Hodge's *Crick Crack, Monkey* (1970), as his pupils stand at attention to sing "Children of the Empire Ye Are Brothers All" (26). This same schoolmaster takes a tamarind-whip to those of the Mother's island children who cannot spell or define "sleet" (67). Hodge's heroine Tee, an African-Trinidadian schoolgirl, attempts to integrate such lessons with the information that her recently deceased mother has "gone to Glory":

> At school I had come to learn that Glory and The Mother Country and Up-There and Over-There had all one and the same geographical location. It made perfect sense that the place where my mother had gone, Glory, should also be known as The Mother Country. . . .
>
> Every Sunday . . . we were given a little card with a picture and a Bible verse—pictures of children with yellow hair standing around Jesus in fields of sickly flowers. . . . I had a pretty good idea of what kind of a place Glory must be, and of what happened to you there; for also at Sunday-school we sang:
>
> *Till I cross the wide, wide water, Lord*
> *My black sin washèd from me,*
> *Till I come to Glory Glory, Lord*
> *And cleansèd stand beside Thee,*
> *White and shining stand beside Thee, Lord,*
> *Among Thy blessèd children.* (30)

The confusion in one girl's mind of England, heaven, whiteness, Jesus, and her own lost black mother is emblematic of the psychocultural dislocations of colonial existence. If every child of the colonial and neocolonial Caribbean is raised by a "mother country," each is, like Michelle Cliff's heroine Clare Savage, "a colonized child" (*Abeng* 77), whose true parentage has been "disremembered" under the "amnesiac blow" of Caribbean history (Walcott, "Laventille" 88).[2]

IN A PROFUSION OF literature since about 1970, Caribbean women writers have undertaken to reimagine the region's history and, in so doing, have conducted an emerging collective recuperation of the figure of a Caribbean mother-of-history that is like and yet strikingly unlike the paradigm we have seen among African-American women writers. For in Caribbean literature the trope of the Mother already had a long and interesting career before the current women writers' boom: first as a figure for the colonizing power, then for a reclaimed precolonial origin, still later for the vexed condition of Caribbeanness itself.

The second half of this book examines the return to maternal history in contemporary writing by Caribbean women. This compendium chapter begins the account just as Chapter 2 did for African-American women's literature: by sketching a history of the figure of the mother. The first section of this chapter demonstrates that the development of a figurative Caribbean

Mother undergirds modern Caribbean literary history, and the second section discusses new formulations of this figure by contemporary Caribbean women writers, comparing them to figures of the African-American mother-of-history. The third section focuses on one recent novel, Jamaica Kincaid's *Autobiography of My Mother*, as an extreme exemplar of the maternal fixation in Caribbean women's historiographic fiction.

Whereas the African-American women's renaissance has produced the remarkably recurrent character type I call the magic black daughter (discussed in the linked readings of Chapters 2 and 3), in the Caribbean region's inherently more diverse literature the shared paradigm of daughterly return to history has produced, instead, a variety of daughterly figures compelled to explore a variety of racial and cultural inheritances. Thus, following this chapter's overview, the Caribbean half of the book devotes each of three chapters to an individual author who has developed a particularly powerful and distinctive rendition of the Caribbean romance with maternal history; these are the Dominican Jean Rhys, the Jamaican Michelle Cliff, and the Guadeloupean Maryse Condé.

The Mother-of-Forgetting

In a 1937 poem by Léon Damas, Guyanese poet of negritude, a young speaker repeatedly urges his mother, who will talk only of bourgeois manners and appearances, "parlez-moi du désastre" ("Hoquet" 35). This disaster of which the Caribbean mother will not speak, the "some" "something" "somewhere" that St. Lucia's poet Derek Walcott does not name (88), is the great repressed that haunts the region's literature. To rewrite Caribbean history is to rehearse a primal rupture, a deep "wound" to collective memory. In his influential study *Caribbean Discourse* (1981), Martinican novelist Edouard Glissant writes that the history of the French Caribbean "began with a brutal dislocation" and that its "historical consciousness . . . came together in the context of shock, contraction, painful negation, and explosive forces." The result is a traumatic condition of "nonhistory," "the erasing of the collective memory" (61–62).[3]

In Damas's poem and elsewhere in Caribbean literature, the sense that primordial, collective memory has failed the children of the Caribbean tends to gather around a figure we might call the mother-of-forgetting. At once matrifocal (positioning mother as origin) and sexist (blaming the mother), this formulation points to the contradictions of Caribbean gender ideologies. But its fusion of rage and longing in this figure of an inadequate, unremembering origin also illustrates the dilemma of Caribbean historiographic desire: born of such a mother, what child could know or tell his or her own history?

Notably, this figure of the mother-of-forgetting is not a significant presence in African-American literature, which tends always to position mothers at the foundation of historical memory. What can account for this difference on the level of primal myth between two cultures with largely parallel experiences of "nonhistory"? Both the African-Caribbean and African-American peoples were formed in the brutal passage to slavery and in ongoing conditions of disenfranchisement and race prejudice amidst the heterogeneous, culturally complex colonial/postcolonial New World. True, one traces such shared historical patterns even while observing how the common legacy is differently shaped by conditions of "majority" status in economically dependent islands under European hegemony over the centuries of imperial rule and beyond, and of "minority" status within the national episteme of the superpower, with its myth of self-realization through Americanization.[4] Years, decades, a century after independence,[5] the colonial legacy holds sway in the Caribbean, hindering economic and social opportunity, balkanizing the islands within the spheres of influence of faraway first-world powers (Glissant 222, 5), privileging metropolitan tongues over Caribbean creoles (the first languages of the majority), maintaining the color hierarchy that still frames Caribbean class structure despite ubiquitous hybridization of peoples, and fostering mass emigrations of students and the educated to Europe and North America. Observing these signs of cultural alienation, Glissant goes so far as to speak of Caribbean peoples' "unstable relationship with their own reality" (5; see also Hodge, "Challenges").

But these social and cultural observations cannot fully explain the literary paradox I mean to delineate: although Caribbean peoples would seem on the face of things to possess their own place—and potentially, their own history—to a greater degree than do African Americans, their literature tends to reflect a deeper sense of dispossession, even homelessness, and historylessness as well. The figure of the mother-of-forgetting precisely embodies this historyless condition, this sense of being "*at* home" in a beautiful place that history yet makes it impossible to claim as one's *own* home.

When Caribbean writers speak of "the struggle . . . to finally inherit the Caribbean," of the need to "establish . . . our own dwelling place" (Hodge, "Challenges" 203; Glissant 4), they agree that reclaiming the Caribbean place would require, above all, reclaiming Caribbean time. "History," John Hearne writes, "is the angel with whom all we Caribbean Jacobs have to wrestle, sooner or later, if we hope for a blessing" (vii). Through a succession of twentieth-century literary movements, Caribbean writing has pursued its historiographic desire. But to do so requires a return to an irrecoverable moment before the colonial education that enables writing, to the maternal realm of all that is forgotten. For Cuban theorist Antonio Benítez-Rojo, the Caribbean text "unfolds its . . . monstrosity toward the void of its impossible origin," seeking above all "to drive the reader . . . to the marginal and ritually initiating territory" he identifies as "the Mother, the Imaginary, the round's absence of violence" (23, 25, 275). Also in a Lacanian vein, Jamaica-born critic Stuart Hall writes that the Caribbean relationship with the past is "like the child's relation to the mother . . . always-already 'after the break.'" Yet the same violent "break" that subjects Caribbean writers to an "endless desire to return to 'lost origins'" also blesses them with an "infinitely renewable source of desire, memory, myth, search, discovery" ("Cultural Identity" 395, 402). The Caribbean mother-quest has been a visionary labor.

Recovering the Caribbean Mother

The modern literary historical career of the Caribbean Mother begins with negritude. Rejecting the maternal authority of the "mother country" in which they resided, Caribbean and African intellectuals in 1930s Europe grounded their ideal of an authentic black culture in the figure of a new Mother: Mother Africa, genetrix in a new myth of origin, dignity, and unity for diaspora blacks (see Wilson 46). But Africa was also a Mother violently violated by Europe, as in a 1946 play by the Martinican Aimé Césaire, *Et les chiens se taisaient* (*And the Dogs Were Silent*):

> Africa is bleeding,
> my mother,
> Africa, shattered, is opening herself to
> a ditch of vermin,
> to a sterile invasion of the
> spermatazoa of rape. (21)

A "Tempter's Voice" serves in the play to articulate the position from which Césaire seeks to liberate his people: "I have no mother I have no past / I have filled in the unmotherly shaft of my navel to the point of / forgetting the dust and the insults" (22). Césaire's enormously influential construction of Caribbean identity depends centrally on the rewriting of the colonial family romance. As A. James Arnold glosses it, "French West Indians [were] . . . the bastard offspring of the European father who will not recognize them and the African mother from whom they have turned away"; "Mother Africa" was "matrix of a tragic myth, part of whose purpose is to deny henceforth the unloving father, Europe" (xxviii).

In the last third of the twentieth century, the ideological attraction of a mythified precolonial Africa, and of the figure of an African Mother, diminished. Indeed, with the post-independence turn to "Antillanité" ("Caribbeanness") by artists, intellectuals, and activists of the past few decades, the Mother undergoes a second major transformation. The enormous increase in Caribbean literary production in this era, called by Barbadian poet Anthony Kellman "nothing short of a renaissance" (xxxi),[6] has generated vigorous varieties of Caribbean postcolonial historiography. In using the much-debated and imperfectly descriptive term "postcolonial" here and throughout the second half of this book,[7] I follow the usage of Ashcroft, Griffiths, and Tiffin and refer not to a precise temporal/historical situation, but rather to an overlap between a text's "material situation" and its "discursive features" (Tiffin 96), that is, to "the discourse of oppositionality which colonialism brings into being" (Ashcroft et al., *Post-colonial* 116). What most distinguishes the postcoloniality of the project to revise the Caribbean trope of the Mother is its engagement of the European colonial heritage in a critical but appropriative, "counter-discursive" relationship (Tiffin 96, see also Emery, "Refiguring" 259).

Thus Glissant offers a historical narrative of Caribbean identity that begins with the European assault on Mother Africa, but then tentatively steps away from both origins, to locate that identity in a contest between homes:

> First the slave trade: being snatched away from our original matrix. The journey that has fixed in us the unceasing tug of Africa against which we must paradoxically struggle today in order to take root in our rightful land. The motherland is also for us the inaccessible land. (160–61)

In this paradoxical vision, Caribbean people must resist a mother's "tug" in order to take root in their "rightful land," which is yet no motherland.

This conflict is resolved, oddly enough, in a bold reconfiguration of the mother by the Barbadian poet and critic [Edward] Kamau Brathwaite, most famous for his Afrocentric or latter-day negritude poetics. While he could still remark in 1974 that Caribbean culture is "really involved with two mothers," meaning Africa and "the Euro-American step-mother" (*Contradictory Omens* 6), Brathwaite makes a momentous symbolic gesture in the preface to his 1977 *Mother Poem*:

> This poem is about porous limestone: my mother, Barbados: most English of West Indian islands, but at the same time nearest, as the slaves fly, to Africa.

Retaining both the influence of England—formerly the "mother country"—and the ancestral pull of Africa—formerly the "motherland"—Brathwaite firmly locates his mother on the island of his birth. This development of the trope, the invention of the Caribbean mother-island, should be seen as one of the defining marks of the last quarter of the twentieth century in Caribbean literature. References to a European "mother country" have become almost exclusively ironic and those to Mother Africa less urgent, more remote, while the Caribbean island itself has become in recent literature "truly the homeland, the motherland" (Morris and Dunn 219).

Problematics of the Caribbean Mother-of-History

While the progression from the figure of the European to the African to the Caribbean Mother presents a powerful psychocultural narrative of decolonization, its linear simplicity conceals complex gendered orderings. On one level, this sequence encodes a phallocentric narrative of nationalism in the form of a claim to the body of a woman. In the literary renderings of this nationalist myth, the "colonized body" tends to be "equated with the mother who has to be rescued from the conqueror and restored to her true identity and her real cultural norms" (Gikandi 198). The writers who originated this narrative, the male authors whose texts dominated the Caribbean canon until the 1970s, generally tended to objectify women and delimit their figural possibilities (see Zimra, "W/Righting" 232). Their representations of the conquered mother-island are in keeping with their depictions of both past and present as realms of male agency, as well as with the heroically self-sacrificing mothers of their fictions, such as the mother in George Lamming's *In the Castle of My Skin* (1953) and the grandmother in Joseph Zobel's *La Rue Case-Nègres* (1950).

Like the maternal clichés of these fictions (Condé, Lectures), the gendered myth of the mother-island presents ideological difficulties for the newly emerging generation of Caribbean women writers. This predicament and these writers' significant revisions are discussed in the second part of this chapter, but it is important to note here that women writers do not tend to reject the mother-island myth outright. Rather, recent texts by women demonstrate some of the most extensive, even obsessive, elaborations of it. Their embrace of the mother-island points to another valence of the myth: its consonance with the tradition of strong mothers in Caribbean folk culture and oral literature.[8] Thus, figures of the mother-island can carry symbolic suggestions ranging from a nationalist (and residually colonialist) privileging of the symbolically male order, associated with domination (see Boehmer 6–8), to a postcolonial, feminist reaffirmation of the culture's deeply maternal consciousness, its shaping maternal myths.

Reading Caribbean modernist novels, Kathleen K. Ferracane identifies an "embracing" maternal presence that "both is, and contains, the Caribbean itself" and that tends to be drawn positively or negatively—on the model of the "good" or "bad" mother of infantile psychology—depending on the writer's "attachment to or rejection of" the Caribbean motherland (3–4, 9). Thus George Lamming (Barbados) and Jean Rhys (Dominica) express yearning for maternal figures, while V. S. Naipaul (Trinidad) portrays a "devouring," "threatening" Mother (10–11, 86, 131). While I concur with this sense of the centrality of maternal presences in Caribbean literature, I would identify a paradigm of more complex and ambiguous figuration, in which the writer positions him or herself as a child torn by conflicting feelings for a mother who is at once "good" and "bad," beloved but terribly problematic. In many variations on this paradigm, the mother-island's natural beauty is warped by abandonment and suffering. This figuration suggests the mother-island trope is a sign not simply of an author's feelings for the island, but more saliently of his or her relationship to the island's *history*. It is her capacity to embody history that associates the Caribbean mother-island, in writings by both men and women, with sickness, death, abandonment, rejection, and failure. Indeed, history's grip on the island gives Caribbean writers one of their central projects: the "ironic reversal of the blessed isle *topos* inherited from the Renaissance" (Zimra, "Calabash" 144).

Writing by Caribbean men tends to transplant the primal scene of the rape of the African motherland to the mother-island, often personified or incarnated in an actual mother. Lasana M. Sekou's poem "mothernation" (1991) is paradigmatic. It addresses the poet's native St. Martin as beauteous mother-island:

For you
a woman like you
sustains us, feeds us, cradles us
nurtures us from small

. . . .

upon the green sunlight of your beauty
fresh woman
like a young mother long abandoned
to breed us all in pain

The poem goes on to link the pain and abandonment of the mother to the scene of her rape, which is witnessed by her children. In the aftermath, the children lament their suffering within the maternal realm: "oh mother of us all / look how mahga [thin] some ah we looking / in all ah this passing richness . . ." (40).

Figurations of the mother-island and her children, found in some of the best-known recent texts of Caribbean literature and criticism, can be startlingly harsh. In his epic novel of Guadeloupe, *Lone Sun* (1989) (*L'isolé soleil*, 1979), Daniel Maximin writes a line of the kind that shatters touristic images of the Caribbean: "lands where the weather is too beautiful are like maternal wombs hostile to rebirth" (10). Maximin goes on to compare the topography of Guadeloupe and its small adjacent island, Désirade, to "a mother whose bared caramel forehead burns with fever" as she gently uses a foot to push her newborn daughter "out of her tepid waters towards the oceans of Africa, the way the slave mothers gently suffocated their daughters at birth . . . so they could discover the road back to Ethiopia" (23). Similarly, the heroine of Condé's *A Season in Rihata* (1987) (*Une saison à Rihata,* 1981), refusing to return home from Africa, complains that her native Caribbean island has "become like a sterile womb, never to nurture a foetus again" (63). Phyllis Shand Allfrey's unfinished novel *In the Cabinet* figures the author's native Dominica as "a young Black mother sitting with her dying baby" (Elaine Campbell 14). In Jamaican novelist Michelle Cliff's *Abeng* (1984), a mad woman who teaches the young heroine about her country's barbaric history concludes the lesson with a striking metaphor:

> They are all gone now—the ones who did these things—gone to their reward. But the afterbirth is lodged in the woman's body and will not be expelled. All the waste of birth. Foul-smelling and past its use. (165)

An even more graphic instance of the maternal-bodied metaphor is Benìtez-Rojo's mapping of the political history of the Atlantic, which was "engendered by the copulation of Europe . . . with the Caribbean archipelago":

> the Atlantic is today the Atlantic (the navel of capitalism) because Europe, in its mercantilist laboratory, conceived the project of inseminating the

Caribbean womb with the blood of Africa; the Atlantic is today the Atlantic (NATO, World Bank, New York Stock Exchange, European Economic Community, etc.) because it was the painfully delivered child of the Caribbean, whose vagina was stretched between continental clamps. . . . After the blood and salt water spurts, quickly sew up torn flesh and apply the antiseptic tinctures, the gauze and surgical plaster; then the febrile wait through the forming of a scar; suppurating, always suppurating. (5)

And in the poem used as epigraph to this chapter, when Walcott recounts a visit to a neighborhood stuck "in the unalterable groove of grinding poverty" to act as godparent at a christening, he describes his people as "bound" in oxymoronic "swaddling cerements"; like infants born in mourning, the Caribbean descendants of African slaves—even the child he has just helped usher into the faith—are prevented by the swaddling clothes of their tragic heritage from emerging fully into the "world . . . beyond" ("Laventille" 88). Though in recent literature the Caribbean island emerges as the only mother there really is, she seems to be an unsuccessful, unnurturing mother for her children, like the mother to whom Damas's child must cry, "Parlez-moi du désastre!"

Certainly a sexist scenario distorts Damas's narrative of repression and revelation as well as many of these other texts, but the metaphor's resonance transcends such limitations. The figuration of the lingering effects of Caribbean history in images of an insufficiently motherly mother, a "hostile," "sterile" womb, or a birth that is a harvest of death, recalls the use of distorted childbirth metaphors to render traumatic history in works by African-American and other ethnic American women writers. Notably, male and female writers alike use this trope in Caribbean literature, rejecting the search for mothers elsewhere and self-consciously attempting to "take root" in the inhospitable soil of an inadequate, historically compromised mother-island.

Many texts, then, envision a renewed and remade Caribbean in the form of a recovered mother. Like Sekou, writers position themselves as children who, "growing tall, wish to care for," "stand for," "wash," "adorn," and "praise" their maligned, abused mother-island (40–42). A key literary recuperation of the mother can be traced from Césaire to Brathwaite to Cliff, writers who find a previously neglected mother in Shakespeare's *The Tempest*, the ur-text that has already given to postcolonial letters the emblematic figures of Prospero the colonizer, Ariel the willing (bourgeois, mulatto) slave, and Caliban the enraged colonial subject who learns the master's language only to curse him.[9] In *Une Tempête* (*A Tempest*), Césaire's 1969 rewriting, the poet retains only one original passage from Shakespeare: that which relates "Caliban's claim of legitimacy (i.e. history) to Prospero's island through his own witch-mother" (Zimra, "Calabash" n45; 155). In Shakespeare's play, Caliban protests: "This island's mine, by Sycorax my mother, / Which thou tak'st from me" (I. ii. 331–32). As Césaire has it, Caliban says to Prospero, "Without you? I'd be . . . king of the island I inherited from my mother, Sycorax" (15). The dialogue continues:

PROSPERO: There are some family trees it's better not to climb! She's a ghoul! A witch from whom—and may God be praised—death has delivered us.

CALIBAN: Dead or alive, she was my mother, and I won't deny her! Anyhow, you only think she's dead because you think the earth itself is dead. . . . Dead, you can walk on it, pollute it, you can tread upon it with the steps of a conqueror. I respect the earth, because I know that it is alive, and I know that Sycorax is alive. Sycorax. Mother. (15)

Fusing island and mother, Césaire creates in Sycorax a figure of uncontestable mythic priority, whose aliveness suggests formidable power latent in Caribbean peoples' connection to the natural world of their home.

Eight years later, Brathwaite's *Mother Poem* invokes a figure he calls "black sycorax my mother," her color even more closely identifying the witch with an African matrilineal inheritance (47). Brathwaite has gradually developed the tropological potential of mother Sycorax into a central element of his work. He has called her a symbol of "the survival potential, the irreducible spirit" of African culture as it endures in Caribbean people (qtd. in Pattanayak 63); he writes a letter to her on a computer in *X/Self* (1987); and in *Barbajan Poems* (1994), he conjures Sycorax as his matrix, muse, typist, style, and the very name of his computer.

Michelle Cliff differently extends the witch's meanings in a 1991 essay in which she calls herself "Caliban's Daughter" and "granddaughter of Sycorax" and also identifies the rebel heroine Nanny of the Maroons as "the Jamaican Sycorax," thus reinventing Shakespeare's witch as a Caribbean feminist precursor ("Caliban's" 40, 47).[10] Yet if, as Ferracane says, "it is through the Mother that [Caribbean] authors identify with the Caribbean, through Sycorax that they claim—or deny—their island" (13), the progress of the mother-metaphor from Europe to Sycorax does not imply complete and happy closure in a maternal embrace. Sycorax is, after all, a minor character in an English play, an always-already dead and absent woman, a mother whose bequest to her child has been violated, and, moreover, a witch, a holder of defamed and eternally oppositional knowledge. To recover such a mother is to claim a subversive identity and mission, not yet to claim sovereignty over one's homeland.

Indeed, this mother's strange name in itself suggests her problematic status. Quite evidently not an African-Caribbean word, not a word from the mother-tongue, "Sycorax" is a vile-sounding name invented by an Englishman for a foreign witch.[11] Given the vexed questions of naming and language that loom large in current Caribbean literary debates, this island-mother's false naming—and the need to rename her—seem emblematic of the Caribbean historiographic predicament. Recent Caribbean fiction, Clarisse Zimra writes, "hides the silent presence of a Mother not yet fully understood" ("Calabash" 157); she urges Caribbeans to "[disregard] the Logos of the Father for the Silent Song of the Mother" (156). Indeed, the work of women writers, according to Jamaican poet and novelist Olive Senior, is now "opening up . . . a completely new approach to the topic of the Caribbean mother—one of our great literary preoccupations—and of our relationship with that mother" (485). As women rewrite the Caribbean mother, perhaps her "Silent Song" will find a tongue and relate her knowledge of life and generation despite "désastre." It is to women's texts that we must look if—like Hodge's young heroine Tee, wondering about her great-great-grandmother—we hope to learn the old woman's "true-true name" (19, 110).

THE CARIBBEAN DAUGHTER'S RETURN

The Caribbean Women's Renaissance

In much the same spirit as recent critical proclamations on African-American women's writing, the 1989 anthology *Her True-True Name* celebrates the "remarkable" output of Caribbean women writers in the 1980s as a "literary blossoming"; other collections announce a "flowering" and "a veritable explosion" (Mordecai and Wilson xi; Davies and Fido 12; Esteves and Paravisini-Gebert xi). The rapid rise of this body of literature makes much of it seem to have "arrived full-grown" to participate in an era of women's worldwide literary emergence (Mordecai and Wilson xvii; Cudjoe, *Caribbean* 6). But the "worldliness" of this renaissance—to use Said's term—should not surprise us, arising as it does within a literature initiated and sustained in the crosswinds of many cultures.

The term "Caribbean women writers" describes an extremely diverse collection of women: women of numerous racial and ethnic groups who reside in many nations and write in at least four European languages and many Caribbean creoles. Even a study like this one, which addresses only anglophone and francophone writers, faces a heterogeneity that defeats simple literary-geographical categories. Perhaps the most acclaimed woman writer of the region, still, is a white woman identified with English modernism, who lived almost all of her life in Europe and died just as the Caribbean women's renaissance was getting under way.[12] The international reputation of Jean Rhys has soared since the publication of her last novel, *Wide Sargasso Sea*, in 1966, aided by American feminist critique in the 1980s, yet the question of her status as a Caribbean writer is still debated among Caribbean critics. The other writers whose strongly matrifocal narratives of Caribbean history are given substantial treatment in this study are citizens or residents of the United States: Jamaica Kincaid, an Antiguan who became known in the 1980s as a writer for the *New Yorker* and seems to be read more as a Caribbean-American than an African-American or postcolonial writer; Michelle Cliff, a Jamaican of mixed-race background, now a U.S. citizen and a writer generally identified with the cultural politics of American lesbian feminists of color; and Maryse Condé, a Guadeloupean who has lived for extended periods in France and Africa, now resident for much of the year in the United States, and usually identified as a postcolonial writer.

This varied reception is the usual course of things for Caribbean writers, who often find more readers overseas than at home, partly because of obstacles to literary production in the islands—including a lack of readership and of literary institutions—that force writers to accommodate foreign publishers and audiences (Shelton, "Women Writers" 347; see also Paris 85).[13] The knowledge that they write for readers far away (Condé, Lectures) encourages a cosmopolitan consciousness in Caribbean women's shaping of local fictions, as does the experience of expatriation, shared in various forms by all the novelists considered in the chapters that follow. While the removal of so many writers to foreign shores registers the lamentable conditions of life in many parts of the region, expatriation can also be a spur to literary development. As Simon Gikandi puts it, exile awoke colonially educated writers to "an irreversible cognizance of their cultural schizophrenia" and thus "constitute[s] the ground zero of West Indian literature, its radical point of departure" (26, 33).[14] Though exiled writers may suffer permanently an "Atlantic-divided mind" and may lament the difficulty of going home again,[15] many have drawn inspiration from "the seed of possibility" in these very conditions (Salkey 182; Glissant 23; Kellman xxix); many have made the shifting perspectives of the exile an essential theme of their work.[16]

American readers are familiar with several Caribbean women writers who have made the United States their home and who have been integrated to varying degrees in the African-American canon. The late 1950s, 1960s, and 1970s novels of Paule Marshall and Rosa Guy, of Barbadian and Trinidadian ancestry, respectively, helped to spark the new African-American women's writing and to make the Caribbean a mythic region of quest for African-American heroines. Audre Lorde, who was the daughter of immigrants from Grenada, has become revered as an African-American lesbian feminist poet and theorist. Other anglophone Caribbean women writers gaining international reputations include Louise Bennett (Jamaica), Dionne Brand (Trinidad-Canada), Erna Brodber (Jamaica), Zee Edgell (Belize), Lorna Goodison (Jamaica), Merle Hodge (Trinidad), Grace Nichols (Guyana–United Kingdom), Marlene Nourbese Philip (Tobago-Canada), Olive Senior (Jamaica), and Sylvia Wynter (Jamaica–United States). Well-known twentieth-century francophone women writers include Marie Chauvet (Haiti), Edwidge Danticat (Haiti–United States), Jeanne Hyvrard, Michèle Lacrosil, Jacqueline Manicom, Simone Schwarz-Bart, and Myriam Warner-Vieyra (all from Guadeloupe).[17] This heterogeneous catalog will suggest why, though some have sought to define literary Caribbeanness on the basis of authorial residence or length of residence, this study presumes that the region's history makes much of such quibbling absurd, that it is in the nature of this literature to describe an exilic, migratory subject, and that many kinds of writers contribute to the polyglot project of Caribbean letters.

MORE THAN ONE critic dates the new era in Caribbean women's literature from the publication of Hodge's *Crick Crack, Monkey* in 1970 (See Cudjoe, *Caribbean*

43; Mordecai and Wilson xvii), the same pivotal year that Toni Morrison, Alice Walker, and Maya Angelou published first books. Before 1970, Caribbean women writers received scant attention in criticism and literary histories, a neglect that has been linked to the sexism of Caribbean nationalisms and their narrow definitions of politically "relevant" work (Esteves and Paravasini-Gebert xvi). But critics would find it hard of late to dismiss a literature that so evidently addresses Caribbean women's lives and history from a new "point of affirmation and self-consciousness" (Mordecai and Wilson xvi). Though "feminism" is a much-debated, problematic term for these writers (often associated with white, middle-class European and American women's politics),[18] Carol Boyce Davies and Elaine Savory Fido argue for the existence of an indigenous feminism in the region, "a long history of struggle" (15), which is borne out in the literature previous to this era.

Caribbean women's renaissance writing presents a feminist mode of the postcolonial counter-discursive literary practice discussed in the first part of this chapter. Recent texts revise a tradition of women's literature that tended to portray female characters in abortive struggle against oppressive colonial social and political orders, in plots dominated by the vexed, socially determinative issue of skin color[19]; the figure of the tragic, often mad mulatta was particularly central to francophone women's literature, the earliest to generate a substantial body of texts.[20] Recently, anglophone women's fiction has emerged from decades of struggle against limitations of race, place, and possibility and toward greater optimism and authority in women's voices, more questioning of gender inequality, stronger bonds among female characters, and "uneasy quests for liberation." Hodge's *Crick Crack, Monkey* "begins the work of rescue" by portraying a heroine rooted in Caribbean culture despite the sway of metropolitan values (Mordecai and Wilson xvi–xvii, xi; see also Niesen de Abruna, "Twentieth Century"). Though old stereotypes die hard, and for the most part "appearance remains essence" in francophone women's texts, these plots, too, have become more complex, heroines tending to seek identity through a quest into a "subversively subjective" history (Zimra, "W/Righting" 233–34).

The turn to history in the work of both groups of writers now presents the recreation of a female past as this literature's most compelling project. But though women have begun to create revisionary histories of "Caliban's daughters," female rebels of Caribbean history, the more difficult problem remains that of Caliban's shadowy mother, the defamed, symbolic embodiment of Caribbean origins, of a longed-for mother-island. Recovering this mother—once mainly a male literary enterprise—has become a key venture for women writers in their moment of renaissance. Clear parallels link their project to African-American women's repossession of a black mother-of-history from received historical and cultural narratives as well as from the tensions of emergent feminism. Yet, Caribbean fictions of daughterly desire for the historical mother engage an even more complex problematics than those of African-American women—and those of Caribbean men as well.

Jamaican poet Lorna Goodison's 1986 volume *I Am Becoming My Mother* and Jamaica Kincaid's 1996 novel *The Autobiography of My Mother* vividly signal the trend toward matrifocal identity in contemporary Caribbean women's writing. Yet the maternal imagery of this literature has been notably contradictory, strong and nurturing mothers coexisting with dead and dying, inhibiting and compromised ones. Women writers created several of the figures of failed, unmothering maternal bodies listed earlier, a catalog of horrors surpassing the outrageous mother-figures of the African-American women's renaissance. These contradictory Caribbean mothers suggest a certain incoherence in the symbolic structure within which Caribbean women render their histories—as if a revered mother source somehow spurns specific daughters, or as if strong human mothers reside in a sick, dying motherland. Maternal figures like these mirror the paradox of reclaiming a history of disaster and disempowerment.

Such is the case in the novel that inaugurates the new women's writing, Hodge's *Crick Crack, Monkey*. The young heroine Tee, who confuses Mother England with her own mother, might be thought to resist her colonizing education, intuitively assimilating the false colonial "mother" to the mother of her primary emotional attachment. Yet the original mother to whom she gives an imaginary apotheosis is dead, and dies—significantly in the motifs of contemporary women's literature—in childbirth. Indeed, this first Caribbean women's renaissance text opens, quite like its African-American counterpart *Jubilee*, with the scene of the young heroine's ignorant witness to her mother's death. Hodge's Tee is not carried in to say goodbye to her dying mother, however, but stands at the window of her house, still waiting for her mother's return from the hospital, calling out to all passersby, "we gettin a baby" (1).[21] Though this opening promises a normative female history, Hodge delivers instead a traumatic narrative of orphanage. In this novel, as in Margaret Walker's African-American epic, the ominous separation of mother and daughter *because of* childbirth inscribes a people's formative historical rupture. Significantly, however, the two novels diverge in their inscription of the power to recover matrilineal memory. While *Jubilee* is founded on the prodigious memory-work of the author's grandmother and ends with the scene of a daughter attending to her mother's call, the strong, adored grandmother of *Crick, Crack Monkey* has "amnesia" (Gikandi 213); she dies unable to transmit to her granddaughter her own grandmother's "true-true," presumably African name, and the novel ends with the girl sent away from the maternal island, to the father who has emigrated to Europe.

The contrast between these first African-American and Caribbean women's renaissance texts points us to the more difficult nature of the Caribbean recuperative project, figured in a more ambivalent relationship to the historical mother. A popular folkloric image casts the Caribbean as "a woman compelled to suckle a snake all night long" (Dukats 745). More dramatically even than the images of distorted island-birth, this image suggests that the problem with the great Caribbean mother is that she has been compromised by colonial history, that she has "internalize[d] the phallic imperative, the condition of her very survival" (Zimra, "Negritude" 73). Zimra elaborates the implications for mother figures:

> The white master's whore is, simultaneously, the locus of both desire and hatred. Unlike European convention, her motherly role cannot redeem her, for there is no telling but that the self-sacrificing mother has also slept in the white man's bed. . . . ("W/Righting" 232)

To be sure, much the same has been said about figures of the African-American mother. But the pervasive association of the Caribbean mother with the beautiful, betrayed *island* itself, and the island's capacity to embody history, makes maternal corruption a more central and consequential symbolic element in the Caribbean than the African-American imaginary. Mothers who are compromised, bad, sick, or dying in this literature are figures for a site of history so perverse that even a returning daughterly imagination finds its mothers suspect.

When the mythic relationship to the mother-island is played out in realist novels by Caribbean women, fictional mothers who carry this larger symbolic connection tend to be, not surprisingly, unsatisfactory mothers for their daughters. Traumatic disruptions of the mother-daughter relationship here, as in African-American women's writing, carry the emotional weight of a psychologically difficult inheritance. Many Caribbean women's texts deal with this ambivalence by treating the middle-generation woman, the heroine's mother, as a compromised or alienated figure, while elevating a grandmother, other mother, or mythic mother figure to the special, honorific status of "good" nurturer.[22] Grandmothers tend to be bearers of culture, connected to the land, idealized objects of the daughterly desire to return. Allied with grandmothers are historical and mythological heroines like the Jamaican rebel leader Nanny of the Maroons, explicitly reclaimed by Cliff and evoked by Condé; Solitude, the Guadeloupean heroine recuperated by André and Simone Schwarz-Bart; and Condé's Barbadian heroine Tituba.[23] These "figures of resistance and survival" (listed by Mordecai and Wilson xvi) recall the heroes and martyrs of Caribbean men's writing but carry a notably different valence as mothers-of-history, who even in death bear hope of futurity.

All matrifocal texts in recent Caribbean literature are indebted to Guadeloupean novelist Simone Schwarz-Bart's *Pluie et vent sur Télumée Miracle* (1972, translated as *The Bridge of Beyond*, 1974), a novel on which critics converge with praise and affection for its unambivalent embrace of a Caribbean matrilineage, its tribute to the spirited, undefeated, poor women of Guadeloupe, and its lyrical rendering of Guadeloupean folklife in what Marie-Denise Shelton calls "a poetry of presence and plenitude against absence and fragmentation" ("Women Writers" 354). Schwarz-Bart's heroine Télumée is abandoned by her mother but is grounded in the love of her grandmother Queen without a Name and in her island, to which she compares herself

(46). This Caribbean home is "not a place to be fled nor a prison" but, rather, "the locus of self-discovery and human realization" (Shelton, "Women Writers" 355). Télumée has no need for a roots-search, Zimra writes; "she is her own genitrix. Therein lies the 'miracle'" ("Negritude" 70). But I would say that the "Miracle" for which the villagers name Télumée is that she becomes her grandmother's heir, that is, the miracle of mythic matrilineal identity overcoming personal and collective trauma. *Pluie et vent sur Télumée Miracle* stands out in a tradition that, while strongly attracted to the matrilineal, has generally been less than confident of matrilineal miracles.

Indeed, viewed from the vantage point of Caribbean women's fiction, the collective African-American vision of daughters determined to recover mothers-of-history registers a degree of imaginative triumph remote from the Caribbean instance. Though recent Caribbean women's writing features multiple daughterly returns to reclaim lost, mythic mothers, it does not generally literalize contact with the past in magic or time-travel. Though magic is often an important maternal property in these fictions, heroines cannot summon it to empower and protect them. Revisionary daughters with less confidence in the romance plot of return, Caribbean women writers perform historical returns without claim to magical mastery of time and loss.

It may be surprising that these fictions should be less magical than the African-American ones, as magic is a vital element of life in many parts of the region and literary magic realism itself has a Caribbean origin.[24] But given the more troubling nature of the symbolic figure of the Caribbean mother-of-history, it is no wonder that she should be less recoverable by the work of the imagination, which, I have argued, narrative magic serves to figure. This resistance to the "happy ending" of magical transformation resonates with the general tendency (in Glissant, Walcott, Hall, Benítez-Rojo, among others) to render Caribbean history as an absence, enduring wound, or object of unrequitable desire, as well as with the venerable literary tradition (in Césaire, Alejo Carpentier, Glissant) that recasts Caribbean history in the form of tragic romance, centered on the relationship of a "suffering hero or anti-hero" to the colonized masses (Kellman xvi; Arnold xv).[25] These traditions reflect not only the grip of a traumatic past but also the disillusionment of postcolonial political and cultural aspirations. Indeed, we might connect the limitations on magic in the novels studied here to the skeptical, non-triumphalist mode characteristic of postcolonial narrative, the tendency of texts "to deny the possibility" of recovering the "wholeness and homeland" for which they nevertheless convey a deep longing (Lima 54, n5).[26] With as strong a desire for the mother-of-history as their African-American counterparts, but with a more chastened hope, these Caribbean daughter-figures must be especially heroic, must sacrifice their lives in anticolonial resistance, pursuing the maternal romance through violence and grief to tragic endings. Their plots signal victory only in symbolic gestures toward futurity, the spiritual mothering of daughters in a new Caribbean day.

Writing a Different Mother-Island

When Caribbean women writers blend the images of island and mother, how do they create mother-islands that differ from those of their male counterparts? How do they revise a male tradition that equates homeland and nation with the fertile female body? This problem has been a particularly live one for feminist critics of African literature, because of the pervasive negritude trope of "Mother Africa," which tended to contrast the passive physical presence of woman/land/nation to the creative force of the male writer, masking male domination in nationalist rhetoric (Stratton 41, 55; see also Goodwin xviii). Susheila Nasta argues in the anthology *Motherlands* that postcolonial African, Caribbean, and Asian women writers do manage to develop "mothers and motherlands" into "a potent symbolic force" while rejecting colonialist and nationalist appropriations (xix). I would agree that the mother-(is)land remains a paradoxically empowering and important figure for Caribbean women writers and add, moreover, that one finds in their literature very little impulse to denaturalize the mother, to separate land and woman.[27] But how, as Elleke Boehmer asks, can women distinguish such images from "those which continue to shore up patriarchal desire and a system of gendered national authority?" (Boehmer 9).

My view is that women writers create distinctive figurations of the mythic mother-island by embedding them in complex, female "relational" connections. Ann R. Morris and Margaret M. Dunn observe that a Caribbean woman's relationship to a "motherland":

> encompass[es] in its connotations her island home and its unique culture as well as the body of tropes, talismans and female bonding that is a woman's heritage through her own and other mothers. The land and one's mothers, then, are co-joined. (219)

Drawing on these symbolic connections, women writers represent the mother-island not in idealized scenarios of "female bonding" but in visions that evoke the range and richness of actual mother-daughter relationships.

Autobiographical reflections by two of the novelists discussed in this study will illustrate this distinction. Maryse Condé speaks of her home:

> The Antilles is my natural mother and it is with her that I have accounts to settle, like any daughter with her mother, before becoming completely an adult. (trans. Gikandi 231; original in Jacquey and Hugon 23)

And Michelle Cliff addresses her native Jamaica:

> I wonder if I will ever return. . . . And this is something I will admit only to you. I am afraid my place is at your side. I am afraid my place is in the hills. This is a killing ambivalence. I bear in mind that you with all your cruelties are the source of me, and like even the most angry mother draw me back. ("Love" 103)

In Condé's portrayal, the mother-island is not static and passive, but alive, talkable to, a difficult woman who is yet capable of engaging in dialogue with her children. Her function does not end with birthing, but is ongoing, a relationship. Similarly, Cliff speaks intimately to "cruel" Jamaica, explaining and admitting, acknowledging the island's active, maternal pull on her grown daughter. These authors' remarks demonstrate a distinctly relational conception of the historical mother, an interactive sense of self and source that—corresponding to female psychology as interpreted by Chodorow and others—makes the mother-island the sign not of a static origin but of a writer's dynamic relationship to her heritage.

When Caribbean women writers revise history, then, they tend to do so in intimate plots that stress less the violated mother than the daughter's violated *relationship* with her mother, especially the separation of a mother and her baby. By contrast, historical recovery tends to be figured in plots of reunion with the mother; birthing and gestation metaphors predominate. Recent fiction offers many variations on this paradigm: returning daughters may seek to contact actual mothers, or to repair inadequate experiences of mothering through mythic union with the mother-island (see Morris and Dunn 221); motherhood and daughterhood may fuse or alternate in a heroine's self-conception; daughterly return may win her a place among the mothers of her people. In almost all cases, women writers link recovery of maternal history with the generation of a hopeful future.

Refusing Motherhood

But in this literature, the connection between recovering the maternal past and creating a future generally avoids the obvious link of a daughter's becoming a new mother in turn. Even more consistently than African-American women's fiction, Caribbean women's texts render the problematics of inheriting "bad history" in the form of the refusal of motherhood. In her early study of francophone Caribbean women's fiction, *La parole des femmes* (1979), Condé discusses heroines whose mothers are central to their plots but who do not become mothers themselves. For Condé this refusal of motherhood is a nuanced form of feminist protest, against the conventional identification of women with maternity and against male progenitorial pride. At the same time, Condé perceives in this refusal an avoidance of generational conflict and thus of symbolic engagement with a heritage. While she calls these heroines and authors "voluntarily narcissistic," she also senses their anxiety about the future, their inability to envision solutions to contemporary Caribbean problems (44–47, translation mine).

My own analysis is close to Condé's. It seems to me that when Schwarz-Bart's Télumée, Cliff's Clare, Jamaica Kincaid's Xuela, and Condé's own Tituba reject motherhood, they do more than "[discard] the biological bond . . . in favor of the free choice of an ideologically autonomous agent" (Zimra, "Calabash" 155–56). Rather, they signal an agonistic relationship to their own maternal pasts, symbolically declaring that the traumatic historical chain stops here.

Such literary refusals echo a documented history of Caribbean slave women's resistance to childbearing for the plantation system's profit (see Mair 56). Indeed, Caribbean heroines who forego maternity attain a state of heroic resistance that allows a transcendent kind of motherhood. Thus Lorna Goodison's portrait of the great Nanny in her African youth highlights the warrior's refusal of biological motherhood:

> My womb was sealed
> with molten wax
> of killer bees
> for nothing should enter
> nothing should leave
> the state of perpetual siege
> the condition of the warrior.

Removed from the possibility of conventional motherhood, Nanny becomes revolutionary nurturer of her people:

> From then my whole body would quicken
> at the birth of every one of my people's children.
> I was schooled in the green-giving ways
> of the roots and vines.

Notably, the denaturalized motherhood of Goodison's Nanny goes hand in hand with a radically revised story of her abduction into New World slavery; she is trained in Africa to lead her people in the New World:

> And when my training was over
> they . . .
>
> . . . .
>
> . . . sold me to the traders
> all my weapons within me.
> I was sent, tell that to history.

Sent, not stolen, the intentional slave-warrior does not give birth to descendants, as in the conventional course of reproduction, but instead inspires heroic followers: "When your sorrow obscures the skies / other women like me will rise" ("Nanny" 69–70).

Goodison's Nanny is one among many childless women who become wise, culture-bearing mother-figures in Caribbean women's literature (Zimra, "Calabash" 156). Last in a formidable chain of mothers, Schwarz-Bart's Télumée adopts a daughter near the end of her story; Condé's Tituba follows suit, choosing a girl who will carry on in her revolutionary spirit. Like their African-American counterparts, heroines in this literature who refuse motherhood become "symbolic ideological Mother[s] to a whole people" (Zimra, "Calabash" 156). Foregrounding maternity by refusing and revising it, these daughters claim new mastery of their relationship to history.

The Horizontal Plot

The recurrent refusal of generation in contemporary Caribbean women's visions of the maternal past is consonant with this literature's greater suspicion of the romance of return, of magically complete retrieval of the mother-of-history. Indeed, as we shall see in the chapters that follow, the paradigm of the magic black daughter does not seem to find a home in Caribbean writers' work—except, interestingly enough, when their fictions imaginatively approach the United States.

But as if in place of the power of magical return, Caribbean women's historiographic fiction has developed a different strength, one that we saw emerging as a secondary thread within the African-American daughterly returns: the plot of cross-cultural connection. Displaced by slavery or exile from the figurative mother who embodies a fullness of historical continuity, fictional daughters of the Caribbean find inspiration, knowledge, and love in transhistorical and transcultural meetings with other women.

In African-American women's historical fictions, we saw this important female exchange occurring most often through the shared experience of motherhood and in scenes of childbirth and nursing. White women help black women to mother their descendants as midwife (*Beloved*) and wet-nurse (*Dessa Rose*), and white and Native American women become surrogate mothers (*The Gilda Stories*). Such generative connections with "other" women counterbalance the powerful, "ethnic" daughter-mother romance plot. Moreover, I would contend that wherever they occur in contemporary women's literature, they serve to register the supporting role of emergent women's voices across the racial and ethnic spectrum in any woman's rise to the imaginative power to recreate her maternal past. To put it in other terms, narratives that feature such connections embed their "vertical" or diachronic visions of particular pasts within a "horizontal" or synchronic consciousness of a multicultural, multihistorical world, a world that writes and reads across national and ethnic boundaries.

In Caribbean women's fiction the cross-cultural vision is more pronounced than in texts by American women. The three novelists examined in Chapters 5–7 demonstrate a strongly "horizontal" interest in relations with the world, which crosses with and helps to shape the "vertical" interest in their own people's history, becoming crucial to the meaning of the past they reimagine. In this aspect, their work accords with the current Caribbean embrace of "hybridity" and "creolization," with the theory that a heritage of violent, disastrous encounters now yields ironic benefits: a creatively multilingual, multiracial Caribbean identity that values cultural complexity and diversity over either "universality" or "purity" (Bernabé et al 892).[28] We might say that in Rhys's *Wide Sargasso Sea*, Cliff's *Abeng* and *No Telephone to Heaven*, and Condé's *I, Tituba, Black Witch of Salem*—all of which display a mix of peoples, races, cultures, and languages—the project of reopening history may be as much about "creolizing" the past, so to speak, as feminizing it.

Seeking a symbolic Caribbean mother-of-history, the heroines of these texts form a distinct genealogy of Caribbean daughters, revising one another's plots as well as earlier English narratives. Yet along the way they also encounter stories of "other" women, adopted mother and sister figures external to their ethnic histories but critical to their own imaginative journeys, who as doubles, role models, or antagonists bear witness to the pan-ethnic contemporary project to recover a female past.

JAMAICA KINCAID AND THE MATERNAL VOID OF HISTORY

Jamaica Kincaid's 1995 novel *The Autobiography of My Mother* is an extravagant contribution to the literature of Caribbean women's history, and of their historically traumatized maternity. In her first two novels, *Annie John* (1983) and *Lucy* (1990), Kincaid dramatizes a young Caribbean protagonist's obsessive love-hate relationship with a devouring mother. This mother embodies the ambivalence of colonial female identity; she is a figure at once of oppression and of potentially liberating origin. Early Kincaid heroines must escape this mother by leaving the mother-island. But in her first venture into the historical imagination, *The Autobiography of My Mother*, Kincaid returns to the island and to the mother's life, reuniting daughter and mother in the tightest knit yet—as suggested by her paradoxical title—and giving the progress of her oeuvre a remarkably circular aspect.[29]

Kincaid's text merits special attention because its very excesses dramatize the profoundly troubled realm of maternal history in Caribbean women's literary imagination. Extending the author's longtime preoccupation with mothers into the genre of historical fiction, this novel demonstrates that an obsession with the "vertical" axis of relationship to the traumatic maternal past can blot out other possibilities, such as a viable future or a "horizontal" plot of cross-cultural relationships. At the same time, then, Kincaid's novel serves as a caution against too-easy celebration of the hybridity born of violent conquest.

Refusal of Childbearing

The Autobiography of My Mother is the first-person narrative of a woman traumatized from the beginning to the end of her life by the loss of her mother. The heroine Xuela begins:

> My mother died at the moment I was born, and so for my whole life there was nothing standing between myself and eternity; at my back was always a bleak, black wind . . . [and] at my end was nothing, no one between me and the black room of the world. (3)

Over the course of the novel, Xuela repeats more than a dozen times—twice on one page—the stark fact of her mother's death in bearing her. In a recurrent dream, the mother descends a ladder toward her but never reveals more than "her heels, and the hem of her gown" (18).[30] This emblematic absence of the Caribbean mother becomes the heroine's most intimate definition of self: "Who was I? My mother died at the moment I was born. . . . This fact of my mother dying at the moment I was born became a central motif of my life" (225).

Kincaid's intense fusion of motherly and daughterly identities therefore carries an entirely negative valence, and, stemming from this formative negation, a tone and a grammar of negation rules the book; "not" becomes the most vital word in Xuela's mother-tongue. On her schoolteacher: "she did not love us; we did not love her; we did not love one another, not then, not ever" (15); on her people's devalued culture: "Our experience cannot be interpreted by us; we do not know the truth of it. Our God was not the correct one, our understanding of heaven and hell was not a respectable one" (37).[31]

The mother whose emblematic death spawns this profusion of negativity was a Carib of the island of Dominica, one of the region's last retreats for the remnants of this indigenous people. Thus Xuela's motherless identity is associated throughout with a brutal, persistent, irreversible history of "defeat" (139). Descended also, on her father's side, from enslaved Africans, Xuela knows only that "the Carib people had been defeated and then exterminated, thrown away like the weeds in a garden; the African people had been defeated but had survived" (16). Time for Kincaid's heroine is inextricable from the thrall of this defeat:

> For me history was not only the past: it was the past and it was also the present. I did not mind my defeat, I only minded that it had to last so long; I did not see the future. . . . (138–39)

Perhaps more relentlessly than in any other text of Caribbean literature, this novel's account of the lives of history's defeated invokes women's failed, traumatized, or refused maternity. Indeed, *The Autobiography of My Mother* gives to the trope of the refusal of childbearing a most graphic, furious, even violent rendering, one that resists the usual consolations of spiritual mothering or historical mastery. The heroine's foremothers fail tragically—her mother dying in childbirth and her grandmother abandoning her infant—and almost every woman in the novel's scope is barren. Xuela herself aborts and otherwise resists pregnancies explicitly so as to articulate and resist her people's ongoing defeat. Though she echoes Morrison's Sula in saying "I chose to possess myself" (174), she intends not simply feminist self-assertion, but a symbolic repetition of a history of maternal abandonments:

> That attachment, physical and spiritual, that confusion of who is who, flesh and flesh, which was absent between my mother and her mother was also absent between my mother and myself . . . how can any child understand such a thing, so profound an abandonment? I have refused to bear any children. (199)

Moreover, Xuela understands her boycott of motherhood as a radical political act: "I refused to belong to a race, I refused to accept a nation. . . . The crime of these identities, which I know now more than ever, I do not have the courage to bear" (225–26). Refusing to bear more racialized history, Xuela makes her reproductive power her weapon; she deploys the power *not* to mother in explicit refusal to make "biological contributions to the 'nation' or the 'race,'" in Judith Raiskin's terms (7).

But while the burdens of history help explain this heroine's attitude toward her fertility, the fury of her words is still shocking:

> I would never become a mother, but that would not be the same as never bearing children. I would bear children, but I would never be a mother to them. I would bear them in abundance; they would emerge from my head, from my armpits, from between my legs. . . . they would hang from me like fruit from a vine, but I would destroy them with the carelessness of a god. I would bear children in the morning, I would bathe them at noon in a water that came from myself, and I would eat them at night, swallowing them whole. . . . I would cover their bodies with diseases, embellish skins with thinly crusted sores, the sores sometimes oozing a thick pus for which they would thirst, a thirst that could never be quenched. I would condemn them to live in an empty space frozen in the same posture in which they had been born. I would throw them from a great height; every bone in their body would be broken and the bones would never be properly set. . . . It is in this way that I did not become a mother; it is in this way that I bore my children. (96–98)

The evident pleasure in this catalog of fantasized tortures cannot be reconciled with grief of a normative kind. Clearly the heroine creates these abortive imaginings out of a depth of anguish and despair that is culture-wide, history-deep, that blights the future and leaves daily life in the thrall of the unspeakable. If in Xuela's narration, Kincaid dramatizes the bearing of history's persistent "wound" more vividly than does any writer discussed in this study, she also shapes this condition into her own distinctive existential torment.[32]

The ending of this novel is also bleaker than any ending discussed here. For, revising important texts of Caribbean daughterly return that came before her, Kincaid's heroine rejects the key symbolic gesture of choosing an adoptive daughter as heir, of becoming mother of a nation. Indeed, she makes no gestures at all toward futurity. Her ending recasts that of Schwarz-Bart's Télumée—who embraces death happy and alone in her own garden—with a longing for death as the one "thing to which I can submit" precisely because it is "not in a book of history," "not the work of anyone human" (228). The "spell of history" (218) so totally envelops Kincaid's heroine that she welcomes death to escape it and can envision no possibility of community outside or after the self. Instead, this novel's speaking self is most fantastically alive with its own blighted internal geneology:

> This account of my life has been an account of my mother's life as much as it has been an account of mine, and even so, again it is an account of the life of the children I did not have, as it is their account of me. In me is the voice I never heard, the face I never saw, the being I came from. In me are the voices that should have come from out of me, the faces I never allowed to form, the eyes I never allowed to see me. This account is an account of the person who was never allowed to be and an account of the person I did not allow myself to become. (227–28)

The Autobiography of My Mother leaves us in a Caribbean present enclosed in the claustrophobia of a traumatized maternal heritage, as it leaves us in the arms of death.

Refusal of Connection

Perhaps the most pointed literary revision performed by *The Autobiography of My Mother* is its rejection of cross-ethnic connections, of the more hopeful multiracial visions now common in Caribbean women's novels. Kincaid's narration self-consciously avoids all use of the terms "black" and "white," preferring non-racializing descriptors like "of the African people and the people from France" (28); skin color, the heroine insists, results from "a mixture of people—not races, people" (117). Yet this apparent desire to even the field is at odds with her knowledge of lingering historical inequities of power:

> His father was a Scots-man, his mother of the African people, and this distinction between "man" and "people" was an important distinction, for one of them came off the boat as part of a horde, already demonized, mind blank to everything but human suffering . . . ; the other came off the boat of his own volition, seeking to fulfill a destiny, a vision of himself he carried in his mind's eye. (181)

When Xuela marries an Englishman, this "history . . . made up of man and people" (185) dooms the interracial marriage: "We could not both be happy at the same time. Life, History, whatever its name, had made such a thing an impossibility" (227). Philip's whiteness entirely delimits her feelings for him; because his skin seems to be only "on its way to being skin," "He did not look like anyone I could love, and he did not look like anyone I should love, and so I determined then that I could not love him and I determined that I should not love him" (152).

Most notably for this study, relations are also impossible between Xuela and Philip's English first wife, Moira. Xuela's account of this failure of women's cross-race relations carries the repetitive excess that signals history's burden throughout the novel:

> I did not like her and I should have liked her, or at least I should have had even a tiny bit of sympathy for her, because like me she also had a broken womb, but I could not tell if like me she had broken hers deliberately or if

> she was born that way. I did not like her; I did not like her, it was impossible, it was an impossible situation. We did not like ourselves, we did not like each other, and so it was impossible to like them. . . . (157–58)

Moira's barrenness might be taken to signify her own inner wounds from an unspeakable heritage,[33] but any possibility of sympathy is eliminated for Xuela by the racialized construction of gender in their world:

> She was a lady, I was a woman, and this distinction for her was important. . . . I was a woman and as that I had a brief definition: two breasts, a small opening between my legs, one womb; it never varies and they are always in the same place. She would never describe herself in this way, she would shrink from such a description. . . . (158–59)

This stark failure stands out among the many female interracial relationships in recent Caribbean women's literature. In particular, Xuela seems to mock the love of Condé's Tituba for a white woman, which is symbolized in a white flower. Not only does Kincaid's narrative associate white flowers with sickness, rot, and death (62), but her heroine actually brings about the death of the white woman with a white flower (an addictive hallucinogen that eventually poisons Moira). It is no surprise that Xuela discovers this plant on "one of my many wanderings while freeing my womb from burdens I did not want it to bear," for the link between her hatred of whites and her resistance to perpetuating her maternal history is clear. But it is surprising that the poisonous flower "turn[s Moira's] skin black before she die[s]" (207). Transformed by Xuela's hatred into that which she herself had hated all her life—into a demonic mirror of the self—Moira is finally and ironically revealed as a cross-race twin, a figure we will encounter repeatedly in Caribbean women's novels, an alter ego central to a heroine's quest for her own identity. In this most dismal of narratives, the alter ego must be punished and destroyed. *The Autobiography of My Mother* remains in the spell of the unnamable force that hovers between the lines of Caribbean literature, the maternal "désastre" that breeds "impossible situation[s]."

Because of its will to absolute negation in the representation of the Caribbean historical legacy, this novel establishes an endpoint on the spectrum of contemporary Caribbean women's historical fiction. Its arrival makes it seem all the more remarkable that both maternal history and interracial women's relationships become sites of desire and of promise in many other texts.

5
Burning Down the House

Daughterly Revision in Jean Rhys's *Wide Sargasso Sea*

> Whether I have any *right* to do it is a question which I'll face later.
>
> Jean Rhys, *Letters*

Alive, in motion, torch in hand, nightmare-wakened, and steeled to the fiery purpose of her dream—thus we remember the figure of Antoinette / Bertha Cosway Mason Rochester at the end of Jean Rhys's 1966 *Wide Sargasso Sea*. A short, stunning novel of spare, lyrical prose, *Wide Sargasso Sea* enacts a radical intertextual design, an "unprecedented and aggressive" revision (Ellen Friedman 117) of Charlotte Brontë's 1847 novel *Jane Eyre* from the standpoint of Rhys's own West Indian Creole culture. In the past two decades Rhys's reimagining of the life of Brontë's Creole madwoman has received extensive critical attention, buoyed especially by Bertha Mason's sudden feminist stardom in the title of Sandra Gilbert and Susan Gubar's influential work *The Madwoman in the Attic*. Indeed, the intertextual pairing of Rhys's revision and its canonical mother text has itself become canonical, has come to typify the late-century feminist relationship of legacy and resistance to traditions of women's writing,[1] as well as the postcolonial appropriation of canonical European texts.

What contribution can be made to Rhys criticism, then, by reading *Wide Sargasso Sea* in the context of late twentieth-century Caribbean women's fictions of return to maternal history? To read Rhys's recreation of Brontë's Bertha as a multilayered allegory of Caribbean daughterly return is to raise a number of questions, first about Rhys's racial and cultural difference from the other writers of both the Caribbean and African-American sections of this study, and then also about the different sort of "return" her novel performs, that is, its primarily literary nature, its interest in reimagining that powerful element of Caribbean (and Commonwealth) cultural history known as English literary tradition. This chapter argues for the value of such a reading despite these differences. For Rhys's text of white colonial daughterly return has become a kind of mother itself: an antecedent and enabler of the Caribbean daughterly "renaissance" Rhys's long life did not quite allow her to see.

Like the heroine of *Wide Sargasso Sea,* Jean Rhys was a West Indian Creole of European, rather than African, ancestry, a racial and cultural identity with complex bearings on both her work and her critical reception. In Caribbean critical circles, Rhys's literary identity was a matter of controversy for years. Most famously, Brathwaite argued in 1974 that she and other white Creole writers cannot "meaningfully identify or be identified, with the spiritual world on this side of the Sargasso Sea" (*Contradictory Omens* 38); in 1992, writing that "Rhys has finally been accepted as a Caribbean writer," Elaine Savory Fido notes that this was "not without long debate and not without some caution as regards some of her work" ("Mother/lands" 347). Long read in English and American critical contexts as a minor modernist, Rhys was claimed by feminist critics, mostly American, in the 1980s. Rhys criticism of the 1990s, energized by the rise of Caribbean feminist critique, has newly emphasized the Caribbean elements of her work, including the early "continental" novels, and has begun to read Rhys in the light of Creole identification and discourse.[2]

The question of the role of writers from white colonies of occupation in postcolonial letters has been a highly charged one, mediated by the changing cultural politics within decolonizing nations. In the work of writers like Rhys or the South African J. M. Coetzee this role can provide an "important—though often highly ambivalent—grounding for discursive interrogations of imperialism's centralising power" (Slemon and Tiffin xix). The phrase "ambivalent . . . grounding" also describes well Rhys's relationship to her colonial home, the mountainous, forested island of Dominica, "a most lovely and melancholy place" (*Letters* 171), which she left early in life and visited just once in adulthood. After a career spent writing fiction set mostly in Europe (but often about female characters originally from the Caribbean), Rhys makes a momentous imaginative return to the Caribbean and its history near the end of her life in *Wide Sargasso Sea.* But this novel demonstrates highly alienated "daughterly" relations to Caribbean origins, more so than do the works by black or mixed-race women writers considered in this study. Speaking to her English husband on their honeymoon, the heroine Antoinette/Bertha says of the island of Dominica:

> It is not for you and not for me. It has nothing to do with either of us. That is why you are afraid of it, because it is something else. I found that out long ago when I was a child. I loved it because I had nothing else to love, but it is as indifferent as . . . God. . . . (130)

The African-Caribbean critics who have doubted Rhys's status as Caribbean writer may have noted that, as Fido puts it, Rhys "writes her distance from her mother-island-home into the voices of every text" ("Mother/lands" 335). Yet I would argue that this condition of having "nothing else to love" but a perpetually distant "mother-island-home" constitutes, precisely, the distinctive Caribbeanness of Rhys's white Creole women. In *Wide Sargasso Sea* the heroine seeks but fails to find sustaining mothering from three potential Caribbean mother figures: the island, her own white mother, and the black nurse to whom she turns in need. Her unfulfilled desires for these Caribbean mothers give the novel the shape of an irresolvable mother-quest.

But *Wide Sargasso Sea*'s revisionary brilliance lies in the way it chooses and engages a fourth "mother": the mother-text *Jane Eyre*. The relationship to this literary antecedent is also ambivalent, suggesting both a cherished "daughterly" intertextual affinity (Delourme 260) and an aggressive attack in which *Jane Eyre* stands in for the colonial's false mother country, England. If neither heroine nor author resolves her ambivalent daughterhood to the Caribbean island, Rhys certainly does claim to be the rightful heir of English literary history—and does so as surrogate for all colonial daughters and, indeed, for many kinds of readers now inheriting English literature.

Resisting Reader, Mother Text

Rhys explained that she first read *Jane Eyre* upon arriving in England from Dominica at age sixteen, "a very impressionable age," and she was "quite shocked" (*Letters* 296–97):

> I thought, why should she think Creole women are lunatics and all that? What a shame to make Rochester's first wife, Bertha, the awful madwoman. . . . She seemed such a poor ghost. I thought I'd try to write her a life. ("Jean Rhys" 235)

Many decades and several novels later, Rhys labored over years of poverty and personal loss to write the novel she originally planned to call "*The first Mrs. Rochester*," knowing that "this book must be done as well as I could—(*no* margin of error) or it would be unconvincing" (*Letters* 50, 253). To imagine a life story for a neglected, marginal character in a famous book one must, indeed, attempt a "convincing" supplement or simulacrum,[3] but Rhys's performance of the life of Bertha Mason goes beyond verisimilitude to demonstrate dramatic and suggestive revisionary uses of intertextuality. Perhaps we most admire *Wide Sargasso Sea* for its daring, the bold way it manages to claim a place, as if in a gap that always awaited it, in English literature. One closes the book with an eerie feeling about the way Rhys has written a text directly "into" literary history—an effect intensified by the way the novel's three sections move the reader progressively "into" contact with Brontë's text. She seems to have stirred the literary universe into animation, to have summoned up and then actually changed literary history.

For many readers, this is a very intimate change. Rhys's "intertextual" revision actually takes place, after all, in our own reading memories; for those who recapitulated literary history by encountering *Jane Eyre* in youth and *Wide Sargasso Sea* later, Rhys's revision marks a developmental stage in our careers as critical readers. We can no longer think of the celebrated heroine Jane Eyre in the same way, once having glimpsed her as Rhys's mad Bertha glimpses her: a pale girl humming to herself as she walks warily through the house of a man who, unbeknownst to her, has crushed the life of the woman who watches her pass. And, of course, we can never think of Bertha Mason in the same way, having read of her lonely Jamaican youth and spurned love, and remembering most of all the way she stands at the end of Rhys's narrative, doomed but triumphant, torch in hand, about to fall once again to the death literature originally gave her—but not just yet. Forever resisting the self-sacrificial closure of her plot in *Jane Eyre*, forever forestalling the closure of Rhys's narrative, Antoinette/Bertha in her last lines advances in furious opposition to her pre-scripted fate, leaving her potential act, and her end, to our memories of literary history.

Experiencing this transformation of our interior canon, readers cannot help but be conscious that it is all due to the act of another reader—one Jean Rhys, who perceived an injustice in English literary history and took it upon herself to rewrite it. The implicit will to action of a self-authorizing reader underlies this revisionary text but becomes most pronounced in the final section, when the sad Creole girl Antoinette is transported to England and becomes the madwoman Bertha, stalking Rochester's Thornfield Hall, plotting and taking her revenge. In this ending Rhys's recuperated and transformed Antoinette/Bertha seems to rebel against her own previous writtenness, to declare the right to tell her "true" story. Her ending plays out the end of Bertha's *Jane Eyre* plot twice: Antoinette/Bertha first dreams of burning down the house, then awakens to interpret her dream's message and set forth, at the very last, intending to carry out its incendiary act. This neatly recapitulates the process by which a person reads a text, interprets it in her own terms, and sets out to rewrite it. Antoinette/Bertha thus embodies in her defiant ending the triumphant revisionist act of Rhys the reader-turned-writer.

Because of this complex of suggestion at the close of a revisionary novel, I want to claim the rebellious heroine Antoinette/Bertha as one of modern literature's greatest figures for the resisting reader[4]—a prophetic figure for Rhys to create in 1966, just before so many female and postcolonial readers began to reject their marginalized relationships to writing and, inspired by a visionary impulse, to re-enter the big house of English literature with a flame. Not to burn it down, as in Bertha's old, self-immolating plot, but rather, as Rhys's heroine puts it in her last words, "to light me along the dark passage" (190)—to help with some difficult rereading ahead.

WITH THE REREADERLY heroine Antoinette/Bertha as its avatar, *Wide Sargasso Sea* "enters and reimagines Brontë's text," as Ellen Friedman puts it, "glossing and subverting, reversing and transforming it" (117). In this act of postcolonial "canonical counter-discourse" (Tiffin 97), Rhys was the contemporary of the first male Caribbean authors to discover in Shakespeare's Caliban a rebel hero and figure for their own radical art, and she was the first to pry open English literary history as a field for Caribbean *women's* revision. Her daughterly heroine—much like Morrison's Beloved—returns into the past as surrogate for her author's own struggles with a violent, racialized inheritance. Reimagining Brontë's monster within the historical context of Caribbean race relations, Rhys returns, too, to the site of her own family's history; the fire set by ex-slaves at Coulibri echoes an 1844 event on the estate of Rhys's slaveholding grandfather.[5]

Thus Rhys restores to the narrative of Empire the suppressed story of its bastard colonial daughter, revealing that the identity of the woman who sets fire to the Great House in *Jane Eyre* was formed in substance by the violent social relations of European colonialism. Indeed, Bertha's marriage to Rochester, central to Brontë's plot, is shown to be continuous with the larger colonizing operations of the British Empire, as Gayatri Spivak has argued. Spivak calls the Creole madwoman Bertha "a figure produced by the axiomatics of imperialism," who must marry a fortune-seeking Englishman, turn into an animal, "set fire to the house and kill herself, so Jane Eyre can become the feminist individualist heroine of British fiction" (266, 270). But Bertha is less an imperialist fantasy of the colonial female subject, as Spivak argues, than, more precisely, a fantasy of the depraved *white* female colonist, "contaminated" by contact with "natives." Rhys's novel thus inserts into English literature a revised white colonial female subjectivity.

And yet, as I have suggested, Rhys is a major precursor to the mostly African-Caribbean women's literary boom that followed her greatest work. Both Michelle Cliff and Maryse Condé, the novelists considered in the next chapters, profess admiration for her and stand in her debt. It may indeed be that Rhys was "the literary mother to the next generation of women writers because she was the first Caribbean woman to create texts dealing with the complex mother-daughter matrix" (Niesen de Abruna "Family Connections" 257). Certainly contemporary women's historiographic texts are indebted to Rhys's rich dramatization of the troubled maternal realm to which a Caribbean daughter must return. For in *Wide Sargasso Sea* this realm of origin contains not only an "indifferent" island and failed mother, but an inescapably racialized history—as well as a colonizing, canonical narrative that would claim to define the heroine's true identity. Perhaps most important, and regardless of its "literary" preoccupations, *Wide Sargasso Sea* bequeaths to Caribbean women's historical writing the potent example of its revisionary courage, its manifest conviction that a daughter's imaginative return can produce revelations of utmost political, cultural, and psychological consequence. Finally, as this chapter's conclusion will relate, Rhys's revision offers a "daughterly" paradigm for literary inheritance itself.

White Daughter and Mother

Providing Bertha Mason with a full, novelistic existence in parts one and two of *Wide Sargasso Sea*, Rhys demonstrates the aesthetics of generically feminist "re-vision."[6] Her account of Antoinette Cosway Mason's youth and early marriage offers "the other side of the story," in Molly Hite's phrase, of the romance plot and the gender and power relations of *Jane Eyre*. To the horrific female creature who shrieks in Brontë's attic Rhys grants humanity, a history, and a narrating voice, and she recasts Bertha's madness as the effect rather than the cause of her rejection by her husband, Rochester.[7]

Moreover, changing the name of Brontë's "Bertha Antoinetta Mason," Rhys creates the defining emblem of her revision, a renaming that makes the original seem to conceal several lies. Bertha, the name of the notorious she-monster of English literary history, in Rhys's text becomes a name imposed arbitrarily by Rochester on his wife to distance her from the name of her mother Annette (Antoinetta in Brontë), whom he believes to be an insane alcoholic. By moving the lovelier name (in its more accurately French form) from second to first position, Rhys at once accuses Rochester of committing an elemental injustice and makes her text seem to correct it: the erasure of the name of the mother from that of the heroine (See Kloepfer 145).[8] The mother who is mentioned in *Jane Eyre* only to suggest a genetic source of Bertha's madness is shown here to have been driven mad, like her daughter Antoinette and under similar circumstances of loss, violence, and exploitation in marriage. While the loss of her mother affiliates Antoinette with orphaned Jane Eyre, Rhys's heroine, unlike Jane, remembers her mother well, and remembers too the pain of losing her. We might say that by reimagining Brontë's monster in the island of her birth, Rhys recuperates for Antoinette/Bertha's plot "a space of privileged contact with the maternal" for which Jane Eyre might have longed (Kloepfer 146).[9]

Strikingly, Rochester remains completely nameless throughout, called only "the man," "he," "husband," and "the man who hated me." That this revision devalues and "suppresses the name of the father" (Hite 40; see also Spivak 271) is also evident in the diminishment of "Mason" to the name of the heroine's mere step-relatives, and the invention of a patronym, Cosway, which becomes the sign for the island's shameful slaveholding history. Rochester is also given no body—no physical description whatsoever; thus "castrating" the formidable lord of Brontë's English manor, Rhys rewrites him as an anonymous, lost voice in a place where the very existence of his fatherland is questioned (Delourme 262).[10]

And yet the maternal space of the island is marked from the first pages by loss and looming menace. Though Antoinette later recalls that she and her lovely mother "were alone in the most beautiful place in the world" (130), the "smell of dead flowers" permeating the garden at Coulibri tells the truer tale (19). The mother-daughter plot in Rhys's oeuvre has been much analyzed, critics often connecting Rhys's biography with her heroines' disrupted relations to mothers.[11] Caribbeanists contribute an allegorical reading of the "alienation of the daughter-island from the mother country" (Niesen de Abruna, "Family Connections" 260). I would invoke Rhys's biography here not so much for the difficult relationship between the young Ella Gwendoline Rees Williams and her mother, but also for the author's lifelong ambivalence about her mother-island (a term she would never have used). This is to say that the failed relationships of Rhys's heroines to their mothers reflect above all the white daughters' alienated relationships with their island homes. For Antoinette's mother, who rejects her daughter several times before going mad and dying, distinctly resembles the lamented, unnurturing mother-island figures that populate Caribbean literature (discussed in Chapter 4). The young widow of a slaveholding planter, Annette cannot sustain herself and her children on a remote estate after Emancipation, amidst the hatred of formerly enslaved blacks. Her inadequacy as the heroine's mother is inextricable from her insecure relationship, as white woman, to the social world of the island (compounded by her being a Martinique Creole woman living in Jamaica). She seems even more compromised and inauthentic than the black mother-island figures of Caribbean literature, who, though seriously flawed, always convey the sense of being in their rightful place.

For like any figure of the mother-island, Annette functions as mother of the heroine's relationship to a traumatic history. In this sense, Antoinette loses her mother in *Wide Sargasso Sea* for the same "reason" that her mother loses her mind; both suffer from the historically coded condition of white colonial women in Rhys's work: a racial alienation within island culture,[12] figured as the alienation from the mother-island and from all possible mothers, white and black.

White Daughter, Black Mother

In order to expose the "true" story of a colonized white daughter, Rhys presents a complex of lives, relationships, and social facts of the colonial island world that are utterly absent in *Jane Eyre*. In so doing, she delineates the heroine's identity within patterns typical of white colonialist and postcolonial writing.[13] A white colonial daughter tends to be sharply aware of her position as less empowered member of the dominating group. While her relationships to white men largely determine her plot and fortunes, her relationships to white women tend to constitute areas of loss, particularly that of the mother, who often seems to have succumbed to the same conditions the daughter faces. Her relationships to black or native men represent the greatest potential for plot crisis, for any disturbance here threatens a specifically sexual danger that could bring down the whole house of cards. But her relationships to black or native women, set in plot segments that remain unfulfilled and subordinate to higher plot demands, tend to be a focus of great desire, of an envisioned "ending" for which the heroine could only wish.

Like many such heroines, Rhys's Antoinette longs for love and community across the barriers of colonial life, and like others undergoes a kind of existential crisis, threatening madness. Recent texts like *Wide Sargasso Sea* and Coetzee's *In the Heart of the Country* (1977) revise the fate of white colonial women in an earlier text like Forster's *A Passage to India* (1924) by progressing through madness to revolt.[14] Though these rebellious white colonial heroines target above all the white man at the top of the social ladder, along the way numerous infractions against colonial "law" occur among the occupants of the lower ranks. The central plot of the white woman tends to generate intimate—though often disastrous—connections with the plots of blacks.

Antoinette's relationship to Christophine, her childhood nurse, is the center of the novel's paradoxical engagement with blackness and, not coincidentally, the locus of its strongest articulation of difference from the precursor text. Christophine provides a countercurrent to the text's attachment to *Jane Eyre*, to the romance plot, and to Rochester. In the paradigmatic black female role in white women's fictions, Christophine holds the paradoxical authority of servant/mother to the white heroine. But while white mothers in colonialist and postcolonial fictions tend to fade away,[15] Christophine is a mother whose racial otherness, perversely, overcomes some of the debilitating effect of her gender. The young white heroine is vulnerable, trapped in the same disempowering role that destroyed her mother, but Christophine, though a servant, is independent, resistant, and unhesitatingly blunt. Her authority is established on the novel's first page, where she is "the first interpreter and named speaking subject" (Spivak 271). Unlike the white heroine and hero, she is given no narrative of her own. But though she speaks only through the consciousness of white narrators, Christophine voices through her containment a scathing critique of Rochester's colonization of Antoinette, becoming the voice of the text's refusal of the authority he cruelly wields over Bertha Mason in *Jane Eyre*: "*Your wife*! . . . You make me laugh. . . . Everybody know that you marry her for her money and you take it all . . ." (152); " 'Now you say you don't love her and you break her up. What you do with her money, eh?' Her voice was still quiet but with a hiss in it when she said 'money' " (158).

A woman who was once a wedding present (from the heroine's father to her mother), Christophine understands Antoinette's love plot as a masked form of economic bondage. Against the "Letter of the Law" (26) that gives Rochester control of his wife's life and possessions, Christophine wields *obeah*, the Caribbean black folk magic/medicine. Her power tends to blur with the power of *obeah*, which creates the crisis in the love plot (when the love potion she gives Antoinette backfires) and disrupts Rochester's control of his narrative and the realist apportionment of narration (see Emery 45–53).[16] Christophine's *obeah* even seems to operate across the intertextual divide—for Rhys implies that her curse causes the blinding of Rochester in *Jane Eyre* (161).

And in a moment of supreme textual subversion, Christophine turns her very illiteracy into a position of resistance. When Rochester orders her out of his house, saying she may write to Antoinette, Christophine replies: "Read and write I don't know. Other things I know" (161). She then walks out of the novel having claimed an existence and knowledge beyond the authority of Rochester and of any text—Rhys's narrative, or any "white writing" that would attempt to represent her.[17] Her untold story is, in Spivak's words: "tangential to this narrative. . . . [and] cannot be contained by a novel which rewrites a canonical English text within the European novelistic tradition in the interest of the white Creole rather than the native." Spivak notes that in Christophine the text "marks with uncanny clarity the limits of its own discourse" (271–72). In this black woman's voice Rhys's revision suggests the need to hear voices that would revise it in turn.

But the treatment of black characters in *Wide Sargasso Sea* operates on a contradictory logic. To the extent that the novel reveals the intimate importance of black people in white peoples' stories and represents at the fringes of the heroine's plot a black social world and even organized black resistance, it can be seen to subvert colonialist narratives. For example, Rhys embeds the romance plot of white hero and heroine in a historical matrix marked by race, power, and money. The conventional madness of white colonial heroines is shown to reflect not only white men's exploitation of their love and money but also the effects of transgressive and volatile interracial relationships.[18]

At the same time, in that the text evokes black resistance while suppressing knowledge of its causes, especially the details of slave history, it can be read as complicit with colonialist exploitation.[19] For Rhys's writing of the madwoman's story represents resistant blacks and violent racial conflict, inevitably, to lend power to its own rebellious textuality.[20]

Moreover, *Wide Sargasso Sea* tends to position black characters as desire's alternative to the entrapping European romance plot. This is evident in Antoinette's longing, even when mad in England, for the black people in her life only: Sandi, Tia, and Christophine. Racism's flip side, the psychosexual desire of whites for blacks or natives profoundly informs the structure of this and many other colonial narratives. In a white colonial daughter's text like Antoinette's, this desire also suggests an impossible wish to heal the awful division in one's social world, to live in relationships free of exploitation. Though her story borrows blackness as a sign of difference and resistance, draws subversive energy from the identification, and foregrounds interracial relationships to help her oppose repressive heterosexual ones, Antoinette's love for black characters and her text's relationship to blackness are not thoroughly or even primarily exploitative. Unlike *Jane Eyre*, *Wide Sargasso Sea* does not villainize the darker woman or require her death; Christophine walks away a free woman, owning her own story—a model of inviolate, self-authorizing female existence.

At the same time, it is in Antoinette's relationships to black women that the double logic of the white colonial heroine's desire is most acutely felt. Unloved or unable to form rewarding relationships with other whites, white heroines in the literature of Empire tend to depend on the black women who serve them for the major emotional support of their lives.[21] The heroines of both *Wide Sargasso Sea* and Rhys's 1934 novel *Voyage in the Dark* express a longing for black mother and sister figures. While African-Caribbean women writers often elevate a nurturing grandmother figure over the figure of a bad or compromised mother, Rhys's Creole heroine instead seeks a substitute by crossing not generations but races.[22] The black mother Christophine is figuratively "older" here in that she is seen to have a more culturally and politically authentic relationship to the island and its history; she is more plausible as mother-island than the weak Annette. But that same history of racialized difference prevents Christophine's full mothering of Antoinette; twice her attempts to help the heroine with *obeah* medicines that are "too strong for *béké*" only make matters worse (153). When Antoinette retreats to Christophine's house after the love medicine fails, she seems nearly to regress to infancy under her care (see Ferracane 124–27). But ultimately the black woman cannot be the Caribbean mother that the white heroine desires, cannot save her from her white colonial heroine's fate. Antoinette's desire for the saving love of black women remains a critical subplot—subordinated to the central romance plot—which reemerges in her story in times of crisis. As she flies down the hallway in the dream of setting Rochester's house on fire, Bertha calls "help me Christophine help me" (189). But her prewritten fate decrees that she must relinquish the plot of Christophine for the plot of Rochester.

White Girl, Black Girl

A similarly doomed plot is that of Tia, the black girl who is Antoinette's only childhood friend, and the precursor of the cross-race female friends who become a key element of the "horizontal plot" in later Caribbean women's literature. When a crowd of blacks burns down her family's house, Antoinette runs to Tia, thinking, "I will live with Tia and I will be like her." But Tia throws a stone at her face. Standing and bleeding, Antoinette sees an identity between them despite the racial difference—or rather, a kind of mirrored pain arising *because* of the race barrier: "I looked at her and I saw her face crumple up as she began to cry. We stared at each other, blood on my face, tears on hers. It was as if I saw myself. Like in a looking-glass" (45). Earlier, on the day of the fight by the pool at Coulibri, when Antoinette calls Tia "cheating nigger" and Tia calls her "white nigger" and steals her dress, Antoinette momentarily must see herself in a black girl's ragged clothes (24–25). And at the narrative's end, when Bertha foresees in a dream the jump from the roof that we know will kill her in *Jane Eyre*, she looks over the edge and sees—of all images she might see—the laughing face of Tia, beckoning from the pool where they played as children, asking "You frightened?" Bertha calls "Tia!" jumps, and wakes, to do her final deed (190).

Clearly, the mirror image of Tia her twin manqué is very close to Antoinette/Bertha's own sense of self, perhaps because the impossible tensions of their relationship crystallize the tensions of her life. When she faces moments of greatest self-confrontation, Antoinette cannot imagine herself into the next plot choice (to leave Coulibri? to jump from the roof?) without the image of union/conflict with the longed-for opposite-race twin, who may very well hate her. This suggests how deeply racial otherness has marked Antoinette's life, and how deeply the division by race has contributed to her emotional ill health. She says to Rochester:

> Did you hear what that girl was singing? . . . It was a song about a white cockroach. That's me. That's what they call all of us who were here before their own people in Africa sold them to the slave traders. And I've heard English women call us white niggers. So between you I often wonder who I am and where is my country and where do I belong and why was I ever born at all. (102)

The distinctive self-questioning of a postcolonial white heroine engages identity in racial terms and generates a subjectivity not merely scarred by racial division, but racially interactive in its very structure, as seen in Antoinette's psychic "twinning" with Tia and the splitting of her plot between the text of Rochester and the text of Christophine.

When the novel moves into its brief final section, in which it "explodes into Brontë's novel" (Ellen Friedman 118) and the transformed heroine stalks Rochester's house, Rhys concentrates the revisionary agendas implicit in the text's first two parts in the act of a furious woman with a torch. The dream of the burning of Thornfield Hall is the moment of Rhys's richest, most dramatic repossession of Brontë's narrative. Infusing color and symbolic power into an event merely reported after the fact by a secondary character in *Jane Eyre*, Rhys invents a nightmare review of Antoinette's life, rendering Brontë's climactic inferno meaningful in terms of the racial dynamics of her Creole heroine's biography (and of her own). She rewrites the house fire that ends Bertha Mason's plot as the mere echo of her novel's original trauma: the burning of the family house at Coulibri by former slaves (which itself echoes Rhys's family history). As Antoinette's hair "stream[s] out like wings" (189–90), she is identified with her mother's parrot Coco, who fell in flames from the second story but saved the family when the crowd retreated from the ill omen of a dead parrot. Rhys extends to her heroine the parrot's desperate entrapment, the fiery fall, the sacrifice for others (Jane Eyre first of all, and then perhaps ourselves), and the recurrent question, associated with both the parrot and the mother in her madness: "*Qui est là*?"—the question of identity.[23]

Coco always answers his own question with his own name: "*Ché Coco*" (41). But Antoinette, about to fall, calls instead to Tia; her black friend becomes "the defining mirror-image whose recognition awakens Antoinette to herself." In this mirroring, Nancy Harrison notes, we see the structure of female relational identity that undergirds the *Wide Sargasso Sea/Jane Eyre* intertextuality, first conceived when "Rhys recognized her own life in that of Brontë's Bertha." Antoinette's call to Tia demonstrates that the text's central question is answered "in responding to one's 'mirror-image,' even if one sees in the looking glass the negative of herself, the other" (Harrison 150, 192). It is the *racially* relational logic of Antoinette's colonial white female identity that causes her to call to Christophine for maternal help, and to Tia for self.[24]

These calls to the black women of another place and time, together with the echoes of the fire at Coulibri, connect Antoinette/Bertha's burning of Thornfield Hall to the legacy of black slave resistance. In relation to

Rochester and to Brontë's novel she thus becomes symbolically a "rebel slave" (as the young Jane Eyre once describes herself) (9); Bertha's fiery assault in *Jane Eyre* is thus rewritten as the revolt of colonized subjectivity against the master text. But the actual distance of Rhys's revisionary text from such a model is evident when Bertha's impossible call to Christophine and Tia, attempting to bring them into the world of Thornfield Hall, registers a poignant absence, suggestive of the absence the young Jean Rhys encountered in Charlotte Brontë's writing of the mad Creole. As Bertha roams Brontë's house these absent black women seem as distant as characters in another book entirely. Just as their prominence in parts one and two helps Rhys to articulate a Caribbean position of difference from Brontë, the absence of black women in part three would seem emblematic of the surrender of Rhys's plot to Brontë's, which deracinates the white colonial woman and sacrifices her desires to its own imperatives (see Harrison 151). Writing just before the collective daughterly return of Caribbean women writers and the rise of feminist literature around the world, Rhys confines her revisionary daughter in a tragic realm, in which she can never fulfill her desires for the Caribbean mother and for interracial female bonds. On the new era's very brink, Rhys's heroine is willing, however, to die trying.

A Model of Daughterly Revision

We may wonder what stopped Rhys from changing the fate Brontë originally gave to Bertha Mason. While she was rewriting, why not cook up an escape from the house, a return to the islands, or at least a Calibanesque moment of articulate defiance of Rochester, or warning to Jane? Rhys's acceptance of Bertha's martyrdom seems an acknowledgement of the tragic nature of literary history—which is, after all, history. Bowing to the historicity of Brontë's plot even while subjecting it to a radical retelling, Rhys frames her intertextual intervention in the irreversible, historic realm in which readers read. But, as Ellen Friedman points out, the very illustration that "her precursor has restricted her to a predetermined narrative" can be liberating (123); when the reader turns to part three and finds that Antoinette has become imprisoned, doomed Bertha in Brontë's house, Rhys has made vivid the oppressions that come with inheriting a tradition and justifies aggressive rewriting. At the same time, she makes the canonical text seem always to have contained the germ of this rebellion, and all literary history, by extension, seem to contain potential transformation, awaiting the right re-reader.

So although the text that opens a space for Antoinette/Bertha in literary history does not save her from her original plot's trajectory toward madness and death, the novel's trajectory moves toward liberation. Resisting the moment of Bertha's original ending, instead giving the force of an ending to the moment *before* the burning, Rhys's unclosed end leaves Bertha's death to the moments after the reader closes her novel and muses in her intertextual memory. In this way, Rhys forces history—that is, Charlotte Brontë—to bear the responsibility of killing Bertha Mason, as Chantal Delourme puts it. When *Jane Eyre* "returns to the surface to write the end of the text born of it" (Delourme 263), Brontë is, as it were, forced to consummate Rhys's heroine's desire for revenge, but also to reduce it to a functional subplot once again, and to reextinguish a life we have come to value.

How do we understand the implications raised by this rewriting for a model of contemporary literary inheritance? Certainly Rhys's novel presents a postmodern challenge to the boundaries of the text, subverting the authority of authorship and privileging the empowering potential of shared readerly knowledge of literary tradition. Self-consciously belated in literary history, *Wide Sargasso Sea* is irreverent about textuality in general—as when the madwoman, chafing at her "written" condition, mocks Brontë's book: "This cardboard house where I walk at night is not England" (181). Treating text as history and history as text, Rhys writes one of the earliest postmodern "metatexts."

But if *Wide Sargasso Sea* is a deconstructing daughter, revising *Jane Eyre* so that "the mother-text is maimed and . . . disarmed" (Ellen Friedman 119), recent criticism reveals a curious and contradictory aspect of the revision. The term "mother text" is sometimes used by critics to refer, as above, to *Jane Eyre*, and at other times to indicate *Wide Sargasso Sea*, as when Mona Fayad writes that "the recognition of . . . [Bertha Mason's] effacement . . . prompts Jean Rhys to produce a 'mother text' for *Jane Eyre* . . ." (442). That Rhys can be seen to produce a mother text for Brontë, so that both texts are "mothers," points to a striking aspect of this revisionary act: though written later, it is not a sequel but a "post-dated prequel" (Baer 132). Rhys undertakes to tell the story anterior to that of *Jane Eyre*, to write *"The first Mrs. Rochester,"* robbing the older text of its position of origin. As Delourme notes, this usurping act transforms the quest for origins into "a fantasy of auto-engenderment": "Just as the mother is born from the daughter, *Jane Eyre* is issued from *Wide Sargasso Sea* and rewrites it." Rhys thus activates intertextuality, in Delourme's terms, as an oscillation between the two texts, "a modality of co-presence" (Delourme 265, 258, 268); or in Friedman's terms, as an "audacious grafting" (118)—the adjoining of a new trunk to an old branch; which is the mother of the life that then blossoms?

This genre of revision differs notably from Harold Bloom's "anxiety of influence," the agonistic struggle of an ephebe for individuation from his literary precursor, or even from Bloom's *apophrades*. A closer analogue is Gilbert and Gubar's "female affiliation complex," in which twentieth-century women writers affiliate with literary foremothers, even while demonstrating anxiety about their influence (*No Man's Land* 1:168–71).[25] The other relevant paradigm is the genre of postcolonial reinscription exemplified by the Caribbean Caliban-texts, which preserve Shakespeare's scenario and the aura of his power while inverting his politics of empire.

Merging feminist and postcolonial impulses in revision, *Wide Sargasso Sea* presents a daughterly difference from the Calibans: a noticeably cozier, "relational" attachment to the mother text. While Rhys rejects and transforms colonialist (and patriarchal) elements of Brontë's novel, in many ways she also honors the "fundamental conversation" between female authors that first gave rise to her novel (Harrison 143). *Wide Sargasso Sea* elaborates an overall structure of mother-daughter romance,[26] privileges dialogue between female characters, and carefully reproduces the structure of its mother text. Among numerous parallels, she takes Antoinette through a series of haunting dreams to match Jane's.[27] Harrison contends that Rhys "pick[s] up the strand of the dream-text of Brontë's novels as the structural principle of her own," inscribing a "sharing-of-the-text" with *Jane Eyre*, weaving a female countertext around the "masculine text" of Rochester's plot, and blending intimate "conversation" with critical revision (Harrison 130–33).

Rhys's letters from the *Wide Sargasso Sea* period reveal mixed impulses to reject and retain the mother text. She describes her mood during the early stages of the writing as "fighting mad," but she also approached her precursor with hesitation and respect, stating in an early letter, "I think of calling it '*The first Mrs. Rochester*' with profound apologies to Charlotte Brontë and a deep curtsey too." Later, when the work became vexed and stalled, she reflected:

> I did not mean to be impertinent about Charlotte Brontë. I admire her greatly. Emily also. And I envy them both more than I can say.
>
> Sometimes I have wondered if Miss Brontë does not *want* her book tampered with! (*Letters* 157, 50, 175)

Though Rhys clearly aimed at a certain independence, announcing in 1962 that her Antoinette "is not Jane Eyre's lunatic at all," she also decided early in the project that, though "it might be possible to unhitch the whole thing from Charlotte Brontë's novel . . . I don't want to do that" (*Letters* 214, 153). The project to write "not *Jane Eyre*'s lunatic" into a text that yet stays "hitched" to *Jane Eyre* is a "misreading" that, (p)revising Bloom, desires a complex kind of individuation, one that embodies the imaginative fusion of daughter-writer with mother. As the novel approaches its ending and the reader reenters Brontë's house, verbal repetitions and structural connections with *Jane Eyre* create an increasing "enlacement of texts," which might be read as "so many denials of separation, of rupture from the body of the other" (Delourme 264–65). In the model of influence suggested by Rhys's revision, the colonial daughter's struggle preserves its matrix, the mother text it both ruptures and reengenders.

But critics do not universally acclaim this privileging of relatedness. An essay by Michael Thorpe begins, "The crucial question *Wide Sargasso Sea*, as a work of art, might seem to pose is whether it can stand and be judged alone. . . ." Thorpe criticizes the 1967 *New York Times* review in which Walter Allen concludes that the text does not "exist in its own right," for it depends on *Jane Eyre* "to complement it, to supply its full meaning." So does another critic, Arnold E. Davidson, who argues vehemently for the text's wholeness, citing as precedents the famous literary borrowings of Shakespeare, Joyce, and others (Thorpe 99; Allen 5; Davidson 16–17).

None of these critics considers the possibility that a work might be whole, and "strong," in Bloom's terms, precisely *because* of the way it remains overtly connected to another, that we might approve a style of revision that departs from what is generally termed the male model of individuation. In contrast to these three critics, none of the dozen or more feminist critics I have read finds it necessary to judge Rhys's text on the "crucial" question of its autonomy; most are interested, rather, in its complex form of attachment to *Jane Eyre*. Similarly, postcolonialists tend to view such linkages to canonical European works as pointed, potent structures of revision; Sandra Drake's ironic terms cast *Wide Sargasso Sea* as "deliberately derivative, an imitation. . . . a novelistic colony" (99). The suggestively grim and awesome imperative that a text "stand and be judged alone" is alien to the model of inheritance implicit in *Wide Sargasso Sea*, which privileges relationships—to a mother first of all and, I shall argue, to daughters to come.

Among Women in the Great House

How oddly perfect it is, one feels upon turning the page to Rhys's part three, that the narrator who locates us in Brontë's Thornfield Hall is Grace Poole. Rhys's unfailing readerly/writerly intelligence locates in Grace the very emblem in *Jane Eyre* of erased, unnarrated female existence. A mystery to Jane in Brontë's novel, Grace is the servant Rochester uses to cover for his cackling wife, with whom she shares the attic abode. Though she rarely speaks in the Brontë text, Grace's voice here provides the most "overt signal of the origin" of Rhys's text and "bridges" the two (Harrison 133), helping the reader to integrate the heroine of *Wide Sargasso Sea* into the known world of *Jane Eyre*. Speaking to another of Brontë's female servants and then to herself, Grace explains why she works for Rochester:

> *The house is big and safe, a shelter from the world outside which, say what you like, can be a black and cruel world to a woman. Maybe that's why I stayed on. . . . above all the thick walls, keeping away all the things that you have fought till you can fight no more. Yes, maybe that's why we all stay—Mrs. Eff and Leah and me. All of us except that girl who lives in her own darkness. I'll say one thing for her, she hasn't lost her spirit. She's still fierce. I don't turn my back on her when her eyes have that look. I know it.* (178)

Rhys's imaginative leap to an English servant woman "knowing" of and sympathetic to her Caribbean heroine follows the "horizontal" logic of female "conversation" and identification-in-otherness that underlies the whole revisionary enterprise.[28] Explaining herself to a female auditor, Grace reveals to the surprised reader that, indeed, she too has a story, and in the clear parallels drawn between her life and Antoinette's—and Mrs. Eff's and Leah's—Grace Poole here seems a candidate for heroine of her own novel, to be written perhaps by a future reader-turned-writer who, following Rhys, might identify with a marginal personage of literary history and take it upon herself to do some rewriting.

Infinite potential recuperation of women's stories is suggested here and all made possible, the reader realizes, by the emergence into activism of a woman reader. It is thus a dramatically energized, radically participatory literary universe that Rhys's work seems to open for us—for her female readers and writers, primarily, because most of the players here are female (Jean Rhys, Charlotte Brontë, Bertha, Jane, Grace, etc.). One closes the book with the sense that all sorts of possibilities exist, which might now tremble into being, that if Bertha Mason Rochester's story can be told with such poignant, searing strength, there is no limit to the number of other characters whose lives might reveal themselves, similarly surprising and compelling, to our reading eyes; Christophine and her knowledge of "other things" seems a foremost possibility.

Antoinette's climactic cry of "Tia!" thus articulates the deep structure of Rhys's revision and of the model she bequeaths to Caribbean (and many other) women writers: "horizontal" identification with and yet against a beloved female other. As a structure of literary inheritance, this female other-embracing recuperative design differs from Bloomian revision both before and behind, reminding us of the mother text and pointing the way to sister texts, daughter texts, future relationality. Whereas Bloom's "strong reading" must "insist upon its own exclusiveness and completeness" to produce other readings, Rhys's strong reading resists such notions, actively producing the germs of future readings (Bloom, *Kabbalah* 97).[29] Harrison contends that Rhys's revision develops the unwritten subtexts in Brontë's novel and then "overtly suggests the presence of its own subtexts," in Christophine, Grace, and other gestures toward yet-to-be-narrated female lives. Rendering female subjectivity as "a multiplicity of selves" and creating a sense of "collaborative authorship, a plurality of narrators or near-narrators," *Wide Sargasso Sea* "invites response and continuation" (Harrison 13, 144, 132)[30]: welcomes further rereadings. And indeed, the chapters that follow will present women writers of several racial and national origins who are Rhys's literary heirs, taking up her model to reimagine the lives of other historical and literary heroines.[31]

Rhys's novel ends, then, not merely with the potential act of its heroine, but with the sense of having generated an expanding female conversation, which includes Brontë and Jane, Christophine and the other island women in Antoinette's memory, and the servants in the English house. *Wide Sargasso Sea* in this sense rejects the Western "feminist individualism" that, Spivak argues, suppresses native female subjectivity and reinforces imperialist ideology in American feminist criticism as well as in *Jane Eyre* (263). It is in the logic of the paradigm offered by Rhys's rewriting of Brontë to value inclusion, not individualism, to honor difference and multiplicity, and even to welcome future response from an unforeseen "other side," which, the text suggests, will always exist.

This vision of community extends ultimately, of course, to the text's readers, we who close the book juggling two novels in our minds. For Rhys's revision constitutes, finally, a tribute to the potentials of a female readership, the traditionally mute but busy builders of a literature. An affirmation of the process of female readerly response, Rhys's text insists that our knowledge of English literary history need not amount to a sentence of imprisonment in the Great House but, rather, is a potentially powerful resource for our own transformational work. Embodying in a cast of reimagined female characters the creative response of a twentieth-century woman reader-turned-writer—thus potentially of ourselves, Rhys declares open house on English literature for all its diverse "servants" and invites us back in together, to reexamine our common inheritance.

"Whether I have any *right* to do it," Rhys wrote of her revision in progress, "is a question which I'll face later" (*Letters* 149). Fully aware of her audacity and of the magnitude of her enterprise, Jean Rhys is a true daughter of Charlotte Brontë and of the upstart Jane Eyre, with whom she shares an undaunted eye on the future, a willingness to "face later." In the remark quoted, Rhys's anxiety is about neither a precursor's influence nor her own ability to be an author, but about enacting what she knows to be a potentially powerful reader's revolt.[32] If she momentarily doubts her right to rewrite, Rhys creates a heroine who declares without hesitation, upon awakening from her dream in the attic of the great house, "Now at last I know why I was brought here and what I have to do" (190). With the courage she inherited from a nineteenth-century heroine's text,[33] Rhys gives us a paradigm for a revisionary art that draws power from the transformations of a century in women's lives, to light a common future passage.[34]

6 Decolonizing Jamaica's Daughter

Learning History in the Novels of Michelle Cliff

THE NOVEL AS *ABENG*

"You taught me language, and my profit on't / Is, I know how to curse" (*The Tempest* I.2.363–64). For Jamaica-born novelist Michelle Cliff, the famous retort to Prospero that inspired a host of twentieth-century Caribbean Calibans "immediately brings to . . . mind the character of Bertha Rochester, wild and raving ragout, as Charlotte Brontë describes her." Feminizing the New World rebel savage, Cliff claims mad Bertha as Caliban's missing sister. To complete the mythic family tree, Cliff declares herself "Caliban's Daughter" and "granddaughter of Sycorax." As for Clare Savage, semiautobiographical heroine of Cliff's first two novels, "Bertha Rochester is her ancestor." And, she adds, "It takes a West Indian writer, Jean Rhys, to describe Bertha from the inside . . ." ("Clare" 264–65).[1] Consciously deriving from Rhys a tradition of West Indian women's literary resistance, Cliff creates in *Abeng* (1984) and its sequel *No Telephone to Heaven* (1987) a heroine whose life story appropriates European "language"—in its genres of historiography, historical fiction, and the bildungsroman—in order to reclaim her maternal history.

Perhaps no contemporary writer has engaged more overtly in the enterprise of rewriting history than Michelle Cliff. Born and raised in Jamaica, educated in England and the United States, resident here for decades, Michelle Cliff is a quintessential New World writer, whose fiction recrosses the Caribbean and the Atlantic to tell the interwoven histories of New World peoples. In Cliff's revisionary project, the problem of colonization is first of all that of the colonization of minds, and liberation first a matter of self-education. We might say then that her two-novel bildungsroman traces the decolonization of the heroine's mind as prelude to her self-education in her own story.[2] Learning her history and her own place in it, Clare Savage can develop from "colonized child" (*Abeng* 77) to revolutionary. Though the novel of her childhood imprisons her in an allegory of colonized consciousness, the novel of her liberation allows Clare to emerge beyond racial division and self-alienation to accept the full complexity of her history, and so to turn a daughterly embrace to the motherland.

In interviews and autobiographical essays, Cliff relates a narrative of her development through successive definitions of racial identity: from a colonial childhood that required her to repress knowledge of her black ancestry; to her education in the "mother country," England, where she deliberately studied subjects remote from her own experience ("Clare Savage" 263); to a political awakening to claim an identity variously termed "Creole" or "black," as mediated by the differing racial politics across the Caribbean/U.S. line (see "claiming"). Yet one critic calls Cliff a "'Jamaica white' (a Jamaican of mostly white ancestry)," even while noting that Cliff "regards herself as black or mixed" and, moreover, that such color terms constitute social and political distinctions in the Caribbean, referring more to class than to melanin (Edmondson 181, n7). That the designation "white Creole" can apply to such a writer as well as to Jean Rhys suggests the elusive yet defining logic of race in Caribbean discourse.[3]

The matter of Cliff's authorial identity has tended to dominate in the critical reception of her work, particularly in the Caribbean, as Sally O'Driscoll has shown. Like Rhys, Cliff has been suspected by some Afrocentric Caribbean critics, including feminists, of inauthenticity and alien influences, her light skin and privileged upbringing "delegitimat[ing]" her claim to a "black" political identity (O'Driscoll 64). Cliff rejects such forms of criticism, both for herself and for Rhys: "It's not really up to Brathwaite or anybody to define Jean Rhys"; "I choose to define myself the way I define myself . . ." ("Art" 59). Complicating matters further is Cliff's outspokenness about her lesbianism, probably a factor in Caribbean critics' notion of her influence by metropolitan cultural politics. To Caribbean people, Cliff explains, "lesbianism is seen as Eurocentric, eccentric, upper-class behavior. . . . decadent and exploitative of Third World women" ("An Interview" 601). The longtime companion of poet Adrienne Rich, Cliff has made a place in U.S. literary circles as a lesbian feminist writer of color. For many Jamaicans, however, she remains "white."[4]

Thus we have in Cliff a writer whose racial, national, and literary status is ambiguous, and whose work elaborates the sources and implications of a creolized—or in her terms, a "crossroads"—identity (see "Clare"). The name of her heroine reflects this condition; "Clare," Cliff writes, means "light-skinned," which "stands for privilege, civilization, erasure, forgetting" ("Clare" 265). In *Abeng* Clare's father intends the name to honor his grandfather's Cambridge college, but her mother Kitty secretly intends to honor "a living woman," a poor, "simpleminded," black country girl named Clary who once saved Kitty's life (141). While "Savage," the name of the white ancestors of whom Clare's father is so proud, betrays the trait that whites have preferred to project onto those they conquered and enslaved, Cliff revalues it to mean:

> the wildness that has been bleached from her skin, understanding that my use of the word *wildness* is ironic, mocking the master's meaning, turning

> instead to a sense of non-Western values which are empowering and essential to survival, her survival, and wholeness, her wholeness. ("Clare" 265)

Clare never learns the hidden meanings embedded in her name, but Cliff makes uncovering the buried history of her heroine's identity central to the novels that tell Clare's life story. This two-part chapter argues that as Cliff dramatizes Clare's development, she also works to assert her right and her qualifications, as the inheritor of mixed histories, to claim the identity of Jamaica's true daughter.

Uses of the *Abeng*

> "To narrate": 1: to know the story.
>
> Roland Barthes, *S/Z*

Cliff's first novel explains its guiding metaphor on the title page:

> *Abeng* is an African word meaning conch shell. The blowing of the conch called the slaves to the canefields in the West Indies. The *abeng* had another use: it was the instrument used by the Maroon armies to pass their messages and reach one another.

This colonial artifact, the *abeng*, bears witness to the fact that history's residue—relics, ruins, cultures, stories, lives—can hold contradictory meanings and be put to opposite uses. "Calls" and "messages" are never neutral but can enforce slavery or advance freedom, depending on the will of the one who holds the *abeng*.

Historical narrative is an *abeng*—it can be used to enslave or to liberate. Cliff shapes her narrative to display these opposed potentials, to make a call for freedom through a textuality of enslavement. For Cliff's Jamaica is the "island which did not know its own history" (96), and her characters, the descendants of slaves and slave-masters (and usually both), living more than a century after Emancipation, are still tragically unable to construct a redeeming collective history. The prominent evocation of the *abeng* signals that this girl's coming-of-age story will be the site of profound contestation; at the same time, Cliff alerts readers to attend to the hidden, promising undersides of things and privileges the revelation of unknown knowledge—especially unknown histories of resistance—as the essential, liberating readerly act. Cliff models her novel on the *abeng*, then, to make an account of a "colonized" girlhood capable of teaching a history of resistance.

Her narrative strategy is strikingly, insistently dual: she thematizes the loss of Caribbean history as she recovers that history, stressing the problem of loss while she unearths historical facts, so that the reader must read through the thick haze of the characters' not-knowing in the process of coming to know. Through this paradoxical structure, *Abeng* represents both the enslaved condition of ignorance and the liberation born of knowledge within the same narrative space, the same girl's life.

Not Knowing History

Readers of the European-American bildungsroman will find that *Abeng* departs from the genre's primary conventions to place a young girl's "life" within a wider vision. Breaking the rule of consistent narrative focus on the maturing hero(ine), Cliff's narration drifts from the story of Clare Savage's girlhood to the history of the people of Jamaica, sometimes acquiring for pages at a time a tone akin to that of flat reportorial "history":

> Three hundred acres was the minimum expanse of land a sugar plantation could measure—in order to make a profit. One slave was required for every two acres—compared to one slave for every five or ten acres on a cotton plantation. This estimate takes into account the fact that the slaves would be worked twelve hours a day and six days a week. At least. (27)

At least. Cliff muddies generic purity to fuse "historical information" with the elaboration of a young girl's story, creating a prose style between those of "history" and "literature" and creating effects perhaps unachievable in either genre strictly defined.[5] The passage quoted above continues:

> Sugar . . . required an unending supply of unpaid labor. . . . But sugar was a necessity of western civilization—to the tea-drinkers of England and the coffee-drinkers on the Continent, those who used it to sweeten their beverage, or who laced these beverages with rum. Those who took these products at their leisure—to finish a meal, begin a day, to stimulate them. . . . People who spent afternoons in the clubs of Mayfair or evenings in the cafés on the rue de la Paix. People holding forth in Parliament. The Rathaus. The Comedie Française. . . . The fabric of their society, their civilization, their culture, was an intricate weave, at the heart of which was enforced labor of one kind or another. (27–28)

Repressed "history" invades "literature" here, revealing essential "plot" information and "characters" left out of the Euro-American novel. Simon Gikandi notes *Abeng*'s "parasitic and subversive" relationship to European historical and literary texts; it "resurrects meanings that both mock and haunt the dominant culture" (236, 241). Cliff's first novel is thus a metafictional text, as Gikandi claims, but of a different sort from either the canonical revision of Rhys's *Wide Sargasso Sea*, or the critical engagement with white history-writers in African-American women's fictions like *Beloved*, *Dessa Rose*, and *Kindred*. *Abeng* instead stages multiple confrontations between written and oral, official and unofficial forms of historical discourse, delivering Caribbean history in the "conjunction between manifest and celebrated Eurocentric meanings and a repressed Afro-Caribbean hermeneutics" (Gikandi 242, 235).

As the novel inserts generically and politically subversive discourse into a girl's life story, it also performs a radical revision of the novelistic subject. *Abeng* "[transforms] the individualistic bourgeois quest plot into a collective struggle for social justice" (Fiona Barnes 23), insisting that the story of one girl's life cannot be read apart from the context of the historical struggle for the liberation of Jamaica and, indeed, of the oppressed all over the world. Cliff's figuration of female development within a vision of collective liberation stands out, even in the traditions of the feminist and the postcolonial bildungsroman,[6] in its insistent juxtaposition of the personal and public, the individual and collective. Indeed, *Abeng* often seems to be *about* such juxtapositions. The novel opens:

> The island rose and sank. Twice. During periods in which history was recorded by indentations on rock and shell.
>
> This is a book about the time which followed on that time. As the island became a place where people lived. Indians. Africans. Europeans.
>
> ---
>
> It was a Sunday morning at the height of the height of the mango season. . . . The Savages—father, mother, and two daughters—were getting ready for church. . . . (3)

The world Clare Savage inhabits is framed in an extremely wide-angled perspective, containing the entirety of the island's history. Though she is dwarfed by that history, she is also positioned as its culmination. To tell this particular girl's story, the opening seems to say, the widest possible view is required; New World nature and its native peoples must be reinstated in chronological priority to Europeans and their empires, and her life must be seen to "record," like rocks and shells, the impressions of a vast history. In such passages, as Belinda Edmondson notes, Cliff "rewrites [the] white creole heritage of privilege and collaboration to integrate it with the unwritten black and Amerindian histories of suffering and resistance" (185). This radically inclusive vision makes it possible for a girl like Clare Savage to become Jamaica's representative heir.

Yet what is most striking about Cliff's presentation of a girl's life in *Abeng* is its relentless enclosure of the heroine in ignorance of the multiple historical connections the narrator constructs. Again and again we read that Clare does not know about the traces of her slave heritage around her, cannot question the race and class structures her world inherits from the past, and is "not ready to understand" (166) the fact that is clear to the widest view, well-known by the implied narrator, and communicated to the reader: that Clare's identity is not unitary but intrinsically bound up in a large and diverse "we."

Indeed, the novel extends this lack of knowledge about collective identity and history beyond the mulatto heroine to all of its characters; the phrase "they did not know" permeates the text, often introducing passages of historical information. This passage follows the Savage family's arrival at a black church:

> No one had told the people in the Tabernacle that of all the slave societies in the New World, Jamaica was considered among the most brutal. They did not know that the death rate of Africans in Jamaica under slavery exceeded

> the rate of birth. . . . They did not know that some slaves worked with their faces locked in masks of tin, so they would not eat the sugar cane as they cut. Or that . . . the grandmothers of these people sitting in a church on a Sunday evening during mango season, had been violated again and again by the very men who whipped them. (18–19)

> They did not know about the Kingdom of the Ashanti or the Kingdom of Dahomey, where most of their ancestors had come from. They did not imagine that Black Africans had commanded thousands of warriors. Built universities. Created systems of law. Devised language. Wrote history. Poetry. (20)

Over the course of the novel the repeated phrase "they did not know" becomes nearly incantatory, and we almost cease to hear its denotation, as if it were an unconscious reflex of the implied teller's, required to announce the delivery of truth from narrator to reader. Truth is always unavailable to those in the inner spaces of this text, while their ignorance is continually evoked, a seeming corollary to the narrator's knowledge. It becomes apparent that this speaker knows the depth, the shape, and the texture of the Jamaican people's "disrememory" of their history as well as she knows the facts themselves.[7]

Separating fictional world from narrative voice by a radical disparity in knowledge and the power to acquire it, Cliff replicates the educated, alienated colonial writer's return to her people's history. The "decolonized" narrator can know what the colonized heroine and characters cannot. Telling us that this child "lived within certain parameters—which clouded her judgment" (77), Cliff reproduces those imprisoning parameters in her prose. The plot of Clare Savage's *Bildung* thus emerges within a markedly conflicted textuality. Inscribing historical loss as it tells the heroine's history, the narrative jumps from Clare to her slave ancestors to her parents and community, generating startling juxtapositions of the personal and collective, the known and not-known, seeming to seek such eruptions and clashes, rather than coherence, balance, or closure. The effect is less the recovery of the full presence of history than a display of authorial will to infuse amassed knowledge into a space of ignorance. "So many veils to be lifted," sighs the narrator of this girl's life, "so many intertwinings to be unraveled" (67).

The schism between narrative knowledge and fictive ignorance is far more severe here than in an African-American novel like Gloria Naylor's *Mama Day*, in which inset texts give the reader historical information the characters do not possess. Whereas Cliff dramatizes the gap in knowledge as tragic outrage, Naylor presents the discrepancy only to undercut it; the prodigious Mama Day does not need the ancient bill of sale for Sapphira Wade to make deep contact with her ancestress. Oral history, memory, ritual, and magic all triumph over written history in *Mama Day* as in many contemporary African-American women's fictions. But Cliff's Jamaican characters seem to have almost no collective memory, no oral record, only a dim recollection of magic. Their loss of history—highlighted by the disjunctive narrative technique that constantly teaches us what "they did not know"—suggests the "amnesiac blow" that causes the "wound" to Caribbean memory in Walcott's poem.

As a novel of education, then, *Abeng*'s first task is to educate readers of the conventional novel of education, to teach us colonial life-reading. We learn that ignorance of history helps uphold the Empire and that historical discourse can collude in a child's colonization, and we become aware, as we read Clare's story, of receiving a counter-education to the one being offered to the developing girl. In her social environs, the most determinate meanings are predicated on skin color. Clare's domineering father looks nearly "white" and her mother, "black," and this polarity fixes the endposts of Clare's identity; defined by her father as "white," Clare is distanced from any sense of African or of maternal heritage. Much of *Abeng* concerns her attempts to grasp the rules that exclude some things and privilege others in her world, but her efforts to understand the meaning of race are always turned aside by adults:

> It was so easy to lose sight of color when you were constantly being told that there was no "colour problem" in Jamaica. Or anywhere in the Empire, for that matter. . . .
>
> Color was diffuse and hard to track at St. Catherine's, entering the classrooms as seating arrangements, disciplinary action, entering the auditorium during the casting of a play. (100)

Like Clare's teachers, Cliff's narrator keeps the child captive within the false structures of a colonial education, while positioning us on the outside looking in, uncomfortably conscious of the privilege of knowing.

The Voice and the Character

Enclosing the heroine of *Abeng* in ignorance, Cliff clearly risks recapitulating the power relations of colonialism. Indeed, we might read her narration as a kind of colonization by the narrator of the character, who become, respectively, haughty describer and enforcer of "native" ignorance, and silent, oppressed slave, with no access to the resources of power or freedom. But why should Cliff erect a panopticon to tell a near-autobiographical story? And how can such an immured and restricted young heroine be a revisionary daughter?

The division of a text into "narrative voice" and "character" is of course merely "an illusion of difference"; though both elements emerge from the same pen, the conventional narrator:character divide tends to persuade us to "[bestow] on the speaking voice an identity distinct from the world it describes" (Hayles 26). Roland Barthes tells us to regard a text as "an iridescent exchange carried on by multiple voices, on different wavelengths," "a glistening texture of ephemeral origins" (41–42). But fiction has historically relied upon the binary distinction to achieve some of its greatest effects, like the highly developed forms of narratorial commentary on a social scene dating from the eighteenth century. Dorrit Cohn's *Transparent Minds* delineates two principal ways of narrating consciousness:

> One is dominated by a prominent narrator who, even as he focuses intently on an individual psyche, remains emphatically distanced from the consciousness he narrates; the other is mediated by a narrator who remains effaced and who readily fuses with the consciousness he narrates. (26)

These differing narrators tend to tell the stories of different kinds of characters, in "a relation of inverse proportion between authorial and figural minds," the more prominent and distanced narrator being less likely to "reveal the depth of his characters' psyches." "It almost seems," Cohn muses, "as though the authorial narrator jealously guards his prerogative as the sole thinking agent within his novel . . ." (25).

The notion that the distinction narrator:character depends fundamentally on a difference in degrees of power and freedom and that the narrator may be, as it were, *interested* in maintaining this difference suggests that beneath the conventional duality of novelistic consciousness rages a concealed struggle for control of the text. Texts that maintain the greatest "dissonance" between the narrator's and character's "minds," Cohn argues, are in an important sense *about* "the narrator's superior knowledge of the character's inner life and his superior ability to present it and assess it" (28–29). A model of "markedly dissonant psycho-narration" (29) might be a grand nineteenth-century novel like George Eliot's *The Mill on the Floss*, and a novel with less such dissonance would be a high modernist text like Woolf's *The Waves*. Indeed, the narrator-character relationship has evolved along with the modern novel, "the growing interest in . . . individual psychology" leading to the disappearance of the "audible narrator":

> It is therefore no coincidence that those writers who first insisted on the removal of vociferous narrators from fiction—notably Flaubert and Henry James—were also the creators of fictional minds with previously unparalleled depth and complexity. (Cohn 25–26)

The narrator of Cliff's *Abeng*, we must acknowledge, is precisely the sort of "vociferous" presence to whom Flaubert and James objected. Maintaining a high degree of dissonance between narrative and fictional minds, *Abeng* sacrifices depth and complexity in Clare's mind to a narrative-historiographic depth and complexity, rendered in the all-knowing, all-teaching narrative voice. What are we to make of Cliff's postmodern regression to an outdated relationship between narrator and character? I would argue that Cliff adapts the old-fashioned, cognitively privileged, morally righteous voice to portray a legacy of the era of Empire that Flaubert and James knew must be swept away before the emergence of modern character, that is, to call our attention to the imperial power relations of knowing and telling, to the historiographic struggle being waged for the life story of a child in the grip of colonialism. Cliff's revival of this "vociferous" narration is, then, what Gikandi calls a "parasitic and subversive" strategy or, as Cliff puts it, a way of "mixing in the forms taught us by the oppressor, undermining his language and co-opting his style, and turning it to our purpose" ("A Journey" 14).

Adding to the strangeness of this narrator-character tension is the autobiographical element; why should Cliff's decolonized narrator-self reinflict colonization on the child-self? If this recalls a marxist antipsychological strategy, it also recalls a feminist/poststructuralist re-reading of the autobiographical subject. Indeed, Cliff's narrative voice seems closer to either of these discourses than to the postcolonial/postmodern parody of narration found in Rushdie or Coetzee. Dramatizing the warring radicalized and colonized aspects of the self, Cliff does not parody the voice of authority and knowledge but steals it, turning it into a voice for rage. Her project in this sense seems a particularly conflicted instance of the postcolonial "dual agenda" noted by Stephen Slemon; *Abeng* at once "[suspends] the referent in order to read the social 'text' of colonialist power" and works urgently "to reinstall the referent," "to allow for the positive production of oppositional truth-claims" ("Modernism's" 7, 5).[8] A voice that silences the "colonized" heroine in order to explode imperial History with the truth of suppressed histories is the voice of an inherently contradictory postcolonial condition. We might say that the pairing of the explicitly colonized heroine and the angry, history-teaching narrator exposes the concealed power struggle of a George Eliot novel in order to tell a radically revisionary story of a girl's life.

A reading of one episode will illustrate. The most notable fact known by *Abeng*'s narrator but not its heroine is an incident that occurred on the plantation of Judge Savage, Clare's famous ancestor, on the eve of the emancipation of his slaves, her unacknowledged ancestors. Clare and her father go to visit the plantation house, now recast as "atmosphere" (37) for an American vacation development called Paradise Plantation:

> And so father and daughter walked through what was once a great house, and they came out into the backyard, where the only signs of a former life were the foundation stones of some of the outbuildings, and faint gullies marking the earth where others had been. These buildings out back, only a few yards from the great house, had once contained molasses and rum and slaves—the points of conjunction of the system known as the Triangle Trade. (25)

This passage introduces a long description of the process of rum-making in British Jamaica, with emphasis on the labor performed by slaves and their horrid conditions of life. The text then finds Clare again, "noting the existence of the foundation stones and the gullies in the earth, but not knowing the former life they represented" (27). Her mind is occupied with her imaginary relationship to England, "that place she knew from her father's stories and her teachers' lessons. Where everyone was civilized and no one had to be told which fork to use" (36). At chapter's end we learn that Judge Savage, hearing that the slaves were to be freed, grew fearful for—of all things—the purity of his race, and so set fire to the slave cabins, burning one hundred people alive. The narrator closes:

> Lest anyone think the judge's action—which became the pattern of foundation stones and thin dirt gullies Clare saw that afternoon behind the great house, rectangles remembering an event she would never know of—lest anyone think the judge's behavior extreme or insane or frenzied, the act of a mad white man, it should be pointed out that this was not an isolated act on the eve of African freedom in Jamaica.
>
> ---
>
> The bones of dead slaves made the land at Runaway Bay rich and green. . . . (40)

The voice that speaks this last passage, telling us what Clare "would never know" about her "civilized" ancestors, has the moral authority and rhetorical force of a George Eliot narrator, and something of its tone—or rather, the tone of an Eliot narrator who would permit herself to be angry. As N. Katherine Hayles has shown, Eliot exploits "the extraordinarily complex interplay between the narrative voice and the 'givens' of the narrator's world" in *The Mill on the Floss* to contain the expression of an unacceptable female anger:

> To the narrative voice is given the female ethic of care and a habitual plea for tolerance; to the givens is entrusted the anger that the narrator banishes from direct vocalization. (26)

Thus the narrator can urge readerly tolerance of Tom's cruelty to Maggie, for example, but a violent event like the flood—which appears "given" to the reader, of a different order from the authorial voice—can enact otherwise unsanctioned rage and kill him, and her as well.

The narrator of *Abeng*, in her moment of high narratorial righteousness and defense of the "given-ness" of her givens ("lest anyone think the judge's behavior extreme . . . it should be pointed out that . . ."), seems a 1980s feminist to Eliot's Victorian; she sounds angry outright and makes no attempt to mute her anger. While Eliot's narrator seeks to create, with her readers, a community of tolerance that contains anger and forgives injustice, Cliff's narrator seeks to create a community of outrage, which will channel anger into the will to change the conditions that enforce her heroine's ignorance. Exposing the violence and injustice "given" in her heroine's world, *Abeng* performs a degree of reader education from which the novel in English has recently demurred, in order to radicalize our reading, to teach us that anger and action are appropriate responses to the novel of education.

Thus this paradoxical narrative, this narrative *abeng*, tells its heroine's story through doubleness.[9] The antithetical voice of a "historian" who separates herself from her characters by her superior knowledge and who forbids readers to interpret her tale as anything less than truth makes us sensible of the injustice of the heroine's entrapment in ignorance and unfreedom, and probably makes us hope for some means of delivery, some revelation that would lead this child to the knowledge her narrator possesses. But though Clare herself begins to desire a clearer view of the world over the course of the novel, Cliff portrays her in the end poignantly on the verge of, but "not ready" for, such knowledge (166).

For Gikandi, Clare is "a schizophrenic and divided subject" (244) and *Abeng* "a schizophrenic text" (235).[10] Yet, I would argue, Cliff also works to redeem what may indeed be a traumatically induced, colonial schizophrenia through the very structure of her two-faced *abeng*: it makes the life of a colonized child capable of teaching revolutionary ideas, and it renders the child herself—though she "does not know" it—a revisionary daughter. By pairing the oblivious heroine with a narrator possessed of historical knowledge and a radical agenda, Cliff enables the text of this girl's life to recover her mother-island's history. Though she is ignorant of her past, her narrator recalls history for her; though she has not inherited a collective memory, Cliff creates "a geo-political space of memory" inside her life story (Edmondson 185).

A girl whose life story can contain all of her history can thus be a powerful textual figure, though a weak social being. Like Gomez's Gilda or Woolf's Orlando, Clare seems the culmination of a long history; it is in her body, her genes—even, one senses, in her untapped collective memory. Her position amidst an assemblage of historical fragments allows a kind of daughterly recuperation of the past, without her awareness—much less time-travel or magic. Any use of the fantastic would be anathema to the realist aesthetic of *Abeng*, which cultivates the impasse between narrative and fictive knowledge where a novel that dramatizes the emerging power of the oppressed might, indeed, deploy myth or magic. But though Clare has stirrings of desire for magic, Cliff does not permit her to overthrow the real of *Abeng*. When she visits Paradise Plantation, "The house was not at all what she had expected. It was as though she had wanted it to be a time machine rather than a relic. A novel rather than an obituary" (36). Clare wishes to contact history through time-travel magic—or to be in the kind of novel that would grant her such powers—but she is enclosed in a realist "obituary," a text that refuses transcendence of history. Such powers must await adulthood and the next novel—ironically, more the "obituary" in that it ends with death, yet a much more novelistic text, more open to transforming possibilities. Readers of Cliff's first novel are likely to wish that the girl who contains all her history within her would awaken to this fact, for her unawareness seems the chief obstacle to significant transformation of her nation. But of the Clare of *Abeng* we must say, adapting Yeats, that she can embody history, but she cannot know it.

Allegorical Daughter

In her capacity to embody her history, Clare is typical of characters in recent adaptations of the bildungsroman from the Caribbean and decolonizing world. Edmondson explains that in Cliff's novels:

the point is not to embody Clare as a character separate from her "plane of emergence" but rather to read that location through the conflicting and multiple identities that are Clare Savage; she is, as such, not a "character" in the traditional sense at all. (185)

Not a traditional character, Clare Savage is an allegorical figure, a daughter who embodies the history that made her.[11] Her bildungsroman, like those of characters such as Merle Hodge's Tee or, more famously and fantastically, Saleem Sinai of Rushdie's *Midnight's Children* (1980), "parallel[s] the formation of the young self to that of the developing nation" (Lima 35; see also Fiona Barnes 29, Gikandi 217). The beginning of *Abeng* seems to locate Clare's origins in her island's eruption from the sea, and the end of *No Telephone* seems to return her to Jamaican nature. Over the course of the two novels she seeks to reclaim Jamaica as the authentic site of its own history, and to reclaim her own identity with Jamaica.

Thus Cliff's novels insist on the appropriateness of a "Jamaica white" as an allegorical daughter of Jamaica, a political claim certain to encounter resistance from several quarters. Any girl will, of course, have a more awkward fit as national allegory, because national identity has tended to be defined by men and figured male (Gikandi 217–18), except of course for the figures of a motherland. Cliff offers, however, the precedent of the allegorical "Maroon Girl," subject of a poem performed by one lucky schoolgirl each year in the country school of Clare's grandmother's parish:

I see her on a lonely forest track
        Her level brows made salient by the sheen
        Of flesh the hue of cinnamon. The clean
Blood of the hunted, vanished Arawak
Flows in her veins with blood of white and black.
        Maternal, noble-breasted is her mien;
        She is a peasant, yet she is a queen.
She is Jamaica poised against attack. (90–91)

This cinnamon-hued figure is the noble product of race mixture, yet the Garveyite schoolmaster chooses Clare's dark-skinned mother to play "Jamaica" in her youth, as well as Clare's darker, poorer friend Zoe, in turn. But the light-skinned, bourgeois, alienated heroine, raised and schooled in the city and not in her mother's native countryside, seems not to fit the part.[12]

A Jamaica that Cliff's heroine could embody must be more various and contradictory than most postcolonial national allegories admit: it must be not only female and male and multiracial, but also multisexual, multicultural, containing multiple political agendas, like the Clare of Cliff's subsequent novel, *No Telephone to Heaven*: "She is white. Black. Female. Lover. Beloved. Daughter. Traveler. Friend. Scholar. Terrorist. Farmer" (91). Moreover, the "maternal" role of the Maroon Girl must be a refusable option for a daughter of the nation who chooses to "mother" history through means other than procreation. The Jamaica figured in the two volumes of Clare's story includes a range of "crossroads" identities, including a lesbian foremother in Mma Alli, a transvestite revolutionary in Harry/Harriet, and a Jewish role model in Anne Frank, which help Cliff to recast the historical character of Jamaica. Her second novel releases Clare Savage not only from ignorance of the past but also from limiting racialized notions of identity, allowing her to own herself as Jamaica's daughter and to carry out her long-delayed maternal return.

BECOMING HISTORY: *NO TELEPHONE TO HEAVEN*

We Making History

In the sequel to *Abeng* an educated, adult Clare Savage returns to newly independent Jamaica, intent on revolutionizing her homeland. To present its radicalized heroine, *No Telephone to Heaven* breaks out of the narrative prisonhouse of *Abeng*. In the opening scene *Abeng*'s wide narrator-character gap disappears, replaced by a speaker very close to Clare's consciousness, even to a group consciousness:

> This dripping group of pale and dark people standing in the back of a rickety, noisy old truck was little more than a band. But their survival dress could make them feel, seem to be, an army. So they hoped. "It is no mystery / We making history," someone hummed in dub. Yes. (5)

The smooth narrative slide from characters' appearance to their feelings and hopes, to quoted song, to this "yes," which is either Clare's, or the narrator's, or both, illustrates the second text's altered texture. This narrator does not possess but withhold knowledge. Rather, she credits her characters' feelings, says "yes" to them and their aspirations to freedom in a way that *Abeng*'s narrator never does. For *No Telephone*'s opening gives us not "colonized" characters but revolutionaries, breaking out of colonial schizophrenia into self-determination. In Cohn's scheme of narrator-character combat, any "fully developed figural consciousness siphons away the emotional and intellectual energy formerly lodged in the expansive narrator" (25). As the adult Clare begins to analyze the forces that controlled the story of her childhood, her narrator diminishes to let her expand.

Throughout *No Telephone* the narrative voice is less obtrusive than that of *Abeng*, less obsessed with teaching and exposing ignorance, and more willing to allow characters free rein to act in and articulate their unfolding reality. Indeed, unlike the first narrator, she seems willing to mingle with that reality, slipping in and out of Jamaican Creole speech patterns and navigating between the metaphors of two cultures, much like the Jamaican-born, English-educated heroine:

> NO TELEPHONE TO HEAVEN. No voice to God. A waste to try. Cut off. No way of reaching out or up. Maybe only one way. Not God's way. No matter if

him is Jesus or him is Jah. Him not gwan like dis one lickle bit. NO TELEPHONE TO HEAVEN. (16)

With this more flexible and democratic voice, Cliff's second novel engages a Jamaica of intersecting discourses, weaving into the saga of Clare's adulthood the stories of other Jamaicans, of other classes and colors: Christopher, the homeless "yardboy" from the Kingston Dungle; Harry/Harriet, the transvestite nurse and revolutionary; Paul, the son of the wealthy family Christopher murders; and Clare's parents Kitty and Boy Savage. Even nature speaks in this multivocal text: at the opening, singing birds seem to question the rebels' purpose in the Jamaican bush, and a bird chorus has the last word (4, 208). The commitment to unity-in-hybridity appears as well in the novel's project of composing fragments—not merely the narrator's task, as in *Abeng*, but one shared here with the heroine: "There are many bits and pieces to her, for she is composed of fragments. In this journey, she hopes, is her restoration" (87).

Yet Clare's story still bears the paradoxical burden of the postcolonial bildungsroman: "both to represent the movement from fragmentation and loss toward wholeness and homeland, and to deny the possibility of such recovery" (Lima 54, n5). Though Cliff in *No Telephone* erupts out of the binary structure of *Abeng* into a more dynamic, heteroglossic narrative, and though Clare Savage emerges from ignorance and passivity into a revisionary daughter's campaign for self-education, healing, and return, *No Telephone* still confronts in every moment Jamaica's entrenchment in poverty, inequality, and racism, its servitude to neocolonial powers, its culture-wide dis-ease. The novel suggests that the admirable simplicity of a quest for "wholeness and homeland" is doomed in the cultural and political minefield of the contemporary Caribbean, but that a returning daughter can and must struggle to "decolonize" her relationship to her home, her community, and her history.

This second part of Chapter 6 will consider how *No Telephone* revises the bildungsroman to narrate adult development as a "decolonization of the mind." Rather than individuation, the course of Clare's life gradually brings her integration with her people, her past, and with human struggle the world over; becoming herself is, in a profound sense, becoming history. This transformation requires above all the allegorical return to maternal origins begun in *Abeng*; Clare's troubled romance with the Caribbean mother becomes the defining quest of her life. Engaged in this daughterly mission, Clare's story deploys unconventional forms of historical inquiry, of novelistic narration and closure, and of cross-cultural or "horizontal" plotting, which position Jamaica's daughter within new relationships to the past and the future.

Motherless Child, Grandmother Country

Her mother could not respond to her. Where had she gone? Where were her ideas? Her beliefs? Where were

> her mind and memory? It seemed impossible that these things could have vanished into thin air.
>
> *No Telephone* (72)

The two-volume narrative of Clare Savage's quest for "wholeness and homeland" is shaped from beginning to end by the imagery and the structure of maternal allegory. Even more obsessively than most Caribbean writers, Cliff renders her country's history in terms of disrupted or problematic motherhood—starting with "the explosive birth of the island" (*No Telephone* 199). To trace Clare's mother-quest, we must look back to the first novel, where Cliff begins the movement toward repair of the violated mother-daughter bond just as modern Caribbean literature began: by deconstructing the colonial appropriation of the term "mother."

In the opening pages of *Abeng*, a confusion of mothers—of origin and identity—comes to poison a scene of childhood joy in Jamaica's natural landscape. It was "the height of the height of the mango season," the narrative begins, naming the season not by Europe's calendar, but after the wild, indigenous fruit stuffed in the pockets of "all the children on the island." "There was a splendid profusion of fruit," so much so that the *Daily Gleaner* editorializes on "God's Gift to Jamaica, and conclude[s] by telling all inhabitants to be hospitable to the tourists." "It was," Cliff adds oddly, "as if the island was host to some ripe sweet plague" (3–4).

The peculiar, unspecified threat hovering over Jamaica's children in this line, recalling history's distortion of island beauty in so many Caribbean texts, comes into focus when Cliff calls the mango "supreme among all other growing things . . . 'Mother Sugar herself'" and on the same page calls England "the 'mother' country" (5). Eating the fruits of two mothers, apparently, Cliff's Jamaicans cannot claim their native bounty. Over the course of the two novels, Cliff dethrones the "mother country" and elaborates Clare's yearning for figures of the Jamaican mother, from her actual mother and grandmother to animal figures, historical heroines, and mythic ancestresses, in the effort to transform her home from the realm of a sick or sickening mother to that of a mother-warrior.

AT THE HEART of the heroine's mother troubles is her own mother, who like many in realist fictions by Caribbean women is symbolically identified with Caribbean history and the island home, yet is an inadequate nurturer for her daughter. Darker-skinned than Clare and holding a deep "love for Black people—her people" (*Abeng* 127), Kitty Savage is one of the few characters in *Abeng* who is said to know something; "she knew"—one paragraph repeats four times—all the plants and herbs of Jamaica that can be used to kill or cure (53). But Kitty shares with Clare neither her traditional female knowledge, nor "her love of darkness"—which Clare suspects (128), nor her feminist, nature-based spirituality:

> Kitty had a sense of Jamaica that her husband would never have. She thought that there was no other country on earth as beautiful as hers, and . . . that there were certain trees hidden in the underbrush which bore the fruit as they, the trees, wished—with no respect for ordained schedules, in a pattern not as God willed it. For her, God and Jesus were but representatives of Nature, which it only made sense was female, and the ruler of all—but this she never said. (*Abeng* 52–53)

Kitty's failure to tell is critical to Clare's failure to know; this breach in maternal teaching makes the child more vulnerable to colonization. Their ruptured relationship, set by the narrator amidst a general, historical failure to transmit African women's culture from one generation to the next,[13] becomes symbolic of the larger cultural loss that tends to associate Caribbean mother-figures with death and mourning.

Indeed, Kitty's story begins in *Abeng* with the Savage family car passing a country funeral. Moved by the ritual, Kitty identifies an African mourning song for her daughters, while her light-skinned, anglophile husband scoffs (50). Throughout the two novels Kitty stands as a mourning daughter of Africa, a figure isolated in her mourning. Continually at odds with her husband, Kitty seems cut off from her own mother's place in the Jamaican bush and from a once-powerful link to African consciousness. Correspondingly, she remains aloof from her daughter. Clare dares not ask her about female bodily changes, or about the pregnant and nursing women she sees in the countryside. At the age of twelve the unhappy heroine "wanted to suck her mother's breasts again and again," so that "together they would enter some dream Clare imagined mothers and children shared" (54).

Kitty is, however, more sympathetic than many middle-generation women in Caribbean women's fiction, because she is herself an alienated daughter who senses her own loss of maternal heritage. When she receives an omen of her mother's death, Kitty grieves not only for her mother but also for the source of her knowledge of such omens: "the magic which had encircled [her] girlhood," the knowledge "held in the minds and memories of old women," but that her schoolmaster had called "false knowledge" (*No Telephone* 69). Ironically, the death of her mother, Miss Mattie, brings Kitty unprecedented physical intimacy with her, when she washes her body for burial. Here Cliff introduces into Caribbean literature a missing archetype: a scene of a daughter's ritual reclamation of the body of the dead Great Mother—usually gone without a trace, like Sycorax. As Kitty caresses her mother's breasts, "this secret thing which had been hidden from her for thirty years became hers." And as she repossesses the mother's body, Kitty catches a glimmer of lost matrilineal memory: "From somewhere came an image of a slavewoman pacing aisles of cane, breast slung over her shoulder to suckle the baby carried on her back" (71). But Miss Mattie's death finally severs Kitty's access to the heritage it briefly reanimates; shortly afterward, Boy Savage moves the family to the United States. In American exile, Kitty always associates the island with her dead mother, yet failing to extend any experience of deep maternal contact to her daughter, she enforces Clare's daughterly exile as well.

Readers of *Abeng* will understand the depth of Kitty's loss in *No Telephone*, for her mother, Clare's grandmother, is the first novel's great mother-figure. Miss Mattie owns the land where Clare spends her summers and from whence she derives her sense of belonging in Jamaica; her presence still permeates the land when Clare returns to reclaim it. The grandmother's centrality to Clare's sense of Jamaica resonates in Cliff's provocative renaming of Jamaica (in an essay) the "grandmother country" ("Caliban's" 49). This coinage, signifying on the imperialist designation of "mother" countries, also helps install as emblem of Jamaica the historical heroine Nanny, who led an army of Maroons (escaped slaves) against the British. Cliff writes Nanny into Clare's story as mythic warrior-ancestress, "the sorceress, the *obeah*-woman," who came "from the empire of the Ashanti, and carried the secrets of her magic into slavery" (*Abeng* 14). Nanny enters *Abeng* in the scene of Jamaicans at church, as another fact the people do not know about themselves: "Some of them were called Nanny, because they cared for the children of other women, but they did not know who Nanny had been" (21). Positioned as the origin of Jamaican womanhood, the lost Mother in whom all other mothers' identities are gathered, Nanny is the Caribbean mother redefined as a warrior:

> Now her head is tied. Now braided. Strung with beads and cowrie shells. Now she is disguised as a *chasseur*. Now wrapped in a cloth shot through with gold. Now she stalks the Red Coats as they march toward her cave, where she spins her Akan chants into spells which stun her enemies. Calls on the goddesses of the Ashanti forests. Remembers the battle formations of the Dahomey Amazons. (19)

Cliff gives Nanny another manifestation in Mma Alli, a lesbian healer and slave leader on Judge Savage's plantation. This subversive figure from the heroine's family history provides a formidable precursor for a rebel daughter—but of course Clare never knows of her existence.[14]

The problem of Jamaica, then, as *Abeng* constructs it, is the "disrememory" of rebellious mothers, figures from Jamaica's history of resistance. The problem with Clare's mournful mother is that she does not know such a history:

> Kitty should have been the daughter of . . . Mma Alli, and Nanny too—and had she known of the existence of these women, she might have shared her knowledge, her extraordinary passion, using its strength, rather than protecting what she felt was its fragility. . . .
>
> Kitty's mistake . . . was casting her people in the position of victim, so that her love of darkness became a love conceived in grief. . . . The revolution had been lost when the first slave ships arrived from the west coast of Africa. . . . For all its tenderness, her vision was sad. (128)

Yet while Cliff criticizes this "sad" maternal vision, her novels remain partly in its thrall, repeatedly identifying Jamaica with figures of grieving or dying mothers and children, whose agony is the mark of colonial history. *Abeng* tells the story of the wild pig who discovers that her newborn piglets have been eaten by a mongoose, one by one, as she gave them birth; "people said you could hear the bellows of her loss sound through the mountains of the countryside—that was how they could tell that Massa Mongoose was close by. . . ." The predatory mongoose, Cliff tells us, is associated with the white landowners who imported it to Jamaica (114). The "bitter and miserable" Mrs. Phillips, to whose care Clare is sent as punishment in *Abeng*, "had buried each of her thirteen children" and "blamed Jamaica" for this, the "greatest loss a woman can suffer" (143). A "day of national mourning" is declared in *No Telephone* for "the grandmothers of our people," "the 167 old women who burned up in a fire started by some bastard" in a Kingston almshouse, victims of political infighting (160). In *No Telephone*'s explosive story of Christopher, the Kingston "yardboy" brutally murders his employers because they will not grant him a plot of land on which to bury his long-dead grandmother—whom he feels was improperly buried and so "did not rest" (45). Christopher's story echoes *Abeng*'s story of Mad Hannah, the mother of a homosexual son whose drowning cries were ignored by vindictive neighbors. Crazed with grief, Hannah is sent to an asylum where she "trie[s] to explain to the people in charge—the light-skinned educated people—about the death of her son and his incomplete and dangerous burial" (66). An incomplete mourning rages in Cliff's Jamaica, among mothers and their children. Its foreboding fury haunts the island at large, emblematic of the people's submerged consciousness of their historical loss.

The central instances are Kitty's mourning for Miss Mattie and, later, Clare's unresolved mourning for Kitty, who dies suddenly in *No Telephone* while Clare is a schoolgirl in America and is buried not at her beloved country home, but in Kingston, "in a cemetery which held no history for her family" (103). When at the novel's end the adult Clare says that she has returned to Jamaica "to mend . . . to bury . . . my mother" (192, ellipses in original), it is unclear whether she intends to mend herself or her mother—or both—when she symbolically reburies her mother. As when Kitty annoints her dead mother's body, Clare's desire to attend to the burial of her mother suggests a desire for a larger maternal restitution. Edmondson writes of Clare's and Christopher's mothers:

> That these maternal bodies have been dead but not buried remind us of the invisibility of black women in the narration of West Indian oppositional discourse, as embodied by Caliban's mother, the absent Sycorax. . . . Therefore, the attempt to "bury" the grand/mother becomes a metaphor for reconciling the "unburied"—that is, unrepresented, ghostly, "magical"—history of the people with the possibilities contained in the land, a fusion which requires violent rupture with present reality. (189–90)

This comment elucidates the link between the colonized subject's awakening to her history—symbolized by grief over the improper burial of mothers—and violent upheaval. Cliff's recasting of the always-already-absent Caribbean mother as one who needs to be buried is integral to her revolutionary vision. Shakespeare's Caliban never attempts to hold a funeral for his mother on the island, but can we imagine a cause more likely to arouse his suppressed fury, or to alarm his European master? As Clare's quest develops into a revolutionary vision for the transformation of Jamaica, it becomes most profoundly the quest to lay the mother's spirit in the land and thus unleash the possibilities of a Jamaica reborn as the mother country it has never been.

Here Is Her

The heroine's path to this return in *No Telephone* takes her from mother to mother, progressing from alienation to intimate knowledge, and from false mother to true. Clare's unhappy years in America and Europe are rendered in an ironic catalog of mothers: in England in her twenties Clare is a "Student of the motherland. Motherless" (88); when London erupts in racist riots, she becomes increasingly disenchanted with "this country she had been taught to call Mother" (111).[15] She is thus "startled" when her friend Harry/Harriet calls Jamaica "homeland" and writes in a letter, "Jamaica needs her children"; "Jamaica's children have to work to make her change" (121, 140, 127). As Clare begins her momentous turn toward the Jamaican motherland, she has a final, indispensable European encounter with the statue of Pocahontas, at her tomb in Gravesend. When she imagines the actual woman and her lonely English death, Pocahontas becomes for her the figure of the original New World Mother, cruelly displaced by the same colonial history that brought Clare to the "mother country."[16] The pity and grief she feels for this suffering mother launch her journey home to rediscover the Caribbean mother's realm.

No Telephone symbolically renders her entrance into this realm in the "Magnanimous Warrior" section, a prose-poem invocation of a mythic woman warrior into whose spirit Clare seems to gain entry (163–64). This section also presents another dramatic fusion of identities: those of the narrator and character. The narrative voice stops telling plot to invoke the warrior-spirit in a voice that is and is not Clare's, a battle cry that fuses heroine and narrator as if in response to Harry-Harriet's imperative:

> The time will come for both of us to choose. . . . Cast our lot. Cyaan live split. Not in this world. (131)

Casting her lot with black Jamaica, the heroine also seems to fuse her purpose with that of Cliff's radical narrating voice, healing *Abeng*'s schizophrenic narration of the "colonized child" and signaling her own coming-of-age. This is the first of two dramatic instances toward the novel's end when Cliff closes the gap between narrative and fictional minds; the second is Clare's interview with a guerrilla leader. These two moments, radical in structure and content, signal one of the trajectories of Clare's development: she is a girl taking control of her own story.

"Magnanimous Warrior" ventures to solve the problem of the lost mother-of-history by recreating her as a warrior. The mother-island cast in *Abeng* as a womb of foul afterbirth is recast here as a fierce, wise, loving fighter. Similarly, the grieving, wild pig-mother of *Abeng* is replaced in *No Telephone* by alligator and snake mothers who perform astounding feats to rescue their stolen eggs (191–92). Recalling the Nanny of *Abeng*, the Magnanimous Warrior is invoked as:

> She in whom the spirits come quick and hard. Hunting mother. . . . Warrior who places the blood-cloth on the back of the whipped slave. . . . Obeah woman. . . . The bearer of second sight. Mother who goes forth emitting flames from her eyes. . . . (163–64)

But the section that celebrates this mythic figure ends by lamenting her abandonment by her children. Asking "what has become of this warrior," the last paragraph describes the sick, abused, old black women of impoverished contemporary Jamaica: "She has been burned up in an almshouse fire in Kingston. She has starved to death. She wanders the roads of the country with swollen feet" (164). "Magnanimous Warrior" suggests that the fallen state of the mother-island lamented throughout Caribbean literature is not a matter of maternal fault after all, but of children's responsibility. "Can you remember how to love her?" the section asks in closing, handing those who would remake their nation the responsibility of re-learning to love an abandoned motherland.

FOLLOWING HER DESTINY back to Jamaica, the heroine is called "the woman who has reclaimed her grandmother's land" and seems to strike maternal bedrock when she vows allegiance "to the place my grandmother made" (91, 189). Yet when she travels to visit Miss Mattie's land, Clare recalls not her grandmother, but her mother:

> I explored the country. First with my mother. . . . it was where she was alive, came alive. . . . I was blessed to have her here. Her passion of place. Her sense of the people. Here is her; leave it at that. (173–74)

Saying "here is her," the heroine reclaims the "grandmother country" as the true mother country, at last. Overcoming the more immediate and difficult familial tension between daughter and mother, Clare privileges over a mythologically perfect—but unreal—Jamaican great mother, a more flawed, more intimately known Jamaican mother, a mother with whom one lives day by day, yet who is, after all, the mother one needs most urgently to restore. When an old neighbor of the family's mistakenly hails Clare by her mother's name, she is "not surprised" to hear their identification sealed (187). And whereas on earlier trips home Clare avoided visiting her mother's grave, Kitty's death now comes to the forefront of her mind. Asked by the interviewer to identify herself, Clare responds: "I am a Jamaican. My mother is dead" (189), and asked what drew her back to Jamaica, she speaks of her intention "to mend . . . to bury . . . my mother."

In a brief, private moment away from the rest of the guerrillas, Clare performs what we might regard as a symbolic burial of her mother, on her mother's mother's land. Crawling beneath her grandmother's house, she finds "her mother's things from childhood"—homemade toys and schoolbooks that represent "a former world": "Things, beings, existed in their rightful place—destiny, order were honored." Gathering these relics of her mother's "colonization" into a sack, she scrapes the ground with a shell—remnant of the island's "explosive birth"—and starts to bury "her mother's girlhood," "placing the piece of shell on top" (199–200). But in the middle of her makeshift funeral, Clare is called away by the rebels, who are ready to act. To interpret this as a scene of burial helps us to see Clare's laying of the spirit of the mother in her grandmother's land as necessary preparation for her climactic daughterly act of self-sacrifice and reclamation. The sense of incompleteness about the burial, however, suggests the inevitable failure of a full restoration.

Inside History

The return to Jamaican origins that moves Clare to mend and bury the mother also impels her to learn the history kept from her in *Abeng*. In place of her mother's colonial schoolbooks, Clare invents a radically new way of educating herself about her past. Indeed, the two novels of her education finally make her a teacher, of "reading and writing and history" (192). "It's the best thing I have done," she says; "It's the only thing I have done" (194–95). Her method of "reading" history's "writing" constitutes a bold postcolonial theory of historiography, one that challenges colonialist versions of her people's history by valuing their oral traditions, memories, and bodily experiences as much as textual records.[17] She explains to the interviewer:

> I have educated myself since my return. Spoken with the old people . . . leafed through the archives downtown. . . . I have studied the conch knife excavated at the Arawak site in White Marl . . . the petroglyphs hidden in the bush . . . listened to the stories about Nanny and taken them to heart. (193)

Asked if "this new sort of history" involves proof, Clare replies:

> It's not as simple as that. I am in it. It involves me . . . the practice of rubbing lime and salt in the backs of whipped slaves . . . the ambush tactics of Cudjoe. . . . cruelty . . . resistance . . . grace. I'm not outside this history—it's a matter of recognition . . . memory . . . emotion. When I study Tom Cringle's silk cotton tree, I wonder about the fact that I have never been able to bear a necklace around my throat . . . not even a scarf. (194)

Clare's intimate notion of history—experienced through physical contact with artifacts, listening to tales, exploring the island, recognition, memory, and emotion—links her to all the returning daughter-figures in this study, who, in one way or another, engage history in bodily form. Free of narrative framing in this passage, Clare's voice tells us that she has abandoned the colonial fiction of objectivity and now pursues a history understood as subjective, which she is in, involved in, which she "reads" with her body as well as her brain.

But this is precisely the kind of history that the narrator of *Abeng* already knows, a history latent in the things of the world around us, ours to read in signs like the "indentations on rock and shell" (3) or "the pattern of foundation stones and thin dirt gullies . . . behind the great house, rectangles remembering an event [Clare] would never know of" (40). The Clare of *No Telephone* joins *Abeng*'s narrator in another sense, then: in embracing a theory of historical reading that displaces the primacy of writing with a new privileging of intuitive, bodily responses to the signs of the world. In her colonized childhood, Clare has inklings of such a method of reading, but she cannot realize their potential:

> She sometimes imagined that the walls of certain places were the records of those places—the events which happened there. More accurate than the stories of the people who had lived within the walls. . . . The walls might not be able to reveal exactly what they had seen, but perhaps they could indicate to a visitor something, if only a clue, about the time which had passed through them. Maybe there were signs marked on the walls each time they heard a shout—like the slashes on the Rosetta Stone. . . . (32–33)

The desire to read shouts on a wall is Clare's response to the "historyless" condition of the Caribbean. In *Return to My Native Land* Césaire writes of the region, precisely, as "these countries whose past is uninscribed on any stone" (54). "Because the collective memory was too often wiped out," Glissant ventures, "the Caribbean writer must 'dig deep' into this memory, following the latent signs that he has picked up in the everyday world" (64); like the adult Clare, he advocates "a plowing up of phenomena that acquire significance when put together. . . . the accumulation of the commonplace and the clarification of related obscurity" (142).

In this new postcolonial historiography, nature has a special place, a special readability. Many Caribbean writers have lamented the alienation from their native landscape and the rote adulation of European natural elements—apples, snow, daffodils—enforced on Caribbean children by their colonial educations.[18] "When our landscape is so tampered with," Cliff asks, "how do we locate ourselves?" ("Caliban's" 37). The vision of nature in the Clare Savage novels derives from a commitment to rewriting the Caribbean landscape as the site of history.[19] The volcanic opening of *Abeng*, Gikandi notes, counters those histories that "posit the 'discovery' as the ground zero of the Caribbean experience" and begins to record history in indigenous terms, "the archeologizing gesture" suggesting alternate "modes of historical knowledge" (242). Indeed, Cliff's narrative strategy itself follows her heroine's new historical method, privileging subjective and idiosyncratic encounters with the homeland over received, written colonialist accounts. Rather than write conventional historical fiction—containing history within a fictionalized past—Cliff engages history as it filters into present-day lives, as people encounter it in their world.

I would argue that in Cliff's novels, and in much Caribbean literature, landscape takes the place of the figure of the black body in contemporary African-American writing, as the primary site of stored historical memory. In this island culture of racial mixture it is the place, and not the body, that most distinctively signifies Caribbean difference. Walcott's Nobel Lecture offers a powerful elaboration of the trope:

> [History] is there in Antillean geography, in the vegetation itself. The sea sighs with the drowned from the Middle Passage, the butchery of its aborigines, Carib and Aruac and Taino, bleeds in the scarlet of the immortelle, and even the actions of surf on sand cannot erase the African memory, or the lances of cane as a green prison where indentured Asians . . . are still serving time. (18)

In the absence of written records, nature becomes the archive of ancestral suffering and survival.

For Clare Savage, historical identity is inseparable from geography; when asked to describe herself, she offers an itinerary of her travels. "You stress place," says the interviewer, and Clare replies, "I thought you wanted to know my history." Similarly, she affirms maternal "allegiance" "to the *place* my grandmother made" (189, emphasis added). Cliff casts the Caribbean place as at once the repository of history and the realm of the mother—that is, of the mothered self, of potential wholeness. She describes the foundation of her own identity: "underneath it all, the granddaughter of Sycorax, precolonial female, landscape, I(s)land: I land" ("Caliban's" 40). Such a landscape, to borrow Edmondson's words, "does not simply contain an unwritten history but also contains the potential to heal that history" (188). Clare Savage's revisionary historical method pursues historical healing by reading the motherland.

Diary of a Young Girl

A particularly dramatic reading of history-through-nature occurs in *Abeng* in the section that relates young Clare's obsession with the story of Anne Frank. Cliff's account of Clare's insistent questioning of parents and teachers about the Holocaust is suddenly interrupted by a narrative interlude:

> The smoke from six million bodies burning had passed across the surfaces of continents and the slopes and peaks of mountain ranges and moved over bodies of water. The bones of six million people had been bleached stark white by the same sun that traveled overhead day after day, its circuits telling time. And when the bones started to crumble in their dryness, some of the

dust had also been carried across land masses and bodies of water—while the rest seeped under the ground to fertilize the earth. The smoke from the bodies and the dust from the bones made a change in the atmosphere—in the air that people breathed and the water they drank. Did no one notice the steady change in their environment—that people were disappearing and returning as smoke and dust? (70–71)

This remarkable passage must be called a distinctly Caribbean, a postcolonial rendering of the Nazi Holocaust of Europe's Jews. Reading history through nature rather than through textual or photographic documentation, Cliff insists that nature has not merely absorbed but registered these deaths, just as the island's rocks and shells and green plantations—fertilized by the bones of murdered slaves (*Abeng* 40)—record Caribbean history. The "they didn't know" of *Abeng*'s narration of forgotten Caribbean history is replaced here by the more accusatory "did no one notice," a child's response to her discovery of mass murder in the world, in her own parents' lifetime.[20] What is most salient in this account is the insistence that the "change in the atmosphere" caused by the murder of others far away can and ought to be sensed by people everywhere.

In this and many other moments, Cliff's historiography draws a cross-cultural connection between the histories of diaspora Africans and Jews that is uncommon in current black and postcolonial discourse.[21] For Cliff this identification is part of a broadly multicultural, antiracist vision of collective destiny, a commitment to a cross-cultural reading of the world's events. As a character in her recent novel *Free Enterprise* puts it: "There is no 'someone else's fight' . . ." (199). The first of two chapters of *Abeng* on Clare's Anne Frank obsession begins with speculations about Christopher Columbus's Jewishness and moves on to the history of the decimated Native Carib or *Galibi* Indians, and then to the Carib cinema, "the first enclosed cinema in Jamaica," its screen framed by "two elongated Galibi warriors" (67–68), where Clare goes to see the film version of *The Diary of Anne Frank*. One obscured history of mass murder is layered over another, with the heroine emerging as detective. The Anne Frank section represents an early attempt by the Clare of *Abeng* to read history by the method she develops, finally, at the end of *No Telephone*. Positioned at the novel's midpoint, these two chapters fuse the themes of cross-cultural solidarity and of self-education through the signs left by the past.

AT SCHOOL THEY TEACH Clare something about tracing relationships in history:

The suffering of the Jews was similar, one teacher went on to say, to the primitive religiosity of the Africans, which had brought Black people into slavery. . . . That is, both types of people were flawed in irreversible ways. . . . She went on to stress . . . the duty of white Christians as the "ordained" protectors of other peoples. And the class of Black, Brown, Asian, Jewish, Arab, and white girls listened in silence. (71)

But as Clare reads and re-reads Anne's diary, the strength of her feeling for the Jewish girl forces her, for the first time, to develop her own, personal relationship to the history of others' suffering. She sneaks into the adult area at the library and reads everything she can find on the mass murder of the Jews of Europe. Cliff presents this as the turning-point in her education:

> This twelve-year-old Christian mulatto girl, up to this point walking through her life according to what she had been told—not knowing very much about herself or her past—for example, that her great-great-grandfather had once set fire to a hundred Africans; that her grandmother Miss Mattie was once a cane-cutter with a cloth bag of salt in her skirt pocket—this child became compelled by the life and death of Anne Frank. She was reaching, without knowing it, for an explanation of her own life. (71–72)

Though her parents discourage what they find an unseemly interest in the subject, Clare persists, for by inquiring about Jews she hopes to decode the workings of racial difference in her world. Her father vehemently resists the connections she wants to draw, insisting that "[a] Jew is a Jew" even if "only half-Jewish," but that Clare, despite her "colored" mother, is "white," like himself. When Clare looks at her body and considers "how she could be white with a colored mother, brown legs, and ashy knees" (73), she has begun to suspect a world of deception. Similarly, the bodily connection she makes with Anne, "a small-seeming dark girl," moves Clare to defy propriety and cling to her book:

> often when reading the diary she would shut the book, her forefinger marking the place, to stare at the face of the writer of the diary and wonder about her and what if she had lived, had survived, and why did they kill her? (68)

With Anne's book in her hands, Clare feels she holds a piece of truth that has survived the adult world's denials: "Anne most certainly had been here. She had left behind evidence of her life" (69). A book that tells the story of a dark girl's life and death can become mighty evidence in the hands of another dark girl, beginning to take her life into her own hands—evidence, potentially, of the validity of her own experience. Yet it is Clare's attachment to Anne's "dark" face, in plain view on the book cover to which she turns while reading, that profoundly mediates this identification. Clare carries the book around with her like a talisman, a sign of the life of a dark girl who wrote to declare that she had lived, before history killed her.

Later in *No Telephone*, Clare carries in her wallet the newspaper photo of one of the young African-American girls killed in the bombing of a Birmingham, Alabama, church in 1963; it is "the picture she needed to see. A girl in a coffin, open" (101). Both instances demonstrate the kind of close, emotional attachment to certain of the world's signs—particularly those marking a place where a dark girl once lived—that comes to characterize the adult Clare's historical method. Sharing with Toni Morrison the fascination with the image of a "dead girl" (and specifically a black girl in a coffin),[22] Cliff puts the image to a more overtly political, less mythifying usage. Her insistence on the "open" display of dead, dark female bodies centers the new historical method upon the recuperation of bodily signs left by dark women.

Moreover, Clare's mind-and-body involvement in another girl's text as an aid to her own search gives us a model for reading, one that resonates in our reading of the story of Clare and Jamaica. After seeing the film, Clare buys herself a diary and begins to write in it, starting with her feelings about Anne and *her* diary—a connection that suggests a future use for the text of her own life. Cliff has remarked that the "Birmingham bombing" "was a huge event in my life" ("Interview" 602); the Anne Frank section, too, is "almost sheer autobiography" ("Art" 68). As a child Cliff was fascinated by Anne and, through her, with the Holocaust; like Clare, she first began to keep a diary after seeing *The Diary of Anne Frank*. "She gave me permission to write," Cliff has said (68). *The Diary of a Young Girl* as text *en abyme* affirms the power of narrative to raise what Clare later calls "recognition" in the female reader, and thus to inspire self-examination and transformation.

Indeed, Cliff's reading of Anne Frank recalls the young Jean Rhys's reading of *Jane Eyre*, for both instances of recognition lead the authors to produce revisionary texts that foreground the imaginative power of women's cross-race identification and that valorize multiple female readings. The "horizontal" impulse in these novels works to establish new imaginative alliances, situating the problematics of a girl's history and identity in a global nexus.

THE NARRATIVE OF THE Anne Frank obsession makes much of Clare's interest in Anne's relationship to her rather distant mother. Clare's longing for her own distant mother and maternal heritage, Cliff suggests, fuels her fascination with the problem of why some women acted in solidarity in the death camps and others did not, and how this affected survival. When she asks herself, "Would Anne have lived to see liberation if her mother had been different?" (*Abeng* 79), the profound connection in Clare's mind between her oppression and her loss of relationship to her mother is apparent, as is her sense that her own liberation might depend on as-yet-unexperienced possibilities of female community.

These possibilities are most poignantly evoked in the section on Clare's curiosity about menstruation, which crystallizes her longing for something beyond the diminished maternal inheritance she receives from Kitty. Taught nothing about her maturing body and given only a brief, graphic description of menstruation from her friend Zoe, Clare develops her own most private feeling about it from a surprising source:

> She had a sense of it as something which would allow no turning back—a "milestone," she called it. But she had a sense of it as a sweetness—a truly private piece of life—like the inscription in Greek on an award she had won at school: "Your possession forever." She had read about menstruation in the

Diary of a Young Girl, because Anne Frank had written about it, in a secretive, unto-herself way; as though it was something she had achieved.

Kitty referred to menstruation as her "friend"—which seemed to Clare, once she had broken her mother's code, a beautiful thing to call it. (106)

In this poignant connection, the text of another girl's life comes as close as a text can to meeting the body of the reader herself. This blood "friendship," the transhistorical, cross-cultural imaginative attempt of a "colonized" girl to overcome the failure of maternal communication in her life through the words left by a murdered girl of another culture, makes a female bodily connection that both inscribes and transcends our century's catastrophic history and gestures, through the wreckage, toward the possibility of sympathy, of communicating the achievement of selfhood.

The degree to which Clare's need for a friend is caused by the colonization of her mother—and of the Jamaican mother-island—is suggested by a curious play on names: "Kitty—the name of Clare's mother . . . was the name that Anne Frank had given her diary":

As if in that attic hiding-place she was writing to a friend. One in whom she had complete trust—she wrote that. Clare did not tell her mother anything which was close to her. She avoided any subject which she thought would make her mother uncomfortable. . . . So she could not take the name Kitty for her diary—she did not know what to call it. (80)

Cliff makes a complicated choice in giving to her heroine's mother the actual name of Anne Frank's diary; Clare's consequently unnameable diary becomes an emblem of her interlaced, unfulfilled adolescent desires—the desire for friendship and for the mother, to share the self and to write. What emerges most profoundly is that Clare's relationship with Anne Frank and her diary, like her relationship with the dead Alabama girl and with her dark-skinned friend Zoe, *substitutes* for the relationship she might have had with her mother.[23] Indeed, when Clare's father confiscates her photo of the dead black girl, saying, "You are too much like your mother for your own good," he refers to the mother and daughter's shared antiracism. But Clare thinks, "It did not matter that the picture was gone—it was in her mind. Connecting her with her absent mother" (*No Telephone* 102). Cliff's heroine makes the vital discovery that imaginative solidarity with other girls can restore a symbolic connection to the lost mother. When news of the civil rights movement comes on the television, Boy Savage tries to distract Clare with talk, "not realizing his daughter could hold two things in her mind at once" (103); we see her emerging from imprisonment in a "colonized" mind into a mode in which she can conceive metaphoric sisterhood under the sign of the mother. It is thus a *maternal* vision of interracial solidarity that Clare's story affirms; bodily identification with other women is doing the unburied mother's work. Clare's revolutionary quest brings her, in place of the lost maternal body, comrades and sisters who share their intimate stories: Anne

Frank, Zoe, Harry/Harriet, the interviewer. The sharing of stories, not by narrative pastiche but through dialogue among diverse characters who identify with one another, becomes an enterprise of revolutionary promise.

New Endings for the Daughter's Story

The ending of a bildungsroman requires the heroine's arrival at some plateau of selfhood where her relationship with knowledge and authority are clear to the reader. Thus, the relationship between narrator and heroine, at issue throughout these readings of *Abeng* and *No Telephone*, is of particular interest at the close of both texts. Both endings diverge remarkably from the conventions for novelistic heroines' fates and present accommodations on the part of the narrator that allow Clare Savage an unorthodox but liberating development.

The end of *Abeng* confronts Clare with tragic female literary fate in the person of Mrs. Winifred Stevens, a crazy white woman out of colonial central casting, whose affair with a black man leads directly to her social downfall and mental collapse. This sort of fate actively threatens Clare,[24] who in an important passage in *No Telephone* identifies with Brontë's Bertha:

> No, she could not be Jane. . . . No, my girl, try Bertha. Wild-maned Bertha. . . . Yes, Bertha was closer the mark. Captive. Ragout. Mixture. Confused. Jamaican. Caliban. Carib. Cannibal. Cimarron. All Bertha. All Clare. (116)

Bertha Mason is, after all, Clare's acknowledged "ancestor," and it is because Clare is "caught in rebellion" that she is sent to live with mad Mrs. Stevens's sister (*Abeng* 150). Like Clare, this madwoman started off as a girl who "surrounded herself with books," who was "too ambitious," "a woman who wouldn't be a woman" (159). A warning of what not to become, Mrs. Stevens is also an alternate model of a woman who rebels, speaks her mind, and will not let her sexuality be policed. She teaches Clare sane, important lessons, relating stark facts about Jamaica's slave history and warning, "don't let them cross you up" (162). She evidently makes a great impression on Clare, because, as Edmondson puts it, "Clare's final destination is not England and a descent into madness, but Jamaica and conscious resistance, though she, like Bertha, dies in the act of resisting" (185).

Despite Clare's differences from mad Bertha, the ending of *Abeng* clearly brings Cliff's heroine into contact with *Wide Sargasso Sea*, much as Rhys's Antoinette/Bertha in her ending enters *Jane Eyre*. Cliff flirts with the fate of the mad white colonial woman, then thrusts her heroine into a final, defining encounter with a black female double, in a dream-sequence that explicitly revises Rhys's famous fight scene between Antoinette and Tia. The plot of Zoe—like the plots of Tia and Christophine for Antoinette—represents for Clare a desired alternative to the entrapping, proper "white" plot. Clare's version of this plot adds overtly lesbian desire, but apart from this difference Zoe's position in her psyche is remarkably like that of Tia for Antoinette.

When Clare dreams that "she picked up a stone and hit Zoe underneath the eye and a trickle of blood ran down her friend's face" (165), she reverses the terms of the *Wide Sargasso Sea* scene, the white girl hurting the black girl (see Edmondson 183). But if Cliff rewrites her precursor "to acknowledge the white woman's relation to power" (Edmondson 183), she also gives the lighter woman a dream-chance to apologize, and heal:

> And she went over to Zoe and told her she was sorry—making a compress of moss drenched in water to soothe the cut. Then squeezing an aloe leaf to close the wound. (165)

True, "Clare must first understand and acknowledge this unequal power dynamic" before she can complete her quest for wholeness in her homeland (Edmondson 183), but this dream of assault, apology, and healing marks the first step on her way. It is as if the encounter with the frighteningly honest madwoman allows the dream of Clare's racially relational identity to rise to the surface and reveal her future mission: to identify the race conflict within her and to work to heal it.

At the end of *Abeng*, however, the narrator is still not ready, as it were, to let the heroine know either her past or her future; she says of Clare, "She was not ready to understand her dream. She had no idea that everyone we dream about we are" (166). But if Clare does not understand her dream, her body does: the blood on Zoe's face becomes, when Clare awakens in the morning, her own blood, her first menses. Clare indeed seems, as Anne Frank intimated, to have "achieved" this "milestone." Her narrator allows her to arrive at the end not at knowledge but at blood, yet blood, evidently, is one of nature's readable signs, the kind that Clare will later learn to interpret. It is a communication from her body, a sign that she contains her own story. A female bildungsroman that ends with menstruation rather than a romance or marriage (or even a less conventional triumph in art) suggests that the telos of this woman's life will be her developing communication with her own body, her contact with the maternal heritage she bears within.[25] This will be the source, we expect, of Clare's awakening to a collective vision, a vision of who "we are."

No Telephone, like *Abeng*, ends with blood. From the moment in *Abeng* when Clare picks up a gun to shoot a wild pig, her self-image as "a daughter who could kill" (115) makes her a girl in search of her fight, in danger of death, and unlikely to become a mother. Like many rebellious heroines of recent African-American and Caribbean women's literature, Clare considers but does not pursue motherhood, repeatedly rejecting this relationship to the future. When Paul is murdered the morning after she has sex with him, Clare "[does] not think of his sperm congregating in her, so that his line might not have ended," but instead, once she gets her period, is glad to be free of him (*No Telephone* 89).[26] When she considers adopting a light-skinned Jamaican orphan girl, so as to "save" her from a colonized upbringing, Clare's motives are scrutinized by a voice that says, "Sharp, very fresh, my girl, but not completely true. Does she think a child will complete her? Make her whole?"; "Had she a child would she be on this truck? On her way to restoration?" (92–93). Vulnerable to conventional feminine myths that her narrator will not let her escape, Clare can yet "call up one fact" only from Jamaican history in a moment of self-examination: "the adamantine refusal of the slave-women to reproduce" (93). She aligns herself, ultimately, with the radical female tradition of refusal to bear children, the tradition of Nanny the warrior, Mma Alli the healer and abortionist, and many others for whom mothering and revolution were mutually exclusive.

After a miscarriage, a "raging infection in her womb" renders Clare sterile (169), so that "in the end she was removed from decision." The narrative voice worries the implications: "Another reprieve from womanhood? Answered prayers?" (157). But Cliff's account of the "women's troubles" that Clare first senses on her shipboard return to Jamaica makes it apparent that her inability to bear children, though not actively chosen, symbolizes her assumption of her heritage:

> She had arrived in Kingston with a high fever, in pain, entering the city on the sea as her ancestors had once done. Some concealed below. Some pacing above, bonnets protecting their finely complected faces from the brutal sun. (168)

The disease of her womb seems the internalization of this brutal, polarized history, her refusal to bear more of it. Though Clare is sometimes "flooded" with sorrowful "thoughts of missed motherhood" (170, 191), she also thinks with irony of the generations-long effort at "lightening up," dead-ending in her: "All that effort for naught" (169). Her removal from motherhood signals a counter-narrative to the quest for the mother-island, one that resists a literalist identification of women with the island and with nature. At the same time, the impossibility of biological motherhood opens up to Clare—as to Caribbean and African-American heroines including Condé's Tituba, Schwarz-Bart's Télumée, Goodison's Nanny, Walker's Meridian, Gomez's Gilda, and Naylor's Mama Day—the potentially greater role of spiritual mother to her people's unfolding history, laboring for the birth of their new era.

THE GRIM CONSEQUENCE of Clare's embrace of a collective destiny in *No Telephone* is her death in the course of a guerrilla assault. Though the journey through the two novels liberates the heroine, it cannot bring about the overthrow of the powers that control Jamaica. Clare's death utterly contradicts our expectations for the ending of a novel of development (Fiona Barnes 30); Cliff ultimately repudiates the individualism that has been an embattled strand in the two novels. Once again rewriting Rhys, she restages the heroine's fiery death in a more explicitly revolutionary context, sacrificing Clare to her people's cause. The fact that the rebels die attacking not a military or government site but the set of a British-American film shoot reminds us that what has been at stake in the Clare Savage novels all along is a contest over the representation of Jamaica, in which cause Clare's struggle for her own story plays a small, heroic part. Though the anticolonial raid is defeated, it brings a certain degree of closure to the plot of maternal return. For it is the Jamaican great mother Nanny whom the moviemakers are defaming in their shoddy "historical" film and whose honor the rebels give their lives to defend. Ironically, history repeats itself when the army moves in to kill the rebels, betrayed like Nanny by some "quashee" (208).

But Clare in her ending finally returns to her motherland in the most intimate way possible. Shot down where she crouches in a bitterbush, she is, Cliff writes in an essay, "burned into the landscape" ("Caliban's" 45) (a line that recalls *Abeng*'s account of the Holocaust). She is buried in the mother-island from whence she came in the first novel's opening. The structure of *Bildung* is finally sacrificed, then, for the structure of ritual that is common in Caribbean novels (Benítez-Rojo 221) and that ends here in a completed burial. In what seems a fructifying return to the motherland, another martyr contributes her body to the island's green beauty.

In her final moments, Clare, her name, and her consciousness virtually disappear from the text, going under cover of the group and its collective fate at the end. Her death is announced in the most impersonal form, signified by a typographical gap: "Shots found the bitterbush. . . . She remembered language. Then   it was gone" (208). With Clare dead the narration gives over entirely to a strange and beautiful performance of bird sounds. At first, presumably while Clare lies dying, we detect phrases with intimate and historical meaning for the dying woman:

> Kitty-woo, kitty-woo, kitty-woo
> Whip-whip-whip-whip-whip-whip-whip-whip-whip-
> whip

But when she dies out of language, "when the cries of birds are no longer translated by her into signifiers of human history" (Cliff, "Caliban's" 46), entirely impersonal, inhuman sounds take over:

> cutacoo, cutacoo, cutacoo
> coo, cu, cu, coo
> coo, cu, cu, coo
> piju, piju, piju
> cuk, cuk, cuk, cuk
> . . . . (208)

Has a novel ever ended like this before? It is as if having killed off the heroine, Cliff leaves a tape recorder on the scene to complete the end of the story—of the rest of the world. One might read in nature's eruption into voice here the kind of subversive, anticolonial noisiness that Brathwaite and Glissant have identified in Creole expressivity. At the same time, when the heroine dies out of the text and into nature, the Caribbean vision of the natural world as archive of human history expands into the novel's consummate truth; dying, Clare enters her natural history, a history that is both sublime and firmly rooted to a place, an apotheosis of place in time.[27]

One line of human language returns, however, at the end: "Day broke." This return of narration with the sun is surprising, for it had seemed narration died when the heroine stopped remembering language, leaving us listening to the world without human consciousness. If the narration imprisons Clare in *Abeng* and moves toward power-sharing with her from that novel's ending over the course of *No Telephone*—the penultimate section of dialogue overthrowing narration entirely—at the end it seems to release her from the text, allowing her to make her choice and to die without authorial intrusion. But it appears, finally, that human language survives. The "mind" that declares that "the island rose and sank" at the beginning of the first Clare Savage novel returns at the close of the second to affirm that her story continues in the continuously narratable natural history of Jamaica.[28] Perhaps the narrator of these two novels is a second developing heroine: she first teaches in an imperialistic manner, then begins to share knowledge and power with Clare, then bows out to allow her her own relationship with her history, respectfully narrates her choice, retreats at her death as if in silent homage, and finally returns to rescue narrative from oblivion, not claiming to have mastered the truth of Clare's story, but taking it up, as it were, as the heroine's inheritor.

No Telephone thus gestures, beyond the impossible daughterly project to reclaim the mother-island and her history, to the future of language itself, signaling "the unharnessed possibilities of discourse" that "remain embedded in the landscape, future potential to reclaim representation" (Edmondson 190), future potential to communicate one's story to others. Cliff sacrifices the daughter who embodies her history, even erases that body, never allowing us to glimpse it once Clare dies into her motherland. Yet like many another "dead girl" in contemporary women's revisionary fictions, from Beloved to Anne Frank, Clare leaves behind not only the "evidence" of her life story but also a newly charged and generative arena of language.

7 Crossing Water

Maryse Condé's *I, Tituba* and the Horizontal Plot

Les gens disent que les esprits n'enjambent pas l'eau.

Maryse Condé, La Vie Scélérate

Because ghosts—so they say—do not cross water, the unhappy spirit of Great-Uncle Bert, who commits suicide in France in Maryse Condé's *Tree of Life* (*La Vie Scélérate*, 1987), must spend eternity an ocean away from his family back in Guadeloupe. Likewise, Tituba and Hester, seventeenth-century friends in Condé's *I, Tituba, Black Witch of Salem* (*Moi, Tituba, Sorcière . . . Noire de Salem*, 1986), must endure separate afterlives because Tituba dies in her beloved Barbados, and Hester in Puritan New England.

The territorial fixity of the dead in the Caribbean maxim makes emotional sense; every ghost haunts his or her own land. Yet Condé's plots consistently take her characters far from their homelands, creating unlikely attachments that must then be broken and unlikely separations that must be suffered eternally. Both Bert and Tituba leave their native islands on paths cut across the sea long before by European colonists: Bert goes to France, like so many twentieth-century Caribbean students, to be educated in the metropole; three centuries earlier, Tituba is sold from Barbadian into U.S. slavery. The difference made by place on the spirit in Condé's fiction is mediated by the dislocations and the place-specific histories of enslavement, colonization, and exile. Embedded in the folk-saying that ghosts do not cross water is a traumatic history of crossings, most importantly the Middle Passage from Africa to the Americas, the departure that left a "wound" in the collective Caribbean memory. While story, song, and speech obsessively record this passage, in a certain, final sense, the culture knows, the "spirit" did not make the crossing with the people who came. Condé's fiction, like so much Caribbean literature, retraces the historic passages of the diaspora, recrossing the waters in the attempt to master and purge historical trauma. In the process, Condé's writing registers the impossibility of full recuperation, scattering spirits around the world, from whence they call out to one another.

In its global span, Condé's work exemplifies the tendency of contemporary Caribbean, postcolonial, and African-American women's historical fictions to sustain a vital "horizontal" plot. Finding the way back to the mother, writers retell the history of the self to include the histories of others, and notions of "ethnic history" are recast as the genre of contemporary women's historical fictions accumulates an interethnic texture. Indeed, in the increasingly global consciousness of recent women's literature—and contemporary culture in general—the simplicity of a 1970s-era roots quest has given way to a "creolized" vision of history, to adapt Glissant, prophet of the increasingly "creolized" world (3). For Homi Bhabha, the "more transnational and translational sense of the hybridity of imagined communities" in our moment means that we must "think beyond narratives of originary and initial subjectivities" and attend to the "'in-between' spaces" where new cultural identities are being formed (5, 1).

In this context, the infatuation of Cliff's Clare Savage with the face of Anne Frank and the desire of Rhys's Antoinette/Bertha for her friend Tia typify rather than contradict the "ethnic" character of the historical consciousness shaping late twentieth-century women's writing: both feminist and "multicultural," it stresses not merely identification across differences, but self-discovery *by virtue of* an encounter with a different woman. And the mediation of the body in these girls' cross-ethnic identifications signals the radically new figuration of history that is the hallmark of this fictional mode. For in the new women's historical fictions, the female body becomes not only the symbolic archive of one people's past, but also a medium of contact with other women, across time and culture.

As the course of this study has taken us from African-American to Caribbean women's historical visions, we have witnessed a stronger and stronger presence of the "horizontal" imagination. The Caribbean world view tends, of course, to be global, international, intercultural, "horizontal"—in a way that the view from the United States rarely is—due to histories of crossings, of creolized cultures and languages, and of existence in small, unpowerful, necessarily outward-looking colonies of European nations. But as North Americans learn to become readers of a globalized literature, we encounter histories of a world we have not known before and find our own histories recast from others' point of view. Indeed, all "histories," wherever in the world they are produced, now find their place in new imaginative geographies as they are read by the emerging global audience.

Anglophone Caribbean literature is still foreign to U.S. English studies, and francophone literature all the more foreign, in the original or in translation. To respond to that foreignness we may project an absolute otherness, an incommensurability that precludes cross-cultural reading, or we may stretch a paradigm to accommodate all sorts of differences in the name of women's literature, or New World women's literature, or the like. Both the insistence on difference and the integrationist categorizations have heuristic merit. But between them, contemporary world literature is making experiments that leave familiar categories behind. In this moment of complex and rapid global change, in which international political realignments, economic changes, communications advances, and mass migrations put peoples and nations into unprecedented configurations, literature, too, generates new cross-currents of response, influence, and alliance. If the close of the twentieth century witnessed the eruption of hitherto untold histories of particular peoples and places, it also witnessed countless simultaneous redrawings of the map of the world.

The work of Maryse Condé has been in this regard an exemplar, gracefully eluding standard literary categories, highlighting intercultural encounter wherever it goes, remaining disconcertingly foreign to a U.S. reader and reflecting foreignness back onto this country, only to astonish us with an intimate, knowing, sometimes furious engagement with our social, political, and literary culture. A complicated history brought Condé to write a daughter's return to her Caribbean inheritance in *I, Tituba* and her novel of the following year, *Tree of Life*.[1] The "diaspora literacy"[2] she has been said to exemplify is a product of her life's journeys, from a bourgeois Guadeloupean upbringing, to education and radicalization in Paris, to a long residence in Africa, followed by a return—physical and literary—to Guadeloupe in 1986, complicated by part-time residence in the United States and an exile's critique of Caribbean culture and politics.[3]

Condé's itinerary is not, of course, a great deal more meandering than that of many Caribbean writers who, Benítez-Rojo asserts, "tend to roam the entire world in search of the centers of their Caribbeanness" (25). As I noted in Chapter 4, Caribbean writers are a heterogeneous group not only in racial, cultural, linguistic, and national terms, but also in place of residence. The fact that Condé, alone among the writers I treat, writes in a language other than English presents a special kind of difference, with the potential difficulties always attendant on the reading of a translation. Yet I have chosen to include Condé's *I, Tituba* because it presents one of the strongest, most interesting articulations of the maternal allegory now common to Caribbean women's historical fictions and, despite (or even because of) the linguistic and cultural differences, makes fascinating comparison with the novels of Rhys, Cliff, Kincaid, and other Anglophone writers. Moreover, Condé's novel itself has much to say about traversing languages, cultures, and nations, in the central plot of Tituba's journeys between the Caribbean and the United States and in her key relationships with Americans; and it comes to our shores in a translation by the author's own English husband.

Of all the writers discussed in this book, Condé is, ironically, the least distant to me, the only one I have met personally. The complex histories of the New World, of contemporary literary academia, and of her life brought her to Virginia, where I was fortunate to study with and interview her. What I learned from her novel *I, Tituba* is that the histories of the world's peoples have been rediscovered as the intersecting currents they always were. But this time, rewritten by late twentieth-century women intensely engaged in revising their own peoples' histories, crossing the waters becomes a mission not only to recover the lives that the first histories scanted, but also to reimagine the world's women as those who would always have transgressed boundaries for the sake of imaginative sympathy, to honor connections of the spirit. Reading *I, Tituba* and, in the epilogue, another feminist, postcolonial, historical novel, I will examine the ways in which they re-cross the waters that the dead cannot cross, to spin a global "spiderweb of permanence" (Mukherjee, *Holder* 96), a new history of connection among the women of the world.

Irony and Return

> Tituba et moi, avons vécu en étroite intimité pendant un an. C'est au cours de nos interminables conversations qu'elle ma dit ces choses qu'elle n'avait confiées à personne.
>
> epigraph to *Moi, Tituba*

Maryse Condé had been musing on a Parisian publisher's suggestion that she write a novel about a Caribbean heroine when, as a 1985 Fulbright Scholar in Los Angeles, she got lost one day in the UCLA library and found herself staring at shelves of books on the Salem witch trials. In one of these she discovered Tituba, a black woman from Barbados who was brought in slavery to Massachusetts and accused and tried in 1692 along with the other Salem "witches," but who subsequently disappeared from history (Scarboro 198–99). Explaining her decision to write *I, Tituba, Black Witch of Salem*, Condé echoes Jean Rhys, a writer whom she avowedly loves (Interview): "I was attracted to write the particular story of *Tituba* because this woman was unjustly treated by history. I felt the need to give her a reality that was denied to her because of her color and her gender" (Scarboro 204).

Like Rhys in *Wide Sargasso Sea*, Condé attempts to redress historical injustice by writing a life of a woman with whom she feels "a strong solidarity" on the basis of shared gender, race, and Caribbean origin. Reconceiving Tituba as "a sort of female hero, an epic heroine, like the legendary 'Nanny of the maroons'" (Scarboro 199, 201), Condé creates a heroic ancestress for Caribbean women—as per the market-savvy publisher's request—and ancestral support for independence struggles like those Condé vocally advocates in Guadeloupe and Martinique (still Departments of France). Yet the voice of Condé's Tituba, as she narrates her life of suffering and revolt, evinces a persistent irony about her emplotment in a doomed historical enterprise. She opens the last chapter, on the eve of her abortive rebellion:

> Do I have to go on to the end? Hasn't the reader already guessed what is going to happen? So predictable, so easily predictable! And then by telling it, I shall be reliving my suffering over and over again. And must I suffer twice? (166)

Recovered from history's margins to inspire by her tale, Tituba finds the role of heroine and martyr not entirely to her taste. For the sake of the revisionary narrative, her author undertakes to "suffer twice" the horrors of her people's history. Yet, having witnessed over a diasporic life the vagaries and failed promises of several great ideological enterprises—negritude, marxism, African nationalisms—it seems, Condé can't quite do it with a straight face:

> I hesitated between irony and a desire to be serious. The result is that [Tituba] is a sort of mock-epic character. When she was leading the fight of the maroons, it was a parody somehow. (Scarboro 201)

Between the commitment to Caribbean self-determination and the lapse into parody, Condé registers a poignant, skeptical postcoloniality, one that undercuts even as it affirms the project of historical reclamation for the neocolonial "postcolonial" Caribbean. "Do not take *Tituba* too seriously, please," Condé warns an over-earnest American interviewer (Scarboro 212).

Condé's remarks in numerous interviews and essays evince this same paradoxical tendency. While she says to one interviewer, "Guadeloupe is home. For me there is no other place I can call home" (O'Byrne 5), she tells a second, "I never felt like an exiled person" in France or Africa; "maybe I experienced exile when I came back home" (Taleb-Khyar 349–50); to a third, she remarks:

> If there is something that I discovered when I settled in Guadeloupe it is that a writer should never settle anywhere. Looking for one's native land, dreaming about it, doing everything to go back, that is a fantasy, a myth. Once one is there, one realizes that one has only one desire: to leave. I dare say that a writer should be perpetually on the move, going from one place to another, searching, trying to understand and decipher things different and new all the time. . . . I discovered that *root* is a very negative word. It ties you down. (Scarboro 208)

"*Ambivalence*," Marie-Denise Shelton aptly notes, "is a key word when one attempts to understand Condé's writing and vision in general" ("Condé" 721). At times Condé seems to "[adopt] a Naipaulesque posture," as Shelton puts it, "[casting] an estranged gaze on the world she had hoped to repossess," so that her return to the Caribbean becomes "a sort of parody of Césaire's famous Return" (719; see also Wylie 763). At other times she seems simply a committed iconoclast, refusing all totalizing formulae and easy sentimentality (see Shelton 721). In this vein, she has declared that "race does not exist, only culture" (Scarboro 209). Asked what her work shares with that of the venerated Rhys, Condé replies, "nothing, except—it's a kind of cliché—the oppression of women" (Interview).

This insistent demystification of her own most serious subjects, this self-consciousness about cliché even while mythifying her people's traumatic inheritance generates in Condé a conflicted, ironic version of the paradigm of daughterly return, one that foregrounds the contradictions of the Caribbean historiographic enterprise. When she declares that rewriting black history "is not history for the sake of history" but "searching for one's self" (Scarboro 203), Condé suggests that her recreation of an ancestress is an allegory of historiographic desire, like the African-American invention of magic black daughters. But while black American women writers allegorize their arrival at a new height of imaginative power, Condé allegorizes her own more ambivalent stance; conscious of the absurdity of a gesture that yet stems from profound commitment, she parodies heroic myths even as she ventures to redeem ancestral stories in a tragic romance. She cannot forget the clownishness of the Barbadian Tituba, her status as a footnote in U.S. history books, even while creating her as a poignant, fully realized, and indeed heroic fictional foremother.

The postmodern crisis of Condé's colonial heroine erupts as she is led to a Massachusetts jail, "racked by a violent feeling of pain and terror," but not because of the miserable cell that awaits her:

> I felt that I would only be mentioned in passing in these Salem witchcraft trials about which so much would be written later. . . . There would be mention here and there of "a slave originating from the West Indies and probably practicing 'hoodoo.'" There would be no mention of my age or my personality. . . . As early as the end of the seventeenth century, petitions would be circulated, judgments made, rehabilitating the victims, restoring their honor, and returning their property to their descendants. I would never be included! Tituba would be condemned forever! There would never, ever, be a careful, sensitive biography recreating my life and its suffering.
>
> And I was outraged by this future injustice that seemed more cruel than even death itself. (110)

A Tituba portrayed in parodic fury about her exclusion from writing is, finally, the refracted voice of an ambivalent historiographic desire, the desire of the author to conjure and retrieve from an "outraged" heritage a single outraged "biography"—a desire that knows its own absurdity, as it knows its fervent emotional and political authenticity.

Tituba's Mothers

Condé's ironic handling of the recuperative project extends to her treatment of the reservoir of maternal motifs shared by this "history" with the others in this study. In a passage cited in Chapter 4, Condé figures her Caribbean identity in terms of an ongoing, unresolved daughter-mother relationship:

> The Antilles is my natural mother and it is with her that I have accounts to settle, like any daughter with her mother, before becoming completely an adult. (trans. Gikandi 231; original in Jacquey and Hugon 23)

No static island-mother, as in the Caribbean men's figurations discussed earlier, Condé's origin is an argumentative mother-of-history, with whom she debates and negotiates her identity. Skeptical of all easy maternal myths, Condé disavows the plot of "looking for the womb" in women's writing; "I don't like it at all," she says, in the fiction of Michelle Cliff. Indeed, Condé criticizes *No Telephone to Heaven* not only for its "artificial," "cold," "nothing-related-to-the-guts" quality, but also for "the obsession with a black grandmother" as muse and source of identity (Interview). She dismisses a theoretical axiom of the African-American women's renaissance too, when she says that "the question of grandmothers telling stories and thus teaching their granddaughters how to become writers is one of the biggest clichés of black female writing" (Scarboro 211–12); "It seems to me that you become a writer because you are in touch with books" (Taleb-Khyar 349).[4] Accordingly, when asked about the powerfully drawn mother-daughter connections in *I, Tituba*, Condé has explained, "As I am very conversant with black female literature . . . I know that in any female epic, some elements must be present, and I deliberately included them . . ." (Scarboro 212). An upholder of women's literary traditions, then, even if she claims to shun essentialist matrifocal myth, Condé ironizes while she reiterates the allegory of daughterly quest for the lost mother-of-history.

For regardless of the author's avowed skepticism of such conventions, it must be said that *I, Tituba* surpasses almost every text in this study in its preoccupation with mother-daughter relations. Moreover, unlike the more realistically depicted heroines of Rhys and Cliff, Condé's heroine lives in a seamless world of maternal magic, in which "death is merely a passageway and the door always remains open" for communication with maternal spirits (124). Tituba is aided on her life's journey by the spirits of her dead mother, Abena, and of Mama Yaya, the witch who trains her in magic. Condé has remarked, however, that "the presence of the invisible (the conversations with the mother and with Mama Yaya) is deliberately overdrawn" (Scarboro 212); though *I, Tituba* employs magic realism, "there is parody there too, so it's a parody of magical realism" (Interview). Could the same be said for her epigraph?:

> Tituba and I lived for a year on the closest of terms. During our endless conversations she told me things she had confided to nobody else. (v)

Here Condé employs the trope of magical authorship prevalent in African-American, other ethnic American, and postcolonial women's fictions. Though she may seem to describe a supernatural intimacy arising simply from a personal relationship rather than from matrilineal descent, the "endless conversations" of the historical witch with the writer who discovers her in the dusty volumes of history strongly echo the intimate dialogues of Tituba with her mother-spirits.[5] Condé conjures mothers, finally, as interlocutors in an impassioned dialogue about traumatic history, its potential meanings and its burdens for a clear-sighted, skeptical, but staunchly returning daughter of the late twentieth century.

MATERNAL HISTORY begins in *I, Tituba* with the rape of the mother on the slave ship *Christ the King* and the heroine's birth from that act "of aggression. . . . of hatred and contempt" (3). Next the mother is hung, for striking the white master who tries to rape her again. The sentence "They hanged my mother" is repeated three times on one page (8), emphasizing the traumatic severance of the mother-daughter bond, the symbolic origin of historiographic desire in this narrative and so many others.

But in the variable, sometimes impetuous course of this "mock"-tragic romance, the initial trauma leads into an ongoing magical discourse with mother spirits, as well as to an obsessive—not to say parodically obsessive—deployment of maternal imagery to describe the vicissitudes of Tituba's emotional life. Like Clare Savage, Tituba abroad is figured as a motherless daughter, struggling to return to her motherland. But the submerged, psychological mother-quest of Cliff's novels is externalized and animated in Tituba's magical world. Returning to Barbados, "like a child running to hide in her mother's skirts," she feels the welcoming physical embrace of maternal and paternal spirits and hears "a soft murmur": "She is back. She is here, the daughter of Abena, the daughter of Mama Yaya. She will never leave us again" (138, 141–42, 147).

Childbirth imagery inscribes historical trauma and repossession here as throughout the novels in this study. In a Massachusetts prison, Tituba's fear is "like a baby in its mother's womb"; "It turns from left to right, then kicks around" (101–2). Her Barbadian home, by contrast, is a land of fruitful maternity: "The calabash tree was showing swellings like the womb of a pregnant woman. The River Ormond was gurgling like a newborn baby" (79). But on the eve of her doomed Barbadian revolt, the pregnant Tituba lies listening as an ominous storm ravages the maternal world:

> Outside the wind had risen. I could hear it hailing mangoes. I could hear it blow through the calabash tree and rap its fruit. I was afraid. I was cold. I wanted to return to my mother's womb. But at that very instant, my daughter moved as if she were calling for my affection. I laid my hand on my belly and, little by little I was filled with a kind of tranquillity, a kind of lucidity, as if I had resigned myself to the final drama I was about to live. (170–71)

Passages like these, set in a time-arrested maternal space, privilege over historical events a transhistorical "conversation" of mothers and daughters—unborn, alive, and dead, connected by the wordless history that is female bodily generation.

Yet the spirits of Abena and Mama Yaya—victim and matriarch, opposing archetypes of the African foremother—as they work together to advise and cheer the heroine, become a comic duo, appearing and disappearing inopportunely, warning her away from men in anachronistically feminist terms: "Men do not love. They possess. They subjugate" (14), and lamenting their limitations. They cannot prevent her sale into U.S. slavery and cannot visit her in that country, for it "take[s] so long to cross the water" and is "so difficult" that Mama Yaya can come to Tituba only in the form of comforting sighs (30). Upholding the rule—so resonant with history—that ghosts cannot cross water, Condé recasts the North American exile of the historical Tituba as a rupture of the mother-daughter bond. "'Cross the waters, O my fathers, Cross the waters, O my mothers, I'm so alone in this distant land!" (69), calls the heroine to her native spirits, in archetypal diaspora lament.

Making Substitutions

The absence of Tituba's maternal spirits from the United States recalls the absence of Christophine and Tia from the English exile of Rhys's heroine. But Condé's exiled slavewoman has several advantages over the madwoman in the attic. Unlike white Antoinette/Bertha, black Tituba has Caribbean mothers who acknowledge her claim on them. And because Condé, unlike Rhys, does not acquiesce to her heroine's prewritten fate, but invents for her a world of magical possibilities, Tituba's Caribbean mothers can send messages of hope, promising that she will survive to return to her island.[6] Most important, in her lonely exile the plucky Tituba discovers the possibility of relationships with other women. Antoinette/Bertha, we presume, is too far gone to note the potential solidarity Rhys suggests in Grace Poole and the other servants at Thornfield Hall. But Tituba develops an exilic logic of substitution to sustain her, a strategy with notable implications for contemporary women's literature.

Missing the medicinal herbs of her native island, Tituba searches a forest outside Boston:

> What was I going to do in this unknown and inhospitable land across the sea? I decided to make substitutions. A maple tree whose foliage was turning red would do for a silk-cotton tree. Glossy, spiny holly leaves would replace the Guinea grass. Yellow, odorless flowers would do for the *salapertuis*, the panacea for all the body's ills, which only grows in the foothills back home. My prayers did the rest. (45)

Tituba makes another creative substitution when she attempts to assuage her homesickness by placing a bowl of water by a window, "so that I could look at it while I busied myself in the kitchen and imagine my Barbados"; "The bowl of water managed to encompass the entire island, with the swell of the sea merging into the waves of the sugarcane fields . . ." (62). This *mise en abyme*, replicating in miniature the novel's recreation of a lost world (the "Caribbean basin"), figures the work of Condé's own exilic as well as her historiographic imagination. An imperfect substitute, the bowl of water reminds us of the evocative but ultimately insubstantial nature of the work of historiographic fiction.

Tituba's substitutive logic does help her, however, to develop a most important new resource: relationships with North American women. She enters the woods—like Kincaid's Xuela—seeking herbs to induce abortion; once again the refusal of childbearing is symbolically linked to a woman's severance from her maternal past. But as she searches, Tituba finds "to [her] surprise that these climes had a certain grace to them," and bending over "a sweet-smelling bush that strongly resembled the many-virtued lemon grass" she hears her name called by a New England witch, a friend sent by Mama Yaya, who proceeds to teach her the "names and properties" of all the local plants (50–51). In this and many other substitutive encounters with women, Tituba demonstrates, like Clare Savage, that the "horizontal" feminist plot of encounter with other women can function—like linguistic substitution for the lost mother's body—as a "substitute" for the lost mother-of-history and the lost motherland. That is, women writers engaged in an impossible literary "substitution" for a lost history "substitute" for return to the mother new relationships with other women, across the boundaries of race, class, and nation. Thus their historical visions inscribe the cross-cultural intertextuality of contemporary literature; postcolonial reading and writing are not merely "vertical" (as in Rhys's rereading of Brontë), but "horizontal" (as Rhys suggests in the community at Thornfield Hall): that is, cross-culturally affiliative.

In *I, Tituba* the horizontal plot of black and white women's affiliation begins on the first page. Tituba's uprooted, violated mother is immediately paired with a white woman, her master's sick wife, "a creature as gentle and desperate as herself," who "hated this brute she had been forced to marry." Mistress and slavewoman "became friends": "They slept together, and while she played with the long plaits of her mistress's hair, my mother would tell her the stories that her mother had told her" (3–4). This startlingly affectionate (and substitutively matrifocal) revision of the mistress-slavewoman relationships in African-American literature finds its opposite in Tituba's contact with her own mistress, the hideous Susanna Endicott, who sells the heroine and her husband into U.S. slavery, and whom Tituba curses with a fatal illness. But again, as soon as Tituba steps on board her new master's ship, she finds a companion in her "fear and aversion for Samuel Parris: Elizabeth, his wife." An even sicker white slave mistress—in this Condé follows religiously the African-American convention—Elizabeth has an illness that has baffled "over twenty physicians," but her compassion for Tituba ("How cruel it must be to be separated from your own family") and her admiration ("How lovely you are, Tituba") causes the slavewoman to say, "impulsively, 'Mistress, let me take care of you'" (38–39). When Parris strikes Tituba and then slaps his wife for protesting, "She too bled," Tituba says, and "this blood sealed our alliance" (41). The blood alliance recalls the blood and tears of Antoinette and Tia, of Clare and Zoe, even of Clare and Anne Frank—a catalog of desire for cross-race sisterhood written on the female body. Tituba's alliances with white women in resistance to the master (and by extension, his version of history) are severely tried in the course of the plot, but her desire for cross-cultural relationships—evidently instilled by her mother—never wanes.

Indeed, such relations multiply in Condé's historical vision, as they do in Cliff's. After the trials, Tituba is bought out of jail by a Jewish merchant, becoming housekeeper and nanny to his motherless children and, eventually, his lover. From their first meeting Benjamin's "look" tells Tituba "that he, too, was from the land of the suffering and that in some undefinable way, we were, or we could be, on the same side"; Tituba feels she "couldn't have fallen into better hands" (121, 123). Benjamin and his family are occasionally parodied as "indifferent" to "anything that did not concern the tribulations of Jews the world over" and for his tendency to engage Tituba in bouts of competitive historical suffering, reeling off the dates of anti-Jewish assaults (123, 127). But their growing love leads Tituba to face the stones of an anti-Semitic mob for Benjamin's sake. When the Puritans burn down his house, killing his nine children, Benjamin interprets his loss as God's judgment on him for keeping Tituba enslaved, but by this point he must persuade her to take her freedom and return to Barbados.

Notably, Condé credits an encounter with a Jewish colleague, a female historian who provided her with material on Puritan culture, for the inspiration to give Tituba a Sephardic Jewish lover in colonial Massachusetts (Scarboro 201–2). It was, literally, the meeting of a Caribbean and a Jewish woman in contemporary Los Angeles that enabled an interethnic romance plot in this vision of New World history; the complex, not uncritical "multiculturalism" of Condé's "history" celebrates, in turn, the cross-fertilizing cultural, political, and intellectual possibilities of the present.[7] Appropriately in this novel's cross-ethnic ethos, it is Tituba's experience in the burning house of Jewish history that finally radicalizes her. She thinks to herself, on board ship, approaching Barbados:

> How many more stonings? Holocausts? How much blood had yet to be shed? How much more submission?
>
> I began to imagine another course for life, another meaning, another motive. The fire engulfs the top of the tree. The Rebel has disappeared in a cloud of smoke. He has triumphed over death and his spirit remains. The frightened circle of slaves regains its courage. The spirit remains. (136)

Like Cliff writing the Holocaust into the Caribbean landscape, Condé writes it anachronistically into New World history, as a lesson for an aspiring Caribbean rebel and martyr.

Yet the novel continually rebukes its own enthusiasm for "horizontal" connections, however, by letting most of its cross-ethnic relationships fail, betrayed by initially well-meaning white women who succumb to the racism around them. When at the pitch of the Salem craze Elizabeth Parris accuses Tituba of witchcraft, Tituba recognizes that she and the white woman do not "belong to the same universe . . . and all the affection in the world could not change that" (63). She begins to fear falling "into the trap of making friends" (95), and the novel might seem to deny the possibility of cross-"universe" friendship if it were not for the one bright exception to the pattern. In a scenario not unlike Clare Savage's encounter with the diary of Anne Frank, Tituba finds the best "substitute" for her lost mothers in a "horizontal" encounter with the white heroine of a famous American book. Being thus "in touch with books," like her author, on a global scale, Tituba hails the transforming potential of the "universe" of literary intertextuality.

In Touch with Books

Perhaps Rhys's Antoinette/Bertha is the "ancestor" not only of Cliff's Clare Savage,[8] but also of Condé's Tituba. For *I, Tituba*, like *Wide Sargasso Sea*, achieves its most powerful revisionary effects by breaking and entering an

English (that is, American English) novel. Another fictional recovery of a marginalized, transgressive Caribbean woman, *I, Tituba* explodes several venerated American texts: the cultural texts of the Puritans and the Salem Witch Trials, Arthur Miller's play *The Crucible*, and, most radically, Nathaniel Hawthorne's *The Scarlet Letter*.

Unlike Rhys, Condé does not seem to wonder whether she has the right to rewrite her precursor. Her thoroughly postmodernized, decolonized relationship to literary history lets her play freely with texts and historical facts. Tituba "magically" predicts events of U.S. history such as the rise of the Ku Klux Klan and the squalor of black ghettoes (177–78). Narration gives way to pastiche when Condé inserts into her text an excerpt of the historical Tituba's actual witch trial deposition—the location of which, in the Essex County Courthouse, Salem, Massachusetts, is indicated in a footnote. Following this bizarre, harrowing confession of conspiracy with the devil, Condé's Tituba breaks into the real to assert her own reality but admits only to a failure of pretense: "It went on for hours. I confess I wasn't a good actress . . ." (106). The treatment of the courtroom testimony as performance and the novel's general irreverence toward the texts of official and popular history suggest that, in narrative contexts of inherent power inequity, one may as well make up stories as attempt to argue truth. The court's corruption makes Tituba's actual guilt or innocence immaterial; similarly, in rewriting the history of New World slavery, her author seems concerned simply to create a strong countermyth.[9]

Condé's intertextual liberties culminate when her heroine, kicked out of a cell by her racist sister "witches" and chained in a prison passageway, hears a kind voice saying, "there's room here for two. Let that poor creature come in" (95). The beautiful, pregnant prisoner who invites Tituba to share her cell gives her name only as Hester. An outrageous redrawing of U.S. literature's first great heroine, this Puritan adulteress is a far more radical figure than Hawthorne's Hester Prynne. Condé's Hester is an ardent U.S. feminist (she even uses the word) who hates her society ("It's not my society," she says to Tituba, "Aren't I an outcast like yourself?" [96]) and yearns to write a book ("but alas, women don't write books!") about "a model society governed and run by women" who would raise and name their children without men (101). This Hester refuses to submit to Puritan justice, planning to kill herself and the daughter she is carrying before they can plant an "A" on her breast. Condé's reentry into the (prison)house of English literature is even more subversive than that of Rhys, for she not only intrudes the character of a rebellious Caribbean woman, but she also transforms the celebrated white heroine herself, seeming to tell *her* true story too, the story her first author suppressed. When Condé's black slave finds Hawthorne's heroine in the next cell, she exposes, behind the walls of U.S. literary propriety, the prison life of Hester Prynne, offering a Foucauldian view of the female gulag between the lines of the American canon, not unlike Cliff's exposure of the slavery in the sugar in every English novelistic cup of tea.

Hester is portrayed as Tituba's sister in revolution. Through their unlikely pairing, Carolyn Duffey writes, Condé "artfully stag[es] the politics of this complicated encounter between first and third-world feminisms" as "an interesting and complex dialogue," rather than a stark or "reductive" "dichotomy" (101).[10] When Hester tends to Tituba's sores, she reverses the interracial women's relations depicted earlier, and when she remarks, "what a magnificent color she's got for her skin and what a wonderful way she has of covering up her feelings!" she displays an ability, found in no other white character, to "see" Tituba inside as well as out. Indeed, with hair "black as a crow's wing" and eyes "black like the benevolent shadow of night" (95), Hester is drawn as much like the black heroine as possible. Their complete solidarity seems to be prevented chiefly by Tituba's milder criticism of men, by which Condé signifies a French Caribbean/black "womanist" distance from white U.S. feminism: "You're too fond of love, Tituba!" says Hester; "I'll never make a feminist out of you!" And Tituba later confirms the charge: "I myself have loved men too much and shall continue to do so" (101, 178).[11]

THE TWO WOMEN'S PLOTS converge profoundly, however, in mutual refusal of motherhood. Tituba and Hester both "kill" children, as Tituba puts it (98), she by abortion and Hester, in a most striking revision of Hawthorne, by killing herself while pregnant. Condé thus rewrites *The Scarlet Letter*—the urtext of U.S. male literary representation of women-in-history—around the signature contemporary female trope for traumatic history: severed mother-child relationships. Scanting the original novel's trauma of sexual trespass, she appropriates *The Scarlet Letter* as a "history" not of tormented American conscience but of the oppression and containment of an American mother.

As for Condé's depiction of the slave mother, it anticipates that of Morrison's *Beloved* (published the following year):

> There is no happiness in motherhood for a slave. It is little more than the expulsion of an innocent baby, who will have no chance to change its fate, into a world of slavery and abjection. Throughout my childhood I had seen slaves kill their babies by sticking a long thorn into the still viscous-like egg of their heads, by cutting the umbilical cord with a poison blade, or else by abandoning them at night in a place frequented by angry spirits. . . . I had heard slaves exchange formulas for potions, baths, and injections that sterilize the womb forever and turn it into a tomb lined with a scarlet shroud. (50)

Like Sethe, Tituba kills her child to protect it from life: "I shall never bring children into this dark and gloomy world" (92). But if it is a text "compelled to repeat the absence and denial of maternity" under slavery (Dukats 747), *I, Tituba* also attempts to revise women's relationships to this traumatic history, and to historical process in general.

Throughout this study I have argued that the varied forms of mother-child separation in contemporary women's texts operate as a system of tropes for "bad history" and for daughterly imaginative return to such inherited pasts. But the meeting of Condé's two characters in a "cell" of intertextual "historical" space to confess mutual infanticide suggests, further, that what *Beloved* has brought to consciousness is a profound, mythic, transgressive female will to imaginative mastery of motherhood, and thus of the power to make meaning in history. Violating the patriarchal script by raising their hands against children, these historical heroines defiantly claim the power to unmake the life they have the power to make, to refuse entrapment in a biological-historical-literary "destiny" and ensure that they enter the historical chain not through domesticated maternity, but by their own articulate agency. One might even ask, could Morrison's Sethe have become a historical heroine had she not picked up the saw? Through such transgressive plots, women writers of the era of accessible birth control reimagine for the mothers-of-history the power to refuse maternity, and so to declare autonomous, imaginative presence.

Condé's Hester wishes, after all, to be a writer. Is it any wonder that, along with refusing to be written upon, she refuses to carry out her prewritten fate? Killing herself rather than be sentenced to wear the "A" or bear the child, this Hester rejects Hawthorne's claim to know what her story means. Preventing her baby from being born as the fairy child Pearl, Hester seems to refuse a legacy of redeeming romance, preferring to make a tragic meaning. Of the child she will not bear, she tells Tituba, "She must simply die with me. I have already prepared her for that when we talk to each other at night" (98). In the face of this tragedy, the novel again invokes a transhistorical maternal dialogue. Hester's conversation with Tituba continues:

> "You know, she's listening to us right now. She's just knocked on the door of my womb to get my attention. You know what she wants? She wants you to tell her a story. A story about your country. Make her happy, Tituba."
>
> Resting my head against this soft curve of flesh, this hummock of life, so that the little one inside could be near my lips, I started to tell a tale and the familiar words of that ever-present, beloved ritual lit up the sadness of our confinement. (98)

Nearly kissing the other woman's womb, Tituba as she tells her story to the other's unborn daughter conjures maternal space, just as she does when called by her own unborn daughter. For her as for Cliff's Clare, physical intimacy and the sharing of life stories with another woman symbolically restores the mother. This prison encounter becomes in memory the heart of the novel, a transhistorical imaginative space not unlike Morrison's 124, where women—mothers and daughters—speak the "unspeakable" to one another across the boundaries of life and death.

It is no surprise then, that when Tituba later learns that Hester has hanged herself, she returns from the substitute to the original source:

> I screamed down the door of my mother's womb. My fist broke her bag of waters in rage and despair. I choked and suffocated in this black liquid. I wanted to drown myself. . . .
>
> Mother, will our torture never end? If this is how things are, I shall never

> emerge into the light of day. I shall remain crouched in your waters, deaf, dumb, and blind, clinging like kelp to your womb. I shall cling so tightly you'll never expel me and I shall return to dust without you, without ever having known the curse of day. Mother, help me! (111)

In Condé's lavish prose, the topos of mother-child separation oscillates from killings of babies to cries for mothers, until the novel's climate resembles the tempestuousness of *Beloved.*

But, unlike Sethe, Tituba continues to regret the loss of her child, so that motherhood weaves itself as an unclosed question through her story. "I had trouble getting over the murder of my child," Tituba says; "the image of that little face whose actual features I would never know haunted me." Though she feels the abortion is "for the best," she cries when the fetus is "carried out of [her] womb in a flow of black blood" and she sees him "wave his arms like a tadpole in distress" (52). Toward the ending she wonders whether this child "would not after all have given my existence a meaning and a purpose." "Hester," she asks her long-dead friend, "did we make a mistake and shouldn't you have lived for your child instead of dying with her?" (152). The symbolic resonance of these sacrificed children deepens when Tituba twice sings a "Lament for my lost child," for her own child and for Hester's:

> The moonstone dropped into the water,
> Into the waters of the river,
> And my fingers couldn't reach it,
> Woe is me!
> The moonstone has fallen.
> Sitting on a rock on the riverbank
> I wept and I lamented.
> Oh, softly shining stone,
> Glimmering at the bottom of the water. . . . (55)

This lyric eruption of maternal desire recalls *Beloved*'s monologue-fugue section, the two interpolations creating similar effects of emotional authenticity—in contrast to the interpolated transcript of the historical Tituba's deposition, which, ironically, strikes a false, alien note in the narrative.

For in these fictions, maternal feeling is stronger than death and truer than recorded history. Moreover, a mother's loss of or reunion with a child arrests time, crystallizing historical trauma and historiographic recovery in a space of maternal desire that conventional historical narratives do not know. Through Tituba's recurrent lamentation for the lost babies, Condé makes absent children the silent present core of her matrifocal history. Though Hester refuses to let her child signify, unborn Pearl—never named—continues as a ghostly presence in our intertextual memory, a notably lost potential, reminding us of the abortive secrets of women's history.

AS FOR THE potential represented by Hester herself, Condé renders the relationship begun in the women's jail even more potent after her suicide. For

Hester magically lives on as another of Tituba's visiting spirits, comforting the heroine along with her Caribbean familiars, but with a difference:

> That night Hester lay down beside me, as she did sometimes. I laid my head on the quiet water lily of her cheek and held her tight. Surprisingly, a feeling of pleasure slowly flooded over me. Can you feel pleasure from hugging a body similar to your own? For me, pleasure had always been in the shape of another body whose hollows fitted my curves and whose swellings nestled in the tender flatlands of my flesh. Was Hester showing me another kind of bodily pleasure? (122)

If the Hester episode as a whole pays (not uncritical) tribute to the influence of U.S. feminism and U.S. women's writing, this moment of homoerotic pleasure offers a startling suggestion of intimacy, both literal and metaphorical, between Caribbean and U.S. feminists. That it occurs only after Hester has shed her living body somewhat tempers the moment's subversiveness; had Condé made the bolder narrative choice of lesbian sex right there in the Salem jail cell, she might have identified U.S. feminists more overtly with lesbianism, or figured Caribbean feminists as "in bed with" them politically. But this "spiritual" sex offers a dramatic figure for enduring closeness across the divide that inevitably separates the two groups. For Tituba and Hester overcome not only distance, race, and heterosexual norms, but death as well (although only the sexual part surprises Tituba!). Their multiply transgressive rendezvous becomes, arguably, a transhistorical "lesbian space" to match the monologues of *Beloved* and, like those passages in Morrison, invites our "destabilizing" lesbian readings (Wilton 135–36, 133).[12]

Late in the novel, Tituba confirms the New England woman's abiding place in her life. Joyfully returning at last to Barbados and to her solitary forest cabin, Tituba brings a chapter to its close with this simple, unanticipated line, "One day I discovered an orchid among the mossy roots of a fern and I named it Hester" (157). Performed after Tituba's return to her motherland, this reverse "substitution" is moving beyond expectations. Calling the native plant after the remembered North American friend (and modifying a formula of Caribbean folklore[13]), this implied gesture toward whiteness as beauty—and its faint recollection of lost Pearl?—reaffirms the heroine's bond with the woman across the waters. These "other" encounters along the way back to the mother matter, we discover here, and are not merely substitutes after all, but something new and valuable in the world.

Daughters and Songs

The magic that sets Tituba's world apart from that of our other Caribbean heroines allows Condé to seal her character's legacy in an extended afterlife. Like Clare Savage, Tituba returns home from abroad a revolutionary, only to be defeated by the regime and then incorporated, in death, into her mother-island. But Tituba's eternal life literalizes Clare's physical fusion with the Caribbean landscape. In a postmortem epilogue she says of her island:

> We have become one and the same. There isn't one of its footpaths I haven't trod. There isn't one of its streams I haven't bathed in. . . . This constant and extraordinary symbiosis is my revenge for my long solitude in the deserts of America. (177)

Tituba's afterlife also literalizes Clare's potential as martyr, for the ex-slave becomes a revolutionary spirit, "hardening men's hearts to fight," "nourishing them with dreams of liberty." "I have been behind every revolt," she says; "every insurrection. Every act of disobedience" (175).

In this radical spirit life Tituba's "one regret" is "having to be separated from Hester" while the two pursue parallel paths, "each . . . on her side of the ocean." When Tituba reports that the immortal Hester is "pursuing her dreams of creating a world of women that will be more just and humane" (178), we assume she does so as the resident muse of U.S. feminism, inspiring heirs to her work. Having refused biological motherhood, both women become adoptive or spiritual mothers to history. Tituba recapitulates Hester's ending when, having become pregnant again, she leads a failed maroon revolt and is hanged. She thus carries—like Hester and like Beloved too—an extra measure of unrealized potential, as a forever-pregnant spirit. Her pregnancy had actually helped inspire her revolt, when she promised herself that "if the world were going to receive my child, then it would have to change!" (159). But when she continues to speak of "my unborn daughter" in her postmortem existence (176), the child she carries seems, together with Hester's unborn daughter, to await an opportunity for a messianic birth—perhaps at the moment of a "renaissance" among their mothers' heirs.

Alone among the Caribbean heroines, however, Tituba is granted a spiritual daughter within the fictional present of the novel, making her ancestral influence more vivid:

> Since I died without giving birth to a child, the spirits have allowed me to choose a descendant. I took a long time making up my mind. I spied into every cabin. I looked at the washerwomen breast-feeding. . . . and finally I found her, the one I needed: Samantha. (176)

Tituba chooses a model revisionary daughter, "with inquisitive eyes and a determined mouth," who asks questions like "why are we slaves and they masters . . . ?", who "[understands] that she [has] been singled out for a special destiny," and who, Tituba reports, "follows me fervently" (177). Selecting such an heir, Tituba celebrates the revision of motherhood we have seen in so many contemporary "historical" heroines: "A child I didn't give birth to but whom I chose! What motherhood could be nobler!" And in her lessons to this chosen daughter, about "the hidden power of herbs and the language of animals. . . . the invisible shapes in the world, the crisscross of communications, and the signs and the symbols" (177), Tituba seems to honor both local "powers" and the "crisscross" of "horizontal" exchange, endorsing for her spiritual heirs Condé's own expansive vision of Caribbean relations with the world.

A STRONG CONSONANCE in the novels of Rhys, Cliff, and Condé studied here is their ending in the heroine's (imminent) death. All three Caribbean daughters go down as martyrs, carrying a torch, as it were, for others to pick up. Yet only Tituba's story explicitly stages its own legacy. In her post-execution epilogue Tituba says, "My real story starts where this one leaves off and it has no end" (175); the real story is Tituba's potential for recovery as Caribbean foremother. Her ongoing presence takes the form of a "song about Tituba":

> I hear it from one end of the island to the other. . . . It runs along the ridge of the hills. It is poised on the tip of the heliconia. The other day I heard a boy four or five years old humming it. . . . Yesterday it was a woman beating her wash on the rocks of the river. (175)

Tituba's afterlife as a popular tune, preserved by oral tradition in the "hearts" and "heads" of a people who "have no need for the written word" (176), is remarkably like and unlike the haunting "loneliness that roams" of Morrison's coda to *Beloved*, which also manifests itself fleetingly, to those who happen to sense her touch as they sleep, or step into her footprint, or glimpse her in a family photograph (274–75). But that lost child is "not a story to pass on"; Morrison's African-American community encounters her spirit only to repress and forget it, whereas Condé's Caribbean islanders do indeed "pass on" their militant mother-spirit to keep their own spirits up. Sometimes Tituba rewards those who sing her song with gifts of their island and their past, tumbling ripe mangoes at the little boy's feet, showing the washerwoman the lovely reflection of her lost youth. Sometimes she "keep[s] a slave from the edge of despair by whispering" a promise of the full inheritance so long denied Caribbean people: "Look at the splendor of our island. Soon it will all be ours. Fields of nettles and sugarcane. Furrows of yams and patches of cassava. All of it!" (178).

In vivid contrast to Morrison's negative delineation of Beloved's legacy in her final lines—describing sounds not of human longing but of ice thawing, wind, "just weather"—Condé's last lines declare the ways that the Caribbean daughter can be certain of Tituba:

> . . . this child of mine has learned to recognize my presence in the twitching of an animal's coat, the crackling of a fire between four stones, the rainbow-hued babbling of the river, and the sound of the wind as it whistles through the great trees on the hills. (179)

Tituba encourages the reading of her active, noisy, twitching, crackling, babbling, and whistling presence, indeed, of her maternal voice, in Caribbean nature, while Beloved, lost to history, is said to be "not" in nature's sounds, unreadable there, recoverable only by a daughter's will to name her absence.

It is striking, then, that while Condé consistently ironizes the myth of return to the Caribbean mother's *body*, she never ironizes the power of the maternal *voice* to inspire revisionary daughters; the Mother, it seems, is less viable for Condé as a destination of return than as a trace in the language, an inspiring undersong, urging action and creation. Indeed, if "the song of Tituba" is a fair sample of the mother-island's voice, perhaps we learn here that Sycorax pronounces her "true-true name" in the form of a call to future daughters. Ending the novel by charging a daughter to assist her suffering people,[14] Condé, like African-American women writers such as Dash, Naylor, and Marshall, and like all of the Caribbean women writers of tragic histories in this study, culminates her "history" by invoking the liberatory potential of daughters to come.

In contrast to the Caribbean heroines, none of the American magic black daughters dies—except the always-already dead Beloved. Comparing the tragic Caribbean endings to the dominant romance pattern of African-American women's historical fictions (Morrison's elegiac *Beloved*, as ever, the complication to the rule), we can confirm that the plot of the magic black daughter's reunion with her mother—this allegory of a generation's powerfully realized historiographic desire—is an African-American paradigm. As such, it not only derives from black cultural politics of the post–civil rights movement era, but also appends itself to a distinctively African-American myth of historical destiny. The Caribbean women's renaissance texts studied here, however, cannot sustain a romance vision of return to maternal history. Neither for Rhys, writing before the boom, nor for Cliff in the emergent radicalism of the Clare Savage novels, nor for Condé in *I, Tituba* is it possible to celebrate the recuperative powers of a revisionary daughter. For that daughter is less an allegory of an ascendant generation than an allegory of her nation or of the Caribbean region,[15] the histories of which remain acutely unresolved. In fidelity to the unfinished work of Caribbean self-definition, nation-building, and healing, these revisionary daughters die back ritually into the maternal arms of their ongoing, still-to-be-redeemed history.

One might even argue that the magic daughter paradigm becomes available to Caribbean women writers to the degree that they engage imaginatively with the United States. Thus Condé's Tituba, discovered in a Los Angeles library as a heroine lost to U.S., as well as Caribbean, history, is reclaimed in a more triumphalist mode. She survives the Puritan persecution, after all, dying only when she goes home and attempts revolution in Barbados; she is a U.S. feminist heroine and a Caribbean revolutionary martyr. The boldest character in the book is Hester, whose vision of women's community and writing registers the confidence of contemporary U.S. feminism.

Similarly, an interest in a U.S. heroine has given rise, for the first time, to a magical aesthetic in the work of Michelle Cliff. Her third novel, *Free Enterprise* (1993), recreates the historical figure Mary Ellen Pleasant, a free, wealthy, nineteenth-century African-American woman who secretly financed John Brown's raid. "MEP" becomes an allegorical figure for the revisionary imagination; she exists in a time-stopped, historicized present in which "everything is here, and now" (154); she is at once mother and daughter, capable of waving to her childhood self from the deck of a ship, and encountering a hologrammatical apparition of Malcolm X. The novel's dreamy, magical reality recalls recent historical fictions by Morrison, Dash, Walker, and others, and in this narrative mode, I would argue, Cliff pays tribute to the historical imagination of contemporary African-American women. Indeed, when MEP adopts as spiritual "heir" the expatriate Jamaican mulatto Annie, who struggles like many Caribbean heroines between a sense of "placelessness" and the "fantasy" of "returning to the place of her origin" (19), this mother-daughter relationship inscribes the Caribbean author's own "daughterly" imaginative relations with Morrison and other African-American novelists.[16]

If *Free Enterprise* contributes to the sense that the contemporary Caribbean idiom of encounter with history is less suggestive of mastery than is the African-American, it also confirms that the Caribbean vision is—to some degree substitutively, I think—more water-crossing, more relational. For it must be said that these thematics of crossing not only rehearse traumatic geographic dislocations, but also take the place of rewriting a profoundly dislocated, unrecollectable, unbearable history. That is, in their strongly spatial, geographic imaginations, and in their "unhomely" postcolonial perspectives (Bhabha 9), Caribbean writers cross water as a "substitute" for crossing time.

In these Caribbean women's "histories" there is less interest, finally, in recovering a lost past than in imagining new ways of inhabiting the world, in mastering "placelessness" and living Caribbeanness as imaginative citizenship in "a cultural meta-archipelago without center and without limits" (Benítez-Rojo 4). As Hal Wylie observes, the continual entrance of Condé's oeuvre into new territories of interrelation, her "transcendental cosmopolitanism" (763),[17] suggests a tireless inquiry into the possibility of meaningful connections—such as the relationship of a Caribbean woman to Africa in *Heremakhonon*, of francophone to anglophone Africa in *Segu*, of Caribbean people to the United States in *I, Tituba* and *The Last Magi*. If these attempts often fail, still they suggest a desire "to become a 'universal' or world writer," perhaps by "groping beyond identity . . . [towards] universal meaning" (Wylie 764, 768) and even—though perhaps Condé would wince—toward a postcolonial humanism.[18]

As Caribbean people work to repossess their homelands, the fiction of Rhys, Cliff, and Condé suggests that it is the world at large that is to be possessed, the world that is at once the matrix of New World identity and the newly reopened territory of imaginative connection, the "crisscross" thoroughfare for fictional encounters, for creative rereading, and for contact with new audiences across the waters.

Epilogue

History, Horizontality, and the Postcolonial Hester Prynne: On Condé, Mukherjee, and Morrison

It is wonderfully emblematic of our literary moment and apposite to this study's conclusion that Maryse Condé's reinscription of *The Scarlet Letter*, translated into English in 1992, was followed the next year by another feminist, postcolonial, historical fiction that performs its own distinctive reinscription of Hawthorne's text, Bharati Mukherjee's *The Holder of the World* (1993). These two novels, by a Guadeloupean and an Indian-American woman writer, overlap like two antique, contradictory maps—or like the two circles of a Venn diagram—to embrace the story of Hester Prynne. I turn, in closing, to the puzzling recurrence of Hester in two contemporary women's texts in order to suggest a further extension of this study's "horizontal plot": the connection between African-American and Caribbean women's revisionary historical fictions and those of women writers of other ethnic and national groups.

Comparing Condé's and Mukherjee's imaginative returns to Salem, I follow a model implicit in many of the works studied here. The invitation Rhys's *Wide Sargasso Sea* makes to further revisions, parallel stories, "other sides"—to an expanded, cross-cultural female conversation—is made in Condé's novel too, Angela Davis suggests in her foreword to *I, Tituba*. Though Davis expresses "profound gratitude to Maryse Condé for having pursued and developed her vision of Tituba, Caribbean woman of African descent," she adds:

> Should a Native American Tituba be recreated, in scholarly or fictional terms, this would be true to the spirit of Condé's Tituba and her revenge. For, in the final analysis, Tituba's revenge consists in reminding us that the doors to our suppressed cultural histories are still ajar. . . . And sometimes there is magic behind those doors, sparkling clues about the possibilities ahead. (xi)

In following Hester out the door of Condé's historical novel and into another, I risk a detour from the historical, racialized site that has been this book's main focus—African-American and Caribbean slavery—but do so for the sake of three goals I hope are "true to the spirit" of Tituba's revenge. First, I mean to delineate the field of global contemporary women's literature as a viable subject of inquiry and as a plane of crisscrossing influence, a relevant, "worldly" context for reading the work of writers usually positioned only within African-American or Caribbean tradition. Second, in pairing these two new Hesters, I want to highlight the fact that a distinctively feminist, cross-cultural vision shapes the "counter-discursive" literary revisions performed by diverse women's "histories." And third, I hope to illuminate the ways that the United States, its literature and its history—key preoccupations of *I, Tituba* and most of the texts in this study—are being repositioned on women writers' newly emerging imaginative maps of the world.

First of the modern postcolonial nations yet the reigning neocolonial superpower, generator of popular cultural myths for all of the world's children, the United States has recently begun to replace Europe as the looming metropolitan presence in Caribbean literature, particularly in Anglophone texts. Caribbean writers have criticized the United States as a nation of obscene wealth and power and as the source of an alien and dominating culture. Its racism is widely held to be worse than that of the Caribbean; when Cliff's Kitty Savage immigrates from Jamaica to the United States only to encounter a sign that reads, "A MAN WAS LYNCHED YESTERDAY," she simply mutters, "Hello, America" (*No Telephone* 54).

For Condé's Barbadian slave, exiled in this country "so hard on the weak, on the dreamers, and on those who do not judge men by their wealth" (170), our saintly Puritans are "monsters" and our Christianity diabolical; she asks in puzzlement, "Perhaps it's because they [white Americans] have done so much harm to their fellow beings, to some because their skin is black, to others because their skin is red, that they have such a strong feeling of being damned?" (68, 47). In the final line of her mortal story, as Tituba is led to the gallows, last of the rebels to be hanged, she notes, "all around me strange trees were bristling with strange fruit" (172). Ending Tituba's life story with the words seared into the popular memory by Billie Holiday's voice, Condé closes her Caribbean "history" with a stinging jab at U.S. racism.[1]

But if it is the land that bears strange fruit, this home of ours also has become the world's home; for legions of Caribbean and other peoples of the former European colonies, the United States has become a new exile of choice. Not the "mother" of their educations but the "uncle" of the foreseeable future, the United States is a place to work and prosper and to "make substitutions" for an unlivable homeland. Caribbean writers residing in the United States have now gained a "place of importance" in Caribbean literature (Davies "Writing Home," 59) and in African-American literature as well. America has become re-conquerable territory, a nexus of postcolonial literature for visitors and new citizens who uncover its historical connections to their own stories and native places: for Maryse Condé, who castigates the United States in the voice of its foremother heroine; for Bharati Mukherjee, who reinvents a worldly prehistory for that foremother, and for her character Venn, an Indian-born computer scientist (whose name inspired my "diagram" metaphor—and perhaps vice-versa for Mukherjee),[2] whose computer "magic" in an MIT lab reanimates a historical link between America and India that encircles, eventually, the life of Hester Prynne.

How do we understand the place of the United States, of U.S. literature, of a character like Hester Prynne, in Caribbean and other postcolonial women's "histories"? What is the allure of America's Hester—standing unbowed with her letter "A," chastened, stalwart first foremother of U.S. fictional heroines—to women writers of the contemporary world? Have they rediscovered her as the first feminist in literature, first female transgressor, first openly sexual heroine? Surely not, for writers whose cultural roots reach into the ancient oral literatures of Africa and India, replete with primally powerful women, not to mention the literatures of England and France, crowded with dissatisfied, aspiring heroines. No, Hester Prynne is simply the first protesting woman in the comparatively infant literature of the United States, but this apparently makes her central to the newly globalized literary universe.

For what has "centrality" come to mean, in the postmodern world? If "the center" continues to dominate and exploit in ways obvious and insidious, from overt hegemony to quasi-appreciative theft, it also becomes the site of multiple recastings, rejections, parodies, inversions—from within and without—texts that may re-enshrine as they condemn, but that alter the face of power by palimpsestic remappings. Revising colonial narratives of their own familial pasts, writers from the margins of Empire seem increasingly interested in negotiating a relationship to the United States's cultural narrative of its historical emergence. At the same time, as Bhabha argues, "the Western metropole must confront its postcolonial history, told by its influx of postwar migrants and refugees, as an indigenous or native narrative *internal to its national identity*" (6). Indeed, in novels like Condé's *I, Tituba*, Cliff's *Free Enterprise*, and Mukherjee's *The Holder of the World*—and, let us add, Morrison's *Beloved*—we are witnessing a phenomenon that the demographics of world migration alone might have predicted: the postcolonization of the American novel.

The Holder of the World

In Bharati Mukherjee's earlier fiction, the contemporary United States is a stage on which postcolonial migrants collide, acquiring American "ethnicity" in tragicomic dramas of seduction and transformation. Her ambitious—if somewhat uneven—1993 historical novel *The Holder of the World* emplots this "horizontal" notion of identity across two centuries. *The Holder of the World* offers an Indian-American parallel to contemporary African-American and

Caribbean women's "histories," in which a daughter's imaginative (and physical) return to her maternal history generates a cross-ethnic axis; it can thus suggest links between women's fictions of New World history and a larger world of contemporary women's historical visions.

Mukherjee's novel takes the contemporary white American heroine Beigh Masters on a quest for her mysterious ancestress Hannah Easton (11), called the "Salem Bibi," who crossed the waters from seventeenth-century Massachusetts to India and back, strewing her traces across the globe. The search for this foremother whose incongruously blond image appears on a series of Mughal Indian miniatures—in one of which she holds aloft an enormous diamond—creates a postmodern double-temporal detection plot reminiscent of A. S. Byatt's *Possession*. Mukherjee presents a wealth of historical debris (books, letters, ship's logs, artworks) through which the twentieth-century heroine must sort in her quest for the story of the historical heroine and her diamond. But Beigh also seeks help from the virtual reality machine created by her Indian-American boyfriend Venn, which promises complete "time-retrieval" (35), cyberspace contact with all the "information" there ever was.[3] Virtual history, we might call this, a gleefully artificial simulation of the past.

Of all the time-transcending techniques employed by returning daughters in the new women's historical fictions—resurrection from death, visitations by spirits of an unborn child or dead mother, vampiric immortality, reincarnation, science fiction time-travel, anachronistic narrative knowledge, dream reality, hologrammatical apparitions, time-stopped visions—Mukherjee's virtual time-retrieval is the only maternal return dependent on technology (and, perhaps not coincidentally, on a boyfriend's help) and is the most interethnic at its core. Inspired by cyberspace versions of reality, Mukherjee's mother-quest becomes an antifoundationalist plot to deconstruct origins. It returns not to one people's past but to the scene of first colonial contact and reveals the sort of meetings between peoples that history and literature have conspired to suppress; on both temporal levels the plot sends white American women into the arms of Indian lovers. *The Holder of the World* takes pleasure above all in "slaloming between *us* and *them*, imagining *our* wonder and *their* dread," asking "What must these worlds have thought, colliding with each other?" (12–13).[4]

Some of the cultural scenarios constructed by Mukherjee's world-crossing fiction are, as Gita Rajan has observed, "predictable" and "stereotyp[ical]" (304). And surely Rajan is right that the novel's exuberant traversals of time and space miss certain imaginative opportunities offered by recent feminist, postcolonial, and postmodern thought, such as the chance to take subjectivity "into surreal, unimagined spaces," producing a "pleasurably insurgent" text rather than one that sometimes reinforces imperial modes of narration, characterization, and spatial ordering (305, 295–97). But this critique misses what I find to be the text's most pleasurable and imaginatively "insurgent" element. For far from being "peopled by women without fellowship," as Rajan has it (305), the novel presents as its key "horizontal plot" the privileged plot we have repeatedly found at the heart of contemporary women's historical fictions: the cross-ethnic relationship of two women.

Hannah's friendship with her Hindu servant Bhagmati begins with a request that echoes the sharing of stories in novels from Cliff and Condé to Morrison and Walker: "Talk to me, please," Hannah says (171). Thus begins a potent comradeship that carries the two women, through a series of improbable and violent events, from the English to the Hindu to the Muslim worlds of India. Plot twists so intensely fuse the identities of these figures—switching their names, clothes, roles, fates, and even bodies—that "horizontal" female identification becomes the great secret, the buried treasure, of the "vertical" quest for maternal origins. When the two women sue for an end to intergroup warfare at the court of the mighty Emperor Aurangzeb—"Holder of the World" and owner of the world's most magnificent diamond—they are imprisoned, but not before the emperor pays tribute to Hannah's bravery by renaming her "Precious-as-Pearl," whereupon Hannah renames Bhagmati "Hester" to honor a girlhood friend.

The plot of Hannah/Pearl and Bhagmati/Hester—having generated the intertextual echo of a daughter-mother relationship—climaxes in an interethnic female bodily connection more daring than any we have seen. Determined to learn the end of her ancestress Hannah's story, Beigh Masters hooks herself up to the virtual reality machine and, a daughterly cyborg, propels herself into the past. "Virtually" inserted into an escape from the emperor in the midst of battle, Beigh finds herself inside a surprising body:

> "Hannah!" I scream against the cannons and flying bullets. I can barely breathe from the sulfur clouds, my eyes burn, and I reach out to hold her, my hand closes on her shoulder and she turns, my hand is brown, with a tinkling gold bangle. (281)

The white American daughter reenters history not in the body of her ancestress Hannah, but in the brown Indian body of Bhagmati; the revelation is not the other woman's face but "my hand," which reaches toward it.

This vision of maternal history as the womb not of ethnic but of cross-ethnic identity is sealed in one further moment. "Virtually" running through a firefight in the body of Bhagmati/Hester, Beigh Masters feels Hannah's "warm hand" pass into her own "a heavy warm glasslike object"—the emperor's diamond, stolen symbol of tyranny's hold on the world. Suddenly she is fatally struck and, on an inspiration, takes out her knife:

> I plunge the knife deep in my belly, watch with satisfaction, and now with the mastery of my pain, the blood bubble from my beautiful brown flesh. More, I think, and plunge the knife deeper. . . . and make a burrow inside me. I feel the organs, feel the flesh, the bowels of history, and with my dying breath I plunge the diamond into the deepest part of me. (283)

Dying there and forever holding in her womb the jewel of the world-holder, Bhagmati/Hester becomes the holder of the world. So does Beigh Masters, who, upon a safe return to the present, knows the whereabouts of the diamond, in Bhagmati's Indian grave (under her adopted English name). And so, most poignantly, does the author, whose name notably resembles that of the character holding the gem, and who seems through the prism of multiple crossings finally to have contacted the history of herself, of her own brown hand, as it reaches to touch the other woman's white hand.

We might say that Bhagmati/Hester follows Condé's Tituba and Hester, dying "pregnant" with a precious gem: the secret, untold in the violent records of nations but often told in the fictions studied here, of the potential of women's cross-cultural camaraderie, and in contemporary terms, of the cross-cultural narrative as a powerful matrix of female identity. As Beigh later puts it, having briefly fused with that "pregnant" historical body, "sometimes I feel in my gut that I really am incubating an enormous diamond" (283).

Recasting the "A"

What *The Holder of the World* contributes to contemporary women's literature of history, finally, is its celebration of the promise of a "crisscrossed" heritage. When the blond bibi returns to Salem, Massachusetts, with a "black-haired and black-eyed" daughter (284)—sired by a Hindu Rajah—to live peacefully on the outskirts of town, doing wildly ornate embroidery, readers realize that her fabulous story was an elaborately invented prehistory of a heroine we know well.[5] Revealing in the end that Hannah was the true Hester Prynne ("Who can blame Nathaniel Hawthorne for shying away from the real story of the brave Salem mother and her illegitimate daughter?" [284]), Mukherjee rewrites Hawthorne's heroine as one who crossed a line not moral but cultural, a traveler "to the uttermost shores" (286). Like Condé and Rhys, she performs postcolonial canonical revision in an affiliative mode, identifying comrades and common struggles while recontextualizing *The Scarlet Letter* in a critical vision of the politics of Empire. Whereas Condé reimagines Hester Prynne as the first American feminist rebel and a friend to New World black revolutionary struggles, Mukherjee reimagines her as an American lover of the East, and a woman whose willingness to traverse the lines of race and nation points toward a creative, culturally hybrid American future. As for her remarkable daughter, called "Black Pearl" by the "town gossips," Mukherjee rewrites her as the child not of sinful adultery but of redeeming race mixture (284).[6]

Yet throughout her world travels, Mukherjee's heroine longs intensely to return to—who else?—her mother. For every historical heroine, we have seen, must have a mother, and must seek to redeem her mother's story. In this thoroughly "horizontal" history, the mother to whom Hannah returns is the first American female boundary-crosser of them all: a Massachusetts Bay Colony woman who also took an "Indian lover," running away with a local Nipmuc while the town of Brookfield mourned her "captivity." In Mukherjee's "history," dependent finally on the pun on "Indian" that derives, like so much of New World history, from Christopher Columbus's mistake, the mother of the first American literary heroine was the primordial New World barrier-crosser, the progenitor of interracial American literature, the mother of us all.[7] Her daughter Hester Prynne, in Mukherjee's refiguration, wears a scarlet badge not of shame but of worldliness, "the first letter of an alphabet of hope and of horror stretching out, and back to the uttermost shores" (286).

WEARING HER SCARLET "A," Hester Prynne can stand at the beginning of any alphabet a contemporary rewriter should care to elaborate, but she will always stand for a female mind unconquered by that which is written upon it. To revisit Hester's story is of course newly to "write . . . a life," in Rhys's phrase, for a heroine whose power seems imprisoned in writing, and who seems to wear her letter in full consciousness of its inadequacy to represent her. That Condé and Mukherjee rewrite Hester Prynne "horizontally," as an ally of their own peoples' antiracist and anticolonial struggles, despite the privileged white American status that might have made her an unwelcome presence in their "histories," suggests the distinctive willingness to see the self in the other that has driven the "horizontal plot" throughout this study. But more particularly, Condé and Mukherjee seem to find in Hester a special potential that mediates their cross-ethnic identification: that of a suppressed foremother *writer*, a reclaimed feminist precursor, Shakespeare's American sister discovered perversely *under* a letter! Both rewritten Hesters are aspiring authors: Condé's dreams of writing books about women; Mukherjee's leaves a memoir, letters, and some extraordinary narrative needlework. As the U.S. heroine these two postcolonial women's "histories" choose to rewrite, Hester Prynne thus becomes the bold foremother of unwriting and rewriting, a figure who embodies a feminist revisionary potential internal to the superpower's own alphabet, a potential that could be released, somehow, only by the advent of third-world women to U.S. imaginative territory. Like Rhys's Antoinette/Bertha, these revised Hester Prynnes make the canon seem always to have contained the germ of its postcolonial revisions. Yet the recreation of Hawthorne's New World Eve carries suggestions that the revision of Bertha Rochester does not. Renewing a figure who was herself conceived in a desire for newness—Hawthorne's reimagination of the Puritan encounter with the American wilderness—Condé and Mukherjee seek to revive and to extend a spirit they still discern within the bloated corpus of the superpower: the revolutionary, anticolonial spirit of America's youth.

The new figurations of Hester Prynne suggest, then, the paradoxical place the United States can be made to hold on the new literary maps of the world: despite its hegemonic position, America is still the home of the will to refuse old histories. Hester Prynne, in her capacity to embody both this revisionary spirit and that of U.S. feminism, is reinvented as a foremother of the radically new historical visions of the world's women. Assigning new values to her letter "A," these writers claim her endorsement of a women's alphabet for a global literature.

Revisiting Salem on their overlapping historical itineraries, Condé and Mukherjee share a healthy sense of irony about the project of redeeming history. Alternately elaborating and undercutting the romance of return to maternal origins, they yet join in affirming the "horizontal" plot, the plot of the other woman's name and hand. Their "histories" articulate this cross-ethnic ethos in female bodily dramas of contact, communication, imitation, and exchange. In the process, their dislocated, water-crossing heroines come to know, as does Cliff's Clare Savage, that they carry history with them in their own breathing bodies. In this sense, the Caribbean and postcolonial daughter-figures in this study embody their authors' revisions of history, just as the African-American magic daughters, returning to "the join" with a history that newly wears the black mother's "face," revise American literature and history from within, themselves embodying its regeneration.

Indeed, Condé and Mukherjee can help us to identify in Morrison's Sethe an African-American rewriting of Hester Prynne that we should have noticed earlier: like Hester, Sethe is stigmatized and emblematically "written" on for another collective American crime: slavery (prior to the crime she commits individually). Imprisoned before the moment of the narrative with her infant daughter, Morrison's independent heroine later lives alone at the town's edge, shunned by the community for unspeakable reasons; at her side always is the uncanny daughter whose presence perpetuates memory of her crime—and who occasionally models her mother's extravagant needlework. Earlier I read Morrison's murderous mother as the sign of the daughter-writer's charged relationship to her traumatic inheritance. To say that Sethe is also an oblique revision of Hawthorne's Hester Prynne is to suggest that Morrison not only reclaims an ethnic past and rewrites her own ethnic literary foremothers, the authors of slave narratives, but also crisscrosses to revise the mainstream U.S. canon. Claiming her place as America's revisionary daughter as well, she intrudes into Hawthorne's New World Eden the unacknowledged sin of its enslavement of her foremothers.

Unlike Condé or Mukherjee, Morrison does not play at encountering the character of Hester Prynne or make explicit intertextual reference to *The Scarlet Letter*. For while their "histories" can spar lightly with elements of the U.S. master narrative in the process of recovering a connection to the story of another homeland, Morrison's must challenge that narrative directly on her own home territory. Rather than reanimate Hester, Morrison appropriates her pariah's position, replacing her with an African-American foremother who withstands ostracism both moral and racial. Rather than have her ex-slave write or envision alternate historical texts, as do Condé's and Mukherjee's writing Hesters, Morrison gives her heroine the rage of one who knows that her illiteracy serves the master's hegemonic texts. "I made the ink," Sethe continues to protest long after Schoolteacher defames her humanity in writing (271), insisting on her indispensable role in a literature that—as Morrison was later to argue in *Playing in the Dark*—has repressed its own debt to blackness.[8] A final difference from Condé and Mukherjee is that while these authors' rewritings both retain (in revised form) the scarlet "A," the mark of punishment on the body of Morrison's heroine is thoroughly reappropriated; moved from front to back and transformed from a public badge of shame to a private tree of life, it becomes an intimately readable sign, a bodily promise of African-American continuity and of imaginative generation.

New Ends of History

The eruption of women's historiographic desire in our literary moment, a logical outgrowth of emerging cultural authority, distinguishes itself among the many contemporary versions of historicity in its passionate preoccupation with the figure of a mother-of-history. As we have seen, the romance of the revisionary daughter with this mother has depended on the gradual invention, within the expressive resources of a traumatic inheritance, of an enabling maternal figure: the black American mother who can become the face of history; the Caribbean island-mother who regains her role from the colonists; the mislabeled white American mother who endorses revisionary writing. Yet all of these mothers are reclaimed, finally, in the service of daughters' new self-definitions, their construction of histories for their own sense of possibility.

This era of unprecedented possibility for minority and postcolonial women writers, arising contemporaneously with an upheaval in historic certainties and the new emergence of previously unheard histories, has generated a literature in which the world brims with to-be-discovered historical meanings, still-potent traces and residues of the past, stories that need telling. Thus Mukherjee's Hannah, standing on the Indian coast, "knows that the world that seems so calm and peaceful this Sabbath morning is full of furious meaning, but refuses to reveal itself" (157). Similarly, the coda of Morrison's *Beloved* suggests that the "weather" around us is pregnant with lost meaning, lost souls, who inaudibly "clamor for a kiss" from the living. The African-American and Caribbean women writers in this study, as well as the other writers whose work has entered into this conversation, posit a clamorous ancestral past, calling for daughterly response. When their fictions of history come to their endings and face the future, as narratives of history must, they tend to foreground the responsibility of writing and tradition-bearing daughters (Allende, Butler, Condé, Dash, Gomez, Kincaid, Naylor, Marshall, Morrison, Mukherjee, Perry, Alice Walker, Margaret Walker, Williams) or revolutionary daughters (Rhys, Cliff, Clifton, Condé). Among these writers, perhaps Kincaid and Morrison most starkly remind us that, despite the urgent labors of a daughter who hears the mother's call, the past, finally, cannot be recovered. It has escaped us, and so must we escape it, if we hope to fulfill its best promises.

The most hopeful aspect of these new women's historical fictions, then, is the collective vision of "spiritual" solidarity arising among daughters returning, through trauma's traces, to so many different historical mothers. Condé's tribute to a white orchid named Hester finds its reflection in Mukherjee's clasp with the brown hand of a woman renamed Hester, of the white hand of another Hester, and in the birth of a Black Pearl. The magic black daughters' recovery of the lost black mother's face—with the assistance of a white mother's "good hands"—finds its parallel in Beigh Masters's growing sense, having fused with the body of a dark woman across water and across time, that she is "incubating an enormous diamond." Of such incubations, such flowerings, such pearls, new histories are now aborning.

Notes

INTRODUCTION

1. See for example Hayden White's reconceptualization of "history" in *Metahistory* and elsewhere.

2. In *The Historical Novel*, Georg Lukacs's reading of Walter Scott develops the connection between historical fiction and nationalism (30–63).

3. Michaels offers a cogent corrective to essentialist forms of nationalist myth but goes too far in concluding that "there can be no real urgency to the study of history" (15). Such an abstract view of history ignores the weight of the past's persistence in the lives of particular peoples, its intimate inherence in constructions of identity—in the sense Stuart Hall means when he writes that "identities are the names we give to the different ways we are positioned by, and position ourselves within, the narratives of the past" ("Cultural Identity" 394). Moreover, as Jameson notes, a certain "kind of past" has been "a necessary component for groups of people . . . in the projection of their praxis and the energizing of their collective project" ("Magic Realism" 310).

4. I refer to Lukacs's notion of the historical novel's task: to produce a *"prehistory of the present"* (337). Notably, the rise of black American women to historiographic authority follows the post–civil rights and women's movement "booms" in black and women's literatures and leads the surge in new feminist "historical" texts across the spectrum of ethnic and postcolonial women's literatures.

5. On matrifocal women's fiction see Hirsch; Washington, "I Sign"; see also Mickey Pearlman's *Mother Puzzles: Daughters and Mothers in Contemporary American Literature* and Suzanna Walters's *Lives Together/Worlds Apart: Mothers and Daughters in Popular Culture.*

Recent mother-daughter anthologies include Patricia Bell-Scott's *Double Stitch: Black Women Write about Mothers and Daughters*, Faye Moskowitz's *Her Face in the Mirror: Jewish Women on Mothers and Daughters*, and Elizabeth Brown-Guillory's *Women of Color: Mother-Daughter Relationships in Twentieth-Century Literature.*

6. At the same time, these writers enrich the limited, one-sided "daughterly feminism" Marianne Hirsch criticizes in *The Mother/Daughter Plot* by setting daughterly ambition within a historical economy of mother-daughter desire (165, 11).

7. The rewriting of history in figurations of childbirth can be seen as a special case of women writers' use of the birth metaphor for literary creativity, which Friedman calls "a defiant reunion of what patriarchal culture has kept mutually exclusive," a yoking of "mind and body, creation and procreation" that refuses age-old denials of women's intellectual and artistic power and affirms "a matrix of creativities based on women's double-birthing potential" (380, 377).

8. For this connection I am indebted to Harry Stecopoulos.

9. On the aims and conventions of the historical novel see Fleishman and Lukacs.

10. On international black women's writing see for example Carol Boyce Davies's *Black Women, Writing, and Identity*, which advances a theory of black women's "migratory subjectivity," and her two-volume anthology *Moving beyond Boundaries*; Cheryl Wall (9); and Filomina Steady, *The Black Woman Cross-Culturally*. On African diasporic literature, see Gay Wilentz, *Binding Cultures*; Bonnie Barthold, *Black Time*; Margaret Busby's international anthology *Daughters of Africa*; and Davies. On "New World writing" see for example Kutzinski, "Commentary" and *Against the American Grain*; Glissant; and Cudjoe, *Caribbean Women Writers* (46). On "inter-American" literature see Stelamaris Coser.

11. Coser demonstrates that African-American writers Toni Morrison, Paule Marshall, and Gayl Jones bridge the continents in their "Caribbean" novels. I would add that Michelle Cliff, Maryse Condé, and many other Caribbean women writers bridge the same divide from the opposite shore.

12. Ballantine's paperback imprint "One World," for example, groups texts by African-American and other ethnic American writers with texts from Africa, India, and Asia under one rubric: "multicultural."

CHAPTER 1

1. Morrison explains the "sixty million" as "the best educated guess at the number of black Africans who never even made it into slavery—those who died either as captives in Africa or on slave ships" (Clemons 75).

2. For Margaret Garner's story see Weisenburger's *Modern Medea*; see also Lerner, 60–63, and Harris's *The Black Book*, which reprints an 1856 newspaper account of the incident (10). Morrison first encountered the story when working on *The Black Book* as an editor at Random House.

3. "No written text is a transparent rendering of 'historical reality,'" write Charles T. Davis and Henry Louis Gates, Jr., "be that text composed by master or slave" (xi). Deborah McDowell observes that "what we call the past is merely a function and production of a continuous present and its discourses. We might even argue that it is precisely the present and its discourses, in heterogeneous and messy array, that the [historical] novel confronts." Recent African-American slavery novels, in McDowell's account, "insert themselves, some by explicit design, into the store of warring texts, of conflicting interpretations of chattel slavery" ("Negotiating" 147, 144).

4. McDowell cites an interview with Morrison conducted by Charlayne Hunter-Gault, *McNeil/Lehrer Report*, 29 September 1987.

5. Carby examines Arna Bontemps's *Black Thunder* (1936) and Margaret Walker's *Jubilee* (1966) and mentions Ishmael Reed's *Flight to Canada* (1976), David Bradley's *The Chaneysville Incident* (1981), Sherley Anne Williams's *Dessa Rose* (1986), and Toni Morrison's *Beloved* (1987). To this list we might add Ernest Gaines's *The Autobiography of Miss Jane Pittman* (1971), Gayl Jones's *Corregidora* (1975), Alex Haley's *Roots* (1976), Barbara Chase-Riboud's *Sally Hemings* (1979), Octavia Butler's *Kindred* (1979), Charles Johnson's *Oxherding Tale* (1982) and *Middle Passage* (1990), Jewelle Gomez's *The Gilda Stories* (1991), J. California Cooper's *Family* (1991), and recent novels of Caribbean slavery, including Maryse Condé's *I, Tituba, Black Witch of Salem* (1992), and Caryl Phillips's *Cambridge* (1992).

6. Historian Roger Wilkins has recalled his mother's explanation for her reluctance to speak about the family's slave past: "I guess it is like the old folks used to say: we didn't like to clank our chains" (Charisse Jones A43). On the difficulty of retelling the past for earlier generations of African Americans see Jane Campbell (xiv, 112, 158) and Christian (326–38).

Hazel Carby explains the relative lack of slavery novels on "an ideology of the 'folk' from fictional representations of sharecropping," which has overshadowed slavery in the black historical imagination, so that the two modes of production blur into "one mythical rural folk existence," repressing black urban experience (126–27).

7. These projects and events continue to multiply. For a few examples, see the following news articles on commemorations of the lives of slaves: Eric Brace, "A Painter Enslaved by History: Rod Brown's Harrowing Lessons," *Washington Post*, 13 Dec. 1993, B7; William Raspberry, "Chronicles of the 'Nameless Grandmother,'" *Washington Post*, 12 Aug. 1992, A21; Eugene L. Meyer, "Backyard Roots: A Mile from Her Affluent Md. Neighborhood, Woman Helps Restore Slave Ancestors' Home," *Washington Post*, 29 Oct. 1995, A1, A8–9; Charisse Jones, "Bringing Slavery's Long Shadow to the Light," *New York Times*, 2 Apr. 1995, A1, A43; Michael A. Fletcher, "By Foot and Rail, Historian Traces Slaves' Secret Flight to Freedom," *Washington Post*, 2 June 1996: A3; Richard Harrington, "Marsalis's 'Blood': The Spirit Moves It," *Washington Post*, 7 Feb. 1997; John W. Fountain, "Taking a Long Walk Back from Slavery," *Washington Post*, 14 July 1998, B1, B4.

8. The original slave narrative, Gates argues, "represents the attempts of blacks to *write themselves into being*" (xxiii), though ex-slaves generally could publish only with extensive supporting documentation by whites, testifying to their authorship, literacy, and even existence. Issues of authority and authenticity are also problematic in the case of the WPA slave narrative project of the 1930s, in which the narratives of elderly ex-slaves were produced in interview situations that approached the power relationships of slavery.

9. Particularly important to recent feminist scholarship has been the authentication by Jean Fagin Yellin of Harriet Jacobs's previously discredited narrative *Incidents in the Life of a Slave Girl*. See also Braxton's essay on Jacobs.

10. On those challenges see, for example, Davis and Gates's volume. Walker's extensive research has proved more solid than Haley's, which has been subject to numerous criticisms (and some rather suspect attacks), even including a plagiarism suit by Walker herself.

11. Paul Gilroy puts the matter acutely; writers like Morrison have "begun the vital work of enquiring into terrors that exhaust the resources of language amidst the debris of a catastrophe which prohibits the existence of their art at

the same time as demanding its continuance" (218). Further, the "minority modernism" of such writers "can be defined precisely through its imaginative proximity to forms of terror that surpass understanding . . ." (222).

12. Fictions of historiographic desire thus strongly resemble the "literature of testimony" created by survivors of catastrophe. Shoshana Felman calls this literature "a performative *engagement* between consciousness and history, a struggling act of readjustment between the integrative scope of words and the unintegrated impact of events" (114).

13. Such characters include Pilate, First Corinthians, and Milkman in *Song of Solomon*; Sula, Eva Peace, and the three Deweys in *Sula*; and besides the ghost Beloved herself, Baby Suggs, Sethe, Stamp Paid, and the three Pauls in *Beloved*.

14. A communal chorus can be heard in the grieving women at Chicken Little's funeral in *Sula*, the various female spirits in *Tar Baby*, and the exorcising women in *Beloved*. An imaginative conflation of "I" and "we," self and community, recurs in Morrison's recorded remarks. "When I view the world, perceive it and write about it," she told Claudia Tate, "it's the world of black people" (118). "I write for black women," she said to Sandi Russell; "we are not addressing the men, as some white female writers do" (46). To Tate again, "My audience is always the people in the book I'm writing at the time. I don't think of an extended audience." And in the same interview, "I wrote *Sula* and *The Bluest Eye* because they were the books I wanted to read. No one had written them yet, so I wrote them" (122). For Morrison, evidently, writing activates communion—among readers, other writers, a community, an ancestry, fictional characters, and the self.

15. Felman and Laub write that in "the intimate and total presence of an *other*" who listens, survivors can begin to articulate and thus "re-externalize" and work toward closure of the trauma that until then traps them in repetition (69).

16. "Disremember" is not a neologism, appearing previously in African-American literary dialogue in Margaret Walker's *Jubilee* (36).

17. Chambers argues that narrative is always a transaction based on "an initial *contract*, an understanding between the participants in the exchange as to the purposes served by the narrative function, its 'point'" (8). The "point" of a given narrative is suggested internally by "specific indications of the narrative situation appropriate to it," such as an inset seduction of a listener, an exchange with the power to "change relationships" (4, 9).

18. Sethe's is a maternalized version of the escape narrative not only in that she gives birth on the run, but also in that her reasons for escape are entirely maternal. She never talks about freedom; rather, she decides to run when she realizes that Schoolteacher plans to sell her children and, after sending the children North, is determined to flee, too, so as to carry her nursing milk to her baby girl.

19. Standing in for the reader as belated receiver of the story of slavery, Denver is sometimes alienated and annoyed: "How come everybody run off from Sweet Home can't stop talking about it?" (13), and often tormented by a story-inheritor's mixed emotions: "She loved it because it was all about herself; but she hated it too because it made her feel like a bill was owing somewhere and she, Denver, had to pay it" (77). And like her author, Denver can only "rememory" her family's stories secondhand: she tells her birth story to Beloved "seeing it" and "Feeling how it must have felt to her mother"; together "the two did the best they could to create what really happened" (78).

20. With a name that suggests the Wild West and a quest for Boston, Amy

evokes a continent of nineteenth-century white American female existence, interestingly represented as earthy and independent, bucking the tide by leaving home, moving away from the frontier, and aiding a slave woman on the run. Morrison draws Amy as like the escaping slave woman as possible: poor and alone, running North, away from a violent father-owner figure, recalling her lost mother.

21. On this controversy see McDowell, "Reading Family Matters."

22. Examples include Cholly Breedlove, Shadrack, Milkman Dead, Son, and Joe Trace.

23. Beloved's monologue (210–14) suggests that she has memories of the Middle Passage, that she carries a vast ancestral memory, and thus is the ghost of many more than one lost soul.

24. This assertion does not contradict Hirsch's claim that in *Beloved* Morrison tells the mother's story and thus "[opens] the space for maternal narrative in feminist fiction" (198), or Liscio's related claim that in *Beloved* Morrison is "Writing Mother's Milk." Rather, as I suggested in the introduction, *Beloved* and related texts turn the "daughterly" feminist plot, in Hirsch's terms, into a project of daughterly return to the mother. Recovering both the (historical) mother's story and "the black mother-infant daughter bond" (Liscio 39), *Beloved* aims to reunite the daughter's and the mother's voices in dialogue.

25. Describing this precursor of Beloved, the dead girl brought back to the world, as a figure for her imaginative work, Morrison uses what would become the language of the coda to *Beloved* in reverse form: writing *The Bluest Eye*, Morrison began the process of "bit by bit . . . rescuing her from the grave of time and inattention," recovering "her fingernails maybe in the first book; face and legs, perhaps, the second time," so that "she is here now, alive" ("Conversation" 217). By contrast, the coda to *Beloved* fragments and dissolves the dead girl back into "time and inattention."

26. When her daughter is restored to her, Sethe's remarks fuse the resentment of a wet nurse and a rape survivor: "Nobody will ever get my milk no more except my own children. I never had to give it to nobody else—and the one time I did it was took from me—they held me down and took it. Milk that belonged to my baby" (200).

27. All three scars form crosses, for the mother has "a circle and a cross burnt right in the skin" (61) and Beloved has a horizontal line across her neck; the inheritance of slavery is, allegorically, these women's cross to bear.

28. Motherlove in *Beloved* is a force stronger than death: "For a baby," Denver says of the ghost, "she throws a powerful spell." "No more powerful than the way I loved her," Sethe replies (4), asserting later in her monologue, "Beloved, she my daughter. . . . my love was tough and she back now." Beyond the grave, powerful foremothers hold sway: "My plan was to take us all to the other side where my own ma'am is," Sethe says of her attempt to kill her children and herself, and when Beloved returns she thinks, "I bet you Baby Suggs, on the other side, helped" (200–203).

29. In reviving the slave mother figure, Morrison reproduces neither the titillating rape scenes predominant in the portraits of slave women in men's narratives (see Foster) nor precisely the archetypal "outraged mother" described by Braxton. Though the pregnant Sethe prepares to devour an assailant, and though she gives birth when nearly dead herself, and rages against the theft of her milk, when she kills her child the archetype is shattered. Morrison's willingness to cre-

ate heroines who break the rules for "positive" representation of the race (see McDowell, "'The Self and the Other'"; Spillers, "A Hateful Passion") here produces the absolute anti-type of the good black mother and of the good daughter while insisting on our sympathy for both. *Beloved*'s ambiguous treatment of the slave woman creates a certain alienation effect; the experience of sympathizing with the slave mother who kills her child may cause readers to feel (as many of my students have felt) that they have begun to realize the full horror of slavery for the first time.

30. Rigney reads this conflagration of voices as an evocation of "the mother tongue," "a semiotic jungle in which language itself defies convention and the laws of logic" and, more specifically, "a black *woman's* jungle" (17–18).

31. I am indebted to Deborah McDowell for this point.

32. Wilton cites Marilyn Farwell (no page), and Sally Munt (xiii).

CHAPTER 2

1. Rich redefines "re-vision" in a passage that has been widely cited by feminist critics: "Re-vision—the act of looking back, of seeing with fresh eyes, of entering an old text from a new critical direction—is for women more than a chapter in cultural history: it is an act of survival" ("When We Dead" 35).

2. The mother-daughter relationship has become the focus in fictions by ethnic women writers too numerous to list; besides the African-American and Caribbean writers studied here, some others include Paula Gunn Allen, Marina Budhos, Ana Castillo, Edwidge Danticat, Cristina Garcia, Gish Jen, Nora Okja Keller, Maxine Hong Kingston, Cynthia Ozick, Leslie Marmon Silko, Esmeralda Santiago, and Amy Tan.

3. The term "renaissance," though an inexact one, has been used by many writers and critics to describe the flowering of letters among the current generation of African-American women whose writings have gained wide notice since 1970. But Darwin T. Turner's 1987 *Black Scholar* essay "Retrospective of a Renaissance" follows Hoyt Fuller in referring to the entire Civil Rights-Black Power era (1954–1970) as a "Second Black Renaissance."

4. For a detailed account of this history see Giddings (300–348). The black women's movement was never as formally constituted or recognized as either of its parent movements and grew slowly from its beginnings in the 1960s. As late as 1977, in her germinal essay, "Toward a Black Feminist Criticism," Barbara Smith laments the lack of any "political movement to give power or support to those who want to examine Black women's experience through studying our history, literature, and culture" (170). These conditions were to change dramatically in the following decade.

5. Brooks won the Pulitzer Prize for the poetry collection *Annie Allen* in 1950; *Selected Poems* was published in 1963. Walker's poetry collection *For My People* was published in 1942, and her novel *Jubilee* in 1966. Hansberry's play *A Raisin in the Sun* was first produced in 1959, when it won the New York Drama Critics' Best Play of the Year Award.

Other established writers included Ann Petry (*The Street*, 1946), and Dorothy West (*The Living Is Easy*, 1948).

6. A list of "renaissance" writers would include at least the following: Maya Angelou, Toni Cade Bambara, Octavia Butler, Lucille Clifton, Julie Dash, Alexis De Veaux, Rita Dove, Mari Evans, Nikki Giovanni, Marita Golden, Gayl Jones,

June Jordan, Audre Lorde, Terry MacMillan, Paule Marshall, Toni Morrison, Gloria Naylor, Sonia Sanchez, Ntozake Shange, Charlotte Watson Sherman, Alice Walker, Margaret Walker, and Sherley Anne Williams.

7. On language see Christian, "Trajectories" 247; Washington, *Midnight Birds* xxi. On redefinitions of black female identity see Henderson xxiv; Christian, "Trajectories" 234, 237.

8. Christian cites rebellious heroines including Walker's Meridian, Marshall's Merle Kimbona, and Morrison's Sula (on whose unconventional character see also McDowell, "The Self and the Other," and Spillers, "A Hateful Passion"), and mobile heroines like Marshall's Avey Johnson, Morrison's Jadine, and Walker's Nettie. Of note here are the three-women households in Morrison (*Sula*, *Song of Solomon*, *Beloved*) and Jones (*Corregidora*). Lesbianism is represented in *The Color Purple*, Jones's *Corregidora*, and Naylor's *The Women of Brewster Place*, among other texts. On this issue see Barbara Smith, "The Truth That Never Hurts."

9. Along with acclaim, African-American women writers have also attracted substantial suspicion and resentment, particularly from black and other male critics. On this subject see McDowell, "Reading Family Matters."

10. Gates explains that contemporary black women have created this new audience by combining "a large and cosmopolitan readership of women" and "the more traditional, but smaller, Black reading audience, male and female" (Preface x).

11. African-American women's literature is linked especially often to a profusion of recent writing produced by black women around the world. On international black women's writing and its varying reception and marketing (which favors African-American women), see Davies's "Black Women Writing Worlds" in volume one of her *Moving beyond Boundaries*; see also McLaughlin.

12. Author Helena Maria Viramontes recently bore witness to this influence on Chicana writers. African-American women writers, she remarked, "paved the way for us, giving us the inspiration to see our personal stories as political stories."

13. Important precursor texts Washington cites are Hurston's *Their Eyes Were Watching God* (1937), Dorothy West's *The Living Is Easy* (1948), and Lorraine Hansberry's *A Raisin in the Sun* (1959).

14. Michele Wallace's *Black Macho and the Myth of the Superwoman* (1979) is an early discussion of the destructive effects of such stereotypes. More recently, Patricia Turner discusses mammies as cultural icons; on mammies, among other slavery-based stereotypes of black women, see Patricia Morton. On the broad cultural influence of such images, see Patricia Hill Collins.

15. De Weever cites Cynthia Davis (341) and Dianne F. Sadoff (25). Two essays in Brown-Guillory's *Women of Color* treat mother-daughter relationships in black women's texts of this era; on poetry see Worsham; on *Sula* see Fultz.

16. The persistent image of the failed or complicit mother in Caribbean literature is a subject taken up at length in Chapter 4.

17. Doyle's argument that Morrison employs an "intercorporeal" strategy, striving "to connect the past with the present in the form of touching bodies" (208, 218), resonates with my paradigm of the black daughter's return to the body of the mother-of-history.

18. The force of this innovation can perhaps best be appreciated in contrast to a text like Hansberry's 1959 *Raisin in the Sun*. Though Hansberry's strong mother Lena Younger is, in Nellie McKay's words, a figure whose "grandeur

takes vengeance for all the black mammies previously presented in American literature" ("Reflections" 250), Lena's relationship with her daughter, aptly named Beneatha, is simply less central to the plot than her relations—indeed her eventual power sharing—with her son, Walter Lee. That is, unlike black women writers of later decades, Hansberry does not focus on the mother as source of strength *for her daughter*.

19. On this subject see Chapter 1, note 6.

20. History may emerge in these fictions in the forms of inset memory and storytelling, histories of places and place-names, or the plot of return to ancestry that restores the spirit in recent texts such as Morrison's *Song of Solomon*. On the prevalence of history in African-American fiction see also Jane Campbell (xiv), McDowell, "Negotiating" (161–62), and Spillers, "Afterword" (257).

The quest for ancestry is undertaken also in Octavia Butler's *Kindred* (1979), Toni Cade Bambara's *The Salt Eaters* (1980), Audre Lorde's *Zami* (1982), Paule Marshall's *Praisesong for the Widow* (1983) and *Daughters* (1991), and Gloria Naylor's *Mama Day* (1988), among other texts.

21. The collective honoring of the mothers in African-American women's fiction finds a parallel in the work of black and other feminist scholars to recover the forgotten work of early African-American women authors. This restoration ranges from Alice Walker's revival of Hurston's writings and famous quest for her gravesite, to the scholarly recovery by Jean Fagin Yellin of Harriet Jacobs's *Incidents in the Life of a Slave Girl* and Henry Louis Gates, Jr., of Harriet Wilson's *Our Nig*, to the republication of out-of-print novels by the Beacon Press's Black Women Writers Series, edited by McDowell, and the Schomburg Library of Nineteenth-Century Black Women Writers, published by Oxford University Press and edited by Gates.

22. Indeed, Washington writes, "so many black women have named their mothers as their literary precursors that much of contemporary writing by black women has to be seen as a response to this oral history" (160). Hirsch offers an analysis close to Washington's (176–77). Similarly, McKay observes that black women "consistently look back to their mothers and grandmothers for the substance and authority in their voices," while "many white women writers say that they are *inventing* the authority for their voices pretty much from scratch in an effort to break the silence of Shakespeare's sisters" (Morrison, "An Interview" 399). On black women writers' debt to the orature of their mothers and African foremothers, see Gay Wilentz; on these writers' deeply intertextual literary relations, see Michael Awkward.

23. This is not to say that the subject of slave women's infanticide is at all original with Morrison; on the documented history of such acts see Hine and Wittenstein; White; Lerner. And on black mothers' killing of their children in twentieth-century novels and plays by black women, see Brown-Guillory.

24. This claim is made by Henderson (xxiv) and Spillers ("Afterword" 250).

25. Christian makes this point about motherhood in contemporary women's slavery novels ("Somebody" 335–39). On fictional treatments of slave motherhood, see Keenan. On slave mothers' historical experience see White; see also Lerner, Dukats.

26. Ozick's *The Shawl* represents the enormity of the losses of the Holocaust in one Jewish mother's anguish over the murder of her baby daughter in a Nazi concentration camp. Just as the rebirth of the haunting, undead child in *Beloved* embodies the return of traumatic history, the ongoing relationship of Ozick's

heroine Rosa with the fantasy of her living, adult daughter signifies inability to emerge from a devastating past.

Likewise, Tan's *The Joy-Luck Club* dramatizes the consequences of war and emigration in mother-daughter separation and the healing of those historical wounds in mother-daughter reunion. After the death of a Chinese-American mother, her daughter Jing-mei learns of an earlier loss: her mother's forced abandonment of twin daughters while a refugee in wartime China. The novel unfolds emotional estrangements and reunions between four pairs of Chinese-American mothers and daughters, ending when Jing-mei returns to China to meet the sisters her mother always hoped to recover. The night before the meeting Jing-mei learns that her mother's name, Suyuan, means "long-cherished wish," and the next day, in a Polaroid photo taken of the three sisters together, Jing-mei believes she sees her mother's "long-cherished wish" taking shape before her eyes (280, 288); the mother herself is re-embodied in her daughters and history is healed.

27. On the place of *Daughters of the Dust* in the black independent film movement, see Bambara.

28. Commenting on this scene, Dash indicates her desire to open new plot possibilities: "Where have you ever seen a Native American win in the end and ride off in glory? When have you ever seen an African American woman riding off into the sunset for love, only, and not escaping?" (49).

29. This is essentially Carpentier's claim in his famous prologue to *The Kingdom of This World* (1949), recently translated as "On the Marvellous Real in America," in Zamora and Faris, ed., *Magical Realism: Theory, History, Community*, a volume that does much to complicate conventional readings of magic realism and the subordinate status it has held in discussions of the postmodern. For a refutation of Carpentier's view, see Amaryll Chanady, in the same volume, pp. 133, 141.

30. Similarly, Caribbean critic Selwyn Cudjoe prefers the term "critical realism," which stresses the work of anti-realist representations to render a history of extreme violence and upheaval (267).

31. Appiah reviews Ben Okri's *The Famished Road* (London: Cape, 1991). "Spiritual realism" might suit as well those texts by African-American women in which the "magic" evokes African spiritual "survivals," including *Daughters of the Dust* and texts by Morrison, Naylor, Bambara, Alice Walker, and others.

32. Spillers points toward this meaning of magic as subversive power in *Jubilee*. She notes that the atmosphere of magic created by Walker's citation of folk beliefs and sayings is connected to the narrative's "theonomous" structure; invoking a God of emancipation, the enslaved oppose magic to tyranny ("A Hateful Passion" 35).

33. The same might be said of the penchant for extravagant, space-age supernaturalism in black popular culture—for example, among jazz musicians like Sun Ra and his Intergalactic Arkestra, who claimed to hail from Saturn, or Abbey Lincoln, who on a recent album sings of her mother's arrival on a spaceship "from 600 trillion miles away." Similarly, Lucille Clifton writes in her poem "note, passed to superman":

> lord, man of steel,
> i understand the cape,
> the leggings, the whole
> ball of wax.

you can trust me,
there is no planet stranger
than the one i'm from. (*Book of Light* 48)

These uses of the extraterrestrial translate a "disremembered" legacy of African displacement, of global crossings, of African "magic," revaluing the difference of the self in terms other than racial ones. Racial and cultural inheritance here become sources of uncanny knowledge and power.

34. The difference of the magical feminist aesthetic—its mythification of the claim to daughterly inheritance—can be seen in the contrast between Allende's redeemed grandmother-text and its precursor: another text *en abyme*, the mysterious parchment handed down through male generations in Garcia Marquez's *One Hundred Years of Solitude* (1967). Marquez's inset text, which turns out to have contained the novel's ending since the very beginning, consumes the family, the town of Macondo, and the novel's entire vision in its last lines. The magical power of writing supersedes rather than celebrates inheritance. But Allende's Alba, left alive and pregnant with a daughter at the novel's end, rewrites her magical grandmother's life so as to produce a text that will bear her descendants into the future.

35. Butler was preceded in the African-American time-travel plot by John A. Williams, who may have originated this plot in his 1972 *Captain Blackman*. Williams's hero, a black U.S. soldier in Vietnam, suffers a head injury and delirium that catapult him into an internal past. He finds himself living the role of African-American soldier in successive ages of American history and into a surprising future, in which blacks take over the U.S. military. The novel's recuperative project differs from that of the magic daughter fictions: it affirms the emergence not of a female literary authority but of a latent, male "black power" within the national might of the United States.

36. Butler's many other novels include *Patternmaster* (1976), *Wild Seed* (1980), *Imago* (1989), *Parable of the Sower* (1993), and *Parable of the Talents* (1998).

37. For example, as she helplessly watches a forefather being whipped, it occurs to Dana that she knows the "name for whites who rode through the night in the ante bellum South . . . torturing black people": "Patrols. . . . Forerunners of the Ku Klux Klan" (36–37). On returns to the present she and Kevin do intensive research—"I brought everything we had on black history. . . . Start hunting"—to learn exactly where she has been and what tools, imitated free papers, maps (torn out of history books), and so on she might gather to put to use there (48).

38. Tiffin derives the term from Richard Terdiman's *Discourse/Counter-Discourse: The Theory and Practice of Symbolic Resistance in Nineteenth-Century France* (Ithaca, N.Y.: Cornell University Press, 1985).

39. The stakes of such a choice may be better appreciated in the context of recurrent comments in contemporary black culture about the dangers awaiting the African-American time-traveler. Sherley Anne Williams writes in her Author's Note to *Dessa Rose*, "I loved history as a child, until some clear-eyed young Negro pointed out, quite rightly, that there was no place in the American past I could go and be free" (ix–x). Comedian Paul Mooney, whose album *Race* was quoted (and edited) in the *Washington Post*, says:

> See, you're white, you can go back. "Back to the Future," they like all that [stuff]. . . . I can only go back so far, then my black [behind] is in chains.

> [Expletive] you, I'm not goin' back. . . . No, I'mo stay here in the '90s where I can tell you to kiss my black [behind].

40. The fact that Dana's "scar"—the most dramatic physical injury suffered by any of the magic black daughters—is not associated with maternity, but only with her own agency, underscores the distance of this novel from an allegory of authorial engagement with a maternal heritage.

41. Dana first practices for the possibility of having to use a knife against an assailant by drawing a ruler across Kevin's abdomen (47). And her early musing about Rufus and his power to call her into the past might stand equally well as an inquiry into the possibilities of a life with Kevin:

> There was nothing in him that reminded me of any of my relatives. Looking at him confused me. But he had to be the one. There had to be some kind of reason for the link he and I seemed to have. . . . What we had was something new, something that didn't even have a name. Some matching strangeness in us that may or may not have come from our being related. (28–29)

42. The struggle for the freedom to love has been a crucial theme in the women's slavery novel tradition. It is the central freedom celebrated in *Beloved* and, in a sense, in *Jubilee*, too, which progresses from the mother's victimization by the white master's rape, to the heroine's choice of a "free" husband from whom slavery separates her, to her ultimate choice between two free black men.

CHAPTER 3

1. Gomez has written on the need to fill the "vacuum" of fictional representations of black lesbians:

> The Black Lesbian writer must recreate our home, unadulterated, unsanitized, specific and not isolated from the generations that have nurtured us. This will serve to create a literary record that is placed in a historical perspective so that we, who have been lost in the shadows of the past, can be revealed and appreciated for the powerful legacy we bear. ("A Cultural Legacy" 122)

2. See Nina Auerbach's *Our Vampires, Ourselves* on the vampire narrative tradition, including the homoerotic element. Auerbach reads *The Gilda Stories* as a "diluted" vampire vision of the Reagan years, "purged of aggression" and thus "present[ing] no threat to established power" (184–85).

3. Roof's discussion focuses on two lesbian novels: Jane Rule's *This Is Not for You* and Rita Mae Brown's *Rubyfruit Jungle*.

4. An extended discussion of the elegiac aspect of the photograph is in Santner.

5. There has long been a multicultural interest in Walker's work; notable are her early novel *Meridian* and her essay collection *Living by the Word*.

6. A recurrent sign of the valorization of interracial relationships in these novels is the willing adoption of white people's names. This surprising reversal of the law of slavery occurs in the naming of Morrison's Denver—ironically, the only one of Sethe's children to be born outside of slavery and the rule of the master's name—as well as in Paul D's retention of his connection to the Garners of Sweet Home. When Denver calls him "Mr. D.," he corrects her: "Garner,

baby. Paul D Garner" (11), when surely he could rename himself anything from "D" to "X." Other instances are Dana's acknowledgement, in Butler's *Kindred*, of Rufus's name in her family Bible; the elaborate plot of cross-race naming in *Dessa Rose*; and Gilda's inheritance of her "creator"'s name.

On Amy Denver's role and her relationship to Denver's plot see also the introduction and Chapter 1.

7. An important difference between these African-American women's revisions of Shakespeare's play and the many Caribbean versions is suggestive: no Calibans here, but rather, heroines identified with the privileged European visitors to the enchanted island, perhaps appropriating their positions rather than re-embodying Caliban's.

8. As black women's texts of this period reimagined a historical mother, they also evinced a growing interest in the stories of older women in general, in novels like Marshall's *Praisesong*; Williams's *Dessa Rose* (1986); Morrison's *Beloved* (1987), *Jazz* (1992), and *Paradise* (1997); MacMillan's *Mama* (1987); Naylor's *Mama Day* (1988); and Walker's *The Color Purple* (1982) and *The Temple of My Familiar* (1989).

9. Coser notes that "avatara," from the Sanskrit, signifies incarnation or embodiment of a deity or person and suggests Avey's embodiment of her aunt's "spirit and her culture" (63).

10. See Brathwaite, "African Presence" (99–100), and "West Indian History," in both of which he praises *The Chosen Place, the Timeless People*. Marshall discusses her interest in recovering historical and spiritual dimensions of diaspora black culture in "Re-Creating Ourselves."

11. For a discussion of a parallel in Caribbean literature, which only gradually moved its spiritual center from Africa to the Caribbean, see Chapter 4. On black heroines' journeys to ancestral places in African-American women's renaissance fiction see Christian, "Trajectories" 243–45.

12. Perry invokes Butler when Lizzie tells the cousin who believes in her reincarnation, "It's nice to have a kindred spirit around" (74); recalls an early scene in *Beloved* when Lizzie's boyfriend Anthony Paul (a descendent of Paul D's?) "runs his tongue over the scars on my back, sliding his arms around me and covering my breasts with his hands" (131–32); and appropriates Julie Dash's central symbol for African-American matrilineal connection: "I'm always surrounded by dust, made of it, always caught up in it as it swirls and resettles and rises again and again to worry the living" (129).

13. Parallel paternal-bodied visions of the African-American past are offered in the rhetorically dazzling (but notably gynophobic) "neoslave narrative" novels of Charles Johnson. *Oxherding Tale* (1982) and *Middle Passage* (1990) share with recent black women's texts both the magical realist repertoire and the emphasis on the black body as the locus of history, but both present submerged father-quests, male embodiments of history, and mythified forms of generation artfully managed by means other than childbirth. See the father-son reunion within the "impossible flesh tapestry" of the Soulcatcher's chest at the end of *Oxherding Tale* and a similar encounter within the body of an African god at the end of *Middle Passage*.

Another notable invocation of a black male-bodied history is Bill Cosby's "three-hundred year old black man," imagined in his introduction to *The Black Book*, the 1974 compendium of documents, facts, and photographs from African-American history in which Morrison as Random House literary editor first encountered Margaret Garner's story.

14. Gaines's Miss Jane Pittman, also childless, adopts a sequence of promising boys as spiritual heirs, becoming a mother to them and to the civil rights movement.

15. In Gomez's vampire creation scenes, as in Sethe's encounter with her mother in *Beloved*, the secret place of maternal signification is a mark "below . . . [the] breast" (192); in both novels a symbolically charged maternal semiosis is located in a bodily place under, hidden by, the visible and conventionally maternal signifier, suggesting deeper forms of maternal nurturance and connection. Only Gilda, however, is privileged to "drink" from this deeper place, and this indeed is part of Sethe's tragedy.

16. In this form of "reproduction" Gomez is indebted to the 1970s feminist vision of sisterhood as a reciprocal, nondominating version of motherhood. Hirsch writes:

> In the 1970s, the prototypical feminist voice was . . . the voice of the daughter attempting to separate from an overly connected or rejecting mother, in order to bond with her sisters in a relationship of mutual nurturance and support among equals. . . . The paradigm of sisterhood has the advantage of freeing women from the biological function of giving birth, even while offering a specifically feminine relational model. . . . In this feminist family romance, sisters are better mothers . . . . (164)

This paradigm suggests an alternate reading of Gilda's flight from slavery—all memories of which center on her mother—to a life among sister vampires, and indeed from the African-American slave narrative to the vampire tale.

17. On the narrative voice of *Jazz,* see my "Impossible Voices: Ethnic Postmodern Narration in Morrison's *Jazz* and Yamashita's *Through the Arc of the Rain Forest,*" forthcoming in *Contemporary Literature.*

18. A difficulty with this theory is that Joe is born in 1873, while Beloved becomes a pregnant fugitive in 1874. But perhaps the linear flow of time ought not to be a concern when the mother in question is Morrison's ghost.

CHAPTER 4

1. Frantz Fanon writes:

> Colonialism . . . did not seek to be considered by the native as a gentle, loving mother who protects her child from a hostile environment, but rather as a mother who unceasingly restrains her fundamentally perverse offspring from managing to commit suicide and from giving free rein to its evil instincts. The colonial mother protects her child from itself, from its ego, and from its physiology, its biology, and its own unhappiness which is its very essence. (211)

2. All citations of Walcott's poems refer to his *Collected Poems*.

3. Glissant's interpretation of the trauma of history in Caribbean culture resembles McDowell's psychoanalytic notion of an African-American "compulsion to repeat" the story of slavery:

> Would it be ridiculous to consider our lived history as a steadily advancing neurosis? To see the Slave Trade as a traumatic shock, our relocation (in the new land) as a repressive phase, slavery as the period of latency, "emancipa-

tion" in 1848 as reactivation, our everyday fantasies as symptoms, and even our horror of "returning to those things of the past" as a possible manifestation of the neurotic's fear of his past? (65–66)

Such a collective psychological analysis would read contemporary Caribbean literature as an ongoing "talking cure" for a people trapped in traumatic repetition.

4. Africans and their descendants in the Caribbean have formed the vast majority of the population since slavery, originally because of the massive labor demands of the sugar plantation system (Fogel 31).

The cultural repercussions of these two different conditions are many and complex. For example, though Caribbean people insist "dat dis / place ain't Uncle Sam backyard" (Nichols, "Caribbean Woman's Prayer" 2), they are constantly exposed to the consumer and cultural exports and the might of "America," without access to the material advantages that shape the aspirations of U.S. minority groups. Islanders may be proud of the independence of a nation they yet experience as the pawn of far greater forces, while African Americans may be and feel disenfranchised within the powerful nation in which, paradoxically, they have attained considerable cultural and political influence and "visibility," both nationally and internationally (Nelson 54; see also Ashcroft 21).

5. Independence dates of the Caribbean nations discussed in this study are as follows:

Haiti	1804 (by revolution)
Jamaica	1962
Trinidad	1962
Barbados	1966
Guyana	1966
Dominica	1978
St. Lucia	1979
Antigua	1981

Guadeloupe and Martinique remain Overseas Departments of France (Source: Balutansky).

6. In a somewhat conflicting designation, the literary period 1950 to 1965 has also been called the "West Indian Renaissance" by Brathwaite (qtd. in Dance 2–3).

7. On the problematics of the term "postcolonial," see McClintock, Olaniyan, Radhakrishnan, and Shohat.

8. Condé observes that the oral folk culture of the Antilles pays homage to women's strength and resilience, celebrating mothers in particular (*Parole* 4, 41). Carol Boyce Davies finds that Caribbean folk proverbs and calypso lyrics, though they demonstrate overwhelmingly negative and even hostile references to women, single out mothers for praise ("Woman Is" 165–67, 180). On this subject see also Perry (247) and Liddell (321). The contradictions among these folk images of women and mothers reflect the conflicted family and gender relations of the region's postslavery social order, in which women have often been single parents and independent economic agents (see Davies, "Woman Is" 185).

9. Caliban has become the emblematic Caribbean in the literary and theoreti-

cal works of a number of writers, including Lamming in *The Pleasures of Exile* (1960) and *Water with Berries* (1971), Césaire in *Une Tempête* (1969), Roberto Fernández Retamar in "Caliban: Notes Toward a Discussion of Culture in Our America" (1971), and Brathwaite in "Caliban" from *Islands* (1969). On the history of Caribbean adaptations of *The Tempest* see Nixon; see also Saldivar's chapter, "The School of Caliban."

10. Critic Clarisse Zimra similarly asks, in 1986, "Did Caliban have a sister?" signifying on Virginia Woolf's question about Caliban's author ("W/Righting" 229). An essay by Sylvia Wynter discusses a hypothetical figure she calls "Caliban's woman"—an ontological absence in Shakespeare's play—who would be the savage's complement and mate, a "model of desire" and source of meaning other than Miranda, whose "'demonic'" terrain Caribbean women writers should newly claim (360, 366).

A recent collection of feminist cultural and sociological essays on Caribbean women is *Daughters of Caliban: Caribbean Women in the Twentieth Century*, ed. Consuelo Lopez Springfield.

11. Sycorax's name is said to derive from the Greek *sys* (sow) and *korax* (raven), and her character to derive from that of a witch who saved Algiers from the siege of Charles I in 1541 (Barton 147–48).

12. As in the case of African-American women's writing (see Chapter 2, note 3), the use of the term "renaissance" here should be understood to refer to a period of collective literary emergence, without necessarily invoking a return of the dynamics of any particular earlier moment.

13. Olive Senior remarks that for Caribbean writers "perceived marketability outside your own country" is the key to publication. Because Jamaica offers few venues or encouragements for creative writing, such as periodicals, grants, and prizes, "to stay at home and write is a considerable act of faith" (486).

Expatriation and contact with the metropole may be more consequential for women writers than for men in this regard. The rise of women's presses and of a market for "third world women's" texts in cities like London, Paris, Toronto, and New York have made it easier for women to find publishers outside of the Caribbean (Paris 85). Indeed, Mordecai and Wilson suspect that the "sudden literary blossoming" of Caribbean women may be "at least in part . . . a flowering of publishing interest consequent on the Women's Movement" (xi). On this subject, see also Davies, "Black Women Writing."

14. Many writers educated in colonial schools "discover they are *different*, become aware of their Caribbeanness" only in Europe (Glissant 23). Césaire's is the paradigmatic instance; among many others who describe this phenomenon, Maryse Condé recalls first realizing she was not French at age sixteen, because of the way she was treated in France (Lectures).

15. For example, Condé has said that she may first have felt like an exile when she returned to Guadeloupe (Taleb-Khyar 349–50), especially since several novels had won accolades and prizes in France, and her first "Guadeloupean" novel *Tree of Life* received negative reviews from a local critical establishment that read it as a political betrayal (Lectures).

16. Lamming's *The Pleasures of Exile* (1960) treats exile as both a curse and a blessing and makes it the occasion for a wide-ranging examination of colonialism. Kellman celebrates the fact that exile "promotes a deeper, broader vision of what it really means to be Caribbean and a part of a pluralistic New World order" (xxix). On exile and Caribbean literature, see also Gikandi, 33–42, and on

the healthy effect of Caribbean writers' migrations on systems of literary categorization, see Davies, "Writing Home" (70).

17. Spanish- and Dutch-language women writers, who do not fall within the scope of this study, have also begun to receive wider notice. See Rodriguez and Phaf.

18. Davies and Fido debate the usefulness of the terms "womanism" and "feminism" for Caribbean women writers in their preface (ix–xix). On the history of Caribbean feminism, see Reddock.

19. American readers often must work to grasp the meaning "attached to relative skin color" in Caribbean literature, as Esteves and Paravisini-Gebert put it: "the polar categories of black and white that characterize race relations in the United States are replaced by a broad spectrum of racial categorizations that runs the gamut between black and white" (xxiv), and in which relative differences have extreme social consequences for women in particular. Mordecai and Wilson illustrate by noting that French Caribbean women writers themselves "range, like the heroines of their novels, over a wide and complexly designated colour spectrum: négresses, mulatresses, capresses, chabines, femmes à peau de sapotille, à peau d'acajou, and so on" (x–xi).

20. On the troubled plots of interracial love affairs, madness, and suicide in francophone women's writing before the present era, see Zimra, "Negritude," and "W/Righting" (240–44); see also Shelton, "Women Writers"; Wilson. On similar patterns in anglophone women's writing see Mordecai and Wilson (xii); and O'Callaghan (104).

21. On this scene see also Gikandi (211).

22. Texts discussed in this study that feature troubled mothers but firm, supportive grandmother figures include novels by Cliff, Condé, Hodge, Rhys, and Schwarz-Bart; in all but the last, the heroine's mother dies. On a parallel tendency in African-American literature, see De Weever (140–42).

23. Historical information on Nanny is given by Davies and Fido (xiii), Mair, and Cliff (*Abeng* 14 and elsewhere). André and Simone Schwarz-Bart's *Un plat de porc aux bananes verts* (1967) is a prelude to his fictional biography of the mulatto heroine Solitude (1972, translated by Ralph Manheim as *A Woman Named Solitude*, New York: Atheneum, 1973).

24. The phrase "magic realism" derives originally from Cuban novelist Alejo Carpentier, who in the prologue to his novel of Haitian history, *The Kingdom of This World* (*El Reino de Este Mundo* 1949), describes life amidst the memories and lingering signs of Haiti's dramatic history as a "marvelous reality" ("Marvelous Real" 84). The early Césaire also celebrated magic as a distinctive and essential attribute of Caribbean black people.

25. See Césaire, *Toussaint L'ouverture: la révolution française et la problème coloniale* (1962) and *Tragédie du Roi Christophe* (1963); Carpentier, *El Reino de Este Mundo* (1949); Glissant, *Monsieur Toussaint* (1961). More recent women's texts in the genre include Condé, *Moi, Tituba, Sorcière . . . Noire de Salem* (1986); Cliff, *Abeng* (1984); Goodison, "Nanny," in *Selected Poems* (1992); Grace Nichols, "The Return" and "Nanny," in *I is a long-memoried woman* (1983).

26. Lois Parkinson Zamora makes a similar distinction between "U.S. and Latin American traditions of counterrealism": whereas "most contemporary U.S. magical realists" manage by the end of their texts to re-integrate ghostly eruptions into "reestablished communities," "most contemporary Latin American magical realists, on the contrary, refuse such consolation: magical

resolutions are considered, then canceled by crushing political realities" (542–43).

27. I see evidence of this impulse in only two limited forms. First, daughterly heroines tend to resist becoming biological mothers themselves. And second, while the colonial allegory of maternal rape does occur in the work of Rhys, Cliff, Condé, and others, women writers tend not to extend the allegory—as male writers often do—to depict a rape of the island itself, refusing that further and perhaps more degrading equation of the female body with the land. On the obsolescence of the rape metaphor for postcolonial literature and especially for feminist postcolonial critique, see Suleri 16–17.

28. On creolization see Brathwaite, *Contradictory Omens*, "History of the Voice," and elsewhere; on his development of this concept in several 1970s essays, see Martini.

Glissant writes of the paradoxical "potential of the slave trade": "a population that is transformed elsewhere *into another people* . . . enters the constantly shifting and variable process of creolization (of relationship, of relativity)" (14–15). An important revision and elaboration of Glissant's "créolisation" is the "créolitude" of Bernabé, Chamoiseau, and Confiant in their *Eloge de la créolité* (1989; translated as "In Praise of Creoleness").

29. For ideas about mothers in Kincaid I am indebted to unpublished essays by Charlene Beh, Tanya McGarry, Eliza Slavet, and Virginia Guckenberger, students in my 1996 Yale senior English seminar. These students helped me read *The Autobiography of My Mother* as a daughterly return not only in that it imagines a Caribbean woman of an earlier generation, and in that the narrating woman "returns" imaginatively into her mother's life, but also in that the novel seems to constitute Kincaid's return to her own mother's story. Certain repetitions link the heroine to the facts of Kincaid's mother's life: the name "Richardson" (Kincaid's given name was Elaine Potter Richardson); birth on Dominica; policeman fathers. Xuela also shares with the mother of *Annie John*—modeled on Kincaid's mother—a brother who dies young of a diseased leg.

Kincaid's third novel thus returns to the mother her early novels reject, fusing daughterly and motherly identities, and in a paradoxical sense finally freeing mother and daughter both. For Xuela, unlike Kincaid's actual mother, is freed from bearing children. And the author is freed when, as Charlene Beh argues, she reclaims writing from the figure of the "writing mother" who composed her life in the early novels, so that the daughter now writes the mother's life.

30. The lost mother's descending heels recall a passage that associates writing with recording the footsteps of forgotten Caribbean women in *Omeros*, the epic poem by Walcott, to whom Kincaid dedicates *The Autobiography of My Mother*. The poet's father tells him of watching the feet of a long line of women climbing a ladder up to a ship in the St. Lucian port of Castries, bearing on their heads "hundredweight basket[s]" of coal. He urges the poet to "[climb] in their footsteps, that slow, ancestral beat," in order "to give those feet a voice" (74–76).

Curiously enough, the autobiography of Jean Rhys (on whom Walcott has written an eponymous poem) recalls the same scene, witnessed on a childhood visit to Castries, a disturbing sight of women's suffering about which the young Rhys was afraid to ask any adult for explanation (*Smile, Please* 45).

31. On negation in the novel see Schine and Kakutani.

32. For this point I am indebted to Rita Felski.

33. Compare Walcott's similar distribution of wounds to colonized and colo-

nizer alike in *Omeros*, read by Jahan Ramazani as a poetics of "cross-cultural affliction" (17).

CHAPTER 5

Reprinted with permission of the University Press of Virginia.

1. Gilbert and Gubar list Rhys among the "twentieth-century women novelists [who] have played variations on the themes of their foremothers in order to strengthen themselves by restoring and revising the past while restructuring the future" (*No Man's Land* 208).

2. Davies and Fido's 1990 anthology *Out of the Kumbla: Caribbean Women and Literature* declares that it is time "to reintegrate [Rhys] with the rest of the women writers . . . who portray Caribbean reality" (16). Also in 1990 Mary Lou Emery complicates the tendency of Rhys critics to fall either into the feminist or Caribbean camps by arguing that Caribbeanness significantly marks Rhys's entire oeuvre (7–20). Recent critics who integrate the two elements include Ferracane, Fido, Niesen de Abruna, Gregg, and Raiskin; these last two offer further discussion of the problem of Rhys's status and treat her as a Creole writer.

As I note in the next chapter, Michelle Cliff has staunchly claimed Rhys as Caribbean feminist precursor, but Cliff's Caribbeanness, too, has come into question.

3. Some other experiments in the genre in English include Valerie Martin's *Mary Reilly*, John Gardner's *Grendel*, Tom Stoppard's *Rosencrantz and Guildenstern Are Dead*, and Robert Browning's "Caliban upon Setebos."

4. I take this term from Fetterley's influential book.

5. In her autobiography *Smile, Please*, Rhys mentions the burning of the Geneva estate (25), an account that has been generally accepted by critics. But see Peter Hulme for a refutation of the anecdote and a reading of it as a "screen-memory" for other, more incriminating stories of Rhys's ancestors' roles in Dominica's violent racial history (82).

6. Critics of *Wide Sargasso Sea* cite Adrienne Rich's definition of "re-vision" with notable frequency (see Chapter 2, note 1).

7. "The other side" is a formulation Rhys herself uses for her reinscription of Brontë; her heroine tells Rochester: "There is always the other side, always" (128).

In rehabilitating as sympathetic heroine a character created by Brontë to be "morally dispensable" (Hite 35), Rhys of course follows Brontë, who demonstrates that a poor, plain governess can prove an impressive romantic heroine.

8. Ronnie Scharfman notes that "Antoinette" is "a combination of Annette and 'toi': a hidden, built-in bond between mother and daughter" (103).

9. Kloepfer links Antoinette's madness to Rochester's "denial of her language, her name, and her matrilineage," but notes that by privileging the maternal, Rhys's rewriting "forces the son to experience . . . [female] psychological and linguistic space" (145, 158). Similarly, Nancy Harrison reads in *Wide Sargasso Sea* the construction of a distinctively female fictional space she calls a "woman's text" (6).

10. Chantal Delourme contrasts this "castrated," nameless man to the "nom-roc," "nom-forteresse" that dominates *Jane Eyre* (262). Translations of Delourme are mine.

Christophine doubts the existence of England because she has never seen it herself (111). It should be noted that Rhys's depiction of Rochester is not entirely unsympathetic; for example, she carefully delineates his legal victimization as a second son under the law of primogeniture.

11. Ferracane argues that in both *Voyage in the Dark* (1934) and *Wide Sargasso Sea*, Rhys's heroines enact a desire for return to a primal merger with the mother through lifelong searches for mother substitutes, ending in death as replacement for the mother (86). On the mother-daughter plot in Rhys's life and oeuvre see also Niesen de Abruna, "Family Connections"; Fido, "Mother/lands".

12. Raiskin argues that Rhys's dominant figure for this condition is zombification (129–43); on Antoinette as zombie see also Drake (110).

13. On representations of white colonial women in fiction see Gardiner.

14. Forster's *A Passage to India* features the "good" colonial Englishwomen Adela Quested and Mrs. Moore, who wish for "friendship" with Indians but whose mind-shattering visions at the Marabar Caves cut short their plots. The white colonial daughter's compromised position is signaled in Miss Quested's absurd name: a person marked as the *object* of quest cannot be expected to *discover* anything much of her own. And in the moment in the cave on which the whole plot turns, when Adela has the predictable hallucination of a sexual assault by an Indian man, her sudden fear is that she is not the quester she has wanted to be, but rather, exactly what they have always called her: quested.

In Coetzee's tragicomic postmodern fable *In the Heart of the Country*, the motherless white heroine Magda makes ill-fated attempts at friendship with the black servant couple on her father's South African farm. Though her failure and her madness are rendered in an ironic, self-consciously literary mode, like Antoinette, she turns madness into violent revolt: she kills her father, sets fires, and saws the house apart. I have discussed these texts in "The Mad Colonial Daughter's Revolt: J. M. Coetzee's *In the Heart of the Country*" (*South Atlantic Quarterly* 93, no. 1 [1994]: 157–80).

15. Among the numerous white mother-figures who die in white women's colonialist or postcolonial narratives, one might recall Scarlett O'Hara's mother in *Gone with the Wind*. In thinking about this phenomenon, we might add to Chapter 4's discussion of the trope of failed or dying mothers in postcolonial women's literature Gardiner's view that white colonial daughters grow up in a home that "demeans women and makes it impossible for them to identify with the mothers they yearn for" (141), and also Adrienne Rich's theory of "matrophobia," the fear of becoming one's mother, discussed in Chapter 2, part 1.

A notable exception to the rule is Caryl Churchill's deconstructive farce *Cloud Nine* (1979), in which, among many reversals, the colonial mother herself turns out to be the heroine.

16. Emery demonstrates that the episode in which Antoinette seeks the drug from Christophine constitutes an eleven-page interruption of Rochester's narrative, part two of the text (45). When Antoinette loses her narrative at the end of part one, it is clear that her marriage has meant the loss of her "voice"; thus her brief narrative interruption of part two can be read as a subversion, powered by Christophine and *obeah*, of Rochester's control of the story of their marriage. Kloepfer reads this interruption as Antoinette's momentary escape from Rochester's discursive frame and into contact with the mother, here the surrogate Christophine (148).

17. J. M. Coetzee's collection of essays on white South African literature is entitled *White Writing: On the Culture of Letters in South Africa*.

18. Most significant here are dramatic acts of revenge by blacks: the burning of the mother's house, Tia's stone-throwing rejection of Antoinette, the black caretaker's sexual abuse of the mother, Daniel Cosway's blackmail letters, Amélie's seduction of Rochester in the room adjacent to Antoinette's. Of these examples, three include elements of interracial sex (for Daniel reports Antoinette's involvement with her half-black cousin Sandi).

Rhys has predecessors among francophone women writers in this drama of sexual madness as the trace of racially volatile history, for example, Marie Chauvet's *Amour, colère et folie*. On this subject see Chapter 4, note 20.

19. Rochester asks Antoinette, on the first page of his narrative, the name of the Dominican village before them:

> "Massacre."
> "And who was massacred here? Slaves?"
> "Oh no." She sounded shocked. "Not slaves. Something must have happened a long time ago. Nobody remembers now." (65–66)

Recently, Jamaica Kincaid has remembered the story of this town in *The Autobiography of My Mother*, correcting the impression Rhys creates of suppressed slave history by revealing a history of Native-European intimacy and violence:

> It was at Massacre that Indian Warner, the illegimate son of a Carib woman and a European man, was murdered by his half brother, an Englishman named Philip Warner, because Philip Warner did not like having such a close relative whose mother was a Carib woman. (87)

Kincaid's novel underscores the living memory of history by having the heroine Xuela attend school in Massacre.

20. On the double-edged representation of blacks in Rhys's Creole text see Gregg.

21. Rather than the many examples of this tendency I'll cite a parody of it from the black heroine's point of view: the relationship between Sofia, the former servant, and Eleanor Jane, the mayor's daughter, in Alice Walker's *The Color Purple*.

22. Though Antoinette's Aunt Cora presents another potential mother, her age, unlike that of black Caribbean mothers, seems to disqualify her. Antoinette in one moment shrinks from her aged, unprettified face and Cora later turns her own face away, Christophine explains, specifically because she is old (46, 114). In this novel, then, age cannot make a white woman a stronger Caribbean mother.

23. Harrison illuminates the connections between the heroine and the parrot (176–77). Scharfman reads the resurgence of the parrot's question as the metonymic reemergence of the mother at this climactic moment (105). Delourme adds that with hair like wings amidst the fire, Antoinette/Bertha is no mere parrot, but a phoenix (263).

24. Lee Erwin describes the dreamed leap from the roof as "a celebration of or fantasized union with a blackness finally seen to have been the desire of her narrative all along" (154), a desire that "can only realize itself in the gaze of the Other, in an attempt to perform the impossible feat of seeing herself from the place from which she is seen" (155).

25. Ellen Friedman notes that Rhys's revision differs from Bloom's model (117) but does not develop a theory of Rhysian revision.

26. Among the details of plot and setting Rhys repeats from *Jane Eyre*, Delourme cites the echo of a telling phrase: "infamous daughter of an infamous mother," Rhys's modification of Rochester's epithet for Bertha, "true daughter of an infamous mother" (Delourme 260).

27. Elizabeth Baer asserts that of all Antoinette and Jane's shared plot elements—lost mothers, nurturance by women servants, narratives of painful progress through five named houses, and so on—the most important are their dreams, "submerged text[s]" that recast the romance plot in nightmare form and "nudge the consciousness" of the dreamers (137–38). Antoinette's final moment of triumph comes, Baer notes, when she "heeds the dream text" in waking life (147). The interpretation of dreams is a major preoccupation of Rhys critics; see also Friedman, 124–27; Kloepfer, 154–58; and Emery, 53–59.

28. In a chapter of *Unbecoming Women* titled "Jane Eyre's Fall from Grace" Susan Fraiman reads Brontë's Grace Poole as emblematic of a potentially emancipatory counterplot of homosocial bonding among working-class women in *Jane Eyre*. Fraiman notes that Jane believes for much of the novel—as do her readers—that the frightening noises coming from the attic are made by a drunken English servant woman. The composite "madwoman" Bertha-Grace can thus be seen to haunt Rochester's house with both a "native" and a working-class woman's rage. In her rewriting, Rhys underscores the potential solidarity of their causes by treating Grace as Antoinette/Bertha's sympathetic keeper.

29. Bloom is citing Paul de Man in this passage.

30. Harrison titles the chapter from which I quote "The Woman Writer as Reader" and argues that Rhys "makes the collective enterprise clear, the reading of ourselves and others that compels our own writing" (132).

Similarly, Gregg discusses the central concern with "rereading and rewriting" manifest throughout Rhys's work in a plethora of "citations, titles of precursory texts, hidden and overt allusions and references. . . . fragments, anachronisms," and so on, which remind us of the distortions of "dominant discourses of empire, gender, and subjectivity" (80).

31. One might also say that Rhys's model of rewriting a received figure is employed, among African-American women writers, by Toni Morrison, Barbara Chase-Riboud, and Sherley Anne Williams, whose *Beloved*, *Sally Hemings*, and *Dessa Rose* develop fictional life stories for historical slave women about whom little is known.

32. These sources of authorial anxiety figure in, respectively, Bloom's theory of the "anxiety of influence," and Gilbert and Gubar's theory of the female "anxiety of authorship," developed in *The Madwoman in the Attic*.

33. See Nancy Miller's *The Heroine's Text*.

34. Harrison writes that Antoinette/Bertha arrives in her ending "at a psychological destination . . . consistent with the overall achievement, both cultural and conceptual, that has been actively at work in women's lives and intellectual pursuits for more than a hundred years" (136–37).

CHAPTER 6

1. For an extended discussion of Bertha Rochester see Cliff, "Caliban's Daughter." Cliff calls Clare Savage "not exactly an autobiographical character" in "Clare Savage as a Crossroads Character" (264).

2. I take the phrase from Ngugi wa Thiong'o, *Decolonizing the Mind*.

3. Edmondson also observes that the fluidity of racial categories in the region is "such that a 'white' creole may choose to designate himself as politically 'black'" and that Cliff "explicitly seeks to revalue black identity in her novels" (181). Judith Raiskin develops a nuanced reading of Cliff's revisionary stance toward racial categorizations such as "black," "white," and "creole" (177–204).

4. On the problematics of Cliff's critical reception see Sally O'Driscoll; see also Lionnet (27–30), and Edmondson (181–82). O'Driscoll writes that critics' accounts of Cliff's work tend to "begin with attempts to locate and define her authorial identity" and often dismiss her work on the basis of an "inauthentic" Caribbean identity (60). Mordecai and Wilson, the editors of *Her True-True Name*, criticize Cliff's heroine and her handling of the creole and claim (inaccurately, I think) that Cliff is unusual among recent anglophone women writers in that she "does not affirm at least aspects of being in the Caribbean place." These editors have a point in placing Cliff along with Rhys "more in the alienated tradition of a 'francophone' than an anglophone consciousness" (xvii), but they are too dismissive of white Creole and mixed-race anglophone writers, whose forms of alienation need not estrange them from the anglophone canon (or disqualify them from political relevance).

5. In this, Cliff anticipates Glissant's vision for a renewed Caribbean writing. "Inherited categories," he writes, "must not . . . be an obstacle to a daring new methodology," in which literature "will not be divided into genres but will implicate all the perspectives of the human sciences," working together to "reconstitut[e]" the "tormented chronology" of the Caribbean (65). Analyses of multigenre collage in Caribbean writing are also in Brathwaite's *Contradictory Omens*, in Davies and Fido's introduction to *Out of the Kumbla* (4–6), in Benítez-Rojo (25), and in Torres-Saillant (276).

6. This second genre might be well described in Selwyn Cudjoe's discussion of African-American autobiography, which "presents the . . . subject emerging as an almost random member of the group, selected to tell his/her tale": "The Afro-American autobiographical statement emerges as a *public* rather than a *private* gesture. . . . superficial concerns about *individual subject* usually give way to the *collective subjection* of the group" ("Maya Angelou" 9–10).

Maria Helena Lima writes that "the novel of *Bildung* has been 'chosen' in virtually all countries undergoing decolonization because it is the Western form of discourse that constitutes identity in terms of a relation to origin"; postcolonial transformations of the genre perform "provisional rewritings of origin and identity" (36).

7. A knowledge-ignorance schism erupts in remarkably similar form in Jamaica Kincaid's *Autobiography of My Mother*, published twelve years later; like *Abeng*'s speaker, Kincaid's heroine figures her people's mental colonization in their ignorant attendance at church. Xuela watches her compatriots "walking in a trance, no longer in their right minds, toward a church or away from a church," and knows they are unaware that the church, "typical of its time and place in every way, was built, inch by inch, by enslaved people" (133).

8. Gikandi similarly observes the postcolonial adaptation of the postmodern in Caribbean literature:

> [On] one hand, the well-known techniques of postmodernism—temporal fragmentation, parody, intertextuality, and repetition—are being used by

> [Caribbean] writers to subvert institutionalized history; but, on the other hand, these writers are striving to establish an authoritative Caribbean narrative of history. . . . [and even] to affirm the continuing urgency of an oppositional history and discourse that strive for the status of a grand narrative. (232–33)

9. Gikandi writes that Cliff's narration "is shaped by the doubleness of Caribbean history itself—the need to simultaneously represent dominant discourse, its referent, figures, and spectacles, and to question its privileges; the desire to psychoanalyze the trauma of history but also to transcend it" (239–40).

10. Self-division is not uncommon among Caribbean autobiographical subjects, Gikandi adds (see 203). Of course, the Euro-American female *bildungsroman* does not tend to present a coherent, unified subject and plot of development. Fraiman describes the heroines' plots in eighteenth- and nineteenth-century English women's novels as an "embattled development," even a "deformation" (xi–xii).

One might, indeed, read the narrator-character split in *Abeng* as a healthy revision of the confused, schizophrenic, or otherwise mad female subjectivities presented in earlier Caribbean women's fiction, including those of Rhys.

11. I draw on Frederic Jameson's controversial position that "Third world texts . . . necessarily project a political dimension in the form of a national allegory: *the story of the private individual is always an allegory of the embattled situation of the public third-world culture and society*" ("Third-World Literature" 69). See also Slemon, "Post-Colonial Allegory."

12. An interesting study of the problem of differing racial characteristics in constructions of Jamaican women's identity is Natasha B. Barnes's "Face of the Nation: Race, Nationalisms, and Identities in Jamaican Beauty Pageants." Barnes cites a 1986 incident in which a white woman crowned Miss Jamaica was booed off the stage by the furious crowd (285).

13. The transmission of African women's culture is evoked in the novel through remnants like the Jamaican tradition of appliqué, which characters in the book do not know has been passed down to them from the Fon women of Dahomey (59).

14. Cliff comments on this figure in the interview with Raiskin, "The Art of History" (70).

15. In an essay, Cliff similarly refers to England as the "mother (*sic*) country"—her pun perhaps intended ("Caliban's" 42).

16. Cliff has called Pocahontas a grandmother-figure for Clare ("Caliban's" 49).

17. Gikandi call this "an *annales* approach to history," one "in which rocks, eye-witness accounts, coffins, and oral forms have as much authority as documents" (242–43).

18. Caribbean fiction offers ironic accounts of the colonization of children's relationship to nature by their instruction in English literature. In Hodge's *Crick, Crack Monkey*:

> Books transported you always into the familiar solidity of chimneys and apple trees, the enviable normality of real Girls and Boys who went a-sleighing and built snowmen, ate potatoes, not rice, went about in socks and shoes from morning until night and called things by their proper names. . . . Books transported you always into Reality and Rightness, which were to be found Abroad. (61)

The apparently frightful tyranny in colonial children's lives of a single English poem, Wordsworth's "I Wandered Lonely as a Cloud"—about the "host, of golden daffodils"—is recorded by Jamaica Kincaid in *Lucy* (17–30), by Cliff in *Abeng* (84–85, 129), and by Jean Rhys in the story "The Day They Burned the Books" (175).

Such instruction in the natural features of a faraway landscape also confuses a white child of the African colonies in Doris Lessing's "The Old Chief Mshlanga." All of these children suffer from the colonial "gap . . . between the experience of a place and the language available to describe it" (Ashcroft 9). In a counter-strategy, *Abeng*'s black schoolmaster inserts into Langston Hughes's "The Negro Speaks of Rivers" the names of the Jamaican rivers he wants his students to know and love (90).

19. Glissant claims that Caribbean people have lacked a historicized vision of their natural environment (see 63, 92).

20. Cliff might be said to follow George Eliot in projecting into these "givens"—the smoke and dust residue of the Holocaust—an anger that cannot be expressed overtly, in this instance because of restrictions imposed both on a child, and on novelistic discourse.

21. This connection recurs throughout Cliff's work: besides the extended Anne Frank episode, in the ruminations about Columbus in *Abeng*; in the storytelling character Rachel DeSouza, comrade of the Jamaican heroine of *Free Enterprise* (1993); in the slur of the southern racist who pronounces the name of Boy Savage's country "Jew-maica" in *No Telephone*; in the story "A Woman Who Plays Trumpet Is Deported," about Valaida Snow, a black American woman imprisoned by the Nazis; and in several interviews and essays. Speaking with Judith Raiskin, Cliff recalls her graduate study with professors who were Holocaust survivors and makes multiple political and cultural connections to Jews and Jewish history (see "Art"; see also "If I Could" 71–72). Cliff's longtime companion, part-Jewish poet Adrienne Rich, has become increasingly concerned with Jewish issues in her work; Cliff has also collaborated extensively with the Jewish lesbian poet and activist Irena Klepfisz.

22. Speaking of the "fragments of stories" that inspired *Beloved* and *Jazz*, Morrison mentions, along with the newspaper article about Margaret Garner, a photograph in Van der Zee's *Harlem Book of the Dead* of "a young girl lying in a coffin" who apparently allowed herself to die rather than betray the lover who killed her ("Conversation" 206–7).

23. Edmondson writes that "Clare's love for Zoe is a manifestation of her more deeply rooted yearning for her mother's love and approval . . ." (188). On postcolonial women's writing and the logic of "substitution," see Chapter 7.

24. On this subject see Edmondson (184). Cliff has remarked that the character of Mrs. Stevens "is almost an exact description of a woman I knew," a neighbor who was mad and, moreover, a poet ("Interview" 616). Cliff has described a traumatic "silencing event" in her childhood, when her parents found and read her diary aloud, to chastise her for the lesbian feelings it recorded (603). While this was going on, Cliff has said, "there's this 'madwoman' over the wall. A poet." She adds:

> I don't have to have an imagination. All I have to do is record things. It's as if Bertha Rochester was next door, and this diary is connected up to writing

and expression of oneself, which was then used to humiliate me, and she's a poet and look what's happened to her. (617)

25. On conventions of the female bildungsroman see Abel et al (8). The episode of Clare's involvement with Bobby, the wounded black Vietnam vet, is unconvincing primarily because the plot of Clare's *Bildung* cannot comfortably accommodate a heterosexual romance, being preoccupied with maternal and historical return to Jamaica. Bobby's most important function is as the literal agent of Clare's symbolic sterility.

26. This is one of the few instances in *No Telephone* when *Abeng*'s rhetoric of not-knowing appears, and the circumstance is notably different. The full passage reads:

> When she heard what had happened to Paul and his people, she felt shock but no real sorrow. She did not think of his sperm congregating in her, so that his line might not have ended. In a few days she bled. She was free of him. Free as a free-martin. (89)

Here, when the narrator thinks of something Clare does not, Cliff articulates not the clear gap in knowledge of *Abeng*, but Clare's gradually and unevenly emerging self-knowledge: she is "free" of a patriarchal narrative that might have entrapped her, but she is also "free" of any understanding of the conditions in her country that have brought about the murder of Paul and his family.

27. A definition of Caribbean culture offered by Benítez-Rojo seems apposite here: "the cultural discourse of the Peoples of the Sea attempts, through real or symbolic sacrifice, to neutralize violence and to refer society to the transhistorical codes of Nature" (17).

28. This return of narrative assertion resonates with the final word of *Beloved*, which also reinstates human presence after a devastating diminishment.

CHAPTER 7

1. In *Tree of Life* (*La Vie Scélérate*) a daughter narrates a multigenerational saga that loosely follows Condé's own family story. Condé represents her generation in the alienated, assimilationist mother, against whom the narrator-daughter (to whom Condé gives her own daughter's birthday [Interview]) rebels. The daughter seeks to achieve peace with her dead, represented by a serene and beneficent foremother ghost, and to retrieve the family story. *Tree of Life* suggests that alienation and exile preclude a plot of reclaimed inheritance among Condé's generation; its ambivalent return to the family paves the way, instead, for a future returning daughter.

2. Vèvè Clark coins the term "diaspora literacy" in an essay on Condé's *Heremakhonon*, arguing that the novel helps to develop such literacy in readers through its use of allusion (303): "Diaspora literacy is the ability to read and comprehend the discourses of Africa, Afro-America and the Caribbean from an informed, indigenous perspective" (304).

3. Condé studied from 1953 to 1959 in Paris, where she developed her anticolonial politics. When she married an African in 1959, she went "back to Africa" with him both politically and geographically. Though the marriage later failed and Condé became disenchanted with African nationalisms (see Taleb-Khyar

352), she stayed in Africa for many years and wrote her first three novels about that continent: *Hérémakhonon* (1976), *Une Saison à Rihata* (1981), and the two-volume historical saga *Ségou: Les murailles de terre* (1984) and *Ségou: La terre en miettes* (1985).

At a moment when she "wanted to turn toward the Caribbean," Condé has said, "Tituba came to me or I came to her . . ." (Scarboro 204). After *Moi, Tituba*, Condé continued a rapprochement with the Caribbean, setting three novels in Guadeloupe: *La Vie Scélérate* (1987), *Traversée de la Mangrove* (1989), and *Les Derniers Rois Mages* (1992). She has also published a collection of Caribbean folktales, six plays, and several works of criticism, including *La parole des femmes* (1979) (for a list, see Scarboro 198).

Remarried to an Englishman who is her translator, Condé now divides her time between Guadeloupe and the United States. Her three grown daughters live (as of 1993) in chosen places along the route of their mother's wanderings: one in Africa, one in Paris, one in Guadeloupe.

4. In an interview, Condé recalls hearing an African-American woman writer recite a "superficial" story of her inspiration by her grandmother (Taleb-Khyar 348–49). Condé's rejection of the myth of the non-writing black foremother as source of the writing daughter's creativity—the thesis of Alice Walker's "In Search of Our Mothers' Gardens," for example—suggests, once again, the more problematic Caribbean figuration of the mythic mother.

5. Elisabeth Mudimbé-Boyi reads the author-character relationship initiated in this epigraph as a "collaborative enterprise" that valorizes orality and Caribbean "*métissage* and pluralism, at the racial, the cultural, and the linguistic levels" (754).

6. The fate of the historical Tituba is unclear; Condé's "Historical Note" to *I, Tituba* cites several myths (183).

7. These possibilities apparently include mutual alienation of ethnic audiences. Condé has cited Philip Roth as the greatest influence on her first novel, *Heremakhonon*: "I wanted to write a book about my community, meaning the West Indian community, which was going to enrage them, to make them furious, as much as I knew that *Portnoy's Complaint* infuriated the Jewish community" (Taleb-Khyar 362).

The appearance of subplots about the protagonist's identification with Jewish history in fictions by two Caribbean women, Cliff and Condé, is especially interesting in contrast to the absence of Jews in the new "histories" by African-American women, a suggestive matter beyond the scope of the present study.

8. Cliff claims only Brontë's Bertha as Clare's ancestor, but it seems clear that Rhys's adaptation of the character figures prominently in her lineage.

9. Here again, Condé's skeptical inclination contrasts with a tendency of African-American women novelists, who generally place more trust in their power to correct empirically false tellings of history. Rhys would seem to resemble Condé in this regard, but not so Cliff, interestingly closer to the African Americans in her tendency to argue fact. And as I assert later in this chapter, in her 1993 novel *Free Enterprise*, Cliff draws closer, too, to the African-American use of magic realism.

10. In this sense the Tituba-Hester pairing resembles Morrison's matching of the runaways Sethe and Amy Denver. Lillian Manzor-Coats claims, however, that the Hester-Tituba relationship parodically "stages the typical power relations . . . between white liberal feminists and women of color in contemporary

Anglo society," focusing on "their different experiences . . . along both racial and class axes" (742).

11. Condé has often espoused feminist views—speaking for example of a "bond" between Caribbean and U.S. women on the basis of their common experience of male domination (Interview), remarking that *I, Tituba* "is more about the discrimination and the ruthlessness against women than against people of color in general" (Scarboro 210) and writing a feminist analysis of Caribbean women's literature in *La parole des femmes*. Yet, she says, Caribbean women "don't relate so much to the hard-core feminists":

> American feminism is for us too alien; there is this idea of war between the sexes that we cannot accept, because we believe that men and women are all victims of colonialism and the two of us have to fight together. . . . We don't believe they are enemies, just spoiled by ourselves.

American feminists, in Condé's view, sometimes have a distorted sense of nature, as seen in an obsession with combating sexual harassment, or as when a group of American feminists told her of plans to bypass men in favor of artificial insemination. "For us," she says, "it is a perversion" (Interview).

12. See Chapter 1, p. 68.

13. As Condé retells the folktale, Ti-Jean's sister Ti-Marie is killed by a wild animal. When her brother goes in search of her he "suddenly sees a flower who sings to him, 'I am Ti-Marie'"; she has been transformed into the flower. When he cuts it, it bleeds and she comes to life again (Interview).

14. Notably, Condé's subsequent novel *Tree of Life* ends with a similar charge.

15. On the tendency of Caribbean characters to symbolize a collective condition see the discussion at the close of Chapter 6, part 1; see also Torres-Saillant (275). The regional conception of Caribbean literary culture advanced by Glissant has recently been advocated in books by J. Michael Dash and Torres-Saillant.

16. Cliff has often spoken of the importance of Morrison's work to her; see "Art" (60, 66) and "An Interview" (618).

17. Wylie notes that the protagonist of Condé's *The Last Magi* (*Les derniers rois mages*, 1992) criticizes the sort of fixation on the past that destroys one's ability to live in the present (766).

18. On a new universalism, see also Lionnet's introduction to *Postcolonial Representations* and Torres-Saillant's concluding chapter. On a new humanism, see Lionnet's chapter "Towards a New Antillean Humanism: Maryse Condé's *Traversée de la mangrove*."

EPILOGUE

1. "Writing Tituba," Condé has remarked, "was an opportunity to express my feelings about present-day America. I wanted to imply that in terms of narrowmindedness, hypocrisy, and racism, little has changed since the days of the Puritans" (Scarboro 203).

2. For this connection I am indebted to my student Susan Stern.

3. When Venn explains his plans for "computer-assisted time reconstruction" based on the creation of "the mother of all data bases" (138), he evokes for contemporary women's literature an entirely new, technologically generated historical "mother." The sardonic allusion to the American defeat of Saddam Hussein and his metaphors betrays the link between Venn's quest for an unprecedented

totalization of knowledge and the world view of a superpower. Yet the fact that it is Venn—and Mukherjee—inventing such a new world matrix suggests, at the same time, an ironic, postcolonized American vision of world history and its mother.

4. An example of the novel's pleasure in spinning out horizontal connections is the Yankee Hannah's romance with a Hindu rajah. When passion overtakes them on a carpet "alive with lion hunters grasping griffins with amber manes" (229), Mukherjee's characteristic turn is to invent a matching textile: the "elaborate knuckle covers" Hannah embroiders for her lover "to use under his shields": "scenes of Nipmuc warriors scalping amber-maned Puritans" and "a field of Massachusetts wildflowers (imagine the consternation of the first Sotheby's catalog, trying to explain the origin of such transcontinental adumbration!)" (230).

5. In addition to *The Scarlet Letter*, Mukherjee's heroine's plot also intersects the Hindu oral epic the *Mahabharata*. Bhagmati recites the story of the epic heroine Sita in her storytelling exchanges with Hannah, while Mukherjee generates extended parallels to Hannah's adventures, providing another literary intertextuality and another rewritten heroine.

6. Hawthorne, in Mukherjee's elaborate conceit, unknowingly honored Hannah's Hindu friend by misnaming his heroine "Hester" and got things wrong again when he called the daughter "Pearl."

7. The plot of Hannah's mother recalls Leslie Marmon Silko's *Ceremony* (1977), in which another white ancestress who willingly allows herself to be captured by Indians (the green-eyed Mexican grandmother of the Native American medicine man Betonie) is positioned as the foundation of the novel's celebration of hybridity. Morrison's "whitegirl" Amy Denver also runs away from her own people, to assist at the birth of a child who seems destined to advance interracial harmony.

8. Citing the argument of *Playing in the Dark*, Woidat does an extended reading of *Beloved* as an Africanist revision of *The Scarlet Letter*, with emphases different from mine.

Works Cited

Abel, Elizabeth, Marianne Hirsch, and Elizabeth Langland. Introduction to *The Voyage In: Fictions of Female Development*. Hanover, N.H.: University Press of New England, 1983. 3–19.

Aguiar, Sarah Appleton. "'Everywhere and Nowhere': Beloved's 'Wild' Legacy in Toni Morrison's *Jazz*." *Notes on Contemporary Literature* 25, no. 4 (1995): 11–12.

Allen, Walter. "Bertha the Doomed." Review of *Wide Sargasso Sea*, by Jean Rhys. *New York Times Book Review*, 18 June 1967, 5.

Allende, Isabel. *The House of the Spirits*. New York: Knopf, 1985.

Anderson, Benedict. *Imagined Communities: Reflections on the Origin and Spread of Nationalism*. Rev. ed. London: Verso, 1991.

Appiah, K. Anthony. "'Spiritual Realism.'" *The Nation*, 3 and 10 August 1992, 146–48.

Arnold, A. James. Introduction to *Lyric and Dramatic Poetry: 1946–82*, by Aimé Césaire. Ed. Arnold. xi–xli.

Ashcroft, Bill, Gareth Griffiths, and Helen Tiffin. *The Empire Writes Back: Theory and Practice in Post-colonial Literatures*. London: Routledge, 1989.

———. *The Post-colonial Studies Reader*. London: Routledge, 1995.

Auerbach, Nina. *Our Vampires, Ourselves*. Chicago: University of Chicago Press, 1995.

Awkward, Michael. *Inspiriting Influences: Tradition, Revision, and Afro-American Women's Novels*. New York: Columbia University Press, 1989.

Baer, Elizabeth R. "The Sisterhood of Jane Eyre and Antoinette Cosway." In *The Voyage In*, by Abel et al. 131–48.

Baker, Houston A., Jr. *Modernism and the Harlem Renaissance*. Chicago: University of Chicago Press, 1987.

Balutansky, Kathleen M. Unpublished bibliography of Caribbean women writers. 1990.

Bambara, Toni Cade. "Reading the Signs, Empowering the Eye: *Daughters of the*

Dust and the Black Independent Cinema Movement." In *Black American Cinema*, ed. Manthia Diawara. New York: Routledge, 1993. 118–44.

Barnes, Fiona R. "Resisting Cultural Cannibalism: Oppositional Narratives in Michelle Cliff's *No Telephone to Heaven*." *Journal of the Midwest Modern Language Association* 25, no. 1 (1992): 23–31.

Barnes, Natasha B. "Face of the Nation: Race, Nationalisms, and Identities in Jamaican Beauty Pageants." In *Daughters of Caliban*, ed. Springfield. 285–303.

Barthes, Roland. *S/Z*. Trans. Richard Miller. New York: Farrar, Straus, and Giroux, 1974.

Barthold, Bonnie J. *Black Time: Fiction of Africa, the Caribbean, and the United States*. New Haven: Yale University Press, 1981.

Barton, Anne, ed. *The Tempest*, by William Shakespeare. London: Penguin, 1968.

Baugh, Edward. "Sometimes in the Middle of the Story." In *Crossing Water*, ed. Kellman. 9.

Bell, Bernard W. *The Afro-American Novel and Its Tradition*. Amherst: University of Massachusetts Press, 1987.

Bell-Scott, Patricia, et al., eds. *Double Stitch: Black Women Write about Mothers and Daughters*. Boston: Beacon, 1991.

Benítez-Rojo, Antonio. *The Repeating Island: The Caribbean and the Postmodern Perspective*. 2d ed. Trans. James Maraniss. Durham: Duke University Press, 1996.

Bernabé, Jean, Patrick Chamoiseau, and Raphael Confiant. "In Praise of Creoleness." 1989. Trans. Mohamed B. Taleb-Khyar. *Callaloo* 13, no. 4 (1990): 886–909.

Berry, James. "The Literature of the Black Experience." In *The Language of the Black Experience*, ed. David Sutcliffe and Ansel Wong. London: Basil Blackwell, 1986. 69–106.

Bhabha, Homi. *The Location of Culture*. London: Routledge, 1994.

Blassingame, John. "Using the Testimony of Ex-Slaves: Approaches and Problems." In *The Slave's Narrative*, ed. Davis and Gates. 78–98.

Bloom, Harold. *The Anxiety of Influence: A Theory of Poetry*. New York: Oxford University Press, 1973.

———. *Kabbalah and Criticism*. New York: Seabury, 1975.

Boehmer, Elleke. "Stories of Women and Mothers: Gender and Nationalism in the Early Work of Flora Nwapa." In *Motherlands*, ed. Nasta. 3–23.

Brathwaite, [Edward] Kamau. "The African Presence in Caribbean Literature." In *Slavery, Colonialism, and Racism*, ed. Sidney Mintz. New York: Norton, 1974. 73–109.

———. *The Arrivants: A New World Trilogy*. 1973. Reprint, Oxford: Oxford University Press, 1992.

———. *Barbajan Poems 1492–1992*. New York: Savacou North, 1994.

———. *Contradictory Omens: Cultural Diversity and Integration in the Caribbean*. Mona, Kingston, Jamaica: Savacou, 1974.

———. "History of the Voice." 1979/1981. In *Roots*. Ann Arbor: University of Michigan Press, 1993. 259–304.

———. *Mother Poem*. Oxford: Oxford University Press, 1977.

———. "West Indian History and Society in the Art of Paule Marshall's Novel." *Journal of Black Studies* 1, no. 2 (1970): 225–38.

———. *X/Self*. Oxford: Oxford University Press, 1987.

Braxton, Joanne M. "Afra-American Culture and the Contemporary Literary

Renaissance." In *Wild Women in the Whirlwind,* ed. Braxton and McLaughlin. xxi–xxx.
———. "Ancestral Presence: The Outraged Mother Figure in Contemporary Afra-American Writing." In *Wild Women in the Whirlwind,* ed. Braxton and McLaughlin. 299–315.
———. "Harriet Jacobs' *Incidents in the Life of a Slave Girl*: The Re-definition of the Slave Narrative Genre." *Massachusetts Review* 27 (1986): 379–87.
Braxton, Joanne M., and Andree Nicola McLaughlin, eds. *Wild Women in the Whirlwind: Afra-American Culture and the Contemporary Literary Renaissance.* New Brunswick, N.J.: Rutgers University Press, 1990.
Brontë, Charlotte. *Jane Eyre.* 1847. Reprint, New York: Norton, 1971.
Brooks, Gwendolyn. *Maud Martha.* New York: Harper, 1953.
Brown-Guillory, Elizabeth. "Disrupted Motherlines: Mothers and Daughters in a Genderized, Sexualized, and Racialized World." In *Women of Color,* ed. Brown-Guillory. 188–207.
———, ed. *Women of Color: Mother-Daughter Relationships in Twentieth-Century Literature.* Austin: University of Texas Press, 1996.
Burch, Beverly. *On Intimate Terms: The Psychology of Difference in Lesbian Relationships.* Urbana: University of Illinois Press, 1993.
Busby, Margaret. *Daughters of Africa: An International Anthology of Words and Writing by Women of African Descent: From the Ancient Egyptian to the Present.* New York: Pantheon, 1992.
Butler, Octavia. *Kindred.* 1979. Reprint, Boston: Beacon, 1988.
Campbell, Elaine. "Phyllis Shand Allfrey." In *Fifty Caribbean Writers: A Bio-bibliographical Critical Sourcebook,* ed. Daryl Cumber Dance. Westport, Conn.: Greenwood, 1986. 9–18.
Campbell, Jane. *Mythic Black Fiction: The Transformation of History.* Knoxville: University of Tennessee Press, 1986.
Carby, Hazel V. "Ideologies of Black Folk: The Historical Novel of Slavery." In *Slavery and the Literary Imagination,* by McDowell and Rampersad. 124–43.
Carpentier, Alejo. "On the Marvelous Real in America." Trans. Tanya Huntington and Lois Parkinson Zamora. In *Magical Realism,* ed. Zamora and Faris. 75–88.
———. *El Reino de Este Mundo.* 1949. Reprint, Santiago, Chile: Editorial Universitaria, 1972.
Caruth, Cathy, ed. *Trauma: Explorations in Memory.* Baltimore: Johns Hopkins University Press, 1995.
Césaire, Aimé. *Discourse on Colonialism.* Trans. Joan Pinkham. New York: Monthly Review, 1972.
———. *Lyric and Dramatic Poetry: 1946–82.* Ed. A. James Arnold. Trans. Clayton Eshleman and Annette Smith. Charlottesville: University Press of Virginia, 1990.
———. *Return to My Native Land.* Trans. John Berger and Anna Bostock. Harmondsworth, Middlesex, England: Penguin, 1969.
———. *A Tempest.* Trans. Richard Miller. 1969. Reprint, New York: Ubu Repertory Theater/Editions de Seuil, 1986.
Chambers, Ross. *Story and Situation: Narrative Seduction and the Power of Fiction.* Minneapolis: University of Minnesota Press, 1984.

Chanady, Amaryll. "The Territorialization of the Imaginary in Latin America: Self-Affirmation and Resistance to Metropolitan Paradigms." In *Magical Realism*, ed. Zamora and Faris. 125–44.

Chase-Riboud, Barbara. *Sally Hemings*. New York: Ballantine, 1979.

Chesnutt, Charles. *The Conjure Woman*. Cambridge: Riverside, 1899.

Chodorow, Nancy. *The Reproduction of Mothering: Psychoanalysis and the Sociology of Gender*. Berkeley: University of California Press, 1978.

Christian, Barbara. "Somebody Forgot to Tell Somebody Something: African-American Women's Historical Novels." In *Wild Women in the Whirlwind*, ed. Braxton and McLaughlin, 326–41.

———. "Trajectories of Self-Definition: Placing Contemporary Afro-American Women's Fiction." In *Conjuring*, ed. Pryse and Spillers. 233–48.

Churchill, Caryl. *Cloud Nine*. 1979. Reprint, London: Pluto, 1981.

Clark, Vèvè A. "Developing Diaspora Literacy: Allusion in Maryse Condé's *Heremakhonon*." In *Out of the Kumbla*, ed. Davies and Fido. 355–72.

Clemons, Walter. "A Gravestone of Memories." Review of *Beloved*, by Toni Morrison. *Newsweek*, 28 Sept. 1987, 74–75.

Cliff, Michelle. *Abeng*. Trumansburg, N.Y.: Crossing, 1984.

———. "The Art of History: An Interview with Michelle Cliff." With Judith Raiskin. *Kenyon Review* , n.s., 15, no. 1 (1993): 57–71.

———. "Caliban's Daughter: The Tempest and the Teapot." *Frontiers* 11, no. 2 (1991): 36–51.

———. "claiming an identity: an interview with Michelle Cliff." With Tacie Dejanikus and Loie Hayes. *Off Our Backs*, June 1981, 18–20.

———. "Clare Savage as a Crossroads Character." In *Caribbean Women Writers*, ed. Cudjoe. 263–68.

———. *Free Enterprise*. New York: Dutton/Penguin, 1993.

———. "If I Could Write This in Fire, I Would Write This in Fire." *The Land of Look Behind: Prose and Poetry*. Ithaca, N.Y.: Firebrand, 1985. 57–76.

———. "An Interview with Michelle Cliff." With Meryl F. Schwartz. *Contemporary Literature* 34, no. 4 (1993): 596–619.

———. "Love in the Third World." *The Land of Look Behind: Prose and Poetry*. Ithaca, N.Y.: Firebrand, 1985.

———. *No Telephone to Heaven*. 1987. Reprint, New York: Vintage, 1989.

———. "A Woman Who Plays Trumpet Is Deported." *Bodies of Water*. New York: Penguin, 1990. 53–60.

Clifton, Lucille. "at the cemetery, walnut grove plantation, south carolina, 1989"; "i am accused of tending to the past. . . ."; "slave cabin, sotterly plantation, maryland, 1989." *Quilting: Poems 1987–1990*. Brockport, N.Y.: BOA, 1992. 11–12, 7, 13.

———. "daughters." *The Book of Light: Poems*. Port Townsend, Wash.: Copper Canyon, 1993.

———. *Generations: A Memoir*. New York: Random House, 1974.

Coetzee, J. M. *In the Heart of the Country*. New York: Penguin, 1982.

———. *White Writing: On the Culture of Letters in South Africa*. New Haven: Yale University Press, 1988.

Cohn, Dorrit. *Transparent Minds: Narrative Modes for Presenting Consciousness in Fiction*. Princeton: Princeton University Press, 1978.

Collins, Patricia Hill. *Black Feminist Thought: Knowledge, Consciousness, and the Politics of Empowerment*. Boston: Unwin Hyman, 1990.

Condé, Maryse. *Heremakhonon*. Trans. Richard Philcox. Washington, D.C.: Three Continents, 1982.

———. *I, Tituba, Black Witch of Salem*. Trans. Richard Philcox. New York: Ballantine, 1992.

———. Interview by author. Charlottesville, Va., 3 May 1993.

———. Lectures. "Caribbean Culture: Post-Colonialism or Post-Modernism?" Department of French, University of Virginia. Spring 1993.

———. *La parole des femmes: Essai sur des romancières des Antilles de langue française*. Paris: Editions L'harmattan, [1979].

———. *A Season in Rihata*. Trans. Richard Philcox. Oxford: Heinemann, 1988.

———. *Tree of Life*. Trans. Victoria Reiter. New York: Ballantine, 1992.

Cosby, Bill. Introduction to *The Black Book*, by Middleton A. Harris. New York: Random House, 1974.

Coser, Stelamaris. *Bridging the Americas: The Literature of Toni Morrison, Paule Marshall, and Gayl Jones*. Philadelphia: Temple University Press, 1994.

Coulthard, G. R. *Race and Colour in Caribbean Literature*. London: Oxford University Press, 1962.

Cudjoe, Selwyn R., ed. *Caribbean Women Writers: Essays from the First International Conference*. Wellesley, Mass.: Calaloux, 1990.

———. "Maya Angelou and the Autobiographical Statement." In *Black Women Writers (1950–1980): A Critical Evaluation*, ed. Mari Evans. Garden City, N.Y.: Anchor/Doubleday, 1984.

———. *Resistance and Caribbean Literature*. Chicago: Ohio University Press, 1980.

Curry, Renee R. "*Daughters of the Dust*, the White Woman Viewer, and the Unborn Child." In *Teaching What You're Not: Identity Politics in Higher Education*, ed. Katherine J. Mayberry. New York: New York University Press, 1996. 335–56.

Damas, Léon. *Pigments-Neuralgies*. Paris: Présence Africaine, 1972.

Dance, Daryl Cumber. *Fifty Caribbean Writers: A Bio-bibliographical Critical Sourcebook*. Westport, Conn.: Greenwood, 1986.

Dash, J. Michael. *The Other America: Caribbean Literature in a New World Context*. Charlottesville: University Press of Virginia, 1998.

Dash, Julie. *"Daughters of the Dust": The Making of an African-American Woman's Film*. With Toni Cade Bambara and bell hooks. New York: New Press, 1992.

Davidson, Arnold E. *Jean Rhys*. New York: Frederick Ungar, 1985.

Davies, Carole Boyce. *Black Women, Writing, and Identity: Migrations of the Subject*. London: Routledge, 1994.

———. "Black Women Writing Worlds: Textual Production, Dominance, and the Critical Voice." In *Black Women's Diasporas*. Vol. 2 of *Moving beyond Boundaries*, ed. Davies. 1–15.

———, ed. *Black Women's Diasporas*. Vol. 2 of *Moving beyond Boundaries*, ed. Davies. New York: New York University Press, 1995.

———. "'Woman Is a Nation . . . ' Women in Caribbean Oral Literature." In *Out of the Kumbla*, ed. Davies and Fido. 165–93.

———. "Writing Home: Gender and Heritage in the Works of Afro-Caribbean/American Women Writers." In *Out of the Kumbla*, ed. Davies and Fido. 59–73.

Davies, Carole Boyce, and Elaine Savory Fido, eds. *Out of the Kumbla: Caribbean Women and Literature*. Trenton, N.J.: Africa World, 1990.

Davies, Carole Boyce, and 'Molara Ogundipe-Leslie, eds. *International Dimensions of Black Women's Writing*. Vol. 1 of *Moving beyond Boundaries*. New York: New York University Press, 1995.

Davis, Angela Y. "Black Women and Music: A Historical Legacy of Struggle." In *Wild Women in the Whirlwind*, ed. Braxton and McLaughlin. 3–21.

———. Foreword to. *I, Tituba, Black Witch of Salem*, by Maryse Condé. Trans. Richard Philcox. New York: Ballantine, 1992.

Davis, Charles T., and Henry Louis Gates, Jr., eds. *The Slave's Narrative*. Oxford: Oxford University Press, 1985.

Davis, Cynthia A. "Self, Society, and Myth in Toni Morrison's Fiction." *Contemporary Literature* 23 (1982): 323–342.

D'Haen, Theo L. "Magical Realism and Postmodernism: Decentering Privileged Centers." In *Magical Realism*, ed. Zamora and Faris. 191–208.

Delourme, Chantal. "La Mémoire Fécondée. Réflexions sur L'intertextualité: *Jane Eyre, Wide Sargasso Sea*." *Etudes Anglaises: Grande-Bretagne, Etats-Unis* 42, no. 3 (1989): 257–69.

De Weever, Jacqueline. *Mythmaking and Metaphor in Black Women's Fiction*. New York: St. Martin's, 1991.

Douglass, Frederick. *Narrative of the Life of Frederick Douglass: An American Slave, Written by Himself*. 1845. Reprint, ed. Benjamin Quarles. Cambridge, Mass.: Belknap/Harvard University Press, 1960.

Doyle, Laura. *Bordering on the Body: The Racial Matrix of Modern Fiction and Culture*. New York: Oxford University Press, 1994.

Drake, Sandra. "All That Foolishness/That All Foolishness: Race and Caribbean Culture as Thematics of Liberation in Jean Rhys' *Wide Sargasso Sea*." *Critica* 2, no. 2 (1990): 97–112.

Duffey, Carolyn. "Tituba and Hester in the Intertextual Jail Cell: New World Feminisms in Maryse Condé's *Moi, Tituba, sorcière . . . Noire de Salem*." *Women in French Studies* 4 (1996): 100–110.

Dukats, Mara L. "A Narrative of Violated Maternity: *Moi, Tituba, sorcière . . . Noire de Salem*." *World Literature Today* 67, no. 4 (1993): 745–50.

Edmondson, Belinda. "Race, Privilege, and the Politics of (Re)Writing History: An Analysis of the Novels of Michelle Cliff." *Callaloo* 16, no. 1 (1993): 180–91.

Emery, Mary Lou. *Jean Rhys at "World's End": Novels of Colonial and Sexual Exile*. Austin: University of Texas Press, 1990.

———. "Refiguring the Postcolonial Imagination: Tropes of Visuality in Writing by Rhys, Kincaid, and Cliff." *Tulsa Studies in Women's Literature* 16, no. 2 (1997): 259–80.

Erwin, Lee. "'Like in a Looking-Glass': History and Narrative in *Wide Sargasso Sea*." *Novel* 22, no. 2. (1989): 143–58.

Esquivel, Laura. *Like Water for Chocolate: A Novel in Monthly Installments, with Recipes, Romances, and Home Remedies*. New York: Doubleday, 1992.

Esteves, Carmen C., and Lizabeth Paravasini-Gebert, eds. *Green Cane and Juicy Flotsam: Short Stories by Caribbean Women*. New Brunswick, N.J.: Rutgers University Press, 1991.

Fanon, Frantz. *The Wretched of the Earth*. New York: Grove, 1963.

Faris, Wendy B. "Scheherazade's Children: Magical Realism and Postmodern Fiction." In *Magical Realism*, ed. Zamora and Faris. 163–89.

Farwell, Marilyn. "Heterosexual Plots and Lesbian Subtexts: Toward a Theory of Lesbian Narrative Space." In *Lesbian Texts and Contexts: Radical Revisions*, ed. Karla Jay and Joanne Glasgow. New York: New York University Press, 1990.

Fayad, Mona. "Unquiet Ghosts: The Struggle for Representation in Jean Rhys's *Wide Sargasso Sea.*" *Modern Fiction Studies* 34, no. 3 (1988): 437–52.

Felman, Shoshana, and Dori Laub. *Testimony: Crises of Witnessing in Literature, Psychoanalysis, and History*. New York: Routledge, 1992.

Ferracane, Kathleen K. "Images of the Mother in Caribbean Literature." Ph.D. diss. State University of New York at Buffalo, 1987.

Fetterley, Judith. *The Resisting Reader: A Feminist Approach to American Fiction*. Bloomington: Indiana University Press, 1978.

Fido, Elaine Savory. "Mother/lands: Self and Separation in the Work of Buchi Emecheta, Bessie Head and Jean Rhys." In *Motherlands*, ed. Nasta. 330–49.

Fischer, Michael M. J. "Ethnicity and the Post-Modern Arts of Memory." In *Writing Culture: The Poetics and Politics of Ethnography*, ed. James Clifford and George E. Marcus. Berkeley: University of California Press, 1986. 194–233.

Fleishman, Avrom. *The English Historical Novel, Walter Scott to Virginia Woolf.* Baltimore: Johns Hopkins University Press, 1971.

Flockemann, Miki. "Language and Self in Opal Palmer Adisa's 'Bake-Face and Other Guava Stories.'" *Ariel* 24, no. 1 (1993): 59–73.

Fogel, Robert William. *Without Consent or Contract: The Rise and Fall of American Slavery*. New York: Norton, 1989.

Forman, Ruth. *We Are the Young Magicians*. Boston: Beacon, 1993.

Forster, E. M. *A Passage to India*. 1924. Reprint New York: Harcourt, 1984.

Foster, Frances. "'In Respect to Females': Differences in the Portrayals of Women by Male and Female Narrators." *Black American Literature Forum* 15 (1981): 66–70.

Fraiman, Susan. *Unbecoming Women: British Women Writers and the Novel of Development*. New York: Columbia University Press, 1993.

Friedman, Ellen G. "Breaking the Master Narrative: Jean Rhys's *Wide Sargasso Sea.*" In *Breaking the Sequence: Women's Experimental Fiction*, ed. Friedman and Miriam Fuchs. Princeton: Princeton University Press, 1989.

Friedman, Susan Stanford. "Creativity and the Childbirth Metaphor: Gender Difference in Literary Discourse." *Feminist Studies* 13, no. 1 (Spring 1987): 49–82. Reprint in *Feminisms*, ed. Warhol and Herndl, 371–96.

Fultz, Lucille P. "To Make Herself: Mother-Daughter Conflicts in Toni Morrison's *Sula* and *Tar Baby.*" In *Women of Color*, ed. Brown-Guillory. 228–42.

Gaines, Ernest J. *The Autobiography of Miss Jane Pittman*. New York: Dial, 1971.

Gardiner, Judith Kegan. "The Exhilaration of Exile: Rhys, Stead, Lessing." In *Women's Writing in Exile*, ed. Mary Lynn Broe and Angela Ingram. Chapel Hill: University of North Carolina Press, 1989. 133–56.

Gates, Henry Louis, Jr. Preface to *Toni Morrison*, ed. Gates and Appiah. ix–xiii.

Gates, Henry Louis, Jr., and K. A. Appiah, eds. *Toni Morrison: Critical Perspectives Past and Present*. New York: Amistad, 1993.

Giddings, Paula. *When and Where I Enter: The Impact of Black Women on Race and Sex in America*. New York: Morrow, 1984.

Gikandi, Simon. *Writing in Limbo: Modernism and Caribbean Literature*. Ithaca, N.Y.: Cornell University Press, 1992.

Gilbert, Sandra, and Susan Gubar. *The War of the Words*. Vol. 1 of *No Man's Land: The Place of the Woman Writer in the Twentieth Century*. New Haven: Yale University Press, 1988.

———. *The Madwoman in the Attic: The Woman Writer and the Nineteenth-Century Literary Imagination*. New Haven: Yale University Press, 1979.

Gilroy, Paul. *The Black Atlantic: Modernity and Double Consciousness.* Cambridge: Harvard University Press, 1993.

Glissant, Edouard. *Caribbean Discourse: Selected Essays.* Trans. J. Michael Dash. Charlottesville: University Press of Virginia, 1989.

Gomez, Jewelle. "Black Women Heroes: Here's Reality, Where's the Fiction?" *Black Scholar* 17, no. 2 (1986): 8–13.

———. "A Cultural Legacy Denied and Discovered: Black Lesbians in Fiction by Women." In *Home Girls: A Black Feminist Anthology,* ed. Barbara Smith. New York: Kitchen Table, 1983.

———. *The Gilda Stories.* Ithaca, N.Y.: Firebrand, 1991.

Goodison, Lorna. *I Am Becoming My Mother.* London: New Beacon, 1986.

———. "Nanny." *Selected Poems.* Ann Arbor: University of Michigan Press, 1992. 69–70.

Goodwin, K. L. *Understanding African Poetry.* London: Heinemann, 1982.

Gregg, Veronica Marie. *Jean Rhys's Historical Imagination: Reading and Writing the Creole.* Chapel Hill: University of North Carolina Press, 1995.

Grewal, Gurleen. *Circles of Sorrow, Lines of Struggle: The Novels of Toni Morrison.* Baton Rouge: Louisiana State University Press, 1998.

Hall, Stuart. "Cultural Identity and Diaspora." In *Colonial Discourse,* ed. Williams and Chrisman, 392–403.

———. "New Ethnicities." In *Black Film/British Cinema,* ed. Kobena Mercer. London: ICA, 1988. 27–31.

Harris, Middleton A. *The Black Book.* With Morris Levitt, Roger Furman, and Ernest Smith. New York: Random House, 1974.

Harris, Wilson. *The Womb of Space: The Cross-Cultural Imagination.* Westport, Conn.: Greenwood, 1983.

Harrison, Nancy. *Jean Rhys and the Novel as Woman's Text.* Chapel Hill: University of North Carolina Press, 1988.

Hart, Patricia. *Narrative Magic in the Fiction of Isabel Allende.* London: Associated University Presses, 1989.

Hayles, N. Katherine. "Anger in Different Voices: Carol Gilligan and *The Mill on the Floss.*" *Signs* 12, no. 1 (1986): 23–39.

Hearne, John, ed. *Carifesta Forum: An Anthology of Twenty Caribbean Voices.* Kingston, Jamaica: Institute of Jamaica and *Jamaica Journal* [1976].

Henderson, Stephen E. Introduction to *Black Women Writers (1950–1980): A Critical Evaluation,* ed. Mari Evans. Garden City, N.Y.: Anchor/Doubleday, 1984.

Hirsch, Marianne. *The Mother/Daughter Plot: Narrative, Psychoanalysis, Feminism.* Bloomington: Indiana University Press, 1989.

Hite, Molly. *The Other Side of the Story.* Ithaca, N.Y.: Cornell University Press, 1989.

Hodge, Merle. "Challenges of the Struggle for Sovereignty: Challenging the World versus Writing Stories." In *Caribbean Women Writers,* ed. Cudjoe. 202–8.

———. *Crick Crack, Monkey.* 1970. Reprint, London: Heinemann, 1981.

Hollinger, David. *Postethnic America: Beyond Multiculturalism.* New York: Basic, 1995.

Holloway, Karla F. C. *Moorings and Metaphors: Figures of Culture and Gender in Black Women's Literature.* New Brunswick, N.J.: Rutgers University Press, 1992.

hooks, bell. "Postmodern Blackness." *Yearning: Race, Gender, and Cultural Politics.* London: Turnaround and Boston: South End, 1991. Reprint in *Colonial Discourse,* ed. Williams and Chrisman. 421–27.

Hulme, Peter. "The Locked Heart: The Creole Family Romance of *Wide Sargasso Sea*." In *Colonial Discourse/Postcolonial Theory*, ed. Francis Barker, Peter Hulme, and Margaret Iversen. Manchester: Manchester University Press, 1994. 72–88.

Hutcheon, Linda. "Historiographic Metafiction: The Pastime of Past Time." *A Poetics of Postmodernism*. London: Routledge, 1988.

Hurston, Zora Neale. *Their Eyes Were Watching God*. 1937. Reprint, Urbana: University of Illinois Press, 1978.

Jacobs, Harriet [Linda Brent, pseud.]. *Incidents in the Life of a Slave Girl, Written by Herself*. Ed. L. Maria Child. 1861. Reprint, New York: Harcourt, 1983.

Jacquey, Marie-Clotilde, and Monique Hugon. "L'Afrique, un continent difficil. Entretien avec Maryse Condé." *Notre Libraire* 74 (1984): 22–25.

James, Cynthia. "The Unknown Text." *World Literature Today* 68, no. 4 (1994): 758–64.

Jameson, Fredric. "On Magic Realism in Film." *Critical Inquiry* 12 (1986): 301–25.

———. *The Political Unconscious: Narrative as a Socially Symbolic Act*. Ithaca, N.Y.: Cornell University Press, 1981.

———. "Third-World Literature in the Era of Multinational Capitalism." *Social Text* 15 (1986): 65–88.

Johnson, Charles. *Middle Passage*. New York: Plume-Penguin, 1991.

———. *Oxherding Tale*. New York: Grove, 1982.

Johnson, Judith E. "Women and Vampires: Nightmare or Utopia?" *Kenyon Review*, n.s., 15, no. 1 (1993): 72–80.

Jones, Charisse. "Bringing Slavery's Long Shadow to the Light." *New York Times*, 2 Apr. 1995, A1, A43.

Jones, Gayl. *Corregidora*. 1975. Reprint, Boston: Beacon, 1986.

Jordan, June. "Gettin Down to Get Over." *Things That I Do in the Dark: Selected Poems*. 1977. Reprint, Boston: Beacon, 1981. 27–37.

———. *Naming Our Destiny: New and Selected Poems*. New York: Thunder's Mouth, 1989.

Kakutani, Michiko. "Losses in the Caribbean, from Birth On." Review of *The Autobiography of My Mother*, by Jamaica Kincaid. *New York Times*, 16 Jan. 1996, C17.

Keenan, Sally. "'Four Hundred Years of Silence.' Myth, History and Motherhood in *Beloved*." In *Recasting the World: Writing after Colonialism*, ed. Jonathan White. Baltimore: Johns Hopkins University Press, 1993. 45–81.

Kellman, Anthony, ed. *Crossing Water: Contemporary Poetry of the English-Speaking Caribbean*. Greenfield Center, N.Y.: Greenfield Review, 1992.

Kincaid, Jamaica. *Annie John*. New York: NAL-Penguin, 1986.

———. *Lucy*. New York: Farrar, Straus & Giroux, 1990.

———. "My Mother Wrote My Life." Interview with Patricia T. O'Conner. *New York Times Book Review*, 7 Apr. 1985, 6.

Kloepfer, Deborah Kelly. *The Unspeakable Mother: Forbidden Discourse in Jean Rhys and H.D.* Ithaca, N.Y.: Cornell University Press, 1989.

Kristeva, Julia. "Women's Time." Trans. Alice Jardine and Harry Blake. In *Feminist Theory: A Critique of Ideology*, ed. Nannerl O. Keohane, Michelle Z. Rosaldo, and Barbara C. Gelpi. Chicago: University of Chicago Press, 1982. 31–53.

Kutzinski, Vera M. *Against the American Grain: Myth and History in William Carlos Williams, Jay Wright, and Nicolas Guillen*. Baltimore: Johns Hopkins University Press, 1987.

———. "Commentary: American Literary History as Spatial Practice." *American Literary History* 4, no. 3 (1992): 550–57.

Lerner, Gerda, ed. *Black Women in White America: A Documentary History*. 1972. Reprint, New York: Vintage, 1973.

Lessing, Doris. "The Old Chief Mshlanga." *The Doris Lessing Reader*. New York: Knopf, 1988. 3-13.

Liddell, Janice Lee. "The Narrow Enclosure of Motherdom/Martyrdom: A Study of Gatha Randall Barton in Sylvia Wynter's *The Hills of Hebron*." In *Out of the Kumbla*, ed. Davies and Fido. 321–30.

Lima, Maria Helena. "Revolutionary Developments: Michelle Cliff's *No Telephone to Heaven* and Merle Collins's *Angel*." *Ariel* 24, no. 1 (1993): 35–56.

Lincoln, Abbey. "Evalina Coffey (the Legend of)." *Devil's Got Your Tongue*. Qtd. in *The New York Times*, 28 Feb. 1993, H28.

Lionnet, Françoise. *Postcolonial Representations: Women, Literature, Identity*. Ithaca, N.Y.: Cornell University Press, 1995.

Liscio, Lorraine. "*Beloved*'s Narrative: Writing Mother's Milk." *Tulsa Studies in Women's Literature* 11 (1992): 31–46.

Lorde, Audre. *Zami: a new spelling of my name*. Watertown, Mass.: Persephone, 1982.

Lukacs, Georg. *The Historical Novel*. Trans. Hannah Mitchell and Stanley Mitchell. 1962. Reprint, Atlantic Highlands, N.J.: Humanities, 1978.

Mair, Lucille Mathurin. "Recollections of a Journey into a Rebel Past." In *Caribbean Women Writers* ed. Cudjoe. 51–60.

Manzor-Coats, Lillian. "Of Witches and Other Things: Maryse Condé's Challenges to Feminist Discourse." *World Literature Today* 67, no. 4 (1993): 737–44.

Markham, E. A. *Hinterland: Caribbean Poetry from the West Indies and Britain*. Newcastle upon Tyne, England: Bloodaxe, 1989.

Marquez, Gabriel Garcia. *One Hundred Years of Solitude*. Trans. Gregory Rabassa. New York: Harper & Row, 1970.

Marshall, Paule. *Brown Girl, Brownstones*. New York: Random House, 1959.

———. *The Chosen Place, the Timeless People*. 1969. Reprint, New York: Avon, 1976.

———. *Praisesong for the Widow*. New York: Penguin, 1983.

———. "Re-Creating Ourselves All over the World: A Conversation with Paule Marshall." With 'Molara Ogundipe-Leslie. In vol. 2 of *Moving beyond Boundaries*, ed. Davies. 19–26.

Martini, Jurgen. "Literary Criticism and Aesthetics in the Caribbean I: E. K. Brathwaite." *World Literature Written in English* 24, no. 2 (1984): 373–83.

Maximin, Daniel. *Lone Sun*. Ed. Clarisse Zimra. Charlottesville: University Press of of Virginia, 1989.

McClintock, Anne. "The Angel of Progress: Pitfalls of the Term 'Post-Colonialism.'" *Social Text* 31/32 (1992): 84–98.

McDowell, Deborah E. "Harlem Nocturne." Review of *Jazz*, by Toni Morrison. *Women's Review of Books* 11, no. 9 (1992): 1, 3–5.

———. "In the First Place: Making Frederick Douglass and the Afro-American Narrative Tradition." In *Critical Essays on Frederick Douglass*, ed. William Andrews. Boston: Hall, 1991. 192–214.

———. "Negotiating between Tenses: Witnessing Slavery after Freedom—*Dessa Rose*." In *Slavery and the Literary Imagination*, ed. McDowell and Rampersad. 144-63.

———. "Reading Family Matters." In *Changing Our Own Words: Essays on Criticism, Theory, and Writing by Black Women*, ed. Cheryl A. Wall. New Brunswick, N.J.: Rutgers University Press, 1989. 75–97.

———. "'The Self and the Other': Reading Toni Morrison's *Sula* and the Black Female Text." In *Critical Essays on Toni Morrison*, ed. Nellie Y. McKay. Boston: Hall, 1988. 77–90.

McDowell, Deborah E., and Arnold Rampersad, ed. *Slavery and the Literary Imagination*. Selected Papers from the English Institute. N.S. 13. Baltimore: Johns Hopkins University Press, 1989.

McKay, Nellie Y. "Reflections on Black Women Writers: Revising the Literary Canon." In *Feminisms*, ed.Warhol and Herndl. 249–61.

McLaughlin, Andree Nicola. "A Renaissance of the Spirit: Black Women Remaking the Universe." In *Wild Women in the Whirlwind*, ed. Braxton and McLaughlin. xxxi–xlvii.

Michaels, Walter Benn. "'You who never was there': Slavery and the New Historicism, Deconstruction and the Holocaust." *Narrative* 4, no. 1 (1996): 1–16.

Miller, D. A. *Narrative and Its Discontents: Problems of Closure in the Traditional Novel*. Princeton: Princeton University Press, 1981.

Miller, Nancy K. "Emphasis Added: Plots and Plausibilities in Women's Fiction." *PMLA* 96, no. 1 (1981): 36–48.

———. *The Heroine's Text: Readings in the French and English Novel, 1722-1782*. New York: Columbia University Press, 1980.

Mills, David. "Island of Originality: Director Julie Dash's New Take on Tradition." *Washington Post*, 28 Feb. 1992, C1–C3.

Mooney, Paul. "Race." Qtd. in *Washington Post*, 16 May 1993, G1.

Mordecai, Pamela, and Betty Wilson, eds. *Her True-True Name: An Anthology of Women's Writing from the Caribbean*. Oxford: Heinemann, 1989.

Morris, Ann R., and Margaret M. Dunn. "'The Bloodstream of Our Inheritance': Female Identity and the Caribbean Mothers'-Land." In *Motherlands*, ed. Nasta. 219–37.

Morrison, Toni. "African-Americans, Part III: Toni Morrison and Trudier Harris." *Soundings*. With Wayne Pond. Radio program, WTJU, Charlottesville, Va., 20 Feb. 1991.

———. *Beloved*. 1987. Reprint, New York: Plume-Penguin, 1988.

———. *The Bluest Eye*. 1970. Reprint, New York: Plume-Penguin, 1994.

———. "A Conversation: Gloria Naylor and Toni Morrison." With Naylor. *Southern Review* 21 (1985): 567–93. Reprint in *Conversations with Toni Morrison*, ed. Danille Taylor-Guthrie. Jackson: University Press of Mississippi, 1994. 188–217.

———. "Interview with Toni Morrison." With Christina Davis. In *Toni Morrison*, ed. Gates and Appiah. 412–20.

———. "An Interview with Toni Morrison." With Nellie McKay. In *Toni Morrison*, ed. Gates and Appiah. 396–411.

———. "Intimate Things in Place: A Conversation with Toni Morrison." With Robert B. Stepto. In *Chant of Saints*, ed. Michael S. Harper and Stepto. Urbana: University of Illinois Press, 1979. 213–29.

———. "It's OK to Say OK." With Sandi Russell. In *Critical Essays on Toni Morrison*, ed. Nellie Y. McKay. Boston: Hall, 1988. 43–54.

———. *Jazz*. 1992. Reprint, New York: Plume-Penguin, 1993.

———. Lecture. Frederick G. Melcher Book Award, Unitarian Universalist Association. Cambridge, Mass. 12 Oct. 1988. *Cambridge Forum*. Radio program, WVTF, Roanoke, Va, 5 Apr. 1991.

———. *Playing in the Dark: Whiteness and the Literary Imagination*. Cambridge: Harvard University Press, 1992.

———. "Rootedness: The Ancestor as Foundation." With Mari Evans. In *Black Women Writers (1950–1980): A Critical Evaluation*, ed. Evans. Garden City, N.Y.: Anchor-Doubleday, 1984. 339–45.

———. "The Site of Memory." In *Inventing the Truth: The Art and Craft of Memoir*, ed. William Zinsser. Boston: Houghton, 1987. 101–24.

———. *Song of Solomon*. 1977. Reprint, New York: Signet, 1978.

———. *Sula*. 1973. Reprint, New York: Plume-Penguin, 1982.

———. "Talk with Toni Morrison." With Mel Watkins. *New York Times Book Review*, 11 Sept. 1977, 48, 50.

———. *Tar Baby*. 1981. Reprint, London: Triad Grafton, 1983.

———. "Toni Morrison." With Claudia Tate. In *Black Women Writers at Work*, ed. Tate. 117–31.

Morton, Patricia. *Disfigured Images: The Historical Assault on Afro-American Women*. New York: Greenwood, 1991.

Moskowitz, Faye. *Her Face in the Mirror: Jewish Women on Mothers and Daughters*. Boston: Beacon, 1994.

Moynihan, Daniel Patrick. *The Negro Family: The Case for National Action*. Office of Policy Planning Research, U.S. Department of Labor, March 1965.

Mudimbé-Boyi, Elisabeth. "Giving a Voice to Tituba: The Death of the Author?" *World Literature Today* 67, no. 4 (1993): 751–56.

Mukherjee, Bharati. *The Holder of the World*. New York: Knopf, 1993.

———. *The Middleman and Other Stories*. New York: Fawcett Crest-Ballantine, 1989.

Munt, Sally, ed. *New Lesbian Criticism: Literary and Cultural Readings*. Hemel Hempstead, England: Harvester Wheatsheaf, 1992.

Nasta, Susheila, ed. *Motherlands: Black Women's Writing from Africa, the Caribbean and South Asia*. London: Women's, 1991.

Naylor, Gloria. *Bailey's Cafe*. New York: Harcourt, 1992.

———. *Mama Day*. 1988. Reprint, New York: Random House, 1989.

Nelson, Emmanuel S. "Black America and the Anglophone Afro-Caribbean Literary Consciousness." *Journal of American Culture*, 12, no. 4 (1989): 53–58.

Ngugi wa Thiong'o. *Decolonizing the Mind: The Politics of Language in African Literature*. Portsmouth, N.H.: Heinemann, 1986.

Nichols, Grace. "Caribbean Woman's Prayer." In *Caribbean Women Writers*, ed. Cudjoe, 1–3.

———. "Epilogue," "Nanny," "The Return," "Web of Kin." *I is a long-memoried woman*. London: Karnak House, 1983.

Niesen de Abruna, Laura. "Family Connections: Mother and Mother Country in the Fiction of Jean Rhys and Jamaica Kincaid." In *Motherlands*, ed. Nasta. 257–89.

———. "Twentieth-Century Women Writers from the English-Speaking Caribbean." In *Caribbean Women Writers*, ed. Cudjoe, 86–97.

Nixon, Rob. "Caribbean and African Appropriations of *The Tempest*." *Critical Inquiry* 13, no. 3 (1987): 557–78.

"Nobel for Toni Morrison." Editorial. *Baltimore Sun*, 10 Oct. 1993, 2E.

O'Byrne, Anne. "From One Shore to Another." *Charlottesville Observer Magazine,* 3 June 1993, 4–5.
O'Callaghan, Evelyn. "Interior Schisms Dramatised: The Treatment of the 'Mad' Woman in the Work of Some Female Caribbean Novelists." In *Out of the Kumbla,* ed. Davies and Fido. 89–109.
O'Driscoll, Sally. "Michelle Cliff and the Authority of Identity." *Journal of the Midwest Modern Language Association* 28, no. 1 (1995): 56–70.
Olaniyan, Tejumola. "On 'Post-colonial Discourse': An Introduction." *Callaloo* 16, no. 4 (1993): 743–49.
Ozick, Cynthia. *The Shawl.* 1989. Reprint, New York: Random House, 1990.
Paris, Arthur. "The Transatlantic Metropolis and the Voices of Caribbean Women." In *Caribbean Women Writers,* ed. Cudjoe, 82–85.
Pattanayak, Chandrabhanu. "Brathwaite: Metaphors of Emergence." *Literary Criterion* 17, no. 3 (1982): 60–68.
Pearlman, Mickey. *Mother Puzzles: Daughters and Mothers in Contemporary American Literature.* New York: Greenwood, 1989.
Perry, Donna. "Initiation in Jamaica Kincaid's *Annie John.*" In *Caribbean Women Writers,* ed. Cudjoe, 245–53.
Perry, Phyllis Alesia. *Stigmata.* New York: Hyperion, 1998.
Petry, Ann. *The Street.* Boston: Houghton Mifflin, 1946.
Perry, Phillis Alesia. *Stigmata.* Hyperion, 1998.
Phaf, Ineke. "Women Writers of the Dutch-Speaking Caribbean: *Life Long Poem* in the Tradition of Surinamese *Granmorgu* (New Dawn)." In *Caribbean Women Writers,* ed. Cudjoe, 357–64.
Philip, Marlene Nourbese. "The Absence of Writing or How I Almost Became a Spy." In *Out of the Kumbla,* ed. Davies and Fido. 271–78.
Pryse, Marjorie. "Introduction: Zora Neale Hurston, Alice Walker, and the 'Ancient Power' of Black Women." In *Conjuring,* ed. Pryse and Spillers. 1–24.
Pryse, Marjorie, and Hortense J. Spillers, eds. *Conjuring: Black Women, Fiction, and Literary Tradition.* Bloomington: Indiana University Press, 1985.
Radhakrishnan, R. "Postcoloniality and the Boundaries of Identity." *Callaloo* 16, no. 4 (1993): 750–71.
Raiskin, Judith L. *Snow on the Cane Fields: Women's Writing and Creole Subjectivity.* Minneapolis: University of Minnesota Press, 1996.
Rajan, Gita. "Fissuring Time, Suturing Space: Reading Bharati Mukherjee's *The Holder of the World.*" In *Generations: Academic Feminists in Dialogue,* ed. Devoney Looser and E. Ann Kaplan. Minneapolis: University of Minnesota Press, 1997. 288–308.
Ramazani, Jahan. "The Wound of History: Walcott's *Omeros* and the Postcolonial Poetics of Affliction." *PMLA* 112 (1997): 405–17.
Ramchand, Kenneth. *Introduction to West Indian Literature.* Middlesex, England: Thomas Nelson, 1976.
Reddock, Rhoda. "Feminism, Nationalism, and the Early Women's Movement in the English-Speaking Caribbean (with Special Reference to Jamaica and Trinidad and Tobago)." In *Caribbean Women Writers,* ed. Cudjoe. 61–81.
Rhys, Jean. "The Day They Burned the Books." In *Green Cane and Juicy Flotsam,* ed. Esteves and Paravasini-Gebert. 173-79.
———. "Jean Rhys: The Art of Fiction LXIV." Interview with Elizabeth Vreeland. *Paris Review* 76 (1979): 218–37.

———. *Letters, 1931–1966*. Ed. Francis Wyndham and Diana Melly. London: Andre Deutsch, 1984.
———. *Smile, Please*. New York: Harper & Row, 1979.
———. *Voyage in the Dark*. 1934. Reprint, New York: Norton, 1982.
———. *Wide Sargasso Sea*. 1966. Reprint, New York: Norton, 1982.
Rich, Adrienne. "Compulsory Heterosexuality and Lesbian Existence." *Signs* 5, no. 4 (1980): 631–69.
———. *Of Woman Born: Motherhood as Experience and Institution*. New York: Norton, 1976.
———. "When We Dead Awaken: Writing as Re-Vision." *On Lies, Secrets, and Silence: Selected Prose 1966–1978*. New York: Norton, 1979. 33–49.
Rigney, Barbara Hill. *The Voices of Toni Morrison*. Columbus: Ohio State University Press, 1991.
Rodriguez, Maria Christina. "Women Writers of the Spanish-Speaking Caribbean: An Overview." In *Caribbean Women Writers*, ed. Cudjoe, 339–45.
Roof, Judith. "'This Is Not for You': The Sexuality of Mothering." In *Narrating Mothers: Theorizing Maternal Subjectivities*, ed. Brenda O. Daly and Maureen T. Reddy. Knoxville: University of Tennessee Press, 1991. 157–73.
Rule, Sheila. "Director Defies Odds with First Feature, *Daughters of the Dust*." *New York Times*, 12 Feb. 1992, C15, 17.
Sadoff, Diane F. "Black Matrilineage: The Case of Alice Walker and Zora Neale Hurston." *Signs* 11 (1985): 4–26.
Said, Edward. "Criticism/Self-Criticism." *Linguafranca* 2, no. 3 (1992): 37–43.
Saldivar, José David. *The Dialectics of Our America: Genealogy, Cultural Critique, and Literary History*. Durham: Duke University Press, 1991.
Salkey, Andrew. "After a Long Time Away." In *Crossing Water*, ed. Kellman. 182.
Santner, Eric L. *Stranded Objects: Mourning, Memory, and Film in Postwar Germany*. Ithaca, N.Y.: Cornell University Press, 1990.
Scarboro, Ann Armstrong. Afterword to *I, Tituba, Black Witch of Salem*, by Maryse Condé. 187–225.
Scharfman, Ronnie. "Mirroring and Mothering in Simone Schwarz-Bart's *Pluie et Vent sur Télumée Miracle* and Jean Rhys's *Wide Sargasso Sea*." *Yale French Studies* 62 (1981): 88–106.
Schine, Cathleen. "A World as Cruel as Job's." Review of *The Autobiography of My Mother*, by Jamaica Kincaid. *New York Times Book Review*, 4 Feb. 1996, 5.
Schwarz-Bart, Simone. *The Bridge of Beyond*. Trans. Barbara Bray. London: Heinemann, 1982.
Sekou, Lasana M. *Mothernation: Poems from 1984 to 1987*. Philipsburg, St. Martin: Nehesi, 1991.
Senior, Olive. "An Interview with Olive Senior." With Charles H. Rowell. *Callaloo* 11, no. 3 (1988): 480–90.
Shange, Ntozake. *for colored girls who have considered suicide / when the rainbow is enuf: a choreopoem*. 1975. Reprint, New York: Collier-MacMillan, 1989.
Sharp, Saundra. *Black Women for Beginners*. New York: Writers and Readers, 1993.
Shelton, Marie-Denise. "Condé: The Politics of Gender and Identity." *World Literature Today* 67, no. 4 (1993): 717–22.
———. "Women Writers of the French-Speaking Caribbean: An Overview." In *Caribbean Women Writers*, ed. Cudjoe, 346–56.
Sherman, Charlotte Watson. *One Dark Body*. New York: HarperCollins, 1993.

———, ed. *Sisterfire: Black Womanist Fiction and Poetry*. New York: HarperCollins, 1994.
Shohat, Ella. "Notes on the 'Post-Colonial.'" *Social Text* 31/32 (1992): 99–113.
Silko, Leslie Marmon. *Ceremony*. 1977. Reprint, New York: Penguin, 1986.
Slemon, Stephen. "Magic Realism as Post-Colonial Discourse." *Canadian Literature* 116 (1988): 9–24.
———. "Modernism's Last Post." In *Past the Last Post: Theorizing Post-Colonialism and Post-Modernism*, ed. Ian Adam and Helen Tiffin. Calgary: University of Calgary Press, 1990. 1–11.
———. "Post-Colonial Allegory and the Transformation of History." *Journal of Commonwealth Literature* 23, no. 1 (1988): 157–68.
Slemon, Stephen, and Helen Tiffin, eds. *After Europe: Critical Theory and Post-Colonial Writing*. Sydney: Dangaroo, 1989.
Smith, Barbara. "Toward a Black Feminist Criticism." *Conditions: Two* 1, no. 2 (1977). Reprint in *The New Feminist Criticism: Essays on Women, Literature, and Theory*, ed. Elaine Showalter. New York: Pantheon, 1985. 168–85.
———. "The Truth That Never Hurts: Black Lesbians in Fiction in the 1980s." In *Wild Women in the Whirlwind*, ed. Braxton and McLaughlin. 213–45.
Sollors, Werner. "Ethnicity." In *Critical Terms for Literary Study*, ed. Frank Lentricchia and Thomas McLaughlin. Chicago: University of Chicago Press, 1990. 288–305.
Spear, Thomas C. "Individual Quests and Collective History." *World Literature Today* 67, no. 4 (1993): 723–30.
Spillers, Hortense J. "Afterword: Cross-Currents, Discontinuities: Black Women's Fiction." In *Conjuring*, ed. Pryse and Spillers. 249–61.
———. "A Hateful Passion, a Lost Love." In *Toni Morrison*, ed. Harold Bloom. Modern Critical Views Series. New York: Chelsea House, 1990. 27–53.
Spivak, Gayatri Chakravorty. "Three Women's Texts and a Critique of Imperialism." In *"Race," Writing, and Difference*, ed. Henry Louis Gates, Jr. Chicago: University of Chicago Press, 1986.
Springfield, Consuelo Lopez, ed. *Daughters of Caliban: Caribbean Women in the Twentieth Century*. Bloomington: Indiana University Press, 1997.
Steady, Filomina Chioma, ed. *The Black Woman Cross-Culturally*. Rochester, Vt: Schenkman, 1981.
Stratton, Florence. *Contemporary African Literature and the Politics of Gender*. London: Routledge, 1994.
Styron, William. *The Confessions of Nat Turner*. New York: Random House, 1967.
Suleri, Sara. *The Rhetoric of English India*. Chicago: University of Chicago Press, 1992.
Taleb-Khyar, Mohamed B. "An Interview with Maryse Condé and Rita Dove." *Callaloo* 14, no. 2 (1991): 347–66.
Tan, Amy. *The Joy-Luck Club*. New York: Putnam, 1989.
Tate, Claudia, ed. *Black Women Writers at Work*. New York: Continuum, 1983.
Thorpe, Michael. "The Other Side: *Wide Sargasso Sea* and *Jane Eyre*." *Ariel* 8, no. 3 (1977): 99–110.
Tiffin, Helen. "Post-colonial Literatures and Counter-discourse." *Kunapipi* 9, no. 3 (1997). Reprint in *The Post-Colonial Studies Reader*, ed. Ashcroft, Griffiths, and Tiffin. 95–98.

Torres-Saillant, Silvio. *Caribbean Poetics: Toward an Aesthetics of West Indian Literature*. Cambridge: Cambridge University Press, 1997.

Turner, Darwin T. "Retrospective of a Renaissance." *Black Scholar* 18 (1987): 2–10.

Turner, Patricia. *Ceramic Uncles and Celluloid Mammies: Black Images and Their Influence on Culture*. New York: Doubleday, 1994.

Viramontes, Helena Maria. Lecture. Department of Spanish and Portuguese, Yale University. 1 Dec. 1993.

Vizenor, Gerald, ed. *Narrative Chance: Postmodern Discourse on Native American Indian Literatures*. Albuquerque: University of New Mexico Press, 1989.

Walcott, Derek. *Collected Poems 1948–1984*. New York: Farrar, Straus & Giroux, 1986.

———. "The Muse of History: An Essay." In *Is Massa Day Dead? Black Moods in the Caribbean*, ed. Orde Coombs. Garden City, N.Y.: Anchor/Doubleday, 1974. 1–27.

———. Nobel Lecture 1992. Reprint in "The 1992 Noble Prize in Literature: Derek Walcott," by Edward Halsey Foster. *Dictionary of Literary Biography Yearbook: 1992*. Ed. James W. Hipp. Detroit: Gale, 1993. 5–19.

———. *Omeros*. New York: Farrar, Straus & Giroux, 1990.

Walker, Alice. "Alice Walker." With Claudia Tate. In *Black Women Writers at Work*, ed. Tate. 175–87.

———. *The Color Purple*. New York: Simon & Schuster, 1982.

———. *Horses Make the Landscape Look More Beautiful*. San Diego: Harcourt, 1984

———. "In Search of Our Mothers' Gardens." *In Search of Our Mothers' Gardens: Womanist Prose*. New York: Harcourt, 1983. 231–43.

———. *Living by the Word: Selected Writings, 1973–1987*. San Diego: Harcourt, 1988.

———. *Meridian*. New York: Harcourt, 1976.

———. *Possessing the Secret of Joy*. San Diego: Harcourt, 1992.

———. "The Revenge of Hannah Kemhuff." *In Love and Trouble: Stories of Black Women*. New York: Harcourt, 1973. 60–80.

———. *The Temple of My Familiar*. 1989. Reprint, New York: Harcourt, 1990.

———. *The Third Life of Grange Copeland*. New York: Harcourt, 1970.

Walker, Margaret. *How I Wrote "Jubilee," and Other Essays on Life and Literature*. Ed. Maryemma Graham. New York: Feminist Press, 1990.

———. *Jubilee*. 1966. Reprint, New York: Bantam, 1967.

Walker, Melissa. *Down from the Mountaintop: Black Women's Novels in the Wake of the Civil Rights Movement, 1966–1989*. New Haven, Yale University Press, 1991.

Wall, Cheryl. "Introduction: Taking Positions and Changing Words." *Changing Our Own Words: Essays on Criticism, Theory, and Writing by Black Women*. New Brunswick, N.J.: Rutgers University Press, 1989. 1–15.

Wallace, Michele. *Black Macho and the Myth of the Superwoman*. New York: Dial, 1979.

Walters, Suzanna Danuta. *Lives Together/Worlds Apart: Mothers and Daughters in Popular Culture*. Berkeley: University of California Press, 1992.

Warhol, Robin R., and Diane Price Herndl, ed. *Feminisms: An Anthology of Literary Theory and Criticism*. New Brunswick, N.J.: Rutgers University Press, 1991.

Warner-Vieyra, Miriam. *Le quimboiseur l'avait dit*. Paris: Présence Africaine, 1980.

Washington, Mary Helen, ed. *Black-Eyed Susans: Classic Stories by and about Black Women*. Garden City, N.Y.: Anchor/Doubleday, 1975. ix–xxxii.

———. "I Sign My Mother's Name: Alice Walker, Dorothy West, Paule Marshall." In *Mothering the Mind: Twelve Studies of Writers and Their Silent Partners*, ed. Ruth Perry and Martine Watson Brownley. New York: Holmes and Meier, 1984. 142–163.

———, ed. *Midnight Birds: Stories by Contemporary Black Women Writers*. Garden City, N.Y.: Anchor/Doubleday, 1980. xiii–xxv.

Weisenburger, Steven. *Modern Medea: A Family Story of Slavery and Child-Murder from the Old South*. New York: Hill & Wang, 1998.

West, Dorothy. *The Living Is Easy*. Boston: Houghton Mifflin, 1948.

White, Deborah Gray. *Ar'n't I a Woman?: Female Slaves in the Plantation South*. New York: Norton, 1985.

White, Hayden. "The Historical Text as Literary Artifact." *Tropics of Discourse: Essays in Cultural Criticism*. Baltimore: Johns Hopkins University Press, 1978. 81–100.

———. *Metahistory: The Historical Imagination in Nineteenth-Century Europe*. Baltimore: Johns Hopkins University Press, 1973.

Wilentz, Gay. *Binding Cultures: Black Women Writers in Africa and the Diaspora*. Bloomington: Indiana University Press, 1992.

Williams, John A. *Captain Blackman*. Garden City, N.Y.: Doubleday, 1972.

Williams, Patrick, and Laura Chrisman, eds. *Colonial Discourse and Post-colonial Theory: A Reader*. New York: Columbia University Press, 1994.

Williams, Sherley Anne. *Dessa Rose*. 1986. Reprint, New York: Berkley, 1987.

Willis, Susan. "Eruptions of Funk: Historicizing Toni Morrison." *Black American Literature Forum* 16, no. 1 (1982): 34–42.

Wilson, Elizabeth. "'Le voyage et l'espace clos'—Island and Journey as Metaphor: Aspects of Woman's Experience in the Works of Francophone Caribbean Women Novelists." In *Out of the Kumbla*, ed. Davies and Fido. 45–57.

Wilton, Tamsin. *Lesbian Studies: Setting an Agenda*. London: Routledge: 1995.

Woidat, Caroline M. "Talking Back to Schoolteacher: Morrison's Confrontation with Hawthorne in *Beloved*." *Modern Fiction Studies* 39, nos. 3 and 4 (1993): 527–46.

Woolf, Virginia. *A Room of One's Own*. 1929. Reprint, San Diego: Harcourt, 1989.

———. *Orlando*. 1928. Reprint, San Diego: Harvest/HBJ, 1973.

Worsham, Fabian Clements. "The Poetics of Matrilineage: Mothers and Daughters in the Poetry of African-American Women, 1965–1985." In *Women of Color*, ed. Brown-Guillory. 117–31.

Wylie, Hal. "The Cosmopolitan Condé, or Unscrambling the Words." *World Literature Today* 67, no. 4 (1993): 763–68.

Wynter, Sylvia. "Beyond Miranda's Meanings: Un/silencing the 'Demonic Ground' of Caliban's 'Woman.'" In *Out of the Kumbla*, ed. Davies and Fido. 355–72.

Yellin, Jean Fagin. "Text and Context of Harriet Jacobs' *Incidents in the Life of a Slave Girl: Written by Herself*." In *The Slave's Narrative*, ed. Davis and Gates. 262–82.

Zamora, Lois Parkinson. "Magical Romance/Magical Realism: Ghosts in U.S. and Latin American Fiction." In *Magical Realism*, ed. Zamora and Faris. 497–550.

Zamora, Lois Parkinson, and Wendy B. Faris, eds. *Magical Realism: Theory, History, Community*. Durham: Duke University Press, 1995.

Zimmerman, Bonnie. "Feminist Fiction and the Postmodern Challenge." In *Postmodern Fiction: A Bio-Bibliographical Guide*, ed. Larry McCaffery. Westport, Conn.: Greenwood, 1986. 175–88.

Zimra, Clarisse. "Negritude in the Feminine Mode: The Case of Martinique and Guadeloupe." *Journal of Ethnic Studies* 12, no. 1 (1984): 53–77.

———. "Righting the Calabash: Writing History in the Female Francophone Narrative." In *Out of the Kumbla*, ed. Davies and Fido. 143–59.

———. "W/Righting His/Tory: Versions of Things Past in Contemporary Caribbean Women Writers." In *Explorations: Essays in Comparative Literature*, ed. Makoto Ueda. Lanham, Md.: University Press of America, 1986. 227–52.

Index